ADENAUER

A Critical Biography

ADENAUER

A Critical Biography

CHARLES WIGHTON

Coward-McCann, Inc.
New York

Copyright © 1963 by Charles Wighton

First American Edition 1964

Library of Congress Catalog Card Number: 64-13060

Contents

Author's Note

WHEN a publisher's reader in the person of an eminent English historian read a draft of the first half of this book in the mid-fifties, the opinion was hazarded that the anonymous author was 'clearly a Central European refugee with political roots in the Weimar Republic'. The distinguished scholar could scarcely have been more wrong.

To remove any ambiguity, therefore, this book is written from the standpoint which might be expected of one who had a Calvinist upbringing, a Scots liberal education, whose political ideas were developed in the Clydeside of the thirties, and who has spent much of the post-war period in Germany.

As is indicated above, this book has been written over a period of approximately ten years. The earlier portion for the period up to 1955–6 was written and rewritten from notes and observations made in Germany as the events took place. Dr. Adenauer's continuance in office, however, for long ruled out all chance of publication, and the completed chapters were laid aside and largely forgotten. It was not until the beginning of 1963, when at last Dr. Adenauer's retirement seemed a matter of months, that the decision was taken to publish this book in the U.K. and Germany. The manuscript was thereupon brought up to date and the additional chapters written in the intervening months.

Over the years I received much help and information, often of a confidential nature, from officials of what was successively British Military Government, the Control Commission for Germany (British Element) and the British foreign service in Germany and I should like to express my appreciation to them. I should also like to thank other Allied and German officials for information which is included in this work.

I also wish to thank the staff of the British Embassy library in Bonn for their co-operation at various times over the past decade, and also the management of *Der Spiegel* in Hamburg for placing their archives at my disposal.

C. W.

Introduction

AT Easter, 1963, Konrad Adenauer, first Chancellor of the West German Federal Republic, decided at long last that he must retire. He announced that he would demit office within a few months by which time he would be far advanced into his eighty-eighth year. Adenauer felt that he should have stayed on until at least the eve of his ninetieth birthday at the beginning of 1966. His party, which for years had been trying to steel itself to dismiss him, thought otherwise. He was forced out.

A fortnight later the party, the Christian Democratic Union, went a step further. In defiance of its octogenarian leader, it nominated as his successor the German Vice-Chancellor and Minister of Economics, Professor Ludwig Erhard. Adenauer, who had opposed Erhard's nomination for four years, in the end capitulated almost without a struggle. His capitulation was a token that at last he had bowed to age and advancing senility. For, since 1959, Adenauer time and again had torpedoed the nomination of Erhard whom he considered to be politically unsophisticated although an economist of the highest distinction.

The C.D.U. decision to nominate Erhard as next German Chancellor was symptomatic. By the spring of 1963 most Germans, and a considerable section of the Western world, were weary of Konrad Adenauer with his old-fashioned authoritarian ways and obsolete Cold War policies. It was time for a change. In the previous few months the C.D.U., as a result of Adenauer's refusal to get out, had suffered a series of electoral reverses. Erhard as 'the man behind the German miracle' seemed their only hope if they were to recover their political fortunes. From the moment of his nomination there were, in effect, two German Chancellors. Adenauer, still in office but increasingly ignored, lingered on for a few months, a shadow of his former self. But, long before he finally disappeared, 'it was evident that the Adenauer era had ended. In Bonn long-standing Adenauer taboos were swept away. Dictatorial powers which he had exercised for fourteen years vanished with the summer breeze. And as though to set the seal on the old man's decline, his equivocal Secretary of State, Dr. Hans Globke, the Third Reich bureaucrat whose continued presence in the Federal Chancellery had become an international scandal, announced that he would retire at the same time as his faithful master.

Adenauer's decision to go could scarcely have been much longer postponed. It was belated by four years. In the middle fifties the octogenarian Bonn Chancellor had been at the height of his power and prestige. Since he had taken office in 1949 as head of the first post-war democratic German Government, Adenauer had achieved great and historic things for his compatriots. He had given them back their freedom.

In long and complicated negotiations with the Western Allies, which sometimes reduced him to near-despair, he had restored sovereignty and independence to the rump of the Reich over which he ruled. He did more. Within ten years of his predecessor's suicide and the unconditional surrender of the German High Command — with the terrible revelations of unparalleled mass crime which followed — he led the Germans back to international respectability. He took his fellow-countrymen back into the comity of Western civilization and transformed a divided, devastated and occupied country into a much-sought-after and respected ally. And while he did all this the Germans gained a standard of prosperity never known before in their history, 'the German miracle' of post-war recovery.

In a post-war era into which Einstein, Richard Strauss and Thomas Mann survived, it would be false to describe Adenauer as the greatest German of the post-1945 period; and whether he was the greatest German statesman since Bismarck, as a famous contemporary asserted, must await the verdict of history. But

unquestionably history will remember him as the greatest German
political figure of the immediate post-war period.

By the second half of the nineteen-fifties he had become an
international statesman of enormous authority. Abjuring all
baits offered from the East, he firmly led the Germans into the
Atlantic Alliance and banished that fear of a new Rapallo which
was the secret nightmare of the Western Governments. His
great service to the Western cause gained for him a prestige
unequalled by any German statesman since Gustav Stresemann.
In developing his pro-Western policies, he became the favourite
ally of the United States. And through his intimate alliance with
the U.S. Secretary of State, the late John Foster Dulles, he had
become the leading exponent of the Cold War in the Western
Alliance. It was a remarkable transformation for a man in his
eighties who, a quarter of a century earlier, had been hounded
from office as chief magistrate of Cologne; an elderly retired
Prussian civil servant who, after narrowly escaping death at
Nazi hands on several occasions had spent the next decade doing
nothing more exciting than growing roses in the garden of his
Rhineland villa.

Had Konrad Adenauer retired in the spring of 1959, as at first
he declared he would, his fame would have been secure. The
death of John Foster Dulles at that moment – which brought with
it the effective end of their Cold War policies – should have
served only to reinforce his decision to demit office as Chancellor. His renown would have remained unalloyed and those less
attractive political characteristics, which he brought from the
municipal to the national political stage, would have been forgotten or at least submerged in the reputation of the great European and German statesman. But, by 1959, after ten years in
office, Konrad Adenauer like other autocrats, constitutional or
otherwise, could not face the voluntary abandonment of absolute
power. Therein lay the tragedy of his later years.

After announcing that he would retire as Chancellor and stand
as C.D.U. candidate in the forthcoming presidential election,

certain that he would end his great public career as German Head of State, Adenauer suddenly changed his mind. He had planned to transform the Federal Republic into a presidential state with himself at its head. Thwarted in that ambition, he decided to remain Federal Chancellor and retain absolute power. For the first time, the great mass of the Germans, and his many international admirers, were shocked into a realization of what had long been obvious to close observers of the German scene; the venerable statesman was obsessed by a Teutonic lust for authoritarian power.

Since he had taken office in 1949 Adenauer, by brilliant exploitation of the weaknesses in the Bonn constitution, coupled with a political flair approaching genius for playing on the instinctive German urge towards the *Obrigkeitstaat* (Authority State), had succeeded in establishing a régime of personal authoritarianism seldom equalled in a constitutional and parliamentary state. In a decade as Bundeskanzler he had treated his ministers as personal assistants, the members of parliament as lackeys, the German Constitutional Court as a personal convenience, and the Bonn Constitution as a device to be amended to suit his own purposes. As he advanced farther into political senility these dictatorial tendencies became ever more pronounced.

In the spring of 1959 he went too far. His ministers, his party and the great mass of the German people were shocked by his cynical use of the highest offices of the German state as instruments of his craving for power. In most other Western states his actions would have led to his dismissal. But, by the exercise of his inflexible will and an open contempt for the normal processes of democratic politics, he suppressed the incipient palace revolution. It was not until four years later that his sycophantic and pusillanimous supporters, goaded by portents of political disaster, at last plucked up courage to force their aged master out of office.

Konrad Adenauer will always be honoured and respected for what he did for post-war Germany. Whether his services to the cause of German democracy were equally great is more questionable; he left behind him a political heritage fraught with danger for the future.

His seizure of authoritarian power in the face of one of the most carefully devised constitutions in modern history and his open disregard and contempt for the normal practices of modern democracy, in combination with the passive acceptance by the Germans of his paternalistic rule, gave a grim warning of what could happen in the future with a German Chancellor less fundamentally benevolent than Konrad Adenauer.

However rigid Adenauer's policies may have been, everything he did as German Chancellor was based on the fundamental tenets of Western Christian culture. In his devotion to the principles of the more progressive papal encyclicals of the past three-quarters of a century he was curiously similar to his fellow authoritarian, Dr. Salazar, with whom he had much in common. His moral standards were high, but like all dictators, democratic or otherwise, he was sure that he knew best. Much of what he did stemmed from the heart-cry which he uttered in 1954 at the time of the European Army débâcle: 'Mein Gott, what will happen to Germany (and the Western world by implication) after I am gone?'

More alarming, however, than even Adenauer's authoritarian rule was the terrifying willingness of ministers, party, parliament and the nominally democratic Germans in the mass to accept his one man dictatorship for so long. That frightening Teutonic obsequiousness to the *Obrigkeit* (authority) of one strong man, after all that had gone before, must raise the fundamental issue – are the Germans, no matter how great the constitutional safeguards, and no matter how cleverly devised their parliamentary institutions, capable of developing a genuine Western democracy? Konrad Adenauer, by his well-meaning but ruthless exploitation of the Germans' most sinister political instincts, certainly did serious damage to the tender plant of German democracy. How serious must depend on Professor Erhard and subsequent successors. Stalin's wartime dictum that 'democracy fits the Germans as a saddle does an ox', comes all too readily to mind.

If Adenauer's authoritarian practices cannot be condoned, the exceptional occupation conditions of his earlier years in office, plus his great achievements for his fellow-countrymen provide some justification. But his determination to ensure sovereignty, prosperity, and what he believed was security, for the Germans west of the zonal frontier was in curious contrast to his apparent indifference to the other 17,000,000 Germans behind the Iron Curtain.

Before he took office in 1949 a British commentator suggested that Adenauer would remain well content with the borders of the West German state created for him by the three Western Allies out of their zones of occupation. That estimate remained as accurate when he decided to retire as when it was written four-teen years earlier. He was a Roman Catholic Rhinelander. All his life he loathed Protestant Prussia and what he regarded as the evil city of Berlin. At heart Adenauer never wanted German re-unification, a sentiment that almost certainly was shared by some of the post-war Occupation Powers.

To a French Ambassador he admitted that he would go down in history as the only German Chancellor who had 'sacrificed the unity of the Reich for the unity of Europe'. That rare epigram contained the essence of what historians may decide was one of the great lost opportunities of history – Adenauer's failure to seize the chance to reunite Germany on comparatively acceptable terms in those early months after Stalin's death in 1953 when, on the authority of Mr. Khrushchev, at least some of the new masters of the Kremlin wished to rid themselves of what they regarded as the incubus of the Communist puppet state in Eastern Germany.

A predominantly Protestant and almost certainly Socialist re-united Germany might well have marked the end of Adenauer's political career. Whether or not the first all-German general election would have swept him from office, a united Reich would certainly have meant the end of Adenauer as a 'great European'.

For he planned to unite *not Europe* but only the 'little Europe' of predominantly Catholic and conservative states of the old Carolingian Reich. To such a concept a reunited Germany was as alien as the liberal and Protestant Scandinavian countries, or his lifelong hate, Great Britain. For Adenauer's profound Francophilia and Anglophobia, which reached their ultimate expression in the historic events of January, 1963, were but different sides of the same coin.

Yet the Franco-German *rapprochement* to which he devoted much of his life, and in the final realization of which he permanently prejudiced his own, if not Western Germany's relationship with the United States proved to be a chimera even while he still remained Chancellor. The Adenauer-de Gaulle honeymoon following the signature of the controversial German-French treaty in January 1963 lasted just six months. When de Gaulle visited Bonn the following July, a few days after the wilting Adenauer had been pushed more and more into the background of the Kennedy hero's progress through Bonn and Berlin, the real worth of his friendship with France emerged. After two days of discussions Adenauer and de Gaulle were only able to reach an agreement to disagree on all major issues.

Final assessment of Adenauer, the Federal German Chancellor and the world statesman must await the verdict of history. He will certainly be much praised for the way in which he led his rump of the Reich back to sovereignty and freedom. He will be honoured as the head of the first post-war government which gave the Germans fantastic material prosperity and restored them to international respectability. And he will be long remembered for his valiant attempt to make what reparation was possible to the Jews. Against these memorable achievements will be set four charges:

1. His authoritarian methods of government and the injury done by his democratic dictatorship to the tender plant of German democracy.

2. His toleration, if not encouragement, of equivocal figures from the Third Reich in high places in his Bonn Republic.

3. His apparent indifference to the ultimate fate, as well as the day to day living conditions, both of the 17,000,000 'other Germans' held in Communist travail and the gallant people of divided Berlin.

4. His determined pursuit of the Cold War, on which much of his power and prestige had been built, to the bitter end, no matter how great the improvement in the Moscow political climate. In consequence he succeeded in maintaining tension in Central Europe, and far beyond, until the very last weeks of his Chancellorship.

The last will almost certainly be the most serious charge of the world at large against Adenauer. For it would appear to have been no coincidence that Khruschev only agreed to take steps to attempt to ease the deadlock between East and West when the Russians were satisfied that, at long last, Adenauer was to go. From the movement in April 1963 when he announced his decision to retire the Soviet Ambassador in Bonn went to ground. Khruschev had written of Adenauer. They were prepared to wait for the disappearance of the man who had so often inserted a spanner into East-West negotiations. The Anglo Saxon-Soviet test ban treaty and the moves which followed may well have been the first consequences of Adenauer's imminent departure.

Whatever the judgement of history on Adenauer his decision to retire brought a sigh of relief, not only to many Germans on both sides of the Iron Curtain, but far beyond.

His decision to go marked the end of the immediate post-war era in Central Europe and the dawn of a new age in the history of Germany. But generations will pass before the contradictions of his character and the enigmas of his policy are finally elucidated, for reasons which are obvious from the story of his life which follows.

CHAPTER ONE

A Border German

KONRAD ADENAUER, like Adolf Hitler, was born both a border German and the son of a minor government official. But the future Chancellor of the Bonn republic was born a dozen years *before* the Führer of the Third Reich. His birth, to devout Roman Catholic parents, took place at the climax of Bismarck's 'Kulturkampf' against the German Catholic hierarchy, within the shadow of Cologne Cathedral, the doctrines of whose prelates were to dominate much of his life.

In the five years which separated the foundation of the Hohenzollern Reich at Versailles from Konrad Adenauer's birth on 5th January, 1876, the Iron Chancellor's instinctive Junker distrust of the Vatican and its ways had developed into widespread religious persecution. During the earlier years of Adenauer's life many of the Catholic sees in Germany lay vacant while their bishops languished in Prussian prisons. In the Catholic Rhineland there was passionate anger against the Prussian Reich and its autocratic Chancellor, and the conflict almost inevitably brought into existence a great Catholic political party uniting men of all classes in defence of their faith. This was the clerically dominated Zentrum party, to which Konrad Adenauer devoted the first half of his public life.

But the 'Kulturkampf' in the Rhineland had much deeper roots than a Junker Lutheran's aversion to papal authoritarianism and Jesuit intrigue. For the Rhineland, unlike the Prussia which administered it, had a long history of Catholic culture and Gallic civilization.

At the Reformation, when the reactionary princes of northern

and eastern Germany adopted the 'Lutheran heresy' and in return
gained that unquestioning obedience to the secular power which
has damned Germany ever since, the Rhineland as the greatest
artery of medieval trade and culture remained Catholic.

From that point onwards the Rhinelanders, a border people of
only partly Teutonic stock, looked towards France or to the
Catholic Habsburg Emperor in Vienna for leadership. The Jaco-
bins of Mainz welcomed the revolutionary French armies with
open arms – an act of 'high treason' long denounced in German
history books. And after Napoleon's defeat the Congress of
Vienna, in its search for a safe secular ruler for the pro-French
Rhineland, pushed the province into the arms of Prussia as compensation for the forfeited portion of Frederick the Great's Polish
conquests. Subsequently Prussia incorporated both banks of the
Rhine into the Province of Rhenish Prussia. Thereafter the
Rhineland Catholics nursed a grievance against both Prussian
autocracy and Junker confessional discrimination.

This digression into Rhineland history is fundamental. It is the
key to much of Konrad Adenauer's character and most of his
actions. At key moments his instinctive support for historic
Rhineland grievances and antipathies would make him a Rhinelander or a Bonn Republican first, and a German afterwards.

It was therefore into an intensely anti-Prussian environment,
in which Francophil leanings were intermixed with clerical
authoritarianism, that young Konrad Adenauer emerged as soon
as he could talk. It was an environment which quickly swallowed
up the pretty, fair-haired little boy and which left marks which
were easily discernible nearly nine decades later.

The Adenauer family was of solid Rhineland yeoman stock
from the Eifel hill country near the Belgian border. Konrad
Adenauer's grandfather kept a baker's shop in the university
town of Bonn, where a century later his grandson was to establish
what was virtually his own private capital.

Adenauer's father had only an elementary education. He was a
professional Prussian N.C.O. who so distinguished himself at the

battle of Koenigsgraetz in 1866 that he was commissioned in the field, an almost unheard of distinction in the Army of Moltke and Roon. He was stern and somewhat unapproachable, not unlike his famous son. But the future Chancellor's mother was a true light-hearted Rhinelander, sixteen years younger than her husband.

Both parents, however dissimilar in temperament, were pious Catholics, who brought up their little family in all the tenets of the Roman faith.

Soon after he married, Adenauer's father retired from the Prussian army, and by the time his third child Konrad was born he had become head of the general office of the Cologne county court and a minor civil servant, like so many other retired Prussian soldiers.

The Adenauer family which was soon augmented to four – three boys and a girl – knew the genteel poverty of a lower middle-class official and the mother was forced to take in lodgers. One of these died and left a few hundred pounds to the Adenauer children, which helped to provide a University education for the three Adenauer sons. But there was little luxury in the simple home in the Balduinstrasse in Cologne. Adenauer's father, though a born Rhinelander, had acquired during his military service the Prussian virtues of thrift and frugality.

Many years later Adenauer recalled how, shortly before Christmas, his mother had been forced to give the children the choice – meat on Sundays during December or a Christmas tree. To a German family the choice was a formality and the Adenauer family had a meatless December. Every penny that could be saved was put aside for the education of the three boys, with notable results. For apart from the future Chancellor one son rose to be a professor of Roman theology and a canon of Cologne Cathedral, while the other became a prominent Cologne lawyer.

After a strict Catholic upbringing at home, Konrad Adenauer, a thin-faced child with fair curls, was first sent to a local council school. By the time he was ten, however, confessional schools had been reopened in the Rhineland and he passed to the Catholic

High School for Boys, the Apostelgymnasium where Bismarck's unrevoked ban on the Society of Jesus did nothing to prejudice the jesuit-type education given to the boys. Konrad Adenauer was an industrious pupil but seldom top of the class. His main claim to distinction, in fact, was that he was the tallest boy in his form.

Adenauer's father decided that Konrad should be a banker, so he became an office boy in the counting-house of an old Cologne financial house – his first association with the great Cologne bankers who were to play a key role in both his personal and public life for over half a century.

Adenauer, however, was never much of a financier, even as Federal Chancellor in Bonn. His distaste for figures was obvious even to his father and he stayed in the bank only a fortnight.

He was determined to study law, for the 18-year-old Adenauer had already been impressed by those autocratic representatives of the Prussian Government who ruled his native city in the name of the Kaiser. He had made up his mind he would be one of them.

There was still a little of the lodger's legacy intact, and his father managed to secure him a scholarship which permitted him to set out for the university of Freiburg, in south-western Germany. From there he continued to Munich, where in his earnest, pious way he enjoyed life. But the student Adenauer, as the man he was to become, throughout his life found it difficult to make friends. He joined a Catholic Students' Corporation and pointedly declined to associate with the roystering, swashbuckling, beer-drinking student corporations, whose duelling scars have left a permanent mark on so many Germans.

From contemporary accounts, Adenauer as a student, in his sober, humourless way, appears to have been something of a prig.

Finally, for his last year of study, he went home to Bonn and it was there at the age of 21 that Konrad Adenauer passed his first State Examination in law. Four years later he passed the final examination with distinction and became a legal assessor. Before completing his training he spent a few months in Berlin, his first experience of the Reich capital. It was then that he acquired that distaste for the city and its inhabitants which he could never entirely conceal as Federal Chancellor, even when its fate became the concern of the whole Western World.

Adenauer's first legal appointment was as an assistant in the office of the Cologne Public Prosecutor – no doubt as a result of his father's influence. He remained there for two years.

He then joined the firm of the leading advocate in Cologne, Geheimrat Kausen, who in addition to being senior partner was also chairman of the important Zentrum Group in the Cologne City Council.

That step was the key to Adenauer's whole future. His background led naturally to the Zentrum and at the age of 28 he began his active association with the Catholic political party in the Rhineland. The Zentrum would continue to sponsor his political career until, almost overnight, it disappeared in 1933. But its methods never left Adenauer when he became Chancellor of the Bonn Republic. For the German Zentrum was unique among the European political developments of the nineteenth century. From the first it was *without rigid political principles*.

It was a confessional party of political opportunists ready to support any political line and co-operate with any political group, no matter how extreme, as long as the rights and privileges of the Roman Catholic Church in Germany were guaranteed. The Zentrum was politically amoral. Great religious party though it was, the Zentrum went so far as to vote for the historic Enabling Act which gave Adolf Hitler complete dictatorial powers in the spring of 1933, almost at the very moment that its faithful servant Konrad Adenauer was hounded out of Cologne.

'The Zentrum had no parallel in any other European country,' states Mr. A. J. P. Taylor in his pungent history of Germany. 'It was prepared to be German or anti-German; liberal or anti-liberal; free trade or protectionist; pacific or bellicose; a party of expediency as unscrupulous as Bismarck himself.' It was in that remarkable organization that Adenauer found his political and spiritual home.

Soon afterwards the handsome young lawyer took another important step. In 1904 he married Emma Weyer, grand-daughter of a prominent Cologne benefactor. In the following eight years three children – two boys and a girl – were born to the young people. Two years after his marriage at the age of 30, Adenauer entered the service of the city of Cologne as junior Beigeordneter – an administrative assistant of the Oberbürgermeister.

Adenauer's boss, Geheimrat Kausen, as head of the Zentrum in the City Council, had originally intended to fill the vacancy with a young lawyer from Saarbrücken. But before he could make a decision Adenauer marched into his office and bluntly asked, 'Why don't you take me? I am certainly as good as this other chap from Saarbrücken.' Kausen was amused. He nominated his young assistant, who was elected to the post by the overwhelming vote of the Zentrum members of the Council.

As tenth administrative assistant, Adenauer was placed in charge of the city's taxation department. He soon numbered among his friends important members of the Cologne banking houses, with whom he was in daily contact.

Six years later the post of First Beigeordneter – actually deputy Oberbürgermeister – became vacant. The Oberbürgermeister of Cologne, the conservative Wallraf, had been watching Adenauer's work with approval. To the intense chagrin of the other deputies, who were all Adenauer's seniors, he nominated his most junior deputy for the post.

The Zentrum, however, was powerful and Konrad Adenauer, in the face of strong opposition from the liberal sections of the City Council, was elected.

The appointment was denounced on all sides. Perhaps the most significant comment came from the National Liberal newspaper which reported that 'The youngest and most *clerical* deputy has been elected.' Others suggested that he was the 'most autocratic' member of the city administration.

That authoritarian, clericalist, conservative politican with big business backing, the figure who ruled Bonn half a century later, had made his first appearance on the German political stage. Even in these days he was well known to be the trusted confidant of both Cologne hierarchies – that which ruled in the twin-spired 'Dom' and the other which controlled the great international banking houses.

Adenauer was not a popular figure. But even his fiercest critics admitted that he was efficient and able to handle men and affairs with unusual craft.

In his new post Adenauer spent all his time reorganizing the out-of-date administrative machinery of Cologne. In these early years of the century, with the international scene becoming steadily darker, von Schliefen and the other chiefs of the German High Command in Berlin became more and more interested in Cologne. The Rhine city was the main pivot of their aggressive plans against Belgium.

In August 1914, the Kaiser's armies moved westwards. Within a short time of the outbreak of war Adenauer took over the key post of City Food Controller.

He took a less optimistic view than others of the duration of the war and is credited with being the first man in Germany to propose food rationing. He was scoffed at. Soon the success of the British Navy's blockade showed the wisdom of his plans. In Cologne food grew steadily scarcer, and Adenauer, quite unfairly, was blamed. His sarcastic brusqueness and autocratic indifference to the complaints of the citizens concentrated on him most of the city's natural resentment. Soon he became the butt of the city with the nickname of 'Graupen–auer' . . . formed from the German word for barley and the latter half of his own name.

At the height of this period of personal unpopularity, Adenauer's wife Emma died after long years as an invalid, leaving him with three young children. Soon afterwards he encountered another calamity as a result of his passion for being driven in motor-cars at high speed, an obsession which was still strong when he had reached the age of 87.

Driving through Cologne after luncheon, Adenauer's chauffeur, perhaps after a glass too many of the good Rhine wine, dozed at the wheel. The civic limousine in which Adenauer was travelling crashed headlong into one of Cologne's tram-trains, which today are still among the hazards of the Rhine metropolis. Adenauer was hurled through the windscreen on to the street, where he lay unconscious. He was badly injured. His face, hands and feet were terribly cut by the smashed windscreen. For weeks he lay in a Cologne hospital while doctors despaired of his life. Finally they performed a series of operations on his broken cheek-bones and severed face-muscles which left him with that Red Indian face, or Genghis Khan appearance, which was to become the joy of cartoonists for decades thereafter.

The accident was also responsible for the insomnia from which he has suffered ever since. He spent a long period in hospital but even after his discharge he was still far from well. He retired to a convalescent home in the Black Forest. There, as a result of the depression caused by his accident and the aftermath of his wife's death, he seriously contemplated retiring from the civic administration and concentrating on the upbringing of his three young children. It was there, in the autumn of 1917 at the depth of his depression, that, to his intense astonishment, he was visited by two representatives from the city of Cologne. For hours his two colleagues chatted about this and that. There seemed no point to the conversation. At last they came to the point.

Satisfied that he was in his right mind and had suffered no serious mental effects from his accident, the two envoys informed Adenauer that the City Council wanted him to be Oberbürger-meister of Cologne.

His chief, Dr. Wallraf, they told him, had been summoned to Berlin to take up the post of Permanent Secretary of State in the Prussian Ministry of the Interior. In the midst of the war the Cologne City Council felt Adenauer was the best man for the

post. He was overcome. Still not quite recovered, he returned to
his native city. On 18th October, 1917, he was elected Oberbürgermeister by the overwhelming majority of fifty-four votes
to two.

He was elected according to Prussian law for twelve years.
Soon afterwards the Kaiser in the last months of his reign honoured the 41-year-old Oberbürgermeister by summoning him to
be a member of the Prussian Upper Chamber – the Herrenhaus.
Adenauer seemed to have reached the summit of his career. Still
in his early forties, he had attained the highest office in his native
city. He had also a salary and allowances amounting to over
40,000 Reichsmarks, worth at least £2,000 in these days and with
a purchasing power far in excess of that amount.

Adenauer's elevation to Oberbürgermeister was particularly
applauded by his clerical and financial friends, and especially
among the latter into whose inner circle – the 'Koelner Kluengel'
or Cologne Clique – he had recently been initiated. There he was
the intimate of some of the most important figures in German
commerce and finance; Louis Hagen, otherwise Levy, the head
of the banking house of Levy and Oppenheim with whose senior
partners Adenauer was to maintain a lifelong association; Banker
Stein, head of the Stein Bank whose successor, Adenauer's friend
Baron von Schroeder, would later achieve international notoriety
as Hitler's collector of funds and go-between in the negotiations
between the Nazis and Von Papen; Dr. Paul Silverberg, director
of numerous great commercial and financial companies; and Otto
Wolff, the internationally-known Cologne industrialist who had
been in the forefront of Imperial Germany's fight with Britain for
the world's metals and markets.

With these men as his intimates and with the Cardinal Archbishop and the rest of the hierarchy behind him, Konrad Adenauer
was a man to be reckoned with.

Adenauer had completed his first year as Oberbürgermeister
of Cologne when at the end of October, 1918, the German
High Seas Fleet at Kiel mutinied. Within a few days the

German High Command had lost control of the situation. Mutiny became revolution.

In the first week of November, with the Kiel mutineers in the van, the revolution spread like wildfire across Germany. In Cologne, Konrad Adenauer and the local military commander watched anxiously. They saw the revolutionaries head towards the Rhineland in a bid to repeat the historic success of the Bolsheviks in Russia a year earlier. The aim was clear. Cologne, as communications hub behind the 100 German divisions still in Flanders, was the key to general revolt throughout the armies on the Western Front.

Adenauer, however, had another interest in the approaching cataclysm. For weeks and months before the Kiel mutiny the captains of industry in Western Germany and their close associates had, like Konrad Adenauer, seen that the war was lost. The Ruhr barons who frequented the Industrieklub in Düsseldorf, where years later Hitler successfully appealed to them for funds, knew that revolution would inevitably follow defeat. The only question was what kind of revolution?

The Ruhr barons, with their financial friends in Cologne, set about taking steps to safeguard their great possessions and the vast profits they had made during the previous four years of war.

Equally appalled by the prospect of a Red Reich were the dignitaries of the Rhineland hierarchy. By the end of October the march of events had brought them all together.

All were convinced that in the event of the establishment of a Bolshevik government in Berlin there was only one possible solution – some form of Ruhr-Rhine West German state set up according to the circumstances existing at the time *but under the protection of the advancing Western Allies*. What exact part the Oberbürgermeister of Cologne took in these clandestine activities will never be known precisely. As Oberbürgermeister of the Rhineland metropolis, however, with close links to both the main props of the project, he could scarcely have been unaware of what was afoot.

When, therefore, the military commander of Cologne warned Adenauer that a train with the Kiel mutineers was approaching the city, Adenauer was prepared to strike the first blow in the counter-revolution.

He proposed to have the train stopped at a siding outside of Cologne and have the mutineers seized by the still loyal Cologne garrison. But the military commander, not quite sure who his legal superiors in Berlin might be within a few days, equivocated. The bureaucrats of the German State railway administration were, as all good German officials always are, undeviating. The train, they said, must run into Cologne main station according to the railway time-table. *It would therefore run according to the time-table.* There could be no question of putting it into a siding.

The mutineers reached the centre of Cologne and disturbances swept across the city. A blood bath seemed imminent. Adenauer, if no one else, kept his head. He persuaded the panicking military commander, who had by this time decided on violent action, that it was too late – it was madness to shoot at the demonstrators, who now included thousands of Cologne workers. He argued that nothing should be done until the situation clarified, in other words, until it became evident whether the Communist revolutionaries or the Socialist workers would come out on top.

Representatives of the Soldiers' and Sailors' Council invaded his City Hall and took over control of the city. They demanded the removal of the reactionary Oberbürgermeister. But the moderate Socialists fought back. They feared a genuine Red revolution almost as much as the Ruhr barons and the Catholic clergy. The Socialists also recognized Adenauer's administrative efficiency. They insisted that he should remain in office, with a 'controller' to see that he did what he was told.

The Socialists took control of Cologne almost at the same time as their comrades in Berlin, Ebert and Schiedemann, took over the government of Germany.

When the Socialist controller reached Adenauer's study the Oberbürgermeister warned him, 'You understand – I don't want you here. You are not welcome.' But the haughty Oberbürgermeister and his Socialist controller soon reached a compromise. In later years this Left-wing watchdog wrote that 'Adenauer is to be thanked that Cologne was saved from catastrophe. As a result of his efforts the revolution in Cologne was never more than child's play'.

Adenauer, however, while attempting to suppress revolution from the Left, was deep in the plot to stage a counter revolution of the Right, which would be sure of support from the French High Command if not from President Wilson and Mr. Lloyd George. And when on 9th November the unhappy Wilhelm II, badgered by his High Command, was finally pushed across the border into Holland, Adenauer lost no time.

Within hours of the Kaiser's departure for exile Adenauer, on the evening of 9th November, summoned seven leaders of the Zentrum in the Rhineland to a secret meeting in Cologne City Hall. Among those who attended were clerical representatives of the Archbishop of Cologne and an influential Catholic editor with personal ties to the French High Command on the Western Front.

The meeting, according to contemporary accounts which have survived, discussed the possible annexation of the west bank of the Rhine by the Allied armies, which seemed likely. Those present went even further. They discussed the possibility of *establishing an independent Rhineland republic*.

Adenauer's action in summoning such a meeting and going on to discuss such a revolutionary possibility was distinctly equivocal. He was the elected chief magistrate of the principal city of the Rhineland. He was, in addition, a high civil servant of the Prussian, and therefore of the German Government in Berlin. He had certainly no mandate either from those by whom he had been elected or from those to whom he was responsible, the Berlin Cabinet, to consider a proposal which in effect meant the

break up of the Reich. Admittedly he acted in a moment of supreme crisis in German history. His Imperial master had just
disappeared. But no one born with that German sensitivity to
legal and constitutional niceties could doubt that the Socialist
leaders in Berlin were constitutionally taking over the government of the Reich.

For the first time Konrad Adenauer had demonstrated that
cynical willingness to ride roughshod over constitutional niceties
– the same cynical opportunism as he showed forty years later in
Bonn when, for a few weeks, he contemplated changing the West
German constitution to make himself a presidential autocrat in
order to attain what he considered a desirable end. In other words,
the end always justified the means, no doubt a sound principle for
a lifelong student of Machiavelli.

In November, 1918, Adenauer, however, would appear to
have been distinctly conscious of the somewhat unconstitutional
and authoritarian course which he was following. And when at
the secret meeting of the Zentrum on 9th November, he was
asked to make preliminary soundings among other parties, he
hesitated. He countered by saying that his thoughts at this
moment of crisis were 'not yet sufficiently clear to undertake
such negotiations and he would need time to think about it'.
What Adenauer did in these next few days to further the counter-
revolution, and still more what he thought, is obscured by events
of the intervening years. Twelve years of Nazi rule, the R.A.F.'s
thousand bomber raids on Cologne, and the ravages of occupation armies both in the Rhineland and in Berlin have blurred the
record for all time.

In spite of his hesitation, Adenauer's mind had cleared sufficiently to permit him a few days after the Armistice to open
secret negotiations with representatives of both the Social
Democrats in the Rhineland and the Liberal parties. By that time
the situation had been clarified for everyone by publication of the
two armistice clauses under which Marshal Foch, as Allied Commander-in-Chief, proposed to deal with the Rhineland:

1. Evacuation of all German forces from the left bank of the Rhine and the bridgeheads of Cologne, Coblenz and Mainz, and the occupation of the whole areas by the Allied armies.

2. Creation of a demilitarized zone, twenty to twenty-five miles deep along the east bank of the Rhine opposite the occupied territory on the west bank.

While continuing to carry on clandestine negotiations, Oberbürgermeister Adenauer was also striving to maintain control of the city. Through British liaison officers, who arrived to arrange for British General Headquarters to be set up in Cologne, he endeavoured to expedite the arrival of British occupation troops in the city. He failed: On 4th December, on the eve of the British arrival, some of the more rabid fanatics of the Zentrum decided to take action while still unencumbered by occupation forces.

On that day Catholic newspapers in the Rhineland demanded a plebiscite of the Rhineland population *preparatory to the establishment of an independent Rhine republic*. The same evening, a few hours before the British arrival, a meeting of the Zentrum bosses was held, apparently with the intention of proclaiming the Rhineland republic.

Adenauer, so far as can now be established, for some days previously had been secretly in touch with the German Socialist Government in Berlin, whether with the consent of his Zentrum friends is uncertain.

A few hours before the Zentrum meeting, Adenauer received a telephone call from Berlin. This warned him that the Government of Ebert and Scheidemann were strongly opposed even to a federal Rhineland Republic. As Oberbürgermeister he was forbidden to issue any such proclamation.

Adenauer therefore failed to appear at the Zentrum meeting. Later, he claimed that he had known nothing about the proposed proclamation. He stated: 'At the Zentrum meeting of 4th December the plan for a separate Rhineland was openly announced, for the first time, to the best of my knowledge. I was completely astounded when I read of it in the newspapers on the following morning.'

At a distance of nearly half a century, one can only presume that on that occasion the memory of Dr. Adenauer was unusually vague. More probably, Adenauer with his usual adroitness had realized that the Berlin Government was more firmly in the saddle than the Rhineland Zentrum had realized, and was covering his tracks to prepare for a retreat in good order.

In fairness to Adenauer, it is certain that leaders of all political parties in the Rhineland at the time believed that French annexation was imminent. All were searching for some solution to avert such drastic French action. For at that time Paris newspapers had openly announced a plan for the division of Germany into four parts, one of which would be an independent Rhineland republic. And in all the intrigues of the period the key question was what was meant by 'independent'.

Within a day or two, the first British Army of the Rhine occupied Cologne after a number of initial encounters in which the Oberbürgermeister first demonstrated that instinctive arrogance towards, and distaste for the British which he was never able completely to conceal in later years.

Three days after the last of the beaten German troops had retreated over the Rhine bridges, a British tank drove up to the door of the Cologne City Hall. Two young officers appeared through the lid on the top. Marching smartly into the Rathaus, they asked in broken German for the Oberbürgermeister. They were shown to Adenauer's study where they were received coldly. They began at once to make arrangements for the peaceful arrival of the main body of the British occupation forces.

As they sat smoking in arm-chairs facing Adenauer's desk, the two young officers let the ash from the cigarettes drop on to the carpet. In the tense circumstances of a first meeting between the chief magistrate of an occupied city and envoys of the occupying power a more tactful German would have ignored the ash on his carpet. But tact was never a virtue of Konrad Adenauer. Ostentatiously he rang the bell on his desk. An attendant appeared and Adenauer announced distinctly in his slow Cologne drawl: 'The gentlemen require ash-trays.'

In Adenauer's authorized biography this incident is reported somewhat gleefully, in an apparent attempt to prove his superiority over the British even in the circumstances of December, 1918.

But Adenauer had not finished with the British. When, a few hours later, the British commanding general reached Cologne, he presented the Oberbürgermeister with a proclamation to the citizens. This imposed various, quite understandable restrictions on life in the city. It concluded by stating that all German men should raise their hats on meeting a British officer.

A stony-faced Adenauer read the document. Frigidly he informed the general, 'I can scarcely believe that a British gentleman would treat a conquered people in this way.'

According to Adenauer's authorized biography, the British general answered in an uncertain voice, 'I have orders to give this to you. What you do with it must be your business.'

Adenauer thereupon most offensively pushed the proclamation into a corner and said: 'I will carry out your order in so far as my conscience allows.'

To this the British general answered, 'And we will treat you correctly as is our duty.'

The details of this first encounter with a British general seem somewhat unreal and clearly owe something to typical Adenauer propaganda. What is surprising is that Adenauer, thirty-five years later, should have permitted these trivial incidents to be published in an authorized biography. His never well-concealed distaste for most things British had become so obsessional in advanced age that not even the normal niceties of diplomatic protocol could prevent the Federal German Chancellor making cheap propaganda at the expense of his British allies.

The British had just reached Cologne at the beginning of December, 1918, when the German Government in Berlin, under political pressure from all sides, decided to examine the future of the Rhineland. On 15th December a meeting was held at Elberfeld in the Ruhr between representatives of the Berlin administration and the principal political leaders in the Rhine, including Adenauer. At the meeting he astounded some of his Zentrum friends by disclaiming all knowledge of what had taken place at the meeting of 4th December – which he had carefully not attended – and publicly blaming them for precipitate action.

Adenauer at this time was almost certainly playing a political double-game, trying to satisfy both the most rabid separatists among his Zentrum associates and, at the same time, to lull the fears of the German Government in Berlin. Following this equivocal line, he held a series of meetings during the next few weeks at one of which he told industrial and commercial magnates that a Rhenish-Westphalian republic was inevitable in the existing state of European affairs.

He also tried discreetly to win over the British to the cause of Rhineland separatism, and had some discussions with an envoy of the then British Foreign Secretary, Mr. Balfour. But Mr. Lloyd George and his colleagues in the British Cabinet, who were highly suspicious of the aims of Clemençeau and Foch, gave little encouragement to the Oberbürgermeister – a failure which was no doubt privately chalked up as another black mark against the British.

Throughout all these dubious and, indeed, somewhat jesuitical proceedings, Adenauer seemed to be searching for some quasi-legal method of establishing a separate Rhineland state without going to the unconstitutional, not to say treasonable, extremes urged by some of his close associates.

At this stage a general election for the new German Parliament at Weimar was held. The Socialists in Berlin gained a substantial, but not complete victory and a coalition with other democratic parties became inevitable.

With broadly based support, the German Government, fortified by the votes of the people and the strong arm tactics of the

new Defence Minister Noske, turned its attention to the various
seditious movements along the fringes of the Reich, including
that in the Rhineland.

It was, therefore, in an atmosphere of increasing Berlin opposition to any radical solution of the Rhineland problem that
Adenauer and other political, industrial and clerical leaders in the
area summoned a 'special parliament' to meet in Cologne on
1st February, 1919. All the Reichstag deputies elected for Rhineland constituencies in the general election a few weeks earlier and
the chief magistrates of the principal cities and towns were summoned to attend. Of the eighty-four invited sixty-five appeared in
the Hansa Chamber of Cologne City Hall.

On the night before the so-called 'special parliament', Adenauer
is alleged to have told a visitor that he had prepared a strong
speech calling for *the immediate proclamation of a West German
State*. Next morning he appeared at the meeting tense and nervous,
and not without cause. For in a Cologne park had been found an
open grave with a rudely inscribed headstone: 'Here lies Konrad
Adenauer, First President of the Rhineland Republic.'

Whatever speech he may have prepared the previous evening,
it was a careful and statesmanlike address, lasting three hours,
which he delivered to the 'special parliament'.

Objectively he examined the attitude of the Western Allies to
the future of Germany, demonstrating a peculiar understanding
of French susceptibilities, as he was to do so often during the
next half-century. 'Germany may recover,' he said, 'and take revenge on France. It is absolutely essential, therefore, that France
should obtain guarantees that would make it impossible for
Germany to take revenge in the foreseeable future.' His solution
was the 'creation of a West German Republic *within* the bounds of
the German Reich'.

'I take the view,' he continued, 'that whatever the circumstances *a West German Republic* must be created in a legitimate
way within the constitution of the Reich.'

Adenauer's speech was most adroit. His Zentrum friends were

franker; they proposed revolutionary measures, but were at once faced by threats from the Social Democrats at the meeting. At the slightest hint of an attempt to secede, warned the Socialists, millions of workers in the Ruhr and Rhineland would come out in a general strike.

For hours the 'special parliament' argued acrimoniously. Finally, the extremists from whom Adenauer had ostentatiously kept his distance were forced to yield. At his suggestion it was agreed to appoint a West German Political Committee to inquire further into the whole question. Adenauer was chosen as chairman.

Its further activities were most succinctly reported in Clemençeau's memoirs:

'The Bürgermeister of Cologne, Adenauer, had taken over the leadership of the (Separatist) movement. On 1st February, 1919, all Rhineland deputies and bürgermeisters of the Rhineland towns were summoned to Cologne. It was intended to ceremonially proclaim the establishment of the Rheinish Republic. What happened? Under the influence of Adenauer a committee was elected to work on the creation of a self-sufficient Rhineland in the association of the German Reich. How often did it meet? Not at all!' Adenauer's private intelligence service, as always, was good. Just before the meeting of the 'special parliament', he had heard a whisper from Zentrum friends in Berlin. For not all German Catholic politicians were Rhineland separatists. Four days after the Cologne 'special parliament', the Social Democrats in Berlin formed a Left-centre German Coalition Government with non-Rhineland *Zentrum deputies* as their principal partners. That no doubt accounted for the initial delay in calling a meeting of the Rhineland Political Committee. Within a few weeks a more sinister and more formidable authority, the revived German High Command behind the Socialist-Zentrum coalition in Berlin, had expressed disapproval of Rhineland separatism.

At the beginning of March, 1919, Adenauer received a visitor from Berlin, a major of the German General Staff who brought from the German High Command a sharp protest against any proposal to establish a separate Rhineland republic. With that lack of tact for which the High Command was notorious, Adenauer was informed that the Rhineland need now have no fear of the spread of Bolshevism as the High Command was again 'completely master of the situation in Berlin and through the Reich'. That was indeed true. Adenauer took the hint.

A few months later when, at the beginning of June, Dorten, a Rhineland quisling in the pay of the French High Command, raised the flag of revolt in his native Wiesbaden, Adenauer's attitude was beyond reproach. Summoned on a Sunday morning to British General Headquarters to consider the consequences of Dorten's revolt, he counselled General Clive, political adviser to the British Commander-in-Chief, to issue an order 'forbidding any change in the form of the British-occupied territory without the permission of the British military government authorities'.

CHAPTER TWO

Separatism Again

In July, 1919, Germany, after much hesitation and intense controversy, finally signed the Versailles Treaty and the intense political
activity of the months following the armistice quickly declined.

Konrad Adenauer had once again time to contemplate his own
personal problems in which his three motherless children stood
in the forefront. The two boys Konrad and Max and his little girl
Ria had become great favourites of their neighbour in Max
Bruchstrasse, Professor Zinsser, who held the chair of Derma-
tology in Cologne University. As a result the Oberbürgermeister,
who even then was an enthusiastic gardener, came to know the
two young daughters of the professor and especially the prettier,
Gussi. It soon became obvious to the professor and his wife that
the 43-year-old Oberbürgermeister was falling hopelessly in
love with their daughter, eighteen years his junior. Her parents,
understandably, opposed the match. For in addition to the question of age there was the problem of religious creeds. But the
much-loved girl was determined to marry the stiff, but chivalrous
man whom she had first met over the garden fence. Finally,
parental opposition was withdrawn.

They were married quietly and, despite the big difference in
age, Dr. Adenauer and his charming wife remained an ideally
happy married couple until the death of the second Frau Adenauer
in 1948, on the eve of her husband becoming an international
personality.

The second Frau Adenauer's father was, in fact, an American-
born German who had returned to the land of his fathers. This
second marriage to a girl who was half American was of profound

importance to the development of German policy forty years later. For it marked the beginning of that feeling of kinship for the United States which, during his Chancellorship, developed with growing fervour until the advent of John Fitzgerald Kennedy transformed the relationship at the start of the sixties. Adenauer became very proud of this American tie and when he first visited the United States, in 1953, with one of the daughters of his second marriage, Lotte, he emphasized to reporters that her grandfather had been an American.

His second marriage also brought political links which, at the time it was celebrated, would have seemed mere fantasy. Frau Adenauer had three American cousins, one of whom was a member of the great Morgan financial empire in New York. His two sisters married two promising young men from the same circle – Mr. Lewis Douglas, later U.S. Ambassador in London, and Mr. John J. McCloy, who by a remarkable coincidence became first U.S. High Commissioner in Germany at almost the same moment as Konrad Adenauer was elected Federal Chancellor in 1949. Mr. McCloy continued to play a key role in American affairs and was one of the chief advisers of President Kennedy at the time of the Cuba crisis in 1962.

Of this second marriage four children were born; Paul, now a brilliant Monsignor certainly marked for preferment in the German hierarchy; Lotte who married an architect after – it was rumoured in Bonn – strong opposition from her father; Libeth, now the wife of a son of the millionaire Wehrhahn family and nephew of her father's great friend, Cardinal Frings of Cologne; and George, a young lawyer married to the blonde daughter of a Swedish industrial magnate whom he met on a ski-ing holiday in the Alps.

By the time of his second marriage Konrad Adenauer, as a result of his Rhineland activity, had emerged as one of the most important political figures in Western Germany.

With the Zentrum in the Government coalition in Berlin it seemed likely that the Oberbürgermeister of Cologne must soon be a national figure. That estimate was correct, although his arrival in high office was to be delayed for some thirty years.

As Oberbürgermeister one of his main pre-occupations was, not surprisingly, with his masters, the British Army Headquarters on his doorstep. For the seven years, between 1919 and 1926, that the British were in Cologne, his main task was often to attempt to find a compromise between the needs of his city and the inevitable demands of the British generals.

Many lasting Anglo-German friendships were formed during these years. But the dour, stiff and very arrogant Oberbürgermeister was the antithesis of the Rhineland personalities whom so many of the British found congenial. British official relations with Adenauer, on the surface at least, remained correct. They were never cordial. For Adenauer's part in the separatist intrigues of the post-armistice months had been fully observed by the British Intelligence services. By the early twenties the British Government was becoming increasingly distrustful of French ambitions on the Rhine and Adenauer's known pro-French sympathies, his extreme clericalism and his narrow authoritarian outlook not unnaturally made him an object of considerable suspicion in Whitehall.

Not all of these suspicions were revealed. But a vast amount of information about Adenauer and his political activities was duly recorded in the British Intelligence files. These were the files which played a big part in relations between Adenauer and the British many years later, and which had become 'top secret' documents by the time he was at the height of his power as Federal Chancellor.

With only the Rhineland occupied British interference in German affairs was much less open after the First World War, than following the unconditional surrender of 1945. So long as Adenauer as Oberbürgermeister carried out Germany's treaty obligations he could do what he liked. And so Adenauer continued to strengthen the political and commercial ties in Western Germany which had always been so important in his public life.

It was during the post-armistice period that Adenauer formed a close friendship with the late Dr. Robert Pferdmenges, a partner in the great Oppenheim banking house. The friendship began during an attempt to settle some minor religious squabble about Good Friday, for Dr. Pferdmenges was a zealous Protestant. It was an association which was to have vital consequences for Konrad Adenauer in days of crisis, and later in his days of power. For Dr. Pferdmenges provided what Konrad Adenauer lacked, an expert knowledge of commerce and economics on which the future Federal Chancellor called many times during the long years of their friendship.

Pferdmenges, son of a wealthy millowner in Mönchen-Gladbach, had served his banking apprenticeship in the city of London. There, during a ten years' stay prior to 1914, he had acquired a wife, and a taste for Scots tweed, Scotch whisky, bowler hats, and British pipe tobacco, plus a pawky sense of humour. He was, in fact, a cosmopolitan of sound high Tory views and the complete antithesis of the reserved Oberbürgermeister.

This friendship led to that with another banker, Baron von Schroeder. For many years the three families formed a compact little group. But in the early thirties their ways parted, as the Oberbürgermeister became increasingly anti-Nazi whilst Baron von Schroeder became the confidant of Ribbentrop, later Nazi Foreign Minister. But when, in 1949, the pro-Nazi Baron was tenderly handled by a German denazification tribunal, British officials indicated that Adenauer had interceded on his former friend's behalf.

In these early years of the Weimar Republic, Adenauer's prestige and influence among the members of the Zentrum party gained him a reputation far beyond Cologne. When it was decided to form a Prussian State Council, or Upper House, as one of the two organs of representative government in Prussia, Adenauer was elected chairman, an appointment he continued to hold throughout the Weimar Republic.

The Prussian State Council was the Federal Chamber to which

various Prussian provinces sent representatives. Adenauer's appointment was clearly a sop to the Rhineland separatists, for he was widely regarded as a particularist who would combat the centralist tendencies of the Prussian lower house and Social Democrat Government.

It was this presidency of the Prussian State Council which put him into the running for much higher office when, in the spring of 1921, he became a potential German Reich Chancellor.

Adenauer was summoned to the presidential palace following the so-called London ultimatum by the Allies of 5th May, 1921. The Western Powers, profoundly dissatisfied by the way Germany was meeting her reparations commitments, had given the German Government six days in which to meet a demand for £600,000,000 of alleged arrears. Failure to pay, the Germans were warned, would lead to the occupation of the Ruhr, a hint of French policy to come. The German Government promptly resigned, and Konrad Adenauer was invited to form a new government which would pay the debts.

He quickly realized that there was only one way to meet the Allied demands – the Germans must work harder. It was on this basis that he set out to form a ministry. Both he and his policies, however, were anathema to the Social Democrats who were an essential part of any German government coalition. His policy meant the abandonment of the Socialists' cherished eight-hour day. So Konrad Adenauer did not become Reich Chancellor.

Adenauer returned to Cologne and a more pliable member of the Zentrum, Wirth, became Reich Chancellor. But the reparations problem remained and, from his exceptional vantage-point in the metropolis of the Western occupied territories, Adenauer watched the position steadily decline. For in the months after Adenauer's failure to form a German government the German reparations problem began to have widespread international repercussions. There was, first of all, the tension between Germany and the Western Allies over the German failure to meet the reparations payments laid down at Versailles. Out of this had grown an almost equally tense situation between Britain and France over Germany's ability to pay.

The British, impressed by the dangers to Europe of a bankrupt Germany (as, with their Allies, they were again after 1945), favoured a moratorium on the reparations payments. But Poincaré, the chauvinistic Prime Minister of France was determined to have his pound of flesh, despite the fact that in midsummer, 1922, Reich Chancellor Wirth warned the Allies that the value of the mark was falling so fast that a financial catastrophe was inevitable.

Adenauer in Cologne had maintained his links with the great magnates of the Ruhr of whom the formidable Hugo Stinnes was by this time the acknowledged leader. Stinnes, with Adenauer acting as a go-between from the occupied Rhineland territories, made an effort to pacify Poincaré. Acting almost independently of Berlin, the 'Titan of the Ruhr', with the Oberbürgermeister of Cologne as his shadow, made an agreement with the French to provide hundreds of millions of gold marks' worth of material from his Ruhr empire for the reconstruction of devastated north-east France.

Adenauer's part in the transaction was certainly motivated by those openly pro-French sympathies which were to persist until they reached their apotheosis when yet another elderly and devout Catholic authoritarian, Charles de Gaulle, was ruler of France four decades later.

Before the Stinnes agreement could come into operation, the situation deteriorated further. Poincaré announced that he would seize the Reich-owned coal mines as security for the unpaid reparations. The British Government was strongly opposed to such a policy. By the beginning of 1923 the *Entente Cordiale* had reached one of the low ebbs to which it is subjected from time to time. A British-French conference to consider the question broke up in acrimony. A few days later Poincaré, backed by the Belgians, poured French troops into the Ruhr. The occupation of Germany's industrial heart had begun.

The Germans countered this drastic policy by a campaign of

Gandhi-like passive resistance, to which the French retorted by 'necessary coercion' and the French and Belgians seized the Rhineland railways.

The British had no part in this. In the British military enclave around Cologne things went on as before. Konrad Adenauer, as Oberbürgermeister of British-occupied Cologne, became almost the sole German high official in the Ruhr and Rhineland free to carry on his normal functions and to take orders from the German Government in Berlin.

Tension in the Ruhr and Rhineland mounted. The German mark plunged still further. It was soon obvious that Poincaré had failed to achieve his objective. The French were not getting the coal, but their occupation expenses soared to astronomical levels. It was a question of which, the French or the Germans, could hold out longer. All indications suggested that the French were the stronger. The Germans, with their national finances in uproar, were quite unable to continue to subsidize the Ruhr and Rhineland, from which Berlin was drawing none of the normal revenue in taxation, etc. The German Government in Berlin in the first place sought some sort of working arrangement to tide over the crisis period – either until British pressure would bring Poincaré to his senses, or his Government fell in the topsy-turvy of Third Republic political intrigue.

The situation rapidly deteriorated. By October, 1923, it was clear that a radical solution must be found. Adenauer, as the most prominent personality still free to function in the Rhineland, was summoned to Berlin. He was asked to help in finding a solution by which the occupied territories would be able to meet their own economic requirements and, above all, to raise their own taxation.

Adenauer is reported to have warned the German Government that it might be necessary in the circumstances to find a more drastic solution than had been even contemplated in 1919; that if the worst came to the worst it might be necessary to set up a *West German State, not necessarily within the framework of the Reich.*

By mid-October the financial situation in Germany, aggravated by the cost of maintaining the occupied territories, was completely out of hand. The main contributory factor was the 'Notgeld' — or emergency money issued in the previous few years. Issued originally towards the end of the First World War to meet rising costs of living, this emergency money had been exploited by German finance and big business to create controlled inflation, which would sabotage the payment of reparations. Eventually, no less than 2,000 municipalities, banks and industrial cartels were issuing their own notes, and what had originally been controlled financial sabotage developed into galloping inflation.

To meet this crisis of the Reich, the great German statesman, Gustav Stresemann took office, for the first and only time, as Reich Chancellor. On 18th October his Government obtained plenary powers to halt the inflation. At this moment Dr. Hjalmar Schacht appeared on the German financial stage and a new currency, the Rentenmark, was introduced. But within a few days it became clear that, so long as the drain on the currency caused by the occupied territories continued, there could be no financial stability. Stresemann had become convinced that he must bow to French demands. On 13th November Adenauer and other West German leaders were summoned to an emergency meeting at the Reich Chancellery in Berlin.

Contradictory accounts of what happened have been given. Adenauer's version has been challenged in material detail by other prominent Germans who were present. What is certain is that both the German Government and the Rhineland leaders knew that the West German occupied territories must be detached temporarily. According to Adenauer's version, Chancellor Stresemann announced that it was necessary to end the policy of subsidizing the occupied territories. The only way out of the terrible dilemma, he is reported to have said, was the creation of an independent Rhineland state, separated in effect, but not legally from the Reich. Stresemann is said to have told the Rhinelanders that they had better go at once to M. Tirard, the French president

of the Inter-Allied Commission at Coblenz and make the necessary arrangements.

Adenauer claims he violently opposed this and told Stresemann
it was the Reich's duty to support the occupied territories. The
Reich Government, however, had other troubles – including the
revolt in Munich headed by Hitler. Stresemann, troubled by a
weak heart, retired to a sanatorium and resigned after '100 days'.
He was replaced by a Zentrum politician, Chancellor Marx who
summoned his colleague Adenauer to Berlin once again. Marx had
apparently been of the same opinion as Stresemann, but after
Adenauer had explained the situation fully, the new Chancellor
seems to have decided that the whole question must again be
thoroughly investigated.

That, according to a statement in Adenauer's authorized biography, is the last that 'we heard of the separation of the occupied
territories'. This appears to be an altogether too simple explanation. According to other, perhaps more objective contemporary
observers, Adenauer was the leader of what has been called the
'cold' separatist movement. In the last week of November, within
a day or two of seeing Chancellor Marx in Berlin, Dr. Adenauer
made another visit, this time crossing from British-occupied
territory into the French-occupied zone, where he met the French
Commissioner Tirard, the very man whom Stresemann had told
the Rhinelanders to meet.

What was discussed is obscure. It may fairly be guessed finance
was the main subject, as the meeting between Adenauer and
Tirard had followed preparatory discussion between the French
and Adenauer's intimate friend of the Koelner Kluengel, the great
banker Louis Hagen. Adenauer's political opponents from the
Left alleged that political questions also were discussed. It was
said in one instance that Adenauer and Tirard unofficially discussed a plan for a Directory to take over the administration of
the occupied territories with Adenauer as *Staatssurrogat* or
Viceroy of Occupied Western Germany.

In other versions it was suggested that Adenauer, with the

backing of Stinnes and the other Ruhr moguls, was negotiating
for the creation of a West German federal state, that this would
have its own international *gendarmerie* and its own diplomatic
representatives overseas, but would remain loosely represented on
a Federal Council in Berlin. The French quisling, Dorten, whose
account must be regarded as highly suspect, alleged that Adenauer
offered Tirard to set up an independent West German republic
and that Tirard when recounting this to his lackey Dorten, asked
cynically, 'Would you be prepared then, Herr Dorten to give up
your place to Herr Adenauer?'

Adenauer's previous adroit manoeuvres and his political
record as Federal Chancellor in Bonn strongly suggest that he
was much too astute to have committed himself so far. From his
conversations with the different Berlin governments he was very
well aware just how far he could go without committing treason,
but there is no doubt that some members of the administration in
Berlin had been willing to go a very long way indeed.

In any case, he almost certainly realized the inevitably
unstable character of the crisis. Just how far the authoritarian
Oberbürgermeister of Cologne would have allowed his ambition
to take him towards his becoming head of a West German State
must remain a question of history unlikely ever to be solved. In
fairness to Adenauer it must be emphasized that in 1933 Goering,
as Prime Minister of Prussia after the Nazi take-over, ordered a
full investigation of Adenauer's alleged separatist activities and
that even the Nazis were unable to obtain sufficient evidence to
proceed with a prosecution – which may, of course, have been
a tribute to Dr. Adenauer's political agility.

What is almost certain is that in the last weeks of 1923 Adenauer
and Tirard did discuss a separate currency for the occupied territories, and the creation of a Rhenish-Westphalian Currency
Bank. This scheme seems to have contained some of the germs of
the plan for German-French economic co-operation which thirty-
five years later, developed into the European Common Market.
So far did the negotiation go that on 1st December Tirard told a

meeting of Rhineland bankers and other interested parties that
the French Government approved this plan. On the same day
Dr. Adenauer gave an interview to a Paris newspaper in which he
stated that a breakaway of the Rhineland from Prussia would be a
great sacrifice, but that it might prove necessary in the interest of
general peace.

He then went on to make a fascinating prediction: peace would
be assured *if a tie up could be created between German and French
heavy industry.* That idea was put away for a long time. But, just
as his anti-British outbursts tended to repeat themselves over the
years, his 1923 proposal for German-French industrial co-operation duly reappeared in 1950 and developed into what became
the European Coal and Steel Community.

After the meeting in Bonn, Tirard made an effort to raise backing in New York for his proposed bank; but he was faced by a
formidable opposition. Dr. Schacht, as Reich Currency Commissioner, had enlisted the help of his friends in the Bank of England
to thwart the plan for a separate currency. Little more was ever
heard of it and no doubt Adenauer chalked up yet another black
mark against the interfering British.

The French plans for political separatism in the Rhineland
eventually had as little success as the project for financial and
economic autonomy. At the end of 1923 Poincaré, alarmed at the
failure of his policies, was forced to accept British-American proposals for two commissions, headed by the British Mr. Reginald
McKenna and the American General Dawes, to investigate the
whole question of German reparations. Among the experts
nominated to assist was a brilliant young Wall Street lawyer who
was already an expert on German affairs. His name was Mr. John
Foster Dulles. Poincaré's policy, in fact, had so strained the
French franc that in the spring of 1924 he disappeared at the
French elections, and with him went Rhineland separatism.

In the months and years that followed, bitter controversy raged
over the part played by Adenauer and other prominent Germans.
Charges of high treason were made and denied. The complete

historical truth will certainly never be known. Historians of the
Weimar Republic have stated that during the catastrophic developments of 1923, many of those who had previously opposed Rhineland separatism became convinced that they must take the fate of
their country in their own hands. This involved a 'sort of cold
separatism' supported by leading Rhineland personalities who
evolved plans for some sort of special state which *temporarily*
would be separated from the Reich. Under pressure of events this
movement extended into circles around Chancellor Stresemann.
Among its leaders were Adenauer and the Cologne banker,
Louis Hagen. This cold separatism became more and more a
legal movement into which finally the Government of the Reich
was drawn.

A much stronger viewpoint was taken by Adenauer's Zentrum
colleague, the former Reich Chancellor Franz von Papen, in his
memoirs written after the last war. Looking back thirty years von
Papen said, 'Certain personalities even advocated the establishment of a new Rhineland republic with its capital in Cologne.
One of these was Dr. Adenauer. Although he held one of the
highest offices of the Reich as President of the Prussian State
Council he seemed to put the interests of his city above those
of his country as a whole.

'At an emergency meeting of the Zentrum party organization I
described the whole idea of a Rhineland republic as *treasonable* . . .
and had some hard things to say.'

Others, too, were critical. Various leaders of the Zentrum,
including the Reich Chancellor Dr. Marx, were most unhappy
about the part played by Adenauer and his associates. After the
German general election in early 1925 he was accused by fellow
party members of having created national weakness and, at a
meeting in Cologne when the party's dirty linen was washed, he
was accused of 'having been ready to let the Rhineland go to the
devil'. Adenauer appealed to the new German Chancellor, Dr.
Luther, to disclose all the facts, but Luther declined on the grounds
of public interest.

For the remainder of the Weimar Republic the Left wing of the Zentrum, in particular, continued to regard Adenauer with grave suspicion and when he took office in 1949 as Chancellor of the Bonn republic, the Communists again raised the old cry of 'Separatist'. Adenauer categorically denied that he had ever been a separatist – either in 1919 or 1923 – and emphasized that the Nazis had gone into the matter and failed to prove anything against him.

Whether Adenauer *was* a separatist depends largely on what interpretation the word is given. He was certainly never a quisling like the French puppets who set up a provisional Rhineland régime with French bayonets and Poincaré's gold, and both in 1919 and in 1923 he had the excuse of some sort of tacit approval from Berlin, however unwillingly it may have been given. But the course which Adenauer followed on those occasions undeniably was the antithesis of democracy. As in his later years, he seemed to show Bismarckian disregard for the views of the millions of Germans whom he autocratically took it upon himself to represent.

With the disappearance of the last vestige of Rhineland separatism Adenauer retired again to Cologne to concentrate on his duties as Oberbürgermeister. There, in the heyday of the Weimar Republic, his sway was almost as unlimited as that of his historic predecessors, the old Prince Bishops of Cologne. He was one of the great Oberbürgermeisters of whom Stresemann wrote in his diary, 'After the great industrialists they were the monarchs of everyday life.'

Elected for twelve years these civic magnates were literally the All-Highest in the area they administered. They often exercised much more influence than the constantly changing Cabinet Ministers of the Weimar régime. With a handsome salary and liberal allowances, they maintained a pomp and circumstance equalled only by the very rich. One British historian of the period has said, 'These men were the rulers of the public rather than their servants – and they felt their role.'

Adenauer was certainly ruler of Cologne and loved it. Among these civic princes of the Weimar Republic the Oberbürgermeister of Cologne was widely recognized as one of the greatest autocrats in the Reich. There was nothing comparable in the Anglo-Saxon civic system, for he was the complete German Pooh-Bah. Not only was he an elected Lord Mayor paid as a high civil servant, he was also Lord Lieutenant, Town Clerk, Commissioner of Police and permanent head of every municipal department in Cologne. Beyond the city he was permanent President of the Prussian State Council, Chairman of the Rhineland Provincial Committee and President of the German Council of Cities. It is easy to understand why his political opponents referred to him scathingly as 'one of the most powerful three men in Prussia'. And through his long-standing friendship with the Ruhr and Rhineland barons, he had begun to acquire important directorships, perquisites which were the subject of much criticism.

His critics, growing in number from year to year, concentrated on his vast income. By the mid-twenties it was reputed to be in excess of £15,000 a year in addition to allowances for houses and other expenses. He was widely known as the 'highest paid official in Germany, drawing more than the Reich President'. And if his emoluments befitted the supreme autocrat so did his actions. In the face of intensive local opposition he pushed forward his personal plan to convert the ground formerly occupied by the ancient walls of Cologne into a 'green belt'. The Socialists felt the ground might have been better used for workers' houses. Thereafter he gained yet another nickname, that of 'The Gardener', which was not meant as a tribute to his undoubted skill in the cultivation of roses.

The longer Adenauer remained Oberbürgermeister the more dictatorial and indifferent to public opinion he became. This reached a climax in 1926 when he demonstrated to the people of Cologne, as he demonstrated in Bonn decades later, that he cared nothing for normal constitutional processes if they stood in his way.

At that time Cologne decided to build a new Rhine bridge on the northern fringe of the city. There was considerable argument between the supporters of an arched bridge, as proposed by Krupp, and a suspension bridge for which another firm had made a tender and which was strongly supported by Adenauer. In the committee with which lay the decision, seven favoured the arched bridge. Two, including Adenauer, favoured the alternative suspension bridge. The arch-bridge plan was therefore accepted. Adenauer had never much respect for democratic procedure and did not accept the majority decision. First he tried propaganda. When that failed an expert was produced who claimed that the Rhine bank was not firm enough to carry the foundations for an arched bridge. Adenauer finally got the bridge he wanted. In due course the Royal Air Force disposed of it.

The British had not been involved in the bridge controversy but they were much in Adenauer's thoughts at the time. After seven years of British supervision the Oberbürgermeister had become somewhat obsessional on the subject of his Anglo-Saxon overlords. His long-standing irritation broke into open venom when in 1925 the scheduled departure of the British troops – for various international reasons – was delayed until the following year. Throwing all discretion to the wind, Adenauer made a speech which both the British officials in Cologne and the Government in London regarded as open offence.

First of all, Adenauer emphasized that the Rhineland was one of the oldest cultural areas in Europe. He attacked the occupation authorities for 'treating the people of the Rhineland in this age of democracy like a nigger tribe in Central Africa which has been deprived of its freedom without being asked'. The spiteful reference to Africa, where only too recently Britain had acquired the mandate over some of Imperial Germany's colonies, left no doubt of the intended target. At this juncture the British Government was preparing the groundwork of what became the Locarno Pact with the greatest German of the time, Gustav Stresemann; so Adenauer's offensive outburst was merely noted, and ignored.

But, if twenty years later, the 1945 successors of the earlier
Cologne military government viewed Adenauer with some suspicion he had no one to blame but himself.

The British were not his only target. He hated Stresemann
almost as much. When Sir Austen Chamberlain, Briand and the
great German Foreign Minister finally signed the Locarno Pact
the narrow, parochial autocrat of Cologne could see nothing
beyond the Rhineland. 'It is nearly seven years since the Rhineland was occupied,' he commented. 'Yet despite all the nice words
one cannot fail to note that no date has yet been given for an end
of the occupation.'

In the midst of these developments yet another Weimar minority government fell. There was talk of forming a majority
administration, to include the Social Democrats, and in a bid to
find a comparatively independent Chancellor some of the Zentrum
leaders proposed Adenauer. He was summoned to Berlin where he
held conversations for some days with various party leaders.
It soon became evident that Stresemann, whose prestige was such
that he must remain Foreign Minister, would have nothing to do
with the narrow-minded, anti-Locarno Rhineland Oberbürgermeister. Once again Adenauer returned to Cologne, to wait
another twenty-three years before his next attempt to become a
German Chancellor.

At the beginning of 1926 the city presented him with his
portrait in oils on his fiftieth birthday but, despite this, he was
scarcely a popular figure. The longer he remained Oberbürgermeister, the more autocratic he became. Criticism of his administration was widespread. The murmuring was far from being confined to his political opponents. The most valid criticisms were
that he rode roughshod over all opposition and that he refused
to give his subordinates any authority, concentrating power in his
own hands and those of his personal assistants. These were faults
which were to lie at the very foundations of his autocratic rule
as German Federal Chancellor. By 1929 when he was due for re-
election there was considerable doubt about his prospects. But the

Zentrum, though it included some of his leading critics, rallied to him. He was re-elected for another year by a bare majority of two votes.

Now, however, Adenauer had other critics beyond those who had appeared in the normal rough and tumble of normal democratic political controversy. The Nazis were steadily gaining strength, and among their principal targets in Western Germany was Konrad Adenauer. His dictatorial régime in Cologne, his lordly way of life, and his directorships provided plenty of scope for that other pupil of the Rhineland seminarists, Dr. Paul Josef Goebbels, who by this time was directing what has been called 'the stream of right-radical filth'.

Details of the Adenauer 'scandals' alleged to have been unearthed by the Nazis may be safely discounted. Adenauer hit back, and the fiercer the Nazi campaign against him the fiercer grew his opposition. In his powerful official position in Cologne and the Rhineland he was soon recognized by Hitler and his minions as one of their chief enemies in Western Germany.

Why Adenauer, almost by instinct, should have shown such early and determined opposition to the Brown-shirt gangsters is a fascinating problem. For in this same year of 1929, he was indiscreet enough to send Mussolini a glowing telegram on the signing of his Concordat with the Vatican – a telegram which was never mentioned in Bonn after 1949.

Like all high officials of Wilhelm II, Adenauer was a tremendous snob in the way that only a German high civil servant can be. Like the German generals, Adenauer almost certainly regarded Hitler and his companions as parvenus. But undoubtedly his opposition to the Nazis had a more profound basis. Konrad Adenauer had a Catholic education and background which, however narrow and authoritarian it may have been, developed in him a formidable logical intellect based on the highest moral values.

Dictatorial Adenauer might be, but he believed firmly in the Christian rights of the individual and the other principles of Western civilization. Inevitably, from the outset he was an anti-Nazi, as so many other fine and decent Germans were. In the last three years of the Weimar régime Adenauer moved steadily away from those of his Zentrum colleagues, like von Papen, who were prepared to sup with the devil provided the rights of the Roman Catholic Church were safeguarded. He became more and more intransigent, like those other great anti-Nazis, Cardinal Faulhaber of Munich and Bishop von Galen of Munster, who openly denounced the Nazis from the pulpit.

The finest tribute to Adenauer's stand against the Nazis was given in 1945 by that distinguished German trade unionist and close friend of Ernest Bevin, Dr. Hans Boeckler. 'During that period,' said Dr. Boeckler, 'Adenauer's attitude to the Nazis was beyond reproach. He was one of those Catholics who, contrary to some others, had no dealing with them.'

The moment that Hitler and the Nazis reached power on that memorable day at the end of January, 1933, it was clear that Adenauer's political, and probably, personal fate was sealed. At least so far as anyone could foresee.

CHAPTER THREE

Fugitive from the Nazis

AT THE END of January, 1933, Adolf Hitler became German Chancellor and the Weimar Republic, in which Adenauer had been an important but seldom a national figure, disappeared.

Germany was in the turmoil of the 'Brown Revolution'. Anyone who, like the stiff-necked Oberbürgermeister of Cologne, had been sufficiently unwise or courageous to proclaim himself publicly an anti-Nazi, was a marked man. The basically Catholic population of Cologne and the Rhineland had not been among Hitler's more fervent supporters, but almost at once Adenauer faced a demand for the Swastika to be hoisted over Cologne City Hall. He rejected this suggestion on the grounds of his political neutrality. His prevarication sufficed only for a week or so.

Hitler decided on an almost immediate general election. Soon he was in the midst of a grand tour of the Reich as part of the Nazi election campaign. In mid-February Rhineland newspapers announced 'Chancellor Hitler to Visit Cologne'. The showdown was approaching. But the 57-year-old Oberbürgermeister, with four small children at home, did not flinch.

Hitler's arrival was announced for 11 p.m. on February 17th. It was usual for the Oberbürgermeister to receive a Reich Chancellor at the airport. That evening Adenauer told one of his deputies, 'Hitler is coming, not as Reich Chancellor but as a party political speaker. Accordingly I have no responsibility as Oberbürgermeister to meet him. You can represent me.'

At eleven o'clock that night Hitler arrived by plane from Essen where he had made another election speech. In the receiving line

stood the heads of the Nazi party in the Rhineland, the commanding generals of the Wehrmacht and all the other local notabilities
except Konrad Adenauer. The city of Cologne was represented by
a junior assistant of the Oberbürgermeister.

As Hitler left the plane his eyes could be seen searching the
reception party. The insult was obvious. Furiously Hitler
marched to his car and headed at high speed for Bad Godesberg
and his favourite Dreesen Hotel, where five years later he argued
with Neville Chamberlain.

On Sunday, 19th February, Adenauer's deputy for police
affairs warned him that Nazi flags were already hanging from the
poles on the great Deutz Bridge opposite the cathedral. The
bridge was civic property. No authorization had been given for the
flags. The deputy telephoned Adenauer at his home and asked
what was to be done. Adenauer needed a few minutes to consider
the problem. Then categorically he gave the order: 'Remove the
Swastikas from the bridge. Send a gang of civic workers to do the
job. Take a squad of police to protect them. I shall have no
objection if you put up the Swastikas in front of the Fair Hall.'

The anti-flag party, with police protection, moved on to the
bridge. At once a group of Nazi Storm Troopers appeared. There
was a fierce argument between Adenauer's deputy and the
Storm Troopers whose chief went to a nearby pub to phone for
further orders. When he came back the Storm Trooper chief
told the Oberbürgermeister's deputy, in front of a tense crowd
which watched this scene, 'All right. Go on. But this is not the
end of it.'

All Cologne believed that Adenauer had virtually signed his
death warrant. But nothing happened. The Nazis were just as sly
as Konrad Adenauer. They always searched in local, as in international affairs to find some quasi-legal ground for action.
So the violently anti-Nazi Oberbürgermeister was left in office –
for the time being. But the Nazis did not attempt to conceal their
venom. The party collectors in the streets of Cologne pushed
their collecting boxes into the faces of passers-by with the shout,

'Another penny, and another shot at Adenauer.' Some former acquaintances, if not friends, began to cut the Oberbürgermeister and, worse still, his wife in the streets.

On the day of the German general election at the beginning of March, a Storm Troop guard appeared round his house in the Max Bruchstrasse. But still the Nazis played cat and mouse. A week later, and almost a month after his open insult to the Führer, municipal elections were held in Cologne. The Prussian government officials pleaded with Adenauer to take at least fourteen days' leave. He refused. But as a precaution he sent his wife and children to a Catholic Caritas home in Hohenlind.

On the day of the municipal elections there was a memorial service to the dead of the First World War, in Cologne. Despite all advice to the contrary, Adenauer decided to attend. During the service an old friend who had become a Nazi on opportunist grounds sidled alongside the Oberbürgermeister.

'You must get out of Cologne,' whispered the not very good Nazi. 'They have plans to murder you. You will be liquidated tomorrow when you arrive at your office in the morning, and your body is to be thrown from the window of your office into the street.'

After the service Adenauer returned to the office he had occupied for so many years, gathered his papers and left it for ever. That afternoon he visited his most trusted friend Dr. Pferdmenges. To fool the Nazi guard, he slept that night at his own home. Early in the morning he slipped past the Storm Troopers, who were sleeping contentedly in the knowledge that Adenauer had ordered his official car for nine o'clock – for his last ride as they thought. In the dim light of the dawn he found Dr. Pferdmenges's limousine concealed in a nearby street. At once he left for Dortmund in the Ruhr. From there he took an express to Berlin.

By that time the Cologne newspapers were carrying the sensational news of the flight of the Oberbürgermeister – 'the cowardly deserter' as the Nazi evening papers described him. Next morning in Berlin Adenauer formally presented himself at the office of his legal chief, the Prime Minister of Prussia, Nazi No. 2, Hermann Goering. He was kept waiting three days. Then Goering received him. He was cool but Goering could seldom forget completely that he had been born a gentleman. Calmly he asked Adenauer sitting opposite, 'And what had happened to the millions of marks that you took with you out of the city funds.'

Adenauer equally quietly replied, 'You know, Herr Minister, just as well as I do, that is complete nonsense.'

Goering did not pursue the matter further. He then turned to the matter of the Nazi flags on the bridge.

'Why did you remove the flags from the bridge, Herr Adenauer – you know that has given great offence to the Nazi comrades?'

Adenauer, stiff necked and arrogant as ever, with a courage that can only be described as reckless, calmly told him, 'Because I had the impression that the majority of the Cologne citizens did not approve. In any case it had been done without the approval of the civic administration.'

Goering, who was quite as intelligent and sly as Adenauer, saw there was nothing to be gained by an argument with the deposed Oberbürgermeister.

'At any rate,' said the Prussian Prime Minister, 'I have given orders for a senior civil servant to begin an inquiry into your activities as Oberbürgermeister and to examine the charges made against you. My further decisions will depend on the result of that inquiry.'

The Nazi attack was not confined to Adenauer; his closest collaborators were also removed from office. In an attempt to shield them, Adenauer wrote from Berlin to the Nazi who had taken over as Oberbürgermeister. In reply he received abuse.

The inquiry ordered by Goering, which examined among many other things Adenauer's alleged separatist activities, lasted a long time. The Nazis were apparently unable to obtain sufficient evidence and Goering let the matter drop. The man who founded the Gestapo had more important things to worry him than the peccadilloes of the arrogant ex-Oberbürgermeister of Cologne.

Adenauer's situation, however, was serious. His salary had been stopped and his bank account blocked. In despair he was wandering from refuge to refuge in Berlin when he had a visit from an old friend with whom he had done business in Cologne, Mr. D. N. Heinemann, an American-Jewish businessman, who had long lived in Brussels. Somehow Heinemann discovered Adenauer's hideout. As he entered, the American said, 'I can imagine that you need money. I have brought 10,000 marks with me. I knew there might be difficulty with a cheque so I brought it in cash.'

Adenauer tried to decline the offer. He said he was in no position to accept such a loan. 'Don't worry,' said his Jewish friend, 'I know that my money is safe.' That action was to have profound consequences for the new state of Israel twenty years later. And in 1953, when Dr. Adenauer, as German Federal Chancellor, for the first time visited the United States, his first visit when he left the ship in New York was to Greenwich Village – to greet his old friend Heinemann.

Adenauer realized that he could not remain in Berlin much longer. He suddenly thought of a school comrade Ildefons Herwegens, at that time Abbot of the Benedictine Monastery of Maria Laachs in the Eifel mountains near the Belgian frontier. He wrote to his old friend. At once came a telegram. 'I shall be delighted to have you with me.'

Frau Adenauer was called to Berlin and agreed with this solution of the immediate problem. They returned together to the West. At Neuss, near Düsseldorf, the limousine of Dr. Pferd-menges once again was waiting. Adenauer, however, was forbidden to enter the limits of Cologne and it was necessary to make a wide detour to reach Maria Laachs and the shelter of the monastery. There, in the comfortably furnished cell of a former Abbot, Dr. Adenauer lived quietly but safely for a considerable time.

It was at Maria Laachs that Adenauer, his wife and all the seven children of both marriages celebrated the Christmas of 1933. But the visit of the family was observed. The head of the Rhine province administration warned the Abbot that Adenauer could no longer find refuge in the monastery. Herwegens would have defied the order, but Adenauer feared to bring the gallant Abbot and his monks into danger. So once again he went to the other side of Germany – to the outskirts of Berlin where at Babelsberg near Potsdam he found a house for himself and his family. It was there on 30th June, 1934, 'The Night of the Long Knives' when Hitler liquidated his storm trooper paladins, that Adenauer was arrested by the Gestapo. He was imprisoned in the Potsdam police station. Adenauer believed his doom was sealed. The Gestapo car in which he was travelling through the woods near Potsdam approached a side road on which everyone in the district knew many Gestapo prisoners had been shot 'while attempting to escape'. At this moment one of the Gestapo men asked a comrade, 'Have you a gun with you?' Adenauer was certain of what was to happen. The car slowed down, and then carried on along the main road. Konrad Adenauer had escaped again.

He was three days in custody before he was released as a result of an order from Hitler that all those arrested and not shot should be freed. He was certain, however, that he was still in danger. As though to confirm his fears a telegram arrived from the Abbot of Maria Laachs, 'Danger threatening. Essential you leave on journey immediately.'

Many years later, in the archives of the Nazi Ministry of the Interior in the possession of the East German authorities, a letter written by Adenauer on 10th August, 1934 to the Nazi Minister of the Interior, Frick, was discovered. And in September, 1962, from his holiday retreat at Cadenabbia Adenauer confirmed the general authenticity of this letter, although not all its details.

In the East German version he wrote, 'I have always treated the Nazi party in an absolutely correct manner; in so doing I found myself repeatedly at loggerheads with ministerial directives and the opinion of the Zentrum faction on the Cologne City Council. For years, contrary to the decrees of the Prussian Ministry of the Interior, I made the municipal sports grounds available to the Nazis, and allowed them to hoist the Swastika flag on the municipal flag-poles at its meetings held there'. He then gave various explanations of incidents for which he had been much attacked by the Nazis, and protested bitterly about being dismissed as 'nationally unreliable'.

It would be a mistake to make too much of a begging letter of a man obviously near the end of his tether. He had narrowly escaped with his life a few weeks earlier. He realized that the Nazis had come to stay and was trying to make the best of it. It ill becomes any non-German who never had to face such a terrible dilemma to offer any judgement on such a letter.

For a time Adenauer travelled to and fro across Germany. Then one of his former colleagues in Cologne, who had also been sacked, found a small house for the Adenauer family in the village of Rhoendorf, on the east bank of the Rhine, south of Koenigs-winter and almost directly under the well-known Drachenfels. The house was old and damp, but Adenauer and his family were only too glad to be able to find such an obscure refuge. Once again they settled down. But the Nazis were still on the watch. After Adenauer quite innocently had taken part in the local 'Schutzenfest' (Shooting Festival) in the village, they again took action. His little house was just within the limits of the administration district of Cologne, from which officially he was banned.

He was told to get out. This time he found refuge four miles away in the village of Unkel, just outside the Cologne administrative district, where Catholic friends arranged for him to stay in a summer holiday home for Catholic priests. There, during the autumn and winter of 1935, his wife or children were able to visit him almost daily.

But, alone in the almost deserted priests' home, he became ever more depressed. He was on the verge of 60, he was without a job or an income. His future seemed hopeless. Constant rain and the mists of the Rhineland autumn increased his despair. Friends said that at that time he even contemplated suicide on one occasion.

After his sixtieth birthday at the beginning of 1936 things unexpectedly improved. In Cologne his fanatical successor had been replaced by a more reasonable member of the Nazi party who admitted to Adenauer's lawyer brother that the former Oberbürgermeister had been badly treated. He was permitted to return to Rhoendorf. After some negotiation in which it is generally believed his banker friends wielded considerable influence, the civic authorities agreed to pay part of the very large pension to which he was entitled as a lifelong Prussian civil servant. He was given a reasonable monthly sum and substantial compensation for two houses he had owned, and he was told that if he did not accept this settlement the Nazis would take new measures against him.

The sum which the Nazi authorities were willing to pay for his two houses was not ungenerous in the circumstances. It was with that money that he bought the site in Zennisweg in Honnef and built the comfortable villa in which he has continued to live ever since – even as Federal Chancellor in Bonn.

Some of his friends tended to criticize the villa, with its considerable number of rooms and big terrace overlooking the Rhine, but Adenauer felt that his political career was at an end. Only retirement faced him and he was determined after the escapes and flights of the previous few years to have a comfortable home for his large family. He personally superintended every detail of the construction while the garden was his own creation. Month after month he trundled stones and planted the roses which to this day are perhaps his greatest joy. He was still living quietly, though seldom far from catastrophe, when war started three years later. As the European scene darkened, however, he took precautions for he was sure that the outbreak of war would be the sign for a new wave of arrests of anti-Nazis like himself.

Late in August, 1939, he and his wife left for a quiet village in the Swiss canton of Valais where they often spent their holidays. His suspicions were correct. As soon as war was declared some of his closest friends were arrested and died in concentration camps. By the time Adenauer returned to Germany a week or two later the Nazis had forgotten him.

The war, apart from its inevitable restrictions on normal activity, brought little change to Adenauer. His garden was his main interest in these years of retirement. Later he was to tell his Cabinet in Bonn, 'On the whole I became a pretty good gardener.' The tall, elderly man in slacks and open-necked shirt with a broad Italian peasant's hat became, in these war years, a familiar figure to the Rhoendorf villagers. Apart from his garden his main interests were classical music and books, and his hobby of collecting clocks.

Surrounded by his family, a non-smoker and virtual teetotaller – he likes an occasional glass of Rhine or Mosel wine – Adenauer lived in solid middle-class comfort. The masterful ways he had developed as Oberbürgermeister of Cologne were difficult to lose and he was certainly the head of the household. No new dress was bought for the little girls or vital culinary decisions taken without the agreement of 'Vati'. Even when the children of his first marriage grew up and left home the retired Oberbürgermeister continued to keep a guiding hand on their lives. This quiet, retired life was only disturbed when his three elder sons, Max, Konrad, and Paul were called up for a service in the Wehrmacht.

If Adenauer had been discreet since settling down at Rhoendorf during the war, he now became ever more careful not to involve himself in public affairs. Some time in 1943 he was approached by a representative of his one-time colleague, the former Oberbürgermeister of Leipzig, Dr. Goerdeler, who was among the political leaders of the German Resistance Plot against Hitler. Adenauer is reported to have rejected any proposal that he should join the conspiracy, on what ground is uncertain. The circle of those who were involved or had some knowledge of the plot was wide – dangerously so. Despite that, there is no mention in the considerable literature of the 20th July conspiracy of any contact with Adenauer. His first Minister for All-German Affairs, Jakob Kaiser, was the chief Zentrum representative in the conspiracy while the future President, Theodor Heuss, was among the subsidiary plotters.

Perhaps the gallant band of muddle-headed leaders of the 1944 plot was not altogether sorry to have been rebuffed by the conservative, clerical politician whose name always evoked memories of Rhineland separatism. It is doubtful if Adenauer would have been at ease among them.

His lack of contact with the 1944 plotters, however, was not un-important for the future. For in Adenauer's Bonn republic two widely divergent views of the plot developed; some Germans, particularly the decent liberal elements headed by President Heuss, believed that the 'men of 20th July' saved Germany's honour at the bar of history. The others, from authoritarian and Nazi-minded groups, considered that the plotters were 'traitors to the Reich'. Adenauer had been neither 'putschist' nor 'traitor' and certainly his peculiar position of neutrality did nothing to preju-dice his rise as Christian Democrat leader.

Whatever the post-war consequences, Adenauer's refusal to join in the 20th July conspiracy did not save him from its imme-diate aftermath. Three days after the unsuccessful attempt on Hitler's life at his Headquarters in East Prussia, the Gestapo raided the Adenauer house at Rhoendorf. He was questioned and various documents and books were seized but no further action was taken.

Exactly a month later, however, on 23rd August the local Rhoendorf policeman and a detective appeared at the door of Adenauer's home. Very apologetically the local policeman announced that he had a warrant 'from higher up' for Adenauer's arrest. He was taken in the local Rhineside tramcar to the Sicher-heitsdienst (S.D.) offices in Bonn. There he found another 200 prisoners, mostly elderly men like himself, who had been rounded up in Operation 'Thunder and Lightning'. They were marched through the streets of Bonn to the station, where a special train was waiting to take them to Cologne.

Back in the city which he had ruled for so long, Adenauer was interned in a temporary concentration camp erected in the grounds formerly occupied by the Cologne fair. Conditions were grim but a veteran Cologne Communist, promoted to a position of authority as a result of long years of internment, took pity on his former Oberbürgermeister. This man had a room to himself and arranged that Adenauer should share it with him.

Anxiety about his family and his own fate plus a distaste for the primitive concentration camp rations soon reduced Adenauer to little more than a skeleton. The kindly Communist tried to cheer him up with concerts, at which forbidden Jewish music was the principal item, and with political arguments which were almost the only thing to rouse Adenauer out of his lethargy and depression.

Adenauer by this time was intensely interested in the post-war world although whether he would survive to see it was highly problematical. Even then, he predicted that the world would be split into two *blocs*. One would be Communist, he said, and the other democratic; the defeated Germany would have to decide whether to join the East or the West.

The Cologne concentration camp was only a holding camp from which at regular intervals transports of prisoners were dispatched to the death camps of Buchenwald, Dachau, Flossenburg and the rest. The Communist, as a leading prisoner, had access to the camp office. One morning he discovered to his alarm that Adenauer was scheduled to leave for Buchenwald the following day. His ultimate fate was not in doubt. At once he returned to his room and warned Adenauer that his name was in the list.

Adenauer was overcome and said nothing. But the indomitable Communist was determined to try and save the former Oberbürgermeister.

'You have got to get out of here, Herr Oberbürgermeister,' he said. It took some time to persuade Adenauer. Finally, the

Communist sought the advice of a prominent doctor among the detainees who helped with the sick in the camp and enjoyed a special position. As soon as he heard the circumstances he agreed to help.

He secured medicine which caused Adenauer's heart to show signs of apparent disease, and then the camp doctor was told that Dr. Adenauer had had a heart attack. The Nazi doctor visited the room where Adenauer was lying apparently seriously ill. Completely deceived, he ordered Adenauer's removal to one of the principal Cologne hospitals.

Adenauer had escaped Buchenwald, but he never forgot those unlucky ones who were sent there. A few hours after Buchenwald was liberated by the Americans a large Cologne bus, sent by Dr. Adenauer to collect the Cologne prisoners, arrived at the camp gates. Meanwhile he was safe in the Cologne hospital where the professor in charge was an old friend. But his refuge could only be temporary. At once Adenauer and his wife, who now visited him daily, sought for another method of escape. The Professor urged that he should simply walk out. But Adenauer rejected this because of the consequences which would follow. Finally Frau Adenauer contrived a plan.

Towards the end of September a Luftwaffe car arrived at the hospital. From it stepped a Luftwaffe major in dark glasses who announced that he wished to take charge of the detainee Adenauer whom he was to take to Berlin for official inquiries. The hospital raised no objections. A few minutes later Adenauer was in the Luftwaffe car, in the back seat of which he found his wife.

The major was an old friend who was only too willing to do anything against the Nazis. He drove Adenauer to Bonn. But, alas, some months later both the major and his son were arrested in connection with Adenauer's escape. Both were killed during the American attack on Cologne in the following spring.

Adenauer did not linger in Bonn but, as 'Dr. Weber' a lawyer on holiday, found refuge in an isolated guest-house in the Westerwald Hills to the east of the Rhine near Koblenz. The Nazis in Cologne were furious. They had twice been completely fooled. They could find no trace of Adenauer. On 24th September consequently two Gestapo men arrived at the Adenauer home in Rhoendorf and arrested Frau Adenauer. They also attempted to interrogate her two young daughters, Lotte aged 19 and Libeth three years younger, about their father's whereabouts.

Frau Adenauer was taken to the Gestapo headquarters in Cologne where the gentle, cultivated woman was put in an underground cellar along with some of Cologne's principal prostitutes, thieves and other women criminals. It was not long before they discovered her true identity. When she showed a natural reserve they turned on her and beat her. Scarcely aware of what was happening, Frau Adenauer lay on the floor of the cellar until, suddenly, she heard her name called. She was pushed upstairs into a brilliantly lit room where she was completely blinded. Before she could gather her senses she heard a voice demand, 'Where is your husband?'

She resolutely declined to answer and was again taken to the cellar where by this time there was no place to lie. For two hours she stood, half crazed, before being summoned for further interrogation.

This time the Gestapo interrogator was more subtle. He had heard about Lotte and Libeth left alone at home with two young sisters-in-law. He warned Frau Adenauer that he would have them arrested and promised that they would be interned with the prostitutes – and worse. It was too much for the sorely tried mother. She capitulated and finally, in a whisper, revealed that her husband was in the guest-house in the Westerwald.

Next day she was removed to the Gestapo prison at Brauweiler in the Rhineland. There, on the day of her silver wedding, 25th September, 1944, she learned that her husband, too, had been arrested and was in the same prison. Frau Adenauer was released soon afterwards, just as her 16-year-old daughter Libeth, after pestering the Gestapo in Cologne, had traced her to Brauweiler.

Frau Adenauer never fully recovered from her experience. In

prison she contracted a blood disease which eventually proved fatal. Adenauer was told by the Gestapo as soon as he was re-arrested that his 'wife had betrayed him'. By not the slightest flicker of a muscle did he betray any feelings. He knew his wife too well, and realized that the poor woman must have been driven to near distraction to admit anything about his whereabouts.

After his previous escapes he was given a particularly unpleas-ant cell. His tie and braces were removed by a Gestapo man who told him, 'Now don't go and commit suicide or I'll get into terrible trouble. After all there is no need. You are 68 and your life is virtually at an end.' The Gestapo man would have thought anyone mad who had predicted that his prisoner nearly two dec-ades later would be one of the world's best-known statesmen.

Adenauer suffered nothing physically in the Gestapo prison, but the constant screams and moans from the cellar below his cell where the Gestapo tortured prisoners was almost too much for him.

In the meantime, his son Max, later Oberstadtdirektor of Cologne, who at the time was a young officer on the West Front, had been given special leave by an understanding commanding officer. After visiting Adenauer he went to the Gestapo head-quarters in Berlin to try and find out why his father was being interned. He had taken no part of the 20th July conspiracy, but the Gestapo chiefs were suspicious because of his flight from the Cologne concentration camp.

But it was November, 1944; the Western Allies were in Aachen. Now Dr. Max Adenauer took a strong line. He bluntly told the Gestapo that he and his two brothers were soldiers and asked them what effect they thought the arrest of his father without cause was likely to have on a soldier taking part in operations. The Gestapo, too, was beginning to think of the future. The head of the Reich Security Office (R.S.H.O.), the brutal Austrian, Kaltenbrunner, later executed at Nuremberg, personally ordered Adenauer's release. He was freed on 26th November in the midst of an American air attack on the Brauweiler region.

By this time Germany had clearly lost the war. Adenauer and his family, like so many other anti-Nazis, awaited with impatience the arrival of their Allied liberators. By the end of February, 1945, Adenauer realized that final German defeat could not be long delayed. Some of his family wanted him to leave Rhoendorf but, after studying the military position, he became convinced that the main allied thrusts would pass by to the north and the south.

On the morning of 8th March, however, his sister who was at Unkel, four miles south of Rhoendorf called him on the telephone. 'We are liberated,' she told him. 'The Americans are here – very nice people.'

There was a break and it was impossible to re-connect the call. His sister by some chance had been able to speak 'across the front lines'. The Americans, in a surprise dash through the Eifel, had reached the West Rhine bank at Remagen. Before the German defenders could realize what had happened they had pushed across the swaying Remagen railway bridge to seize the Remagen bridge-head, the first Allied foothold beyond the swiftly running river.

The war had come to Adenauer at last. That night the whole family, fourteen of them, took refuge in a small air-raid shelter which he had built in a cave on the Drachenfels, behind his home. For a week the Adenauer family was under fire. The house at Zennisweg was damaged by American shells. Worse still, some of his roses were destroyed.

On the morning of the seventh day the noise of the shellfire stopped. From his vantage-point on the hill he could see a column of camouflaged tanks – all bearing a white star. Joyfully he told his family, 'The war is finished, for us at least.'

Next day an American jeep appeared in Zennisweg and two American officers knocked at the door of the Adenauer house. Adenauer, with pruning shears in his hands, invited them in and asked, 'What can I do for you, gentlemen?' In perfect German the Americans announced that they came on the orders of the Allied Commander-in-Chief, General Eisenhower.

'We wish to know, sir, whether you are willing to take over the administration of Cologne. If so we should propose to appoint you Oberbürgermeister with the full approval of the Allied Military Command.'

Adenauer was astounded. He had not appreciated that the Allies had in their possession lists of prominent anti-Nazis likely to be willing to co-operate with the liberators. He forgot that the British knew a great deal about him. He scarcely knew what to say. His joy at the thought of again becoming Oberbürgermeister of his native city was clouded by the thought of his three sons. They were still German soldiers fighting against these same Western officers who were asking for his co-operation.

After some thought Adenauer told the Americans, 'I am most willing to co-operate with you. But my co-operation must in the meantime remain secret. Until there is an official German surrender I can only act unofficially as an adviser. My sons are still in the Wehrmacht.'

The American officers were understanding. They agreed at once. A quarter of an hour later Dr. and Frau Adenauer were on their way back to Cologne, where in the east bank district of the city the battle was still going on.

CHAPTER FOUR

Oberbürgermeister Again

TWO MONTHS AFTER Adenauer returned to Cologne the war ended. In the interval he had prepared a memorandum of his ideas for the future of Germany which showed remarkable identity with current American opinion. Within a few hours of the German High Command signing the surrender terms in the first week of May, Konrad Adenauer was appointed Oberbürgermeister for the second time.

But Cologne in the summer of 1945 was not the city from which he had fled in 1933. His Rathaus was no more. He set up his office in the still intact Allianz insurance building in the Hohenzollern-Ring. The great Rhineland metropolis itself, which he had once ruled with an iron hand, was nothing but a battered and burnt-out shell. Scarcely more than 50,000 of the city's normal 750,000 inhabitants remained in the cellars and air-raid bunkers hidden below the wreckage. Most of the streets were blocked. There were no trains. The great Rhine road and rail bridges had disappeared, either as a result of the R.A.F.'s attentions or the efforts of the retreating Wehrmacht sappers. Communication between the two halves of the city was by strictly controlled military emergency bridges.

Thousands of breaks in sewerage, gas and water systems were a serious danger to health and the occupation authorities feared epidemics – which for some strange reasons never came to the wrecked German cities. The great twin spires of the cathedral survived. The building itself was torn and battered but the fabric remained fundamentally sound.

To attempt to restore even a modicum of order amid this

appalling chaos was a fearsome task for a man approaching seventy, but Adenauer set to work. To his assistance he summoned the former Oberstadtdirektor, his brother-in-law Dr. Suth and his former Social Democrat opponents who, like himself, had suffered under the Nazis. When one of the German Socialist veterans questioned whether they could work together *permanently* Adenauer with characteristic dryness commented, 'As to *permanently* I don't know, but for the moment we must.'

Conditions were made more difficult by the unbending attitude of the Allied conquerors. Non-fraternization with the Germans was rigorously enforced. Adenauer's contacts with his American military superiors were strictly formal. No political activities were allowed among the Germans. Some of Adenauer's former Zentrum friends had begun to think of the future, but he himself declined to take any part in these political manoeuvrings so long as they were officially banned.

Some of the weaker brethren among the former Zentrum members were, however, responsible for his first move to persuade the Allies to change one of their main policies, denazification. During the Nazi period a certain number of Zentrum supporters had, for opportunistic reasons, become Nazi fellow-travellers, while in the Rhineland there were other rather curious ties between the supporters of Adolf Hitler and the Catholics. Within a few weeks of his appointment as Oberbürgermeister, Adenauer submitted a memorandum to the Americans.

This document, which eventually went to General Eisenhower as Allied Commander-in-Chief, suggested, not without reason, that the more drastic measures against these Nazi fellow-travellers might be eased. It was a truly Christian approach to those who had ill-treated Adenauer's family and himself. In subsequent years it would find a parallel in the charity which he extended to former Nazis who were given high office in his administration in Bonn. But among Left-wing Germans who had suffered equally, his charity smacked of confessional discrimination, and his old

Social Democratic opponents began to revive their suspicions of his political aims.

At the end of June the Americans left Cologne and once again, after twenty years, Konrad Adenauer became responsible to a British military government. Unlike the first occupation, when Cologne had been the British Headquarters, in 1945 it was merely a bombed-out Rhineland city on the extreme south-western fringe of the British Occupation Zone, far removed from the main centres of activity. All important developments were centred in Berlin and in the almost unscathed small towns of east Westphalia where Montgomery had established his headquarters, 200 miles beyond the Rhine.

The transfer of authority from the Americans to the British in Cologne arose from decisions of the Four Power European Advisory Council subsequently confirmed by the Yalta Conference which laid down the zones of military occupation. Adenauer watched the departure of the Americans and the arrival of the British with acute dejection. It brought back memories which he would sooner have forgotten.

All eyes in Germany were turned on the forthcoming meeting of Churchill, Truman and Stalin at Potsdam. Adenauer, more anxious apparently about Germany's future than Cologne's present, seized the occasion to issue his first post-war political statement. The Germans, he announced to anyone who cared to listen, were accustomed to being told what to do. Now, more than ever, they must be told what to do. He then put forward a four-point programme, which was eminently reasonable but seemed somewhat beyond the immediate scope of the Oberbürgermeister of a terribly bombed German city. Adenauer urged:

1. That the German currency should be established.
2. That a central German Government should be established with the co-operation of the Allies.
3. That the Germans should be told what parts of the Reich were to be annexed.

4. That a Federal German State consisting of the four occupation zones be created.

By the beginning of August, as the Potsdam Conference ended, Adenauer was acutely depressed. In the British general election the Labour party had gained a landslide victory over Churchill. Adenauer had become the servant of a government which embodied the two characteristics which instinctively he most deplored; it was Socialist and British. Already he had begun to fall foul of the British military government officers, who probably were not supporters of the Labour Government. To the British Adenauer did not seem to be getting on with his job of trying to convert the ruins of Cologne into shelters for the thousands of returning citizens before the onset of winter. The immediate task was to clear up the mess. But even before the British arrival Adenauer had conferences with architects to discuss long-term civic-planning projects.

The British were also inclined to feel that the veteran Oberbürgermeister talked too much. He would be better employed doing the job he was paid to do than in sticking his nose into political plans which were the sole concern of the four occupying powers.

Then the British in their practical, pragmatic way committed an unforgivable sin. To find fuel for the people of Cologne the military government cut down the trees in Adenauer's 'green belt', the creation of which he had pushed through in the face of fierce opposition twenty years earlier. He retaliated by attacking the British requisitioning of the Ruhr coal.

At the beginning of August the Oberbürgermeister had a somewhat tense meeting with one of Montgomery's most able staff officers Colonel (now Sir John) Barraclough who had been appointed to command No. 808 Military Government Detachment for the administrative district of Cologne. The British commander told Adenauer that he was dissatisfied with the progress made in putting roofs on buildings, clearing the streets and generally making preparations for the winter, which everyone knew would hit the Germans badly.

Adenauer took this badly, but he was stung to make such a determined effort to clear the streets that he gained yet another nickname – 'The City Scavenger'. Colonel Barraclough's deserved rebuke, however, had aroused all Adenauer's dormant instincts about the British. Relations steadily deteriorated.

Finally, 5th October, 1945, Adenauer was visited by two Allied correspondents, one British and one American. He complained of the fuel crisis threatening the citizens of Cologne in the coming winter. He also attacked the Allies, meaning the British, for their failure to provide fuel. He predicted the death of great numbers of people through illness – epidemics and general weakness. He then turned to international problems and Germany's future. The best solution he said would be to split with the Russians and *to set up a Federal State consisting of the three Western Zones*. He also returned to his idea of thirty years earlier for a *close link-up between German, French and Belgian heavy industry*.

Next day he was summoned to Colonel Barraclough's office and handed a letter summarily dismissing him. In this letter the Cologne military government commander recalled his previous complaints to Adenauer two months earlier. While acknowledging the great difficulties facing the German civic authorities, Colonel Barraclough stated that if Adenauer had shown more energy he could have accomplished more. And he bluntly told Adenauer that he had not carried out his duty to the people of Cologne. The colonel informed Adenauer's temporary successor, his brother in law Dr. Suth, that Adenauer had been dismissed because he had not pursued military government policy with sufficient energy and foresight.

There was a background to all this which, while not the concern of the British military government officers in Cologne, played some part in the confirmation of his dismissal by Field Marshal Montgomery's headquarters. This was the explanation given some time later by British Intelligence Officers to the author as an accredited correspondent in the British Zone.

During the weeks immediately prior to Adenauer's dismissal, while relations in Cologne had been deteriorating, certain organs of the British security service whose function was to watch all Germans came to suspect that the Oberbürgermeister had renewed his associations with the French. The representatives of the de Gaulle Government were stationed in the French Zone just south of Bonn, and had easy access to Cologne. The de Gaulle administration, having virtually annexed the Saar, was already demanding the 'internationalization' of the Ruhr and the Rhineland. As was the case after the First World War, there was a certain British suspicion of French motives.

In normal circumstances British Intelligence Officers would not have been interested in contacts between a known German demo- crat and the French, but the British Intelligence Officers had at their disposal the files built up by their Secret Service predecessors in the Rhineland during the previous occupation. The British Secret Service, therefore, kept a watch on Adenauer and in due course they received reports from agents which alleged that either Adenauer himself or his representative had had a meeting, at the Abbey of Maria Laachs inside the French Zone, with a high envoy of the de Gaulle administration in Paris.

Similar reports reached the British at the same time from German Left-wing circles as a result of the long-standing friend- ship between the new Foreign Minister, Ernest Bevin and German trade union leaders who had returned home after spending the war in the U.K. Whether Adenauer, in fact, met a French repre- sentative is uncertain – the British Secret Service seldom issues Press handouts – but that some such incident occurred was well known to Adenauer's political opponents in Bonn.

Whatever the truth of this alleged meeting, when proposals to dismiss Adenauer for inefficiency reached the British headquarters there was the strongest disinclination on the part of the then Director of Military Government, General (now Field-Marshal)

Sir Gerald Templer and his staff to interfere with the decision of Colonel Barraclough. Some members of the British Diplomatic Service then serving as advisers in Germany who had more knowledge of German political personalities than the military officers, opposed Adenauer's dismissal, but they were overruled.

Nine months later, when a young political officer of the British Control Commission wrote a profile of Adenauer in the official *British Zone Review*, he was quite obviously aware of some of this background.

'Removed in October 1945 . . .' wrote this Ernest Bevin protégé. 'Rumour had it that *Adenauer was removed because the military government disapproved of his having been a separatist after the First World War*. In fact the reason was rather that he was not sufficiently vigorous in getting on with the urgent task of carrying out first aid to damaged houses, partly because of his advanced age *and partly because of his pre-occupation with long-term projects*.' It seems curious that this official commentator, writing for a restricted readership, should have recalled the far distant days of Rhineland separatism if some more recent and related event had not aroused the interest of the authorities in Adenauer's long past separatist activities.

Whatever the facts, on the long view it was an unfortunate incident. For Adenauer's dismissal, coupled with his long-standing Anglophobia, seriously prejudiced relations between Bonn and London for most of the fourteen years Adenauer was Chancellor, despite his public assertions to the contrary.

Years later, when Adenauer had become a major figure in the Western World, it became fashionable among British Foreign Office officials who knew nothing of the facts, to blame 'these generals' for what happened. The officers singled out for particular censure were Colonel Barraclough and his military superior, Sir Gerald Templer. That was grossly unfair. Both officers would have been failing in their duty if on the facts they had not acted as they did.

Field-Marshal Sir Gerald Templer was the man who in the

months immediately after defeat got the Ruhr and the British Zone back on its feet. Colonel Barraclough, now an important industrial figure in the Midlands, who for considerable periods was Acting Military Governor of the Ruhr after leaving Cologne, was one of the outstanding successes of the British occupation. Neither, however, was a particularly patient man. Neither was prepared in those months of extreme crisis to let any German block their efforts. To them Adenauer was just an elderly Rhineland bureaucrat who was awkward and difficult for one reason and another. 'Control' was the watchword of the time. The situation was so grave that no Allied senior officer had time to examine the motives of the Germans who opposed their wishes. It was a rough and ready method but it worked, and modern Germany owes much to the Allied officers who 'controlled' them.

It would have been remarkable foresight indeed for the British military government in October, 1945, to have seen in an elderly and extremely awkward German official on the eve of his seventieth birthday, the future German Federal Chancellor. Much later, Adenauer admitted to Sir Ivone Kirkpatrick, then British High Commissioner, that he had no grudge against Field-Marshal Templer. 'On the contrary, I owe it to him that I am Chancellor and not Oberbürgermeister of Cologne,' he said in his dry way.

Adenauer, however, never forgave the British for one personal circumstance arising from his dismissal. In the letter removing Adenauer from office Colonel Barraclough had ordered him to leave Cologne within a week, and to take no further part in the public life of the city or the North Rhine province.

Unfortunately, Frau Adenauer was seriously ill. After months of attempting to commute between her husband in Cologne and her young family in Rhoendorf, she had been removed to the hospital where Adenauer had taken refuge a year earlier. She was suffering from the serious blood infection, contracted in the Gestapo prison, which would eventually prove fatal. She must remain in Cologne for special treatment. Adenauer asked the

British authorities for permission to be with his wife. The request was granted, but Adenauer's authorized biography complains that he was permitted to visit Frau Adenauer 'only twice a week and for an hour on each occasion'.

This might seem reasonable enough. Frau Adenauer, the British were informed, was not critically ill or in immediate danger. Permission to visit Frau Adenauer was granted most willingly, therefore, on what to the British mind seemed normal hospital visiting days. Anglophobe Adenauer, however, was bitterly resentful. He remained so. In subsequent years at private dinners – particularly to French guests – he frequently quoted this incident as an illustration of the 'inhuman' methods of the British occupation authorities.

The British, by removing Adenauer from the restricted field of Cologne in the autumn of 1945, certainly did him the greatest service of his political career. Freed from all administrative responsibilities, Adenauer at once plunged into the reviving political life of Western Germany where other elderly gentlemen from the dim Weimar past were brushing up their recollections of party politics.

Adenauer was in a key position. The other former leaders of the Zentrum were widely scattered; Ex-Chancellor Brüning was a professor in the United States, von Papen was before the Nuremberg court which eventually acquitted him, and Adenauer's old separatist friend and one-time party leader in the Reichstag, Monsignor Kaas, occupied high office in the Vatican.

In his long retirement Adenauer had thought deeply of the weakness of the old Zentrum and of its ignominious support for the grant of dictatorial powers to Hitler in 1933. He was convinced that the future lay with a Christian rather than a narrow Catholic party – a view which was strongly supported by his Protestant crony, Dr. Pferdmenges who had returned to the Rhineland after being 'liberated' by the Red Army. Similar views were held in other parts of Germany and, indeed, throughout Europe.

In the autumn of 1945 political leadership in Germany was wide open. It was almost anyone's for the grasping. Backed by the two formidable figures of the Cardinal of Cologne and the great banker Pferdmenges, Adenauer seized his opportunity. In the last months of 1945 he began to throw out feelers to similar groups which had appeared in other parts of Germany; to the American Zone where the American military government was already looking with favour on Christian Democrat movements; and to Berlin, where the movement was led by Jakob Kaiser, the Catholic trade union representative in the 1944 conspiracy against Hitler. By sheer personality, coupled with considerable exercise of his great gifts of intrigue and political manoeuvre, Adenauer steadily consolidated his position in the Rhineland and the neighbouring Ruhr.

In December, only two months after his dismissal from Cologne, he received a visitor at his Rhoendorf home a British officer who wished to discuss political matters with him. Somewhat curtly Adenauer pointed out that he was expressly forbidden to do any such thing by the orders of the British military government in Cologne – Rhoendorf was within the Cologne administrative district. The officer assured him that this ban would be lifted at once. It was, and by the end of 1945 British official documents reported that the Christian Democratic Union was one of the strongest parties in the British Zone and *that Konrad Adenauer was among its foremost figures.*

The first zonal meeting of the party was in Bad Godesberg. Thereafter, a second meeting took place at Herford, at that time part of Montgomery's headquarters, where Adenauer is reported to have taken over the chairmanship by the somewhat sharp practice of announcing that he was 'the oldest person present'.

Finally, at the end of February 1946, the first C.D.U. congress in the British Zone was held, in a nunnery on the eastern fringes of the Ruhr. Meanwhile Adenauer had beaten down all opposition to his leadership in his usual authoritarian manner and he was elected chairman of the party for the British Zone.

His election was far from popular with the Catholic Left wing which exercised strong influence among the Ruhr workers. For Adenauer, even then, was recognized as the leader of the extreme Right and the nominee of the clergy and of big business.

About this time the official *British Zone Review* commented that the C.D.U. was definitely 'right of centre and very active in the Ruhr and Rhineland where the outstanding figure is Dr. Konrad Adenauer. Some of the C.D.U. leaders are prepared to go far to meet the leftward trend . . . but this is strongly opposed by Adenauer and the more conservative members'.

Some time later, when there were moves to form a national C.D.U., a Swiss newspaper commented cynically that the Christian Democrats 'in Berlin are Socialist and radical, in Hamburg capitalist and reactionary, in Munich counter-revolutionary and particularist *and in Cologne clerical and conservative*'.

The British Foreign Secretary, Mr. Ernest Bevin, was scarcely pro-German and progress towards political life was much slower in the British Zone than in the territory to the south occupied by the Americans. In the spring of 1946, however, the British finally decided to form a zonal advisory council to which prominent Germans were invited. Adenauer, as zonal chairman of the Christian Democrats, after considerable doubt took part in the first meeting. His Cologne dismissal was still much too close to let him foregather willingly with the British military government chiefs.

The sombre figure in a dark, clerical-grey suit and high starched white collar who arrived in Hamburg in a battered Lincoln driven at high speed from Cologne, was scarcely an impressive figure. He took little part in the first meeting. His look of sullen resentment left no doubt that he viewed personal association with any British senior officer with supreme distaste. At the meeting that followed, his dour, unfriendly personality was completely overshadowed by the Social Democrat leader, Dr. Kurt Schumacher and the cheeky, irrepressible leader of the West German Communists, Max Reimann, who had some of the personal characteristics which for so long endeared the late James Maxton to British political life.

German politics in these early post-war years tended to be a somewhat academic pursuit. In the first three years of the occupation the big problem was food. Time after time, new food crises spread over the British Zone. Rations were at starvation level, despite the considerable imports paid for by the British and American taxpayers. In later years Adenauer was to admit frankly that 'it was intolerable that the British taxpayer should go on paying for Germans' food'. At the time his attitude was singularly unhelpful.

His anti-British psychosis could see no good in anything the British did. He was sure that one day the British must return some measure of authority to the Germans, and towards that day he devoted all his energies. By the aid of practices which would have gained acclamation in Tammany Hall he grasped more and more power over the Christian Democratic party into his own hands. So much so that by the summer of 1946 he was considered sufficiently important to merit a full page in the *British Zone Review*.

'By force of his quiet and dignified personality,' stated the writer, a British political officer, 'he has emerged as the outstanding figure of the C.D.U. in the British Zone. He regards himself as a statesman rather than as a politician . . . and exerts influence not at crowded meetings but in private conversation.'

Emphasizing that there was a considerable split in the C.D.U., the official British Review continued, 'The Conservative wing led by Adenauer consists of business-men, industrialists and the farming community. The Left wing on the other hand is prepared to co-operate with the Social Democrats. The conservatives in the British Zone, however, are in the ascendant and Adenauer's position is virtually unchallenged. His opponents accuse him of separatism – and *of opposing the reunification of Germany*. He denies this, but adds that the only future lies in the formation of a United States of Europe. His attitude to the occupying powers is critical in some respects – but he enjoys his power and, for all his apparent detachment, he is one of the astutest and most experienced politicians in Europe.'

That was a remarkable preview of Konrad Adenauer, Federal German Chancellor and world statesman. Seventeen years later the salient points were as accurate as when it was written.

By the summer of 1946, only a year after the Potsdam Conference, Adenauer as zonal chairman of the C.D.U. was the most important anti-Socialist political leader in the highly industrialized British Zone.

It was in that capacity that, along with his principal opponent, Dr. Schumacher of the Social Democrats, he was flown to Berlin in an R.A.F. transport plane to discuss a revolutionary British plan. The two men were received by the acting British military governor, General Sir Brian (now Lord) Robertson. He told the Germans that he wished to know their reaction to this plan which would end for ever the permanent political problem of Prussia.

The British authorities had decided, said Robertson, to combine the former Prussian administrative districts of North Rhine and Westphalia into a single *Land* or federal province. By the stroke of a military government pen they proposed to create a great industrial state stretching from the middle Rhine to the Weser with population and resources greater than those of Belgium.

Schumacher, at that time the darling of the British Labour Government, bluntly rejected the plan. Adenauer later commented cynically, 'He's a Prussian.' And to British astonishment he accepted the plan. Whatever other motives he may have had, he was sly enough to see its significance for his future. By the creation of the new double province his own political importance would be much increased. He would be as head of the C.D.U. in the greatest and wealthiest German state, a formidable contender for national leadership of the Christian Democrats when that came to be settled. Once again, the hated British had done him a good turn.

Following the creation of North Rhine-Westphalia, the British formed a coalition government in the province in which Adenauer ostentatiously took no part. In the election campaign that followed Adenauer seemed to have but two irreconcilable aims: (1) to attempt to tar his Socialist opponents with the Nazi brush. (2) at the same time to suggest that these same Social Democrats were the lackeys of the British Labour Government.

It was during this campaign that Adenauer began his long fight with Dr. Schumacher, which was only brought to an end by the latter's tragic death in 1952.

Adenauer found it easy to combine his traditional anti-Socialist approach with his unconcealed anti-British rancour. To the correspondent of a New York newspaper Adenauer announced that 'he feared that the preference of the British for German Social Democracy was in danger of bringing the S.P.D. into discredit as lackeys of the kings of England'.

He took up the same theme soon afterwards when he addressed the students at Marburg University.

'The S.P.D. in the British Zone,' he said, 'is the Royal British Social Democratic party, supported by the British Labour party. In the British Zone the S.P.D. with military government assistance has succeeded in edging its members into influential positions.'

The references to the British royal family were unmistakably offensive. The British Government certainly thought so. Adenauer's remarks did nothing to improve his relations with the British. Soon afterwards he returned to the attack, when he travelled to the Social Democratic stronghold at Hanover to make another election speech.

'The S.P.D. is the military government party,' he declared. The S.P.D. at once retorted, with justice, that in the American Zone the C.D.U. was already the favourite political organ of General Lucius D. Clay, the powerful American military governor.

Adenauer went on to accuse his Socialist opponents of being 'arch-reactionaries, dogmatists and enemies of the church'. And if that were not enough he attempted to link them with the Nazis. 'The source of the catastrophe which enveloped Germany,' he said, 'was national Socialism. But the ultimate source lay in the materialist, i.e. the Marxist world outlook. Believe me, to an old politician like myself, *it is all the same thing . . . Socialism or national Socialism.*'

The exaggerations of electioneering are proverbial. But Social Democrats like Schumacher, who had been twelve years in a Nazi concentration camp, had shared with Adenauer the persecution and cruelties of Hitler. Adenauer's speech, therefore, came ill from a man whose party was already beginning to accept in its ranks the denazified small fry who were creeping back into public life. Adenauer's propaganda achieved little, for although the Christian Democrats attained a majority, it was insufficient to form a government. The left-wing Christian Democrats, led by the late Dr. Karl Arnold, therefore supported the continuation of the coalition government with the Social Democrats in North Rhine Westphalia. But Adenauer would have nothing to do with such a plan. Government-making went on for weeks while a deadlock existed between Adenauer and Arnold. Finally Arnold, a man of broad liberal sympathies, in open defiance of Adenauer, formed a coalition government. Adenauer in high dudgeon remained a back bencher in the North Rhine–Westphalian parliament.

Adenauer never forgave Arnold, his fellow Catholic and fellow Christian Democrat. When forming his administrations in Bonn in 1949 and later, Adenauer ruthlessly excluded the Ruhr Premier from office, and from the German Cabinet.

In the meantime, international developments of great importance to Adenauer's future career were taking place, not only in Germany but in Washington and London. By late 1946 both the British and Americans were agreed that some effort must be made to sort out the German economic tangle, caused by the division of Germany into four divided zones, which was the fundamental cause of the repeated food shortages in the British Zone.

The signal for the new policy was given in a speech at Stuttgart by the then U.S. Secretary of State, Mr. James Byrnes, who emphasized the need for German economic unity. Soon afterwards Mr. Byrnes and the British Foreign Secretary, Mr. Ernest Bevin, met in Washington to work out a solution. There was hard bargaining but, as a result of the Anglo-American accord, the British and American Zones were loosely combined for economic affairs from the beginning of 1947. This fusion of the so-called Bizone was taken a further important step in mid-1947 by the establishment at Frankfurt-on-Main of a Bizonal Economic Council of leading Germans elected from the provincial parliaments in the two zones.

At the same moment as the Economic Council was established General Clay, the American military governor, issued a new policy directive aimed fundamentally at building up Western Germany as an ally for what was now recognized as the inevitable showdown with the Russians.

The two events together marked an important milestone in the history of the creation of a West German state, and in the political rise of Konrad Adenauer.

By the Bizone arrangement, the food supplies of the largely pastoral American Zone were made available to the workers of the highly industrialized British Zone. In return the Americans reached a goal towards which they had long striven – a foothold in the Ruhr.

At the American military government headquarters in Frankfurt, and in Washington itself, however, other influences were developing which would prove even more important to Adenauer.

Behind General Clay in the policy of converting defected Germany into a cold war ally stood the American Economic Adviser, Major General William Draper. In civil life he was a senior partner of a great Wall Street banking house which, in the twenties, had played an important part in providing American finance to Germany. Both General Clay and General Draper, men of great ability, made little effort to conceal that they were

Republicans and supporters of the traditional big business party in American politics. To those, who, like the author, moved in American military government circles, it was well known that as a result of some bipartisan horse trading in Washington the control of policy in Germany had become the prerogative of the Republicans. And behind the Republican party stood its foreign affairs adviser, Mr. John Foster Dulles. In this way originated the influence of the late John Foster Dulles on Adenauer's rise to world fame. At the time of the abortive Foreign Minister's meeting in Moscow early in 1947, Mr. Dulles, as foreign policy adviser of the Republican party, announced that 'the Americans want Germany to use its own resource of skilled manpower, energy and industrial capacity to rebuild the network of trade on which European prosperity depends'. The real aim of the Dulles policy was to make Germany an American bastion in the cold war – a policy of which Adenauer would become chief exponent.

Adenauer, by mid-1947, through a combination of sly intrigue and aggressive thrusting, had become the acknowledged leader of the C.D.U. throughout the British and American Zones. Only in Bavaria the loosely allied Christian Socialists remained semi-independent and, often, critical.

Up to that point, Adenauer's political rise had been largely fortuitous, owing something to good fortune – for instance, his dismissal by the British – and still more to the elimination of potential rivals in the Nazi extermination camps. His rise was almost inevitable. With his traditional conservative and big business backing, he became the chosen vehicle of the dominant Allied Power in Western Germany. Adenauer personally, of course, at that time meant little or nothing to General Clay in Frankfurt, and still less to Mr. Dulles and the Republican pundits in Washington. He merely happened to be an elderly German Conservative who, by one way or another, had become the head of the chief anti-Socialist party in Western Germany.

The Republicans, through long-standing and unbroken links with German business friends, soon learned that Adenauer was the acknowledged and trusted political representative of big business and high finance in the re-emerging Germany. At this point Fate almost seemed to intervene on Adenauer's behalf. After the failure of the Foreign Ministers' meeting in Moscow in April, 1947, the four occupation powers decided to make another bid to reach a common policy. At the Foreign Ministers' Conference held in London in December of the same year Germany was again considered. The meeting reached complete deadlock over Molotov's persistent demand for reparations from current production. That was as good an excuse as any for the breakdown. For the Western Powers by this time recognized that agreement with the Russians over Germany would be impossible for years to come.

Four-power control of Germany was virtually at an end. The victorious Allies had gone the whole way 'from Potsdam to Partition'. The Communist *coup d'état* in Prague a few weeks later marked the real beginning of the Cold War in Europe. From that point, as a very distinguished but cynical British diplomat once remarked, 'Stalin was Adenauer's best friend.'

Without Stalin and the Soviet policies which made the Cold War inevitable Konrad Adenauer almost certainly would never have become German Chancellor. Had a United Germany passed from four-power Allied control to a democratic German government, as still seemed possible up to the end of 1947, powerful C.D.U. leaders in Berlin and Eastern Germany would almost certainly have ousted the narrow, clericalist, big-business conservative from the Rhineland. More decisively, there was almost certainly a Socialist majority in the whole of a united Germany, a fact which the crafty Adenauer, the 'Autocrat of Bonn,' never forgot.

After the breakdown of the London Conference, what followed was inevitable. On 19th March, 1948, Marshal Sokolovsky, the Russian military governor, walked out of the four-power Allied Control Council in Berlin, clearly on orders from Stalin.

The partition of Germany had begun.

Little more than a fortnight later, the British military governor,

General Sir Brian Robertson told the parliament of North Rhine-Westphalia, including a quiet, sad-faced Dr. Adenauer who was mourning the death of his second wife, that the Western powers had decided to set up a provisional West German state.

The decision had been a particularly difficult one for the British Labour Government. Washington was already in favour of such a move. The French Government in Paris was vacillating as usual. The decisive factor, therefore, was the attitude of the British Government. The Foreign Secretary, Mr. Bevin, was known to be 'pathologically anti-German'. He was reluctant to take any steps to recreate German power in Europe. But as Russian policy in the winter of 1947–8 developed, Bevin realized that a decision must be taken. With that simple clarity which he often possessed he saw that the issue was clearcut: either Western Germany must be incorporated into the western world, or the whole of the Reich would fall like a ripe fruit into the Russian basket.

The proceedings of the British Cabinet are secret but, according to one of his closest collaborators, it was the advocacy of the much troubled British Foreign Secretary which finally swayed the doubting members of the Attlee Cabinet, and made the Chancellorship of Konrad Adenauer possible.

At the beginning of June, 1948, a six-power conference on Germany – Britain, America, France and Benelux agreed on two major points: 1. That a West German Government should be set up as soon as possible. 2. That the three Western occupation powers along with the Benelux states – as a sop to ever-present French fears – should set up a six-power international authority to control the distribution of the Ruhr coal and steel.

The agreement also provided for the establishment of a provisional German constitution. Adenauer, narrow-minded as ever, at once criticized the Allies' plan. The future constitution, he said, could have little expectation of expressing the inner feeling of the German people if it must obtain the approval of the military governors. He asked aggressively whether any German of whatever party could reconcile his conscience by co-operating with 'this increased and continuing restriction on freedom'. Not for the first, or last time, Adenauer's political judgement was completely wrong. He was quite unable to see that the Western Powers had in fact created the charter for his own rise to power.

These moves did not go unmarked by the Russians. As late spring passed into early summer, the Russian authorities placed ever-increasing difficulties on Western communications with Berlin, in the heart of the Russian-occupied Zone, more than a hundred miles from the nearest point in Western Germany. By midsummer the Berlin blockade was in force.

On 20th June the three Western Powers, convinced that four-power agreement was impossible, took the revolutionary step of introducing a new and much devalued currency in the Western Zones.

The partition of Germany was complete. At the same time, by a draconian devaluation which no German Government could have dared to make, Western Germany was set on the road to prosperity and 'the German miracle' of a few years later.

At the beginning of July, 1948, the three military governors met the eleven prime ministers of the Federal States or *Länder* of the three Western Zones and instructed them to summon a German constituent assembly, or pre-parliament. Adenauer was not present, because of the pique with which he had retired to the back benches of the North Rhine–Westaphalian Parliament fifteen months earlier. The Christian Democrats were represented at the meeting by the Premiers of the *C.D.U. governed provinces*. But Adenauer exercised considerable influence through the party machine.

The Western Allies accepted the view of the German premiers that a parliament should draw up a constitution. It was agreed that members should be nominated by the eleven federal parliaments and the pre-parliament should meet in Bonn on 1st September. Adenauer was chosen by the parliament of North Rhine–Westphalia as one of its delegates to the Parliamentary Council. And so Konrad Adenauer went to Bonn.

CHAPTER FIVE

Chairman of the Pre-Parliament

THE BERLIN BLOCKADE was at its height when, at noon on 1st September, 1948, the first post-war German representative assembly met in Bonn.

Sixty-five delegates, most of them elderly, chosen by the parliaments of the future federal provinces, along with important Allied and German personalities, met in a museum of Bonn University to celebrate this important step with a solemn *Festakt*. The author can recall the inevitable Bach and Beethoven and the equally inevitable long, platitudinous speeches. The company then adjourned for a ceremonial luncheon at the nearby British Officers' Club in the Villa Hammerschmidst – soon to be transformed into the official residence of the German Federal President. Then the delegates moved to a white-concrete extra-mural college on the banks of the Rhine, which was later to become the garish seat of the West German Parliament.

First business was the election of a chairman of the pre-parliament, or Parliamentary Council as it was officially described. The two main parties, the C.D.U. and the S.P.D. had an equal number of delegates. To the astonishment of most of the on-lookers Adenauer, scarcely the most popular figure in the assembly, was elected Chairman. He had owed his selection mainly to the support of non-Socialist groups such as the Free Democrats with whom he was to maintain bitter-sweet relations for many years thereafter.

A leading Social Democrat, when asked why no serious opposition had been organized to Adenauer, remarked, 'We wanted to put him on ice. The real business will be done in committee.'

That facile comment seriously underestimated the man and also the office to which he had been elected. For whatever his political opponents may have felt, Adenauer, garbed in the dignity of Chairman of the Bonn Parliamentary Council, soon came to be regarded by the three western military governors as the spokesman of German democracy. Although at the time unknown to the 50,000,000 West Germans, Adenauer, by the simple fact of his election, became a German national figure and an international personality.

As though to emphasize the change, Adenauer at once adopted his most statesmanlike guise, for a time at least. In his speech of acceptance he said, 'We are going to create a constitution not only in the interest of the German people but in the interest of Europe and the world. But the unity of Germany is, and will remain our primary aim.'

That was a far cry from his bitter denunciation of the Allied plan for a West German Government three months earlier, and caused much comment. This was but the first manifestation of that contradiction inherent in Adenauer's political character, the Jekyll and Hyde-like alternation between the narrow, biting party politician and the world statesman.

For the first few months of the Parliamentary Council Adenauer was at his most courteous with his Social Democrat colleagues. This, no doubt, was largely due to the fact that his opposite number, Dr. Schumacher was ill and Professor Carlo Schmid, a distinguished international legal scholar from southern Germany, acted as S.P.D. leader.

This bulky son of a German father and a French mother, born at Perpignan in the Catalan borderlands, is a positive Friar Tuck of a man. His good humour and Mediterranean culture made co-operation between the two main parties easy. Even this easy relationship could not restrain Adenauer's vindictive tongue. Professor Schmid was having considerable difficulty with Dr. Schumacher, who issued instructions from the hospital bed where he had just had a leg amputated – a disability the more serious because of his earlier loss of an arm. Adenauer was churlish enough to make the cheap gibe that the S.P.D. suffered from 'dictation from a sick bed'.

The Western Powers had directed that the future constitution must be of a federative character, and the real negotiations centred on the interpretation of federalism. The S.P.D. aimed at a constitution which would ensure equality of rights for all without giving support to capitalist or clericalist interests. They also hoped for the strongest possible central government, strong enough to put Socialist economic and social policies into operation without too much interference from the federal provinces.

Adenauer and his C.D.U. colleagues had a more traditional approach. They desired a constitution with a Christian basis which would leave economic forces to operate with a minimum of state interference.

By a curious political paradox it was the S.P.D., with its recollections of the frustration of the Weimar coalition, which produced the constitutional device, which would prove Adenauer's trump card in the repeated political crises of his Chancellor's life.

Under the Weimar constitution the German Chancellor alone was responsible for the policy of his government. This was far from the cabinet collective responsibility known to British democracy, but had some kinship with the principle embodied in the presidential powers in the United States constitution. In 1948 Adenauer had no very strong views on this. Without much discussion, therefore, this vital clause was lifted bodily from the Weimar constitution into the Bonn Basic Law. The S.P.D., with memories of the constantly falling German governments in the twenties, proposed a revolutionary addition. By this new clause, in the Bonn constitution a motion of censure against the Federal Chancellor *could only be carried if in the same motion a new Chancellor was nominated.*

These two clauses together, during the next fifteen years, provided the instrument by which Konrad Adenauer autocratically disregarded the views of his own Cabinet and rode rough-shod over the members of his own coalition. On a number of occasions in those years, notably in the summer of 1959 and at the time of the *Spiegel* crisis in 1962, a majority might well have been found to throw him out of office, but his opponents were unable to agree on the nomination of a successor.

By the end of 1948 the Western Powers had wearied of the interminable talk of the German politicians. Adenauer and his colleagues were summoned to Frankfurt to meet the three military governors and told to get a move on. As a conse-quence, there flared up what was to be known as 'the Frankfurt affair'.

Adenauer, as the German spokesman, explained the differences among the German parties to the three military governors. A few hours later his opponents turned on him. They accused him of attempting to get the military governors to settle matters which were purely of German concern. On this occasion Adenauer was blameless. But Dr. Schumacher, quite as astute and wily as Adenauer, from his hospital bed had begun to contemplate the approach of a German general election. His relations with the British Labour Government up to that time had been most cordial. The S.P.D. leader nevertheless had no wish to let Adenauer develop the 'British lackey' innuendo. The S.P.D., therefore, tried to turn the tables and make out that Adenauer was already in the pocket of the three military governors.

Chauvinism, for want of anything better, is always a sound line in a German election. In the six months that followed both Schumacher and Adenauer were to exploit that expedient to a very high degree.

At this time, the dismantling of the Ruhr industrial potential was at its height. This was done by British officers and officials, *acting on Allied dismantling instructions*.

In German eyes it seemed that the British were trying to eliminate German competition, a view which received much encouragement from visiting Republican industrial magnates from the United States, some of whom subsequently became ministers in the Eisenhower administration. Vast Marshall Plan funds were being pumped into Germany and as a result American big business, with large capital investments in Western Germany, began actively to interfere with the dismantling programme.

Both Schumacher and Adenauer, with their eyes firmly on the struggle for power in the forthcoming general election, rushed headlong into the fray. No holds were barred. In the case of Adenauer his traditional Anglophobia only served to intensify his ardour.

There had certainly been abuses in dismantling by both American and British officials, some of the latter representing industries in the United Kingdom which might expect German competition in the future. To a large extent, however, as ministers of the Ruhr provincial government were willing to admit in private, much of the dismantling agitation was shadow boxing on the German side.

The more intelligent German leaders agreed completely with the British officials who cynically pointed out the advantages which would accrue to German industry as a result of the dismantling. Even then, it was obvious that with Marshall Plan and other forms of American aid, West German heavy industry would soon be re-equipped with newer and better equipment than their competitors, a fact which provided part of the explanation of the 'German miracle' in the next decade.

In the meantime, largely as a result of internal squabbles between the French and their Allies on one side, and similar rows inside the German pre-parliament itself, progress towards the future German constitution had almost come to a standstill. Adenauer became increasingly frustrated.

At the height of this period, at the end of March, 1949, Adenauer was invited to Switzerland to address a meeting of the Inter-parliamentary Union in Berne University. There, on historic neutral soil, to the intense embarrassment of his Swiss hosts,

Adenauer seized the opportunity to make a violently chauvinistic anti-Allied speech.

The 'pale lean German with the hard Tartar face', as a Swiss
newspaper described him, complained with some justice that the
dismantling policy was irreconcilable with the Marshall Plan.
He went on to attack the activities of certain British industrial
officials in Germany, particularly for their part in dismantling
the Black Forest clock industry. And even the normally untouch-
able Americans came in for the rough side of his tongue when he
accused American big business of stealing German patents.

The climax of his speech was sensational. Adenauer claimed
that only the German Wehrmacht but not the German people had
'unconditionally surrendered in 1945' – a portion of the speech
which is not included in his authorized biography. From that
premise he went on to question the legality of the victorious
Allies taking over the civil power in Germany at the time of the
armistice.

There was an immediate uproar. He was sharply condemned in
the entire Western Press for attempting to start a 'new stab in the
back legend'. When he returned to Bonn he claimed, as he always
did in a similar situation in the future, that he had been mis-
reported. He issued a corrected version, which Allied officials
said was just as bad as what had been reported from Berne:
The Allies have wrongly interpreted the unconditional surrender
of the Wehrmacht to mean that the entire German sovereignty
passed into the hands of the occupation powers.

In Western newspapers he was described as 'The Wolf in
Sheep's Clothing' and in the more serious journals on both sides
of the Atlantic he was firmly rebuked. In the House of Commons
the British Labour Government formally deplored his outburst
at this key moment for the future of Germany.

He was scarcely back in Germany before he made a new attack.
It was the British again. In the course of border rectification
negotiations with Holland, they had ceded a few yards of Rhineland territory. 'It is a Diktat,' shouted Adenauer at a C.D.U.

meeting, 'quite contrary to those so often repeated Allied claims about respecting the rights of the individual and of nations.'

It was in the midst of this anti-Allied clamour that the affairs of the pre-parliament at Bonn came to a head. There were considerable differences of opinion among the Germans, chiefly between the S.P.D. and the non-Socialists over the financial rights of the federal provinces. The Socialists wished to make sure that a future German government would not be hamstrung in carrying out socialization plans by financial interference from the provincial governments.

The Allies, too, were divided. The British were fairly indifferent. They were cynically willing to accept American views of federalism. The French were against any strong central German government. In addition, the Gaullist French military governor, General Pierre Koenig of Bir Hakeim fame, was frequently in open conflict, not only with his British and American colleagues, but with his own Government in Paris. The dispute was remitted to the three Western Foreign Ministers for settlement.

At the beginning of April, 1949, the N.A.T.O. treaty was signed in Washington. After the meeting the Foreign Ministers of Britain, France and the United States sat down to hammer out a solution of the problem of the future West German State. They bargained for six days. At the end the Foreign Ministers produced two letters which were to be sent to the military governors.

The first letter was straightforward. It indicated that when the West German Government was established, the Western Powers proposed to reserve their rights in regard to demilitarization and dismantling, foreign policy and currency control, and the six power Ruhr authority. The Foreign Ministers promised, however, that military government would be abolished and a High Commission set up. They declared that the proposed Occupation Statute which would embody these points would be reconsidered after eighteen months. Otherwise, the Foreign Ministers more or less accepted the German constitution drawn up by the Parliamentary Council headed by Adenauer.

The Foreign Ministers were well acquainted with the S.P.D. opposition. But by this time, for reasons of the Cold War, they were becoming desperate to establish a West German government. They realized the S.P.D. could hold up progress indefinitely. Accordingly, they prepared a second emergency letter which virtually accepted all the S.P.D. financial demands. The military governors – of whom General Clay, the American was chairman of the month – were told to keep this second document secret, and in reserve. Only if the S.P.D. proved intransigent and blocked immediate establishment of a West German government should the second letter be produced. Secret diplomatic negotiations had already begun with the Russians to end the Berlin blockade, and the Western governments were anxious to face the Russians with a *fait accompli*.

The letters were rushed to Germany. On 10th April, Adenauer, as Chairman of the Parliamentary Council, was summoned to Frankfurt. From General Clay he received the first letter which he was asked to place before the Parliamentary Council. At once the Social Democrats demurred. Professor Carlo Schmid said no decision could be reached until after the S.P.D. party conference to be held in Hanover on 20th April.

When the S.P.D. conference did meet Dr. Schumacher refused point blank to accept the Allied terms contained in the first letter. He repeated the S.P.D.'s well-known financial demands and intransigently announced that the Socialists were not prepared to accept an 'Allied Diktat' but would fight 'for German rights'.

There were hurried private consultations between the three military governors. On 22nd April General Clay, faced with the S.P.D. intransigence on one hand and the Foreign Ministers' demands for the immediate creation of a Western German government on the other, produced the second letter, conceding the Socialist demands.

Dr. Schumacher, despite the effort of Clay to act as Adenauer's guardian angel, had won for the time being. Adenauer's fury was unbounded. It was directed chiefly at the British. For in Bonn there was a widespread rumour that a British official had privately told Schumacher of the existence of the second, and secret letter from the Foreign Ministers. That may well have been true for both the British and Americans were dabbling in German politics at the time.

Adenauer's chagrin was understandable. What followed is less easy to explain. The British newspapers quite objectively reported the facts of Schumacher's victory – and of Adenauer's defeat. When they reached Bonn the Chairman of the Parliamentary Council boiled over, and nothing could restrain his Anglophobia.

On the afternoon of the following day all British correspondents in Western Germany, suddenly received a summons from Bonn. By telephone they were told by British liaison officers that Adenauer wished to see them. Most of the correspondents at this time had offices in Düsseldorf and there was some discussion as to whether to make the fifty-mile trip to Bonn.

In view of the fact that Adenauer as Chairman of the Parliamentary Council was the leading representative German, and because he was an old man, the British correspondents decided to go. At the end of a long drive the British correspondents were faced by a furious Dr. Adenauer accompanied by his party secretary, the ex-Ribbentrop diplomat, Dr. Herbert Blankenhorn, who later was to be a West German ambassador.

Adenauer at once attacked the British pressmen and their newspapers for stating that Schumacher had gained an important victory. He was particularly offensive about a leading article in *The Times* which had said just that. He alleged, as he was to do again in later years, that the attitude of the British Press towards him was endangering German political unity. He went on to complain that the S.P.D. were using British Press dispatches as propaganda, which was scarcely the concern of British newspapers.

The British pressmen were astonished. Some of them very pointedly told Adenauer that British newspapers were not in the habit of taking their views of events from foreign party politicians, however distinguished they might consider themselves. On that note the meeting ended. The encounter was reported privately to the respective Fleet Street offices concerned. Not a word of these private memoranda was ever published. Almost certainly the confidential memoranda contributed to the very critical attitude which many British newspapers continued to show to Dr. Adenauer for a long time to come. And no doubt memories of Adenauer's only direct attempt to muzzle the British Press were revived in after years when, at regular intervals, the Federal Chancellor returned to the attack.

Secret negotiations at the United Nations in New York to end the Berlin blockade had meantime reached an advanced stage. Still the military governors in Frankfurt and Adenauer's pre-parliament dithered about the future German state. The patience of the Governments in London and Washington became exhausted. Highly placed envoys from both capitals arrived in Frankfurt and, somewhat peremptorily, told all parties concerned to get on with it. At midnight on 8th May, 1949, exactly four years after the German surrender, the pre-parliament finally approved the Bonn Basic Law or provisional constitution by fifty-three votes to twelve. Four days later Adenauer and the other German delegates were summoned to Frankfurt. To their astonishment all formalities for the establishment of the West German State were completed by the military governors that same night.

Almost at the same moment the Berlin blockade came to an end. During these heroic months in the history of Berlin, Adenauer did nothing to increase his reputation. At the height of the Russian siege, when world statesmen were arriving almost daily in the beleaguered city to cheer the gallant Berliners, the attitude of the Chairman of the Parliamentary Council in Bonn became something of a scandal.

His attacks on 'the heathen city of Berlin' in Weimar days were widely quoted in the Berlin newspapers, which emphasized that he had never visited the city since the war.

'Adenauer is a stranger to Berlin,' wrote one newspaper, 'and he never visits it. He lives on the beautiful Rhine but he should not forget that Berlin too is in Germany.'

Alarmed by these attacks, Adenauer flew to Berlin on the Allied airlift. He was never at his best when surrounded by the Cockney-like Berliners whom the dour narrow Rhinelander cannot tolerate. At a giant C.D.U. rally held only a few hundred yards from the Russian sentry posts at the Brandenburger Tor, he made a speech which Berliners of all persuasions found intolerable. In the midst of the beleaguered Western sectors which were living from hand to mouth on what the American Air Force and the R.A.F. were flying in every four minutes, Adenauer chose to express the view that *Germany's future lay in playing off the Western Powers against the Russians.* He announced, without any hesitation, that it would depend on the future attitude of the Western Powers as to whom the Germans would co-operate with in the future. That was not a view which found sympathy in Berlin, even among his party friends.

Adenauer never repeated that indiscretion. At the height of his power any reference to the sensational policy which he had advocated in Berlin in early 1949 was best forgotten. But the advocacy of a policy of playing off the West against the East must inevitably raise the question of Adenauer's fundamental aims in the months immediately prior to his taking office as Federal Chancellor. And the Berlin speech provokes fascinating speculation on what Adenauer *might* have done if the Americans had not – for their own reasons – built him up into the 'favourite ally'.

Soon after the Berlin blockade ended Mr. Bevin had an hour's discussion with Adenauer at a Westphalian *schloss.* It was polite, but scarcely a success. It did nothing to prevent Adenauer plunging with gusto into his campaign for the forthcoming general elections, a campaign in which inevitably British occupation policy was the main target of his chauvinistic attacks.

He was not alone in this. Dr. Schumacher, jettisoning his old friendship with the British Labour party, vigorously tried to outdo even Adenauer in the vitriol of his anti-British utterances. The British dismantling of German industry was all too easy to attack and Adenauer exploited the widespread anti-British feelings of many Germans to the uttermost.

In the early summer of 1949 the West German State, in the creation of which Adenauer had played such an important role, formally came into existence. The first general election was scheduled for early September.

On the eve of the poll Adenauer, in a moment of rare frankness, revealed what were almost certainly his innermost thoughts.

'It is no longer France which is the enemy,' he said, '*it is Britain which is the real enemy now.*'

In the years that followed, and especially during the Churchill and Eden Governments in London, he tried hard to conceal his basic Anglophobia. But as he grew older and older, and drew closer and closer to de Gaulle in the last year of his Chancellorship, Adenauer left little doubt that he still held the view which he so indiscreetly admitted in the summer of 1949.

CHAPTER SIX

The Bundeskanzler

ON A HOT Sunday in mid-August, 1949, West Germany went to the polls for the first time since the Nazi general election in 1933. The fundamental contest was clearly between Adenauer and his anti-Socialist Christian Democrats, and Schumacher at the head of his Social Democrats on whose victory foreign observers offered odds of two to one.

Polling was tranquil despite alarmist rumours to the contrary. Almost eighty per cent of the West German electorate demonstrated their appreciation of the importance of the event by going to the polls.

Adenauer adopted his usual pose of cold indifference. On the night of the poll, after hearing that he had been elected deputy for the Bonn constituency by a big majority, he quietly went to bed without waiting to hear how his party had done throughout the country. By early next morning it was clear that, contrary to all expectations, the Christian Democrats had won by a narrow majority over the Socialists. The balance of power lay largely in the hands of the Free Democrats led by Professor Theodor Heuss and smaller Right-wing parties.

By a combination of guile, ruthless suppression of opposition and great good fortune Konrad Adenauer at the age of 73 at last became German Chancellor, more than thirty years after his first attempt to form a Reich government.

His victory was a success for the conservative, clericalist and, in many cases, reactionary forces in Western Germany, who had given their support, and still more their money, to the Christian Democrats. Outside of Germany this was clearly recognized and there was some uneasiness. For few in 1949 predicted that the old man who had just become Chancellor, in the fourteen years which followed would ruthlessly dominate the near-Nazi business-men, the Catholic prelates, the Protestant churchmen and the south German liberals who formed the motley collection around him.

In the weeks before the election Adenauer had drawn support from many peculiar quarters. His old crony, Dr. Pferdmenges by this time the dominant figure in West German commerce and industry had been an indefatigable collector for the C.D.U. fight-ing fund. It was no secret that he had obtained powerful financial support from the big business barons of the Ruhr whose similar financial support had turned the tide for Hitler in 1932.

By the curious combination of direct votes and proportional representation under which the Germans had gone to the polls, Adenauer's parties, the C.D.U. and Bavarian Christian Socialists, obtained 139 seats in the Bundestag, or German lower house, against the 131 of the Social Democrats. The Free Democrats had 52 and the German Party and the Bavarian Party each 17.

Adenauer therefore faced an immediate dilemma. He could form either a 'Big Coalition' to include the S.P.D., a course which most non-Germans expected in view of the fact that the Bonn Government would be under the tutelage of the Western Powers for a considerable time to come; or he could form a 'Little Coali-tion' of his own C.D.U.C.S.U., the Free Democrats, and the other right-wing and semi-nationalist splinter parties.

His own preference was easy to guess. The prejudices of a life-time and his personal animosity towards the equally awkward Dr. Schumacher ruled out an association with the S.P.D. But Aden-auer in these days was still only leader of a democratic party. On the Left wing of the C.D.U. headed by the Premiers of the Ruhr and Rhineland Palatine, Dr. Arnold and Dr. Altmeier, there was considerable support for a national government including the S.P.D.

Some of the S.P.D. also favoured a broad fronted administration. But in initial soundings Schumacher demanded the post of Economic Minister, with all that such an appointment implied for the Social Democrats. That was more than Adenauer or his big business friends could stomach. With characteristic arrogance and without consulting his party leadership, Adenauer decided on a 'Little Coalition' with the Free Democrats.

He had still to persuade the C.D.U. executive and a meeting was summoned for the Sunday after the election in Adenauer's house at Rhoendorf. From the outset, the left wing of the party made clear that they favoured a national government with the Social Democrats. Adenauer firmly opposed them. The former leader of the C.D.U. in Berlin and the Russian Zone, Jakob Kaiser, survivor of the bomb plot against Hitler, who might well have been German Chancellor in a united Germany, also favoured a broad front government. Adenauer made strenuous efforts to persuade the party leaders to accept his view. They were still unconvinced when the talks were interrupted for a meal. During the break, Adenauer received an envoy from the Vatican in the person of an American Army chaplain, in an American Army staff car. The place of a Right-wing Germany in future plans for a 'little Europe' was close to the heart of the German speaking, German-loving Pope Pius XII.

After the meal the executive meeting was resumed. Adenauer, without further parleying, suddenly announced that a 'Little Coalition' with the F.D.P. and the splinter parties would be formed. Taken completely by surprise, no one opposed him. No one even appears to have demanded a vote, for German politicians, as Hitler demonstrated and Adenauer as Chancellor confirmed, are often like sheep. Faced by yet another strong man who knew what he was going to do, the whole of the C.D.U. executive pusillanimously capitulated. Adenauer had begun the authoritarian rule over his party which he never lost – not even in the midst of his disgraceful manœuvres in the early summer of 1959 when, for a few short weeks, he contemplated transforming himself into an executive president in American terms.

One of the subdued C.D.U. leaders nominated him formally as Chancellor. Then Adenauer announced that in return for F.D.P. support he proposed to make the F.D.P. party leader Federal President. Asked by one of the astounded party leaders if he had had the politeness to ask Professor Heuss, Adenauer coolly answered 'No'. In fact, the first that distinguished German liberal is reputed to have heard of his future high office, which he filled with such distinction for the following ten years, was in a C.D.U. newspaper.

After some days of 'horse trading' Adenauer struck a bargain with Professor Heuss and the leaders of the other Right-wing minority parties. By these agreements Professor Heuss became Federal President and his party deputy, Franz Bluecher, became Adenauer's deputy Chancellor. To find jobs for all the parties Adenauer's ministry, originally planned to have eight members, was swollen to a cabinet of fourteen.

In choosing ministers from his own C.D.U., however, Adenauer was as ruthless as at the party executive meeting. All party opponents who might provide an alternative leader, Dr. Arnold the foremost, were excluded from office. Adenauer's only concession to the Left wing was the appointment of Jakob Kaiser as Minister of all German Affairs to look after the interests of the Russian Zone.

As Economics Minister Adenauer appointed Professor Ludwig Erhard, a chubby Bavarian economist who had kept clear of public life during the Nazi period. Professor Erhard, a very recent recruit to the C.D.U., was the former head of the Bizone economic administration in Frankfurt and his so-called 'Market Economy Policy' of largely uncontrolled free enterprise had formed an important part of the C.D.U. election programme.

Adenauer's somewhat devious activities in forming a government took a considerable time. It was not until 15th September, a month after the election, that the Bundestag formally elected Adenauer as Federal Chancellor of the new West German State. He was elected by 202 votes from a total of 402, a bare majority of one, and was widely known as 'the Chancellor who had elected himself'.

His election was received by the Western Powers with a marked lack of enthusiasm, even by the Americans who backed the Christian Democrats. His uncompromising personality and sour criticism had scarcely endeared him to the American officials with whom he had had contact so far; the glorious days when he was to be Mr. John Foster Dulles's favourite ally were still some years ahead.

The French, despite his reputed pro-French background, were suspicious of any German leader and in the first few months he had some sharp passages with the new French High Commissioner M. André François-Poincet.

To the British his election was a frank disappointment. The Labour Government, and Mr. Ernest Bevin in particular, had hoped for a Social Democrat Chancellor who might be expected to carry out nationalization measures in the Ruhr. In addition his all too recent election call, 'Britain is the enemy now', still rankled in Whitehall. In the ensuing weeks he indicated to the British, unofficially, that they 'must make a gesture' which would wipe out the ignominy of his Cologne dismissal four years before. Mr. Ernest Bevin saw no reason to make any such gesture. Relations between the German Federal Chancellor and the British Government remained frigid, therefore, until the appearance of the Churchill administration two years later.

All these doubts were expressed in a penetrating profile of the new Chancellor which appeared at the time in the London Sunday newspaper, the *Observer*.

The author of this well-informed appraisal suggested that the new Chancellor, in his heart of hearts, was well satisfied with the borders of the new West German State, a view which Adenauer's policies in the following fourteen years tended to confirm.

'His horizon,' stated the *Observer* writer, 'through no fault of his own has remained narrow. According to his lights he is a good European – but it is a Europe which ends at the borders of the old Roman Empire and excludes a great part of his own country. *He will be satisfied to pay lip service to the ideal of German unity without pressing for it too strongly.'*

That remarkable prediction was as true fourteen years later as on the day it appeared in September, 1949.

His Cabinet had only been completed for a few hours when Adenauer presented it to the Bundestag. And at once he plunged into a long policy statement. Much of it was unexceptionable. It was punctuated by shafts of that curious dry irony which with Adenauer passes for humour. When one of the Communist deputies accused him of being 'nothing but an American general', Adenauer in a flash retorted, 'All right, you, stand at attention when you address me.'

He even went out of his way to defend the new Allied Occupation Statute, due to come into effect with the advent of the Bonn Government, although it had been attacked by a considerable section of the German Press as an 'Allied Diktat'.   He then went on to foreign affairs. He announced in the clearest terms that his hours-old Government refused categorically to accept the Oder-Neisse Line, and so at the very outset of his career as Chancellor, he threw down his glove to both Poland and the Soviet Union. He formally laid claim to the great eastern territories of the Reich which Stalin had handed over to the Poles in 1945, and recalled with emphasis that both Britain and America had declined to recognize the *de facto* western frontier of Poland at the Potsdam Conference.

This foreign policy declaration, however much London and Washington might sympathize over the Oder-Neisse line, seemed a peculiarly provocative act for the head of a German government within hours of taking office. It caused concern in the Western capitals. In London *The Times* was constrained to refer to the 'unusual emphasis' with which Adenauer had referred to the Oder-Neisse line.

'Whatever may be thought of the justice or the injustice of the line,' stated *The Times*, 'it must be clearly understood from the

start that if Germany is to be welcomed into the European union
it does not follow that Europe accepts and supports all Germany's
claims for frontier revision.' But Adenauer had more shocks
prepared for the Western Powers.

Twenty-four hours later came his second broadside. He chose
the opportunity afforded him by the presentation of his new
ministers to the recently installed Allied High Commissioners,
who had taken the place of the military government; the American Mr. John McCloy, the Wall Street lawyer and banker who had
served in the Roosevelt administration and who was Adenauer's
distant relative by marriage; M. François-Poncet, the brilliant
French Ambassador in Berlin during the Hitler era; and Sir Brian
Robertson minus British uniform and military rank, the only one
of the military governors to survive as a civilian.

The Occupation Statute, which came into effect at that precise
point, gave Adenauer and his Government very considerable
powers; very much greater than anyone in 1945 would have
believed possible four years after the surrender. With characteristic Teutonic lack of taste Adenauer at once told the surprised
High Commissioners, 'We hope that the Allied Powers will make
use of the revision clause of the Occupation Statute and hasten
further political development.'

The French High Commissioner, as chairman of the Commission for the month, at once retorted, 'You know very well the
principles which govern our relations. These are clearly defined in
Occupation Statute which becomes effective at this moment. As
you suggest, this Statute *can* be revised. The more scrupulously
the Statute is observed the earlier will be the date and the wider
the scope of its revision.'

Adenauer was unimpressed. He had started on his long process
of wearing down the Western Powers. He told his confidants,
'We must have patience. I think that patience is the sharpest
weapon of the defeated. I have a great deal of patience. I can
wait.'

That seemed a remarkable maxim for a superannuated Prussian

high official approaching his seventy-fourth birthday. But history was to prove the correctness of his estimate.

His start had scarcely been promising. Adenauer, with that narrow Rhineland bitterness which so often characterized his actions, even as a world statesman, seemed determined to antagonize the Western Allies from the outset. It may have been a hangover from his unfortunate anti-Allied and anti-British election campaign, or it may very well have been but an indication of his own uncertainty in high office for the first time.

His grievances, however, were forgotten as he faced his first fierce struggle over his future capital. Nearly six months earlier the Parliamentary Council had agreed that Bonn, where it met, should serve as a provisional capital. Thereafter a fierce battle developed between the Rhineland University city, where Beethoven had been born, and the former German Imperial city of Frankfurt-on-Main. The Social Democrats strongly favoured the latter because 'it was farther away from Cardinal Frings and Adenauer's other reactionary friends'. The C.D.U. favoured Bonn because as Dr. Pferdmenges, one of the main protagonists in the inter-city battle, later explained, 'Adenauer was an old man and he happened to live across the river.'

It seemed a strange way to choose the capital of a state of 50,000,000 people, but Adenauer's view prevailed. Bonn was chosen as the capital of the West German State by a majority, and the German ministers and foreign ambassadors alike had to suffer its narrow provincialism in the years that followed.

In the midst of this absurd controversy the continued Allied dismantling of German industry became a major issue. The situation in the British Zone, 100 miles or so from Bonn, was almost out of hand. Posters demanding, 'Who are the traitors?' were plastered across the Ruhr, threatening revenge on Germans who carried out British dismantling orders. British protection had to be given to workers employed by the dismantling contractors.

The Adenauer Government scarcely attempted to conceal its support for the agitators. The Western Powers faced a dilemma.

Either they restored order and in the process probably strangled the infant German Government at birth, or they must make major concessions and increase the prestige of the Adenauer Government among its own people.

By this time both the British and American Governments were reaching the conclusion that the Allies had retained too broad reserved powers under the Occupation Statute. Sir Ivone Kirkpatrick, at that time head of the German section of the Foreign Office in London, has stated that both Governments recognized that if the Adenauer administration was not 'to perish of inanition, it must be given more power; something must be done to meet the Germans on the two issues of dismantling and the restrictions on German industry'.

The Truman administration in Washington had long been convinced that the dismantling programme and the restrictions on German industry were anachronisms. The Labour Cabinet in London underwent an 'agonizing reappraisal' before it accepted such a decision.

The British Foreign Secretary, Mr. Bevin, had observed with growing anxiety the establishment in the Russian Zone of an East German Communist administration as counterpart to the Adenauer Government in Bonn. With much hesitation, he decided that the punitive provisions of the Potsdam Agreement could no longer be reconciled with the necessities of the Cold War. And it was the often anti-German Bevin who persuaded his Cabinet colleagues to make major concessions to Adenauer, thereby building up the prestige of the infant Bonn Government.

By early autumn London and Washington were agreed that major concessions must be made on dismantling and easing the restrictions on German industry. But the always-suspicious French had still to be persuaded.

At this juncture Adenauer heard a whisper, but not from the British, of what had been agreed in Washington and London. At once he embarked on what was to be his classical technique during the remaining years of the Allied occupation.

Through his C.D.U. newspapers he launched a campaign demanding, often in offensive terms, precisely those Allied concessions which, he was tolerably certain from the hints of his American friends, were to be granted within the next few weeks. His main demands were the end of dismantling and the lifting of restrictions on shipbuilding; the Germans should be permitted to open consular and commercial relations with foreign powers and Germany must join the Council of Europe and certain other international bodies. Germany, in return, must agree to join the Ruhr authority and *undertake not to re-arm.*

The three High Commissioners in Bonn were told to begin negotiations with the Germans. Adenauer, who by the Occupation Statute was the only German Minister with whom the Allies dealt, was summoned to the High Commission headquarters on a hill above Bonn. For three weeks hard, and sometimes acrimonious bargaining went on. At the key moment Adenauer played the card that was to become familiar in all negotiations with the Occupation Powers in the following half dozen years. He warned them that he was 'a weak Chancellor' with a narrow Parliamentary majority. He was not in a position, he argued, to push radical or unpopular measures through the Bundestag.

This astute device of inverse blackmail worked. In the next few years Adenauer used the same trick over and over again against the Western Powers. The French High Commissioner, the witty M. François-Poncet, summed up these first negotiations with Adenauer by commenting in private, 'It's always a difficult business making gifts to the Germans, and a thankless task at that.'

At last, on 24th November, little more than two months after taking office, Adenauer drove downhill to the Bundestag to announce triumphantly that he had got 'ninety per cent of his demands'.

To his cheering supporters he announced that he had extorted major concessions – which his American friends had assured him all along he would get.

In conclusion he announced that he had signed a declaration expressing 'the earnest determination of the Federal Republic to maintain the demilitarization of Federal territory and *to endeavour to prevent the re-creation of armed forces of any kind*'. That declaration was perhaps the most cynical undertaking Konrad Adenauer ever gave. But its importance was overlooked temporarily as the rage of Dr. Schumacher burst at what was clearly a major victory for Adenauer.

During the evening, after Adenauer's statement, the temper of the Bundestag rose steadily. It reached boiling-point when Adenauer produced a telegram of support from the German Trade Union Congress which Schumacher at once characterized as a forgery. The stormy session seemed on the point of closure when suddenly a Communist shouted at Adenauer, 'Are you still a German? Speak for once as a German Chancellor.'

Dr. Schumacher could contain himself no longer. 'A German Chancellor,' he shouted at Adenauer. '*He's the Chancellor of the Allies.*'

Uproar followed and the sitting was adjourned in disorder. When it resumed at six o'clock in the morning Schumacher was suspended for the next twenty sittings. Adenauer never forgave that taunt. And that marked the virtual end of any chance of co-operation between the two main German parties, so long as Dr. Schumacher survived. Some point was given to Schumacher's taunt when the British High Commissioner, Sir Brian Robertson publicly announced that the Allies 'had made far-reaching concessions in order to promote the prestige of the German Government and remove sources of friction'. The inference was obvious.

But the British High Commissioner, in words clearly directed at Adenauer, added, 'We do not expect this agreement should be a stepping-stone for further demands.'

Adenauer was indifferent to such admonitions. Sir Brian Robertson had merely confirmed what Adenauer had already discovered would be the secret of his future success. From his first negotiation and discussion over the so-called Petersberg Agreement he had discovered that in a final showdown the Western Powers, and particularly the Americans, were willing to pay an unlimited price for Germany's support in the Cold War. That was a momentous discovery. In the fourteen years that followed the old man exploited it to the ultimate.

In the months after the signing of the Petersberg Agreement Adenauer's relations with the Western Powers steadily deteriorated. He was misled, perhaps, by the comparative ease with which he had gained his first success as Federal Chancellor. For although the Western Powers were indeed willing to pay a considerable price for German support in the Cold War, they were not prepared to capitulate, immediately and unequivocally, to any demand Adenauer might care to make. During the following months, until the Korean war revolutionized the situation, Adenauer's development as Federal Chancellor was marked by a steady series of crises with the Occupation Powers. In the six months after the Petersberg success he became disillusioned by the constant series of rebuffs that he received. On at least one occasion he seriously contemplated resignation.

In these same months, however, there appeared from time to time rare flashes of genuine statesmanship. Within a few hours of making a bitter and wounding attack on one of the Western Allies, the old man would be found advancing a statesmanlike project which gained general approval.

All this no doubt was part of the slow development of the narrow, reactionary Rhineland Oberbürgermeister into the equally conservative German Chancellor – a sort of political adolescence at advanced years. It was a difficult period for both Adenauer and the Western representatives, with whom his regular meetings sometimes descended into open acrimony.

His first rebuff was not entirely his own fault. It will be recalled that in the Petersberg Agreement he had signed an undertaking to maintain a demilitarized Germany. He did this although both Adenauer and the American High Commissioner,

Mr. McCloy, were very well aware that the senior American generals in the Pentagon were already clamouring for a new German army. At the same time, the Americans had set up near Munich a vast Cold War secret service, headed by the former German intelligence general Reinhard Gehlen, where the future leaders of Adenauer's army were already secretly working on plans for what became the Bundeswehr.

As Adenauer's authorized biography points out with justice, no one took the trouble to ask either the German people or the new German Chancellor what he thought.

Foreign affairs and defence were officially forbidden subjects for the new German Government. But the Americans were anxious to launch a propaganda campaign in favour of a new German army, and when sometime later they offered Adenauer a chance to express his views, he seized the opportunity with both hands.

He willingly accepted an American suggestion that he should receive a visiting correspondent of the Cleveland *Plain Dealer* and talk about German rearmament. Somewhat coyly Adenauer told the visiting American that, while he was basically against the creation of a new Wehrmacht, should the Western Powers wish the Germans to take part in the defence of Europe, he would not be opposed to a self-sufficient German army, particularly in a European defence force. Within a few hours there was an uproar throughout the western world. He claimed, as usual, that he had been misquoted. But within the next few days, he clarified his views and made it clear that he would have nothing to do with any project for German mercenaries in an international force.

The interview brought joy in the Pentagon, but among the liberal Democrats of the Truman administration, Adenauer's activities were certainly not approved. In Bonn, a senior American diplomat told the author that 'Adenauer is going much too far and his opinions are inappropriate at this stage for a German statesman'.

The White House and the State Department in fact had no

doubt that 'Adenauer had been running up trial balloons and with each subsequent amendment of his declaration the balloon becomes more visible'.

Adenauer took note. His campaign for a new army stopped abruptly; in public at least. Some weeks later, American intelligence officers who had been ordered to keep a watch on him reported that he had been having private meetings with former senior officers of Hitler's Wehrmacht. Why Adenauer should have embarked on this propaganda campaign at this moment is still obscure. At the time Dr. Pferdmenges told the author that Adenauer was 'an old pacifist'. Apart from obvious incitements from military supporters of the Republican party in Washington, the most probable explanation is that the sly political operator who had become Federal Chancellor had been quick to realize that, in view of American military demands, an army would be the strongest card in his hand in his future negotiations with the Western Powers.

The commotion over his German rearmament propaganda had scarcely died down before Adenauer fell foul of the French over the Saar. Again the fault was not entirely his although his typically tactless approach did much to aggravate the situation.

In the years following 1945 successive French Governments had followed a chauvinistic policy which had led to the establishment of what was little better than a French puppet-government in Saarbrücken. The French seemed to aim at the eventual incorporation of the rich Saar industrial basin in France.

Early in 1950 the then French Foreign Minister, M. Robert Schuman, later to be one of Adenauer's closest collaborators in the European movement, visited Bonn. At once, differences over the Saar became apparent. Adenauer rushed into the open and, at a Press conference, announced belligerently, 'If the Saar government attempts to separate the Saar from Germany, with French agreement, then there may be developments of which no one can see the consequences.'

For months afterwards there were pointed exchanges between

the Federal Chancellor and the French High Commissioner. In this case Adenauer stuck to his maxim of patience. By a steady wearing down process over the years he eventually gained the complete return of the Saar to Germany in the middle of 1959.

It was the Saar dispute which also revealed, for the first time, the dictatorial methods by which Adenauer was already controlling his Government. As in Cologne a quarter of a century earlier, the more important Adenauer became, the more autocratic his rule. Time after time, in negotiations over the Petersberg Agreement, in talks with the French over the Saar and in smaller matters, Adenauer just did not trouble to tell his Cabinet.

He repeatedly gave interviews and made policy statements of which his Ministers knew nothing until they read them in the newspapers. It was often difficult to ascertain whether Adenauer spoke as German Chancellor or as the backbiting C.D.U. party boss. The old autocratic habits of the Prussian Oberbürger-meister died hard, if at all. The whole German Government, apart from the economic and financial affairs which he did not understand, were soon completely identified with the personality of the old man in the Federal Chancellery. Within six months of taking office Adenauer had become what he remained for the rest of his long period of office – a one-man government or, more succinctly, a democratic dictator.

To achieve his ends he embarked in these early months on a system which remains one of the most serious indictments against his years as Federal Chancellor. Less and less were the opinions of his Ministers considered while he encouraged the semi-political salaried heads of departments to become his personal assistants in their respective ministries. Ministers, unless they were specialists like the Economics Minister, Professor Erhard, meant little. For Adenauer reverted, consciously or unconsciously, to what might be called a modern adaption of the autocratic system of his great predecessor Bismarck. Adenauer's methods were a brilliant development of that Bismarckian system of rule through personal assistants. But the Bonn Chancellor carried through this system in the face of much stronger parliamentary opposition probably than the Iron Chancellor ever had to face.

It was this skill in creating a one-man government which drew from a witty, if somewhat cynical British diplomat this *bon mot*: 'There are three kinds of democracy nowadays – the good old-fashioned parliamentary democracy of the Anglo-Saxons; the one-party People's Democracy of the Communists, and the authoritarian democracy of Konrad Adenauer'. It was all too true, for the Adenauer 'dictatorship' was based on a foundation of impeccable constitutional democracy.

With the terrible example of Adolf Hitler in the immediate background, the 'democratic dictatorship' of Adenauer provided yet further testimony to the ease with which one ruthless deter-mined autocratic man can regiment sheeplike German democrats, and a warning of what can happen in the future should one of his successors be basically less paternal and benevolent than Konrad Adenauer.

Adenauer was quick to realize his strength under the Bonn constitution and he revelled in it. At an early stage, when the American High Commissioner, Mr. McCloy, inquired about the views of his Cabinet, he retorted, 'Don't worry about my Ministers. I am at least seventy-five per cent of the Cabinet!' After the 1953 and 1959 general elections when he gained an overall majority, there was little which could be done to oppose his autocratic will. It was only after the sharp reverse which he and the C.D.U. suffered in 1961 that Dr. Schroeder and others succeeded in putting a brake on him.

The arrogance and determination which intimidated Ministers and members of the Bundestag had the contrary effect on the Allied officials with whom he came into contact in the first months of his Chancellorship. On some occasions tension between him and top Allied officials seemed near breaking-point. Some of the British, at least, would have been happy to see him resign in these first few months. But Adenauer was not always to blame.

Some Allied officials, accustomed to issue unchallenged orders to the Germans for the previous five years, frankly resented the appearance of a German Government and continued to show little regard for it. Too often, Adenauer and his Ministers were treated as reformed criminals on probation. The High Commission as a whole was often gauche and exhibited a complete disregard for that inevitable German super-sensitivity which was to reappear at regular intervals in the succeeding decade at every crisis of confidence between Germany and the Western Powers.

Adenauer, of course, was arrogant and awkward. The unhelpful and unsympathetic attitude of many Allied officials seemed to bring out the worst in him. In public he seemed unable to restrain his acid tongue. On more than one occasion he seemed to go out of his way to give offence.

With the furore over rearmament momentarily forgotten and the Saar situation continuing to simmer, a new row developed over the German economic situation.

Adenauer, who did not understand economic matters, had taken little interest up to the point in early 1950 when serious difficulties arose, chiefly because Professor Erhard all too zealously followed his American Marshall Plan friends' advice to 'liberalize trade'.

So well, in fact, did the Bonn Economic Minister follow his own instincts and American advice, that within a few months of the Bonn Government taking office, he had almost run Western Germany into bankruptcy, a state of affairs glossed over by the subsequent success of his 'German miracle'.

To some extent Erhard was the victim of divided American counsel. While the Republicans controlling the Marshall Plan administration agreed with him that more and more dollars should be pumped into the German economy, the Truman Democrats in the State Department took a much more restrained view. The American High Commissioner, Mr. McCloy, therefore, delivered a speech largely written in the State Department in Washington.

'The United States has already done so much for Germany,'

said the High Commissioner, 'that it is difficult to think of what more we can do.' This speech was followed by a sharp Allied note telling Adenauer and Erhard that a solution of Germany's economic problem must be found.

Adenauer was furious. He showed little inclination to do anything but accept Erhard's advice and demand more dollars. He was proved right. The influence of his big business friends was clearly stronger than that of the State Department. And the official State Department rebuke became a damp squib when the Marshall Plan authorities, apparently in complete defiance of the State Department, provided the necessary millions of dollars.

Adenauer's most bitter squabbles, however, in these early months of his Chancellorship were reserved, as might have been anticipated, for the British.

Dismantling, which both sides had agreed in the Petersberg Agreement should continue where work was already started, was the cause of the first Adenauer-British row. Fierce resentment flared up over the removal of machinery from the Hermann Goering steel plant near Brunswick, and it became necessary to send British troops to control the anti-dismantling rioters. Adenauer for some reason sent to the scene his ineffective Labour Minister, Storch. In what were, indeed, a 'few ill-chosen words,' Storch announced that 'British soldiers have been given orders to fire on the rioters'.

That was untrue, but typical of the Adenauer Government propaganda of the time. Storch had not had time to get back to Bonn before Adenauer was summoned to meet the British High Commissioner, Sir Brian Robertson. The Germans said the conversation was 'long and satisfactory'; British officials reported that it was 'sharp and terse'. Whatever the details British-German relations slumped still further.

Mr. Ernest Bevin, who some months earlier said he would never again trust a German, became increasingly irritated with Adenauer. In the House of Commons he observed that National Socialism had been an expression of what had always been latent in the German character, a view shared by many objective observers of German history.

Adenauer knew very well that the British Foreign Secretary was hitting at him. He hurried to Munich, the birthplace of National Socialism, and for once abandoned his icy calm. To a party meeting he literally shouted, 'I categorically reject the accusation of the British Foreign Secretary. Germany owes it to her own self-respect to reject such a charge.'

He then accused the British Foreign Secretary of stirring up trouble between France and Germany and rounded on the Allies collectively by demanding further concessions.

He seemed intent on staging a showdown with the Western Powers, but his attacks on the British Foreign Secretary had a more personal background. Some weeks earlier German Post Office engineers attempting to remedy frequent faults in the Chancellor's telephone, found connections under his official residence which they could not identify. They started to trace the wires. After a long search they found that the connections disappeared into a British-occupied building where the German engineers were only too well aware the British Secret Service operated a telephone monitoring service. The Germans were appalled. A year earlier the German Post Office engineers would not have dared to report that the British were spying on a German. But with the establishment of a government confidence had been restored. Adenauer was informed. His pent-up hatred of the British exploded. Sharp but unofficial protests were made. Apologies followed. It was all a mistake and nothing but a carry-over from the occupation days!

The whole affair was hushed up. Some Intelligence Officers were sharply reprimanded for having committed the unforgivable sin of being found out. In late 1962, during the *Spiegel* crisis, Adenauer told the Bundestag that his phone was still being tapped. The British at once denied having anything to do with it.

The scene of Adenauer's next row with the Western Powers

was Berlin, on the occasion of his long delayed first visit as Federal Chancellor. He had never been at his best in the old Reich capital, where the spirit of the Berliners brought out the worst in him. Once again, his visit was unfortunate.

The British, as usual, were his first target. He denounced a leading article in the British-founded and controlled German newspaper, *Die Welt*, which he alleged had demanded that 'his Government must give further proof of having abandoned its tendencies towards Soviet Russia'. That was merely the twist he gave to the article. He went on to say, however, that he trusted the statement in *Die Welt* was not the view of responsible British statesmen and asked, 'What more must Germany do to convince the Western Powers of its attitude?' He then demanded new concessions from the three Western Foreign Ministers who were about to meet in New York. He concluded by denouncing Allied interference which, he said, 'is extraordinarily great and not welcome to the Germans'.

These polemics caused considerable embarrassment, not only to his hosts, the Social Democratic administration of the city, headed by the distinguished and gallant Oberbürgermeister Professor Ernst Reuter, but also to the three Allied Commandants of the city who were present.

Adenauer had still more shots in his locker. At the end of his address he stepped to the front of the platform, told the astounded audience to sing *Deutschland über Alles*, and persuaded the orchestra to start the melody. Up to that time the German national anthem had seldom been sung since 1945 except at extreme nationalist or neo-Nazi gatherings, and such gatherings were not fashionable in divided Berlin. Some of the audience half-heartedly followed Adenauer's lead. Others remained silent. Some of his official hosts ostentatiously marched from the platform, while the three embarrassed Western commandants remained seated.

The incident caused much anger in Berlin, where the blockade had firmly cemented Allied-German friendship and the British

Commandant, General Sir Geoffrey Bourne, said bluntly that Adenauer's actions were 'incorrect and in bad taste'. A leading article in *The Times* summed up Western opinion: 'The temptation to win easy applause by insisting on Germany's rights and by such cheap devices as calling for the third verse, harmless enough in itself, of *Deutschland über Alles* was strong. Unfortunately he (Adenauer) did not resist it. If the result offended the Social Democrats, annoyed the three Western Commandants and failed to arouse much enthusiasm among Berliners in general Dr. Adenauer has only himself to blame.'

No official notice of the incident was taken by the Allied High Commissioners in Bonn. Two days later, however, in the course of the normal approval of German laws, the three Commissioners vetoed a new income tax statute which they felt was not in accordance with Germany's undertakings under the Marshall Plan. There was no connection between the Berlin incident and the veto but Adenauer and his Ministers, touchy as ever, took strong offence. The two Ministers concerned, Professor Erhard and Dr. Schaeffer, the Finance Minister, threatened to resign. Adenauer unofficially let the Allies know that he, too, was contemplating resignation.

A few days later, at a C.D.U. meeting in Düsseldorf at which Adenauer again incited the audience to sing *Deutschland über Alles*, he put his cards on the table. 'Does it pay,' he asked, 'to treat those who have taken over responsibility in this way? The attitude of the Western Powers towards Germany is beyond understanding. Many influential people feel we should tell the Occupation Powers to take back the authority they have given to the German Government.'

Once again he was ready to resign, this time on a clear-cut issue. But the rising note in his anti-Allied speeches was not unassociated with the fact that important provincial elections were due to be held a few weeks later in the summer of 1950. As a year earlier, Adenauer was quite prepared, despite what the Western Powers had done for him personally, to outbid the opposition with anti-Allied outbursts to win German nationalist votes.

His speeches and actions caused sharp misgivings in the Western capitals. It was still a far cry from the days when Konrad Adenauer would be described as the 'strongest bastion of the Western World'. The Western Foreign Ministers were due to meet in Paris at the beginning of May. They were expected to rebuke Adenauer.

On the eve of the Foreign Ministers' meeting, however, German-Allied relations were revolutionized. On 9th May, 1950, a special envoy arrived in Bonn from Paris. He carried a letter from the French Foreign Minister, M. Robert Schuman, to Adenauer urging that in the interest of world peace Franco-German enmity must be brought to an end. He therefore proposed that, as a first step, French and German heavy industry should be brought together under an international authority. These were the proposals known at the time as the 'Schuman Plan'. They were the first step towards European unity which led first to the European Community for Coal and Steel and, eventually, to the European Common Market.

The French Foreign Minister was only one of several 'Europeans' behind this revolutionary plan. Adenauer for some time had been contemplating some sort of Franco-German co-operation. It will be recalled that as far back as 1923, at the height of the separatist period, he had a similar idea. And during the Bizone period in Frankfurt his personal representative, Dr. Pferdmenges, discussed such a project with top American officials, which caused the famous banker to admit subsequently that he might have been 'the grandfather of the Schuman plan'.

By the early months of 1950 the plan had been taken up by such famous Europeans as M. Jean Monnet and M. Schuman in France, and, with powerful backing from the Vatican, by Catholic party politicians in Germany, France and Italy.

Some weeks earlier Adenauer had dispatched Professor Erhard on a reconnaissance to Paris. It is alleged that he carried the

German proposals typed on the notepaper of the great Vereinigte Stahlwerke, the huge steel cartel nominally broken up by the Allies of which by this time Dr. Pferdmenges was chairman.

Another envoy of Ruhr big business, along with envoys from Paris, were sent to London where they got a somewhat frosty reception from the Labour Government, from important British business circles, and from the T.U.C., which, in retrospect, was a mistake.

The proposals for Franco-German industrial co-operation certainly exercised a restraining influence when M. Schuman met his British and American colleagues in Paris a few days later. The rebuke intended for Adenauer was quietly forgotten. The Foreign Ministers agreed to set up a committee to consider further changes in the Occupation Statute. But the final communiqué very succinctly expressed the doubts which continued to exist:

> Progress will depend on the degree of confidence and frank co-operation shown by the Government and people of the Federal Republic . . . the Foreign Ministers earnestly hope that the Federal Republic will fulfil the hopes placed on the wisdom of her people *and of her leaders.*

Adenauer was still on probation – but he was showing signs of improvement.

CHAPTER SEVEN

Signs of Statesmanship

NEWS OF THE Communist attack on South Korea in midsummer, 1950, hit Western Germany like an atom bomb. In the Federal Republic, with its 250 miles of frontier along the Iron Curtain, a wave of panic spread along the 50,000,000 West Germans. The parallel between Korea and divided Germany was only too obvious. The cause of the German alarm was understandable. Both countries as a consequence of the Cold War had been split into two parts – one Communist and one under Western guidance. In the Communist portion of both countries the Russians had built up strong armed forces. And in Korea these forces had gone over to the attack.

Many Germans sought to re-insure themselves with the Russians whose twenty-two divisions in the East Zone were expected on the Rhine within weeks. The always politically-pusillanimous Ruhr industrialists began to place advertisements in Communist newspapers in Eastern Europe. Only four feeble Anglo-American divisions and a travesty of an air force stood between the Red Army and the Germans.

Adenauer, who was recovering from pneumonia on the day of the Korea attack, like millions of his fellow Germans feared that a Communist coup against the Federal Republic was imminent. From the Federal Republic the Chancellor, and the chief staff officers of the British and American armies watched helplessly the movement of the Communist Bereitschaften, the 150,000 Communist emergency police armed with Soviet tanks and guns, who were expected to be used for a sortie across the zonal frontier.

Adenauer, at the head of a disarmed and occupied country, could do little but appeal to the Western Powers for help. The Western Governments in turn felt almost as helpless as Adenauer as they surveyed the handful of formations to which the occupation armies had been allowed to dwindle.

Six months earlier, Adenauer had asked for an Allied security guarantee. With justice, he had emphasized to the Western Powers that as they had disarmed Germany they must now defend the Germans. Allied lethargy and financial stringency, combined with Adenauer's uncompromising hostility to the Allied Powers, had prevented any positive steps being taken. At the end of June the Western Powers and Adenauer were suddenly faced with the necessity of formulating radical new policies – and quickly.

Adenauer, now in his seventy-fifth year, was exhausted by the task of his turbulent first year as Chancellor and by his serious attack of pneumonia. So while the Western military staffs grappled with organizing emergency measures to meet the expected Communist attack, he retired to Lake Lucerne in Switzerland for a much needed holiday.

There he pondered deeply on the previous twelve months and the future ahead of him. Some time in these weeks of heart searching his basic logic and background were shocked into reasserting themselves. In the new circumstances created by the war in Korea, he came up against the fact that his political guerilla campaign against the Western Powers must end. Faced with a Communist threat, the lifelong reactionary, clericalist enemy of Bolshevism had no other choice. He must align himself with the West. That meant much fuller and more active co-operation with the Western Powers than he had ever contemplated. With a lifetime of political activity behind him the old man was able to appreciate that because the Western Allies were also the Occupation Powers, his new policy must involve sacrifice and restraint.

These weeks amid the Swiss mountains marked the turning-point in Adenauer's career as Federal German Chancellor. He

went to Lucerne a narrow carping local politician blown up by
accident into a national prime minister. He returned to Bonn the
same autocratic, awkward, wily and often exasperating old man;
but a subtle change had begun to take place. He was starting to
become a European statesman whom the years would mellow,
until extreme age would revive some of his less desirable political
traits.

The weeks in Lucerne, although long enough to reach a fundamental reappraisal of his basic policies, were too brief a time in
which to lose all his less attractive political habits. In the months
which followed, when he was thrown into ever closer association
with the representatives of the Western Powers, there were many
occasions when his acid comments and lack of tact caused deep
resentment.

He gradually became more ready, though, to appreciate the
overriding reasons for Western policies which sometimes were
hard for the Germans to bear. Tolerance and understanding in
international affairs developed but at home there was no noticeable improvement in his dictatorial method of government. He
never lost his autocratic flair for one-man rule, not that the
Western representatives seriously objected. It was much easier to
deal with one man, however obstinate and awkward, than a whole
covey of German Cabinet Ministers. The Western Powers, therefore, had little inclination to carp at his methods.

On the Allied side, in these weeks after the start of the Korean
war, there was an equal reappraisal of policy. The Western Powers
realized that Western Germany could no longer be left as a sort of
second-class colony in a military and political vacuum. Their
dilemma was obvious. Should Western Germany, weak, defenceless, *but harmless*, be left to drift? Or should the Federal Republic
be integrated as closely as possible into the Western community
by political, economic and *inevitably military ties*?

The Americans had long favoured the second policy. The
French, as always, and despite the Schuman proposals, were
intransigent on any concessions to the Germans. The pragmatic

British, mid-way between the two as on other occasions, tended to hold a decisive role. Up to the time of the Korean war the policy of the London Government in Germany had been to 'hasten slowly'. To a man the British Labour Ministers abhorred German militarism. In the previous five years they had done much to remove any opportunity for its revival. If the Korean war caused Adenauer to revise his fundamental thinking, the reappraisal within the British Labour Cabinet was equally agonizing.

The Foreign Secretary, Mr. Bevin, in his solid commonsense way, had been steadily moving towards the American point of view ever since his initiative at the time of the Petersberg Agreement. When the Korean war started he appreciated that it was fundamental to the West that the Federal Republic, with its great industrial resources and manpower potential, should become an equal partner.

This radical change in British policy towards Germany by complete chance coincided with an important change in the British administration in Germany. Shortly before the start of the Korean war, General Sir Brian Robertson, the first British High Commissioner had left Germany to resume his distinguished military career. His successor was Sir Ivone Kirkpatrick, the head of the German Department in the Foreign Office, who, as a result of years in the Berlin Embassy during the period, was one of the outstanding British experts on German affairs.

The change marked the beginning of better relations between the British and Adenauer, relations for so long clouded by his dismissal by the soldiers in 1945. Gradually Adenauer learned to cloak his Anglophobia as Sir Ivone, with diplomatic tact and vast understanding of Teutonic touchiness, removed points of friction between British and Germans. (The truce endured until the advent of Mr. Harold Macmillan as Prime Minister, when the old Anglophobia reappeared.)

Sir Ivone Kirkpatrick in his memoirs has told of his improved relations with Adenauer:

'In negotiations I always found him a redoubtable but charming adversary. He certainly enjoyed the clash of wits at the conference table. He was always quick to detect any weakness in an opponent's armour and to drive his weapon through the chink; and he was equally quick to recognize generally the strength in an opponent's case. He is always the rational man. The tall figure sits stiff as a ramrod at the table. In carefully articulated German the sentences fall from his lips — impassive authoritative sentences with a flavour of Chinese detachment. But from time to time events seem to provoke him to anger. I once told him he must never allow himself to get angry, because the excitement was bad for his health. "On the contrary," he replied with an impish grin, "that is what keeps me young."* He must often have been angry in the next dozen years'.

Appropriately enough, it was Sir Ivone Kirkpatrick who, in Berlin just a fortnight after the start of the Korean war, gave the first hint of the coming revolution in Allied policy.

'An attack on the Germans is an attack on all of us,' he said to a surprised audience. 'What we have to do is to organize ourselves in a rational manner.' The next decade and more was to be largely occupied by the Western Powers and Adenauer together 'organizing themselves in a rational manner'.

In Switzerland Adenauer gave much thought to the problem of Germany's defence and what part his fellow-countrymen might take in it. Then, in the Swiss morning newspapers on 11th August, he read an electrifying report. At a meeting of the Council of Europe in Strasbourg, Sir Winston Churchill had urged the creation of a European Army, *including a German contingent.*

A few days later, Adenauer returned to Bonn, a new man in body and spirit. He knew by this time that the Western Powers were thrashing out the problem of German defence. At once Adenauer put up a trial balloon to test German and world opinion. To a correspondent of the *New York Times,* which he knew was well read in the Pentagon, he indicated that he wanted

* *The Inner Circle,* Sir Ivone Kirkpatrick. Macmillan 1959.

a West German police force equal in size and armament to the 150,000 strong People's Police in the Russian Zone.

'We recognize the necessity, of setting up a powerful German defence force,' he said, using a pregnant phrase which was widely interpreted as his first move in the demand for a new German army. But he was careful to qualify his remark. He said he would speak neither of a police force or an army but of 'forces powerful enough to prevent the possibility of Korea-type aggression by the Soviet Zone Police.'

The interview had its intended effect. A few days later he was invited to discuss the matter with the three High Commissioners. He asked that the Western Powers should strongly reinforce their garrisons in West Germany, and said that his Government was prepared to raise a security force equal in strength and armament to the Communist People's Police. He proposed the creation of a German Volunteer Force of up to a maximum strength of 150,000 men.

In reply to a direct question from the French High Commissioner, he said he had hoped to spare the German people the problems of remilitarization. He added, however, that he very much favoured Sir Winston Churchill's plan for a European army *with German participation.*

For some unexplained reason, Adenauer went straight from this confidential meeting to a Press conference, where he gave some indication of what had passed, and where he referred to the three High Commissioners as 'The Trinity on the Petersberg'. Adenauer had often difficulty in restraining his normally caustic tongue; the instincts of the Oberbürgermeister were sometimes too much for the good intentions of the Federal Chancellor. His offensive reference to 'The Trinity' was resented. The Allied diplomatic representatives told him that his present methods 'were not conducive to securing support for his proposals in Britain and the United States'.

Adenauer's rudeness patently could not be permitted to interfere with basic Allied policy. A meeting of the Western Foreign

Ministers had been arranged to be held in New York in mid-September. Adenauer was asked to put his proposals in writing.

On 29th August he submitted two memoranda, on six typewritten pages. The first dealt with the German security. In this he requested the urgent reinforcement of the Allied garrisons in Western Germany. He added that in the event of the creation of a European army, the Germans would be ready to contribute a contingent. But he rejected the remilitarization of Germany *through the re-establishment of a national army*. He also proposed the creation of a Federal Defence Police Force equal in strength and armament to the Communist People's Police.

The second memorandum referred to relations between the Federal Republic and the Occupation Powers. His two main requests were that the state of war between the Allies and Germany should end, and that relations between the Occupation Powers and the Federal Republic should be placed on a treaty or contractual basis.

He forwarded these two top policy documents to the Western Foreign Ministers *without submitting them to his Cabinet*. The explanation in his authorized biography is that he had intended to let his Ministers see the two memoranda but he did not have time to do so! The American High Commissioner left Bonn at short notice, and Adenauer gave them to him without troubling to tell the German Cabinet. Some of the German Ministers learned of the contents of the two memoranda from foreign newspapers on the following morning. In any other democratic country the Cabinet would have resigned in a body. But political integrity and courage were never attributes of the Bonn Ministers, as the next dozen years of this Adenauer autocracy were to prove. If these qualities had been more evident the history of Germany might have been different.

Adenauer's Minister of the Interior, the Lutheran Church official, Dr. Heinemann, who *did have enough character to resign* in basic opposition to remilitarization, a few weeks later stated in a Swiss newspaper that 'the rearmament memorandum was part of Adenauer's private policy drawn up without the consent of the people, the Parliament, or the German Cabinet being asked'.

Whether or not it was an accident on this occasion Adenauer, right up to the last months in his office, never hesitated to take equally important policy decisions without reference to his principal ministers, and sometimes in open defiance of what most of them thought.

In mid-September the Foreign Ministers met in the Waldorf-Astoria Hotel in New York. Before the talks started, Mr. Ernest Bevin stated that 'Germany naturally must be brought back into the family of nations but giving weapons to German troops is not the right way to achieve that object'.

Adenauer's proposals for a security police force were strongly supported by the British Foreign Secretary despite his deep-seated suspicion of any Germans in uniform. But the Americans had no interest in Adenauer's military policemen. The generals in the Pentagon wanted stout German divisions. The American Secretary of State, Mr. Dean Acheson, produced what he called a 'package deal':

1. That the United States would send substantial reinforcements to the N.A.T.O. forces in Europe.
2. That General Eisenhower would be appointed Commander-in-Chief of all the N.A.T.O. forces in Western Europe.
3. *That Germany should be allowed to raise an army.* He said that the first two depended on acceptance of the third condition.

The British fought hard for Adenauer's police force. It seemed a good solution. The French were petrified by any thought of Germans in uniform. The Americans were adamant.

The British Foreign Secretary placed fundamental importance on major reinforcements being sent to Europe and to the return of General Eisenhower as Commander-in-Chief. He was prepared to pay the price and reluctantly gave way, against his own better judgement, on the issue of German armed forces, which both the Americans and British believed could be integrated into

N.A.T.O. Sir Ivone Kirkpatrick, who acted as Mr. Bevin's principal adviser, has since commented that events proved the British right and the Americans wrong. The Americans wanted to bring about German rearmament as quickly and effectively as possible. If they had accepted Adenauer's request for a police force they would have got 150,000 German armed men at least seven years earlier than resulted from the weary, long-drawn negotiations for a German army.

The three-power meeting dragged on for ten days. Towards its close, Adenauer received a sudden telephone call from New York. 'Are you prepared to agree to a German participation in European defence?'

He was. But he also was well aware of the widespread pacifist feelings among large sections of his fellow-countrymen after defeats in two wars. For once he was strictly constitutional. 'That is a question for the Bundestag,' he told the caller from the Waldorf-Astoria.

When the conference ended two days later, the Foreign Ministers said they were agreeable to the creation of a Federal police force. The creation of a German *national* army was in the interest neither of Germany nor of Europe, but the question of the Federal Republic's participation in an integrated European defence force would be further examined.

The Allies, however, announced important concessions to Adenauer. The Foreign Ministers agreed to a further revision of the Occupation Statute and the list of forbidden or restricted industries, and authorized Adenauer to open diplomatic relations with other countries except the Communist *bloc*. Most important, the Western Powers announced that any attack on Western Germany – *or on Berlin* – from any quarter would be treated as an attack on the three Western Powers. That declaration remained the cornerstone of Allied military policy in Central Europe so long as Adenauer was Chancellor.

Discussions about the future German participation in European defence continued during the following weeks through diplomatic channels. A month later, in October, Adenauer told his C.D.U. Party Congress, at Goslar, a few miles from the zonal border, that the German people must be ready to take its share of the burden of the combined defence of the West against armed threats from the East.

The French Government in Paris in the meantime had been seriously studying the whole question of a European army. 'The Europeans' in the French Cabinet had been much impressed by Adenauer's statesmanlike co-operation during the negotiations in the previous few months for the establishment of a six-power European Coal and Steel Community. Five days after Adenauer's speech to his party congress, the French Prime Minister, M. René Pleven suddenly revolutionized the whole question of German remilitarization.

In the French Chamber he announced a plan, which afterwards bore his name, for a European army in which Germany would take part. His plan provided for severe restrictions on the size of the German units, on their use of heavy arms, and on the employment of German senior officers. German nationalist critics and some of Adenauer's intimates described the whole concept as a 'glorified Foreign Legion'.

The 'Pleven Plan' was a long way from the American, and Adenauer's concept of a European army. In Bonn, Adenauer indicated confidentially that much of the French plan was unacceptable. But in public he was discreetly non-committal.

The Americans and the British were becoming irritated by French hesitation and prevarication. And when the N.A.T.O. Council met in Brussels at the beginning of December, they pressed for immediate action. As a result of Anglo-American insistence, the High Commissioners in Bonn were told to take two radical steps:

1. To start immediate negotiations with Adenauer aimed at integrating Germany into the common defence effort. (As a sop to the French it was agreed that an Allied-German conference

should meet in Paris early in 1951 to discuss the plan for a European army.)

2. To consider what changes in the occupation arrangements would follow the creation of German defence forces. No one at Brussels in December, 1950, would have believed that it would be more than four years before any of these projects got beyond the paper stage.

By his seventy-fifth birthday, at the beginning of 1951, Adenauer could take stock with quiet satisfaction. In the fifteen months since he had become Federal Chancellor, Western Germany had gone far under his leadership. But how much Adenauer had contributed to that sensational transformation from an occupied enemy country to the status of a near-ally was problematical in the extreme. After he had become a world figure the Adenauer propaganda machine attributed the transformation entirely to the work of the old man. In truth, events had shaped the man, and not the contrary as latter-day flatterers attempted to suggest. For after those first terrible nine months, when he attempted to carry on a sort of cold war against the Occupation Powers, Konrad Adenauer was saved by world events, principally by the outbreak of war in Korea. His not inconsiderable political skill and sagacity enabled him to exploit that situation. But the transformation in the international status of Western Germany between June and December 1950, and the sharp rise in his own prestige were almost entirely due to changes in Western policy caused by the Korean war.

The future status of Western Germany had been assured and his own prestige enhanced by the two important decisions taken at Brussels a few weeks before; to integrate a German armed force into Western defence, and to modify radically, and eventually to end, the occupation of the Bonn Republic.

Adenauer was certain that the turning-point in Germany's immediate post-war history had been reached. Within a few months at most, he believed he would be transformed into

Chancellor of a nearly-sovereign state and a partner in the Western Alliance, with German troops to use as a trump card in future
negotiations.

He felt firm ground under his feet at last. For the first time since
Potsdam he was becoming convinced of the good intentions of
the Western Allies. It would take many years for him to lose, if he
ever did, his fear of the 'nightmare of Potsdam' agreement between East and West at the expense of Germany. His new feeling
of satisfaction with Western policy showed itself immediately in
his personal relations with the representatives of the Occupation
Powers.

He was united with the Western Powers in basic policy, and
however much his sharp tongue and sly manœuvres may have
caused irritation in the Western capitals from time to time, there
was never any real doubt about his fundamentally pro-Western
outlook. And so, for the next dozen years, the story of Adenauer
was largely the history of Germany. From the beginning of 1951 –
officially he became German Foreign Minister two months later –
Adenauer's constant pre-occupation was foreign affairs.

His influence on internal German affairs remained decisive;
he was too much of the autocrat to permit effective control to pass
out of his hands. But he was content to be an overlord, to leave
day-to-day domestic issues to others, and to confine his interference to major decisions of policy.

Adenauer was also shrewd enough to interfere as little as
possible in Germany's fantastic industrial recovery, which was due
more to the Germans' sensational willingness to work, coupled
with American financial support, than to policies of his Economics Minister Erhard. At this point, however, Adenauer made
one important contribution to internal economic affairs which
played a large part in maintaining the industrial peace which
continued throughout most of his Chancellorship.

Early in 1951, under the personal guidance of Adenauer, the
Bundestag passed the sensible Law for Co-Determination in the
heavy industries of the Ruhr. The law, which seemed to derive

something from Adenauer's study of past papal encyclicals on social relations, provided for representatives of the German trade union participating in the management and sitting on the board of directors of the new heavy industry companies established under Allied decartelization legislation. The law was not welcomed by Adenauer's big business supporters. In practice it was to prove a notable success. Not only did it give the workers a direct say in the management, but it seemed to inspire a sense of responsibility which made strikes a rarity. This German legislation certainly provided an interesting alternative to Britain's outright nationalization. The Co-determination Law for which Adenauer personally carried out almost all the main negotiations with the representatives of the German trade unions, also emphasized that his was the master hand controlling all major policy emerging from Bonn.

In March, 1951, his ideas for one-man government were carried even further. At that time the modified Occupation Statute, agreed by the Western Powers in the previous autumn, came into operation. This permitted Germany to appoint a Foreign Minister and to conduct its own foreign affairs, except with the Eastern *bloc*.

Adenauer, amid violent protests from all sides, including his own party, combined the Foreign Ministry with the Chancellorship. His decision in fact was not unreasonable. He was the only minister who could negotiate with the Western Powers, and his new portfolio did little more than formally confirm his existing practice. Even the presidential office was becoming uneasy about the Adenauer autocracy. President Heuss's official spokesman admitted with astonishing frankness that the President 'had agreed to Adenauer's appointment as Foreign Minister with great reluctance'.

This top-level disapproval stemmed from more than merely the question of the Foreign Ministry. A few weeks earlier Adenauer had seized another department into his all-embracing grasp. This was the embryo Ministry of Defence which had started to plan the future German army in accordance with the Allied decisions at

Brussels. The normal course would have been to appoint a senior minister to handle this vital new aspect of German Government affairs, but Adenauer had no intention of letting the army slip from his grasp. He merely made the future Defence Ministry a department of his Chancellor's Office, and in true Bismarckian fashion appointed as State-Secretary a colourless Catholic trade union official with the name of Blank. By the spring of 1951 Adenauer was the Pooh-Bah of Bonn. In his own hands he held four key appointments which gave him effective control of a great part of the Bonn Government:

1. Federal Chancellor – solely responsible for policy and removable only by a vote of confidence which appointed a successor.
2. Foreign Minister.
3. Defence Minister in charge of Germany's rearmament.
4. Special envoy of the Federal government to the Allied High Commission as specified by the Allied Occupation Statute.

At a time when the two most important aspects of the Bonn Government's activities involved the three Allied Occupation Powers in the rearmament of Germany, these appointments made Adenauer, in effect, the German Government. In any other Western country his ministers would have rebelled, but by this time the sheeplike Cabinet seemed mesmerized by the formidable old man.

It was as the one-man government of Western Germany, therefore, that in March he was invited for the first time to make an important international speech to the Foreign Press Association of Bonn, a revival of the custom by which the Reichskanzler had addressed similar functions in Berlin.

In the presence of the Allied High Commissioners he donned for the first time the garb of the European elder statesman and mused on his fellow-countrymen.

'What the Germans do and think must often seem enigmatic and incomprehensible to you,' he told his foreign hosts. 'For in general the Germans are unrealistic people – the Latin races are far more realistic than we are. The Germans have a tendency to go to extremes, in good as well as in bad. That has its advantages as well as its disadvantages. If the Germans could only be left alone they would really prefer to stand outside of politics. But the conflict of East and West does not permit of that and we must choose.'

He let there be no doubt of his own personal choice, whatever his views in Berlin two years earlier. 'Korea taught people to see the immense danger to Western civilization'.

During the first six months of 1951, Adenauer's main activities were concerned with the parallel, and sometimes contradictory talks about the future German army carried on in Bonn and Paris, and the complicated negotiations on the final details of the Shuman Plan.

It was in the last named negotiations that he proved most successful. Scarcely a day passed without a meeting between the three main figures – Adenauer, the French High Commissioner, M. François-Poncet, and the American Commissioner, Mr. John J. McCloy, who, like Adenauer, had become an outspoken advocate of European unity.

The British took little or no part, an omission which cost them dear a decade later. Their only interest was how it would affect Western Germany in which they were an Occupation Power. The British authorities were unhappy about the reorganization of the Ruhr heavy industry proposed in the Schuman Plan.

They felt with considerable justification that the Schuman Plan left the Ruhr largely in the hands of the same forces which had contributed so much to two wars. In partnership Adenauer, with his half a century association with German finance, and Mr. McCloy, a distinguished Wall Street lawyer and banker, formed a formidable opposition and the British finally accepted Adenauer's views with minor modifications.

All difficulties having been finally overcome, Adenauer in his role of German Foreign Minister travelled to Paris in April to sign the Schuman Plan treaty. It was an historic occasion. For the first time since Hitler days, a German Foreign Minister appeared at a great international conference.

It was peculiarly fitting that the German representative should have been Adenauer. In his great labours for the Schuman Plan he first demonstrated that belief in European unity for which he was later to become deservedly renowned. He was firmly welcomed in Paris. He took the opportunity to discuss the Saar at the Quai d'Orsay, with the usual result; a high-sounding communiqué which meant nothing. A fortnight later he had another foreign success when he travelled to Strasbourg, where Western Germany had finally been accepted as a member of the Council of Europe.

It was during these two foreign visits that he began that association with two other European statesmen from the German language borderlands, M. Schuman of France and Signor de Gasperi of Italy, that was later to be known disparagingly as 'The Black Front'.

After these two foreign successes Adenauer at last agreed to move towards the long delayed *rapprochement* with Britain. Mr. Herbert Morrison, now Foreign Secretary, made a brief visit to Bonn. He was received with all honour, but at the official reception for him in the Federal Chancellery, it was easy to observe Adenauer's marked restraint towards this envoy from the British Labour Government. Six months had elapsed between the Western Powers' decision at Brussels to rearm Germany and Mr. Morrison's visit, but in the intervening period little progress had been made.

In Bonn, Allied representatives went over draft plans for the future German forces with Herr Blank and his two military advisers, Generals Speidel and Heusinger. In Paris, other former Wehrmacht officers carried on abortive arguments with members of the French High Command about the proposed European army.

German rearmament was in the doldrums. The Americans

began to lose patience. The U.S. High Commissioner, Mr. McCloy, was recalled to Washington for consultations. On the way he talked over the situation with General Eisenhower, N.A.T.O. Supreme Commander in Paris. In the previous few months the Americans had tended to regard the Pleven Plan as unworkable, but by the summer of 1951 Mr. McCloy and General Eisenhower had come to the conclusion that a European army of some sort was the only basis on which the French would accept German rearmament, if they would accept it at all.

With General Eisenhower's consent, Mr. McCloy 'sold' the European army plan to the Pentagon and the State Department in Washington. Late in June he returned to Germany with orders 'to get on with it – and get Adenauer's agreement'.

First move was a garden party at Frankfurt within a few hours of his return, when the American High Commissioner sounded out Adenauer's military advisers, the civilian-suited Generals Speidel and Heusinger, on the American plans. Next day Mr. McCloy drove to Bonn to see Adenauer. American diplomats frankly admitted that 'McCloy is going to put some American drive into the business'. The American High Commissioner's bustling activities and his bilateral conversations with Adenauer in place of the customary joint negotiations were viewed with some suspicion in London and Paris. The Americans were given orders to 'play the thing down'.

Adenauer, well informed as always on Allied thinking, realized just how desperate the Americans were to get on with the job and get a German army in the field at any cost. The crafty old man in the Chancellery raised his price. He told Mr. McCloy in private talks that as it was a year since the start of the Korean war and nothing had been done, he now questioned whether the Western Powers *still wanted* a German army. If they did, he said, then they would have to make much greater concessions to German opinion than when the project had first been mooted a year ago.

He enlarged on the old story of his weakness within his Cabinet, which no one believed, and the difficulties he would face in Parliament. Then he produced the inevitable demand. He would only be able to gain support for German rearmament at this stage, he claimed, by very wide concessions from the Western Powers amounting to a virtual restoration of German sovereignty.

'Political questions must be solved first,' he announced. 'If we are to be included in Western defence it can only be if we are granted the same rights and the same equality as everyone else.' Pointedly he warned the French, 'We don't intend to be mercenaries,' and then gilded the pill for Washington and London by adding, 'Of course we belong to Western Europe – and the fate of Western Europe will be ours.'

The Americans were not so diplomatically naïve as the Chancellor believed. A few days later Mr. McCloy told the Germans with some asperity, 'No doubt we can defend Europe a little farther to the east *with the Germans than we could without them.*'

Adenauer's German critics felt that the old man was overplaying his hand. Adenauer never played poker but he certainly completely outbluffed the Americans. He was sure that they were so determined to have a German army that they would pay virtually any price he asked. He was sure that they would somehow push the British and French into agreement. History was to prove his estimate completely correct except in one major detail – it was the British who eventually pushed the French willy-nilly into acceptance of German rearmament.

Adenauer was now well into his stride as a diplomat. He had estimated the Americans correctly, he was still uncertain about the British, and he believed that by using all his old pro-French sympathies he could win over France. He therefore dispatched to Paris his assistant for defence affairs, Blank, with the conditions which were now his price for German participation in European defence. The price was:

1. A Wehrmacht of 250,000 men based on a two years' conscription period.

2. Twelve divisions, four panzer, four motorized and four infantry.

3. A Luftwaffe of approximately 2,000 aircraft, chiefly fighters.

4. A coastal navy.

5. A German general staff under a civilian defence Minister – himself.

French staff officers, who had been negotiating with the Germans for six months, were appalled. The conditions went beyond anything remotely contemplated in the Pleven Plan. Other European officers at the talks whose countries had also been ravaged by Hitler's Wehrmacht shared the French alarm. The British and Americans took no part. They did not wish to join the European Army.

Compromise was inevitable. Adenauer again showed diplomatic skill far in excess of what he had demonstrated previously. At once he proposed that Eisenhower should decide – completely satisfied from his secret contacts that McCloy and Eisenhower were united in a firm determination to force through the European army project at any cost. Soon afterwards, General Eisenhower made a speech in London giving open support for the European army plan. As always, his prestige in London was deservedly high. The British Labour Cabinet, which had never really been enthusiastic about German rearmament except as a sort of necessary evil, accepted Eisenhower's views.

By the time the three Western Foreign Ministers again met, in Washington in the autumn of 1951, it was widely known that both the British and American Governments were backing the integration of German armed forces into a European army along the lines that Adenauer had laid down during the summer. Eventually the French Government appeared to have been talked into accepting that Germany should be rearmed within a European army. No details of how Germany was to be incorporated into the future European army, were, however, announced because the three powers could not agree.

Adenauer got his reward. At the end of the long-drawn-out meeting, the Western Allies told him that Western Germany would get almost everything he had asked in the previous few months. The Foreign Ministers announced two major concessions:

1. The end of the Occupation as such.
2. That the Western Powers would stop their interference in the domestic affairs of the Bonn Republic.

The Foreign Ministers added as a rider, which was to become the paramount issue in Europe for the following three years, and which was to prove the despair of their successors in office. They told Adenauer that the Contractual Agreement by which they proposed to end the Occupation, would come into effect *only at the same time as the agreement on the European army of which Germany would be a member.*

Adenauer was elated. With an almost British masterpiece of under-statement he told a party conference that 'he had every reason to be satisfied'.

Unlike some of his previous victories, this time he had deserved his success.

CHAPTER EIGHT

Lost Opportunities

BY THE LATE autumn of 1951, Adenauer was understandably satisfied with what he had achieved. He believed that within a few months the occupation of Western Germany would end and that the Federal Republic would start to rearm.

His success in ostensibly securing agreement among all parties to German participation in a European army had caused widespread misgiving, particularly behind the Iron Curtain.

Up to that point, Adenauer had exercised little influence on the Western Powers' relations with the Soviet Union in connection with the four-power control of Germany. All German questions and all matters relating to German unity were handled by the Western Powers – as officially, at least, they would continue to be throughout his Chancellorship. As Foreign Minister, he was expressly forbidden to enter into diplomatic relations with the Eastern *bloc*. Adenauer was now the most important figure in democratic West Germany and it is necessary to examine his attitude, if not his policy towards Eastern Germany and towards the Russians up to that time. In his first policy statement in 1949 Adenauer had asserted that his Government would never recognize the Oder-Neisse line, an undertaking to which he remained faithful. When the Russians set up a puppet state in the East Zone Adenauer retaliated by claiming that the Bonn Parliament was the sole democratically elected German representative body within the boundaries of the former Reich.

Adenauer claimed that his Government was the sole legitimate German constitutional authority. At the same time, he formally announced that one of the basic aims of his Government was the

re-unification of Germany. His opponents in Germany, notably
the Social Democrats, and his critics among the Western Allies
took leave to doubt these protestations. Whatever lip service
Adenauer might pay towards the concept of German unity, many
objective observers felt that he had little real urge to take any
active step to secure German reunification. The history of his
fourteen years as Federal Chancellor may well be held to prove
the justice of that early view. It might be claimed that in his
obsession for a 'Little Europe' in the West he forgot about the
rest of the Reich in the East.

So widely held was this view in the first months of his Chancellorship that in March, 1950, in a bid to offset this damaging
criticism, he issued proposals to secure German unity. They were
almost a complete echo of American proposals made a short time
previously. Adenauer proposed:

1. That the four Occupation Powers should permit all German
elections, under four-power or U.N.O. control, to elect a constitutional assembly which would draw up a German constitution to replace that of Weimar.

2. That during these elections there must be complete freedom of the individual, the Press, and of all parties in all four
zones.

The Western Powers duly passed on his memorandum to the
Russians in Berlin without result. The Soviet Government had
opposed the establishment of the Bonn Government and denounced Adenauer as a 'separatist', but otherwise had done little.
But the Brussels decision in December, 1950, agreeing to the
rearmament of Western Germany drew immediate fire from the
Kremlin. The Russians launched a diplomatic offensive. The East
Zone Premier, Otto Grotewohl, a renegade from the S.P.D., sent
a letter to Adenauer proposing the establishment of an all-
German constituent assembly to prepare a constitution. Like all
similarly inspired Russian offers, it was full of traps. Grotewohl

seemed naïve enough to believe that West Germany, with three times the population of the East Zone, would accept fifty-fifty representation.

Adenauer denounced this manœuvre as 'pure propaganda'. A fortnight later Grotewohl tried again, and this time made vague threats about Adenauer's policies 'leading to civil war'. This was equally unproductive. Finally, in February, 1951, Grotewohl offered to meet Adenauer personally. And he coupled this offer with a lack of pre-conditions almost unparalleled in Communist diplomatic communications. The Russian Zone puppet Prime Minister said he was ready 'for a clarifying discussion without agenda, rules or pre-arranged conditions'.

At once Adenauer, quickly echoed by his American friends, shouted 'Propaganda'. Maybe it was. But some of Adenauer's normally firm supporters and a number of important Allied officials felt he was singularly ill-advised to adopt such a rigid negative approach.

Soviet policy in 1951, towards the end of the Stalin period, may well have been so firmly set that nothing would have altered it. What Adenauer could have lost by meeting and talking to Grotewohl, say in West Berlin, at this point, however, is difficult to see. Probably nothing would have happened. But some slight progress towards alleviating the condition of the 17,000,000 Germans in the Russian Zone might have occurred. At any rate, a positive approach would have freed Adenauer from the taunt, which would continue as long as he was Chancellor, that at heart he was opposed to German reunification. The truth was that Adenauer was opposed to reunification on anything but his own stiff, rigid terms, which were unacceptable to the Russians even in their most-accommodating post-Stalin period.

The Russians carefully took up Grotewohl's offer on a higher level. As a result, the deputies of the four Foreign Ministers held the famous abortive conference in the Palais Rose in Paris, where absolutely nothing was accomplished after seventy meetings.

Following the meeting of the Western Foreign Ministers in New York in the autumn of 1951, the Russians renewed their offensive. Again Grotewohl was the chosen medium.

The Russian Zone Premier proposed the creation, this time, of an all-German council to prepare the framework for all-German elections. Moreover, Grotewohl abandoned his claim for equal representation for West and East Germany.

Adenauer was even more cautious than on the occasion of Grotewohl's first trial balloon. From the Foreign Ministers' meeting in New York he had gained solid advantages. He knew the Americans were backing the idea of German armed forces with all the ammunition they possessed. He described Grotewohl's offer as 'a will o' the wisp, another contrivance which would be a prey to Communist mischief'. He may well have been right. But the persistence of Soviet moves at the time showed that Stalin was genuinely alarmed by the thought of Germans back in uniform. Some advance towards German re-unification *might* have been possible. But Adenauer, backed by the Americans, was not even prepared to try and find out. In retrospect no one can judge how serious the Russians may have been, but it is just possible that Adenauer in these months sacrificed German unity for what, in the ultimate, proved to be a dozen German divisions.

In any case, serious negotiations with Grotewohl or his Soviet masters was becoming more and more alien to Adenauer's mind. He was developing that doctrine of 'negotiation from strength' of which, with Mr. John Foster Dulles, he would eventually become the leading exponent. Until Western Europe was rearmed, with German forces forming a substantial portion of the shield, he saw little profit in attempting a deal with the East.

The Russians by this time regarded Adenauer as an incorrigible American puppet – which was not true. Their tactics were altered. The Soviet Commander-in-Chief in Germany, Marshal Chuikov, gave a carefully staged interview in which he made

what, on the face of it, seemed a sensational offer. He proposed
that there should be all-German elections to elect an all-German
parliament and government, and then all four occupation armies
should leave Germany.

The snag was obvious. The Red Army would retire to the
Polish border thirty miles east of Berlin. The British and the
French troops would go home and, the Russians appeared to
hope, the American army would go back across the Atlantic. It
was naïve to believe that the Kremlin was not as well aware of that
snag as the Western Powers. Some senior Allied officials felt,
therefore, that the ostensible offer of all-German elections and the
establishment of an all-German government were at least worthy
of further investigation.

Adenauer almost certainly did not agree. But that Allied view,
coupled with the criticism which he was receiving for his cavalier
rejection of the Grotewohl offer, forced him to take the initiative.
In the Bundestag he proposed that free and all-German elections
should be held under the supervision of a U.N.O. Commission.
If the Grotewohl offers had been hypocritical they were almost
certainly matched by this offer. Adenauer must have been fairly
sure when he made the proposals that the Russians would not let
a U.N.O. Commission move unrestrained through the Russian
Zone. Subsequent operations in Africa suggest that they may have
been wise. After six months a U.N.O. Commission did reach
Germany and, as Adenauer almost certainly anticipated, the
Russians refused to let them enter the Soviet Zone. It was obvious
that there was shadow boxing on both sides.

Adenauer at this point never believed any negotiations with the
Russians on German re-unification were possible. And he turned
with relief to building up the West German State he had created,
by launching into negotiations with the Allied High Commissioners to end the Occupation.

He believed that the bargaining could be completed in a few
weeks. He soon discovered his error. And after the first few meetings he sensed that the terms of reference of the High Commis-

sioners were much narrower than had been indicated by the Western Foreign Ministers in their communiqué. At once the negotiations ran into squalls.

Adenauer had sensed correctly. The Western Powers and, most important, the American State Department had begun to have second thoughts about Adenauer's Federal Republic. While the generals in the Pentagon remained as single-minded as ever in their obsession for a German army, the wiser and more politically conscious officials of the State Department had become anxious at developments in the Federal Republic.

American officials in Germany pointed to the number of former diplomats from Ribbentrop's Nazi Foreign Ministry employed in Adenauer's personally controlled Foreign Office in Bonn, where they remained for a very long time; the emergence of noisy mass organizations of ex-servicemen led by more equivocal former generals; and the support gained by the neo-Nazi party of General Remer, the key figure in suppressing the generals' revolt against Hitler on 20th July, 1944.

The Allied-German negotiations moved at snail's pace. Adenauer became more and more annoyed, and sometimes he did not attempt to hide it. At one rather stormy meeting the Americans told him that 'the United States would not budge from the principles for which she fought the war . . . for all the German divisions in the world'.

Adenauer knew that he held the cards. His private contacts with the Pentagon, probably through the massive American-financed Secret Service headed by General Reinhard Gehlen, assured him that the American generals were behind him no matter what the State Department might say. And at a meeting of his closer collaborators he stated, 'Time is on our side. American insistence on a German army will eventually force the Western Powers to accede to our demands.'

Adenauer decided to force the pace by his customary adroit use of propaganda. In an increasingly strident Press campaign he announced that West Germany would be 'independent by

Christmas' which he knew to be impossible. Then he learned that
the Western Foreign Ministers would meet in Paris in November,
1951. So inflated was his vanity by American support, that he
now insisted that he should be allowed to attend the Foreign
Ministers' meeting. By ways best known to himself he saw that
this request duly reached Washington. The by-passed High
Commissioners in Bonn capitulated and advised their governments that he should be invited to Paris. By astute political
manœuvre and incessant and insidious propaganda, he had won
another success. Now, he openly boasted that he dealt only with
the Foreign Ministers and not with underlings.

Adenauer was invited to the last day of the Foreign Ministers'
meeting where he expatiated on the now hoary theme of being a
'weak Chancellor'. He claimed that his Free Democrat allies
would cause a crisis for his coalition if he did not return home
with something to show. In view of his hardy treatment of his
F.D.P. associates in subsequent coalition crises, this crisis was
clearly but another aspect of the propaganda.

The Foreign Ministers were polite but they were not to be
panicked. They were anxious to help him nevertheless. And they
did sign a draft agreement which was, in fact, nothing more than
the preamble to the long and complicated Bonn Treaty which
was not signed finally until six months later. But they emphasized
that the real treaty, the so-called Contractual Agreement was still
to be signed. When he got back to Bonn Adenauer indulged in a
little adroit political bamboozlement. He acted as though the
whole treaty was now signed and announced, 'We now stand in
the West with all rights and obligations.'

At this juncture his old enemy, the British Labour party was
defeated in a British general election. The Conservatives, under
Sir Winston Churchill, returned to power.

He was delighted. And with a lack of tact that cannot be completely explained by lack of experience he announced with some
venom; 'The British people have shown great patience with the
Labour Government. I am not surprised that the Conservatives

have won. We now hope that Britain will follow a more active and positive policy in European questions.'

To mark his approval of the changed face of British political life, he soon afterwards accepted an invitation to visit London for the first time. His visit, however, was scarcely the success which he had anticipated as a result of his reception in other capitals. On the day of his arrival the attitude of the British Press ranged from dignified reserve to open hostility.

The Conservative *Daily Telegraph* commented that 'it would be unrealistic to regard Dr. Adenauer's arrival . . . as symbolizing a close and established cordiality between the two countries'. Other papers referred to his, by then, well-known Anglophobia. And the *Manchester Guardian*, peculiarly well informed by its correspondent in Bonn, commented that 'the Federal Chancellor has neither forgotten nor forgiven the Cologne incident'.

When Adenauer reached Downing Street he was greeted with cries of 'Heil Hitler' and 'Adenauer Go Home'. As his official biography admits, he was surprised by the demonstration which was the least friendly he had ever encountered in a foreign country. Sir Winston Churchill, as one of the first great 'Europeans', greeted him with courtesy and cordiality. But, according to the Adenauer version of their conversation, the Prime Minister left no doubt as to where Britain stood. He agreed that Britain was a 'neighbour of Europe' but not 'in' Europe. That was to sum up the attitude of successive Conservative Governments for nearly a decade.

To that Adenauer replied that it would be beneficial if Britain would make clear beyond doubt where her sympathies lay. The Prime Minister told him that Britain would do everything possible to further Franco-German friendship, but that Adenauer must never forget that Germany was stronger than France, and Britain must always create a counterweight. Adenauer then returned to what he described as his 'nightmare of Yalta'. This was the Adenauer obsession, which dominated and damned all East-West negotiations throughout the years he was Chancellor;

that the Western Powers, above all, the British would do a deal with Soviet Russia behind Germany's back and at Germany's expense.

At what price, he asked, did Churchill seek an understanding with Russia, at what price to Germany? The British Foreign Secretary, the then Sir Anthony Eden, intervened to emphasize that Britain then, and in the future, would never sell out Germany. They would only negotiate with the Russians with the knowledge of Western Germany. The Prime Minister was stirred. British honour was in question. He assured Adenauer, 'We will never betray you. We stand by our word. Have complete faith in England. We will not do business behind your back.'

He emphasized, however, that the desire for peace and fear of Russia was so great among all people that the door to an understanding with Russia must be kept open, but not at the cost of Germany. If the Federal Republic stood by the West the United States and Britain 'would honour such conduct'.

'If we are not united we shall all perish,' concluded the Prime Minister. 'But if we hang together we shall, God willing, come through.'

The ailing King George VI interrupted his convalescence to receive Adenauer. The high civil servant of his Imperial Majesty Wilhelm II was deeply impressed by the audience. After five days Adenauer departed somewhat bewildered, to judge from his authorized biography, by the British, their institutions, and their ways.

Soon afterwards Adenauer journeyed to Strasbourg, the headquarters of the Council of Europe, where he found more congenial company, his fellow 'Europeans', M. Schuman and Signor de Gasperi, both devout German-speaking Roman Catholics from the Teutonic borderlands.

With representatives of the three Benelux countries, they considered future developments in European co-operation following the success of the heavy industry negotiations. The same six countries at this time were also taking part in the semi-moribund negotiations still dragging on in Paris for the formation of a European army.

Adenauer was deeply impressed by the success of the Coal and Steel Community project and the concept of an integrated European fighting force. It seemed to mark the beginning of the fruition of his ideas of a quarter of a century earlier. He was as determined as his French and Italian friends to push forward the European idea. As they discussed economic and military co-operation, Adenauer put forward a revolutionary suggestion. To the representatives of what would soon be known as 'The Six' he proposed the establishment of a European Political Authority and a European Parliament. These, he suggested, must be created to control the heavy industry community, the supra-national European army, and the many other 'European' projects of which much was heard at the time.

Adenauer and his European friends were at once strongly attacked by liberals all over Western Europe for attempting to set up a 'little Europe'.

Some months earlier, when Adenauer had made his first visit to Rome, the Left-wing Press in Britain and elsewhere had strongly condemned what was called the 'Adenauer-Schuman-de Gasperi triumvirate'. More pointed critics linked them with Pope Pius XII whose household was largely German-dominated. The triumvirate were accused of 'attempting to establish a Catholic-dominated alliance after the pattern of Metternich's Holy Alliance, aimed at delivering Europe to a reactionary-clerical despotism'.

That was an extreme exaggeration. But there can be little dispute that the Germans, French and Italian 'Europeans' of the early fifties, consciously or subconsciously, did aim at the re-creation in modern form of the old Carolingian Empire, of a modernized Holy Roman Empire comprising Catholic, or part-Catholic Italy, France, Germany and the Benelux countries.

To such a concept, Britain and the equally Protestant, demo-cratic Scandinavian countries had little or nothing to contribute. In the middle of the struggle over Britain's entry into the

Common Market a decade later it became a commonplace to blame
Britain for failing to seize earlier opportunities. That was partly
true. But the hesitation of successive British Governments of both
political persuasions stemmed largely from an all-too-true assessment of the rigid, narrow, clericalist Europe which was being
planned.

Adenauer knew very well that he was planning a 'little Europe'.
Under attack by his political opponents, he said, 'The policy of the
Federal Republic is the unification of Europe. But why should
there not be a "lesser solution" if it gives hope that it will lead to a
"greater solution?"' The key question was – What did Adenauer
mean by 'Europe'?

This may well have been one of the great lost opportunities of
modern European history. A broader minded, less sectarian, and
more liberal German – such as the First Federal President,
Professor Theodor Heuss – as Chancellor of the free democratic
segment of a Reich that was predominately non-Catholic, might
have considered it his national duty to steer the infant European
movement into a grand, broad concept embracing, at least, all
free and democratic countries west of the Iron Curtain.

But the 'Kulturkampf' was in Adenauer's blood. Prussia, which
as a Rhinelander he hated so much, and which was Protestant, was
submerged in the Marxist flood. So in the vital formative years,
Adenauer was content to take the rump of the Reich into his
'little Europe'.

Adenauer was a curious political contradiction. At the same
time as he sought to restrict a future united Europe to his own
narrow sectarian concept, he strove with all the statesmanship
which formed the other side of his political character to achieve a
lasting reconciliation with France to remove the centuries-old
tension between Germany and France. In this latter policy he
seemed to don the mantle of his great contemporary, Gustav
Stresemann who was actually two years younger than Adenauer.
Their backgrounds were contrasted, but not dissimilar. Both came
from extreme and narrow circumstances – the Protestant Prussian

and the Rhineland Catholic. And the earlier careers of both gave little indication of their later distinction – for Stresemann was the Whip of the German High Command in the Reichstag during the First World War. Adenauer may well owe much of his international success to Stresemann. For the Western willingness to encourage and conciliate Adenauer in the early months of 1952 stemmed largely from the terrible consequences resulting from Stresemann's failure. If the Allies, and above all the French, in the early twenties had offered to Stresemann those same concessions which, all too late, they made to Bruening and von Papen in the early thirties, there might have been no Adolf Hitler.

History had certainly taught the Western Powers, and notably the British and the Americans, one salutary lesson. It was wiser to make concessions to the 'good Germans' like Adenauer, however awkward these might prove to be, than be forced to fight the not-so-good Germans later.

It was to this history lesson that Adenauer owed much of the great reputation as a wise and able statesman which he built up in his negotiations with the Western Powers, in the first six months of 1952. Because of history, and because of the Cold War, the Western Powers made Adenauer no less than 122 major concessions in the so-called Contractual Agreement alone. In vulgar parlance, he was given his much vaunted success over the Allies 'on a plate'. And in private, to the High Commissioners, he admitted it.

When the American High Commissioner, Mr. McCloy, with a certain amount of cynicism made the one hundred and twenty-second concession, Adenauer in his droll Cologne accent quipped, 'I have been reading in the foreign Press that I have been following blackmail tactics in the jackboots of Bismarck. But, gentlemen, let me assure you – they are too big for me.'

At the beginning of the year, despite the claims a few weeks earlier that all was settled, Adenauer was deeply depressed. The negotiations in Bonn over the end of the Occupation and the parallel talks in Paris over the European army were in the doldrums. The European army project, in fact, was in serious difficulties as a result of a burst of renewed French intransigence over the Saar.

Towards the end of January, for no apparent reason, the French Government announced that the French High Commissioner in the Saar, M. Grandval, had been appointed Ambassador in Saarbrücken. This seemed to imply recognition of the Saar as a separate state. As Grandval appeared to enjoy the status of a viceroy, and had been the source of much Franco-German friction in preceding years, there were sharp reactions in Bonn.

Adenauer protested at once: 'We can go no further in the European Defence Community if Germans of all parties have misgivings about French aims in the Saar. In all frankness, let me say that I find it full of danger that at a moment when negotiations are in progress for E.D.C. (European Defence Community) trust and confidence should be destroyed in this way.'

Convinced of the goodwill of his 'European' friend, M. Schuman, the French Foreign Minister, Adenauer dispatched a special envoy to Paris. He came back with an evasive answer — M. Schuman's 'pro-German sympathies' were suspect in the French capital.

Professor Hallstein, later President of the European Common Market, but at that time Adenauer's 'personal assistant' in the Bonn Foreign Office, then exploited a meeting of the E.D.C. negotiators to put forward a claim that Germany should be permitted to join N.A.T.O.

There was another storm, this time in Paris. M. Schuman replied in terms which led later to a special German undertaking in the London and Paris agreements. He pointed out that N.A.T.O. was a *defensive* alliance. The entrance of Germany would alter its fundamental character as Germany had important territorial claims against the Eastern *bloc* for the return of the Oder-Neisse territories and possibly East Prussia, apart from the question of the Russian Zone.

It was unfortunate that Adenauer, at that point, did not abandon E.D.C. and press forward his ideas for membership of N.A.T.O. That was to prove the ultimate solution in 1955. And had Adenauer been less of a 'good European' and abandoned E.D.C. he would have got the army for which he worked so desperately three years earlier than he did.

The French action over the Saar which precipitated this E.D.C. crisis was clearly no accident. It was incredible that the accomplished diplomats of the Quai d'Orsay should have blundered in such a situation. By this time the French had begun to have serious doubt about the wisdom of the whole European Army Plan because Britain had declined to join in it, a curious contrast to the later attitude of de Gaulle over the Common Market.

While the E.D.C. situation deteriorated, Adenauer ran into more difficulties in his negotiations with the High Commissioners in Bonn. He was under strong pressure from the Bundestag which was demanding the immediate end of the Occupation, full German sovereignty, abolition of all Allied controls and release of the war criminals. The High Commissioners in Bonn had no authority to make such far-reaching concessions. Once again, the negotiations reached deadlock, just as they had done the previous autumn.

At this moment, King George VI died. The American and French Foreign Ministers were chosen to lead their respective countries' delegations to the funeral. Taking advantage of their presence in London, it was agreed at short notice that there should be a Foreign Ministers' conference in London immediately after the Royal funeral.

Adenauer, faced with deadlock in Bonn and tension in Paris, decided to gatecrash the funeral and, more significantly, the Foreign Ministers' meeting. To the amazement, not to say annoyance of some of the Allied Commissioners, he persuaded President Heuss to let him lead the official German delegation to the Royal funeral. It was not a duty which might normally have been undertaken by a Chancellor. Once in London, Adenauer realized that it was inconceivable that the Western Foreign Ministers would refuse to meet him.

His tactics were so blatant that the anger of some of the Allies at what was clearly a characteristic Adenauer stratagem was made public. Members of the French High Commissioner's staff announced without any of the usual reservations that he 'would be unwelcome in London at the talks'. The British, being more intimately involved, were less open but some of them held similar views.

In these circumstances he was less than tactful when, on the eve of his departure, he held a private and unexplained meeting with the American High Commissioner. British officials said openly he was 'trying to split the Allies by playing off one against the other. And the High Commissioners can neither agree among themselves, nor with the Germans'.

Adenauer flew to London, still without any official invitation to the Foreign Ministers' meeting. His estimate of the situation proved correct. With Adenauer established at Claridge's and the American Secretary of State insisting that the German Chancellor 'must have a success', the British and French could only accept the *fait accompli*.

His presence was restricted to the final sessions of the conference. But in the few hours he was present, with the formidable support of Mr. Dean Acheson, the U.S. Secretary of State, he was able to secure a number of concessions. The American Secretary of State had previously made it plain to his two colleagues that the U.S. Congress, and still more the generals, were becoming very restive over the slow progress of German rearmament. Something had to be done.

Adenauer's gatecrashing operation, however, was completely unnecessary. A member of the British Foreign Office delegation at the time informed the author, 'There was nothing agreed that could not have been quite as well carried out by the High Commissioners if they had been given the necessary instructions by their governments. But Mr. Acheson was adamant that Adenauer must have a success. And it did no harm to let Adenauer take part.' Added this somewhat cynical diplomat: 'It satisfied his vanity to feel that he was now negotiating with the Foreign Ministers. He is susceptible to such influence and his presence at the Foreign Ministers' meeting will merely make him more amenable to Allied policy.' If the British diplomat had said 'to American policy' he would have been proved correct.

Adenauer, indeed, felt his visit to London had been worthwhile. When he stepped from a British aircraft at Bonn he told enthusiastic German reporters that the Foreign Ministers had agreed to 'end the Occupation' in return for German troops. He added that the Occupation 'would end in a few weeks'. He was perhaps over-optimistic. The Occupation was not to end for another three years, due largely to the French whom he had so annoyed by gatecrashing the Foreign Ministers' meeting.

His principal gain was an Allied promise to set up four-power clemency boards to consider the cases of the German generals in the war crimes prisons.

He was worried, however, by the rising wave of opposition to German rearmament in Britain and France. Exasperated by these foreign opponents, he said in a broadcast, 'Try and think of something else other than German divisions. Why should everyone keep recalling that it was a German army that has invaded France three times in the last three quarters of a century? These German divisions are becoming an obsession. Think of something else.'

Adenauer, of course, had gone right to the heart of the matter. It was just the vision of new German divisions which filled so many people in Europe with foreboding.

The foreboding was not restricted to the West. On 11th March, Mr. Vishinsky, then Soviet Foreign Minister, handed a Note to the Western Ambassadors in Moscow. It proposed, as many other Russian Notes in the future would propose, that a German Peace Treaty should be signed. It then gave Stalin's ideas of the peace treaty:

1. All Occupation Forces should be withdrawn from Germany within a year of the treaty becoming operative.

2. Germany must pledge herself to remain neutral.

To these conditions the Soviet Government added what could only be described as a sensational concession to German militarism. The Russians proposed that the united Germany should be allowed 'limited national defence forces' with permission to manufacture sufficient arms for such a force.

The Western Powers and Adenauer felt that the Russian offer was nothing more than a Soviet bid to hold up the negotiations for a German army. They were probably correct. And in view of what has since been revealed of Stalin's megalomania in the last months of his reign, it is doubtful if anything could have been achieved even although negotiations had been started. The opportunity would come in the months *after* Stalin's death.

The Russian Note achieved one thing. It made both the Western Powers and Adenauer realize that they must terminate the never-ending squabble in Bonn and Paris about Germany's future. For the following two months, therefore, both sides made an all-out effort to complete the two vital treaties, the Contractual Agreement being negotiated in Bonn, and the European army treaty in Paris.

Adenauer felt confident of the result. And in the negotiations in Bonn, in which he personally took part, he showed surprising restraint and a growing degree of statesmanship. He left the acrimony to his Finance Minister, the stubborn Bavarian Dr. Schaeffer, in the negotiations over the financial support of the Allied Forces after the end of the Occupation. Day after day, and often night after night until well into the morning, the negotiations went on. Adenauer had completely convinced the Allied negotiatiors that he was a changed man when his schizophrenic political personality intervened.

In the midst of the negotiations he suddenly announced that the third verse of *Deutschland über Alles* would henceforth be the

National Anthem of the Federal Republic. Its words, 'Unity, Justice and Freedom for the German Fatherland' were unexceptionable. But it was scarcely the most tactful moment to make such an announcement. The President, Professor Heuss, shared that view. He issued a letter indicating that he had agreed to Adenauer's announcement 'with reluctance' only after a 'gentlemen's agreement'. The Allies, however, had come to know Adenauer so well that they completely ignored the incident.

Finally, after long night sessions which reduced both Adenauer and the Allied negotiators to near exhaustion, everything was agreed – except the difficult question of the extent of German financial support for the Allied troops in Germany after the end of the Occupation. It was agreed that the financial question be left until the arrival of the Western Foreign Ministers in Bonn to sign the Contractual Agreement at the end of May.

On 23rd May, Mr. Acheson, M. Schuman and Sir Anthony Eden arrived, a visible token of the prestige Adenauer had gained for his country in his two and a half years as Chancellor. At the eleventh hour the French, as so often in post-war negotiations, threatened to sabotage what had already been achieved. They wanted further guarantees from Britain and America, in case Germany should 'desert' from the European army. There were frantic telephone calls to Paris, London and Washington. Adenauer, in the meantime, in a mood of deep depression, was left to kick his heels in his Chancellery.

The Foreign Ministers worked through the week-end. When everything at last seemed to have been agreed there was a second bombshell. The Russians chose this psychological moment to issue a Note on German re-unification, making threats of what would happen if the Contractual Agreement and the E.D.C. Treaties were signed. But Soviet diplomatic sabotage had lost its novelty. And late on the night of Sunday, 25th May, the Western Powers and Adenauer announced that they would sign on the morrow.

CHAPTER NINE

So Near and Yet So Far

AT THE END of May, 1952, Adenauer believed that he had reached the goal towards which he had been striving ever since he took office as Federal Chancellor nearly three years earlier.

Within twenty-four hours, in Bonn and Paris he signed two treaties which, if they had been ratified by all concerned, would have given his Bonn Republic virtual independence, with the right to arm within a European army.

In Bonn the old man, solemn faced as ever, and surrounded by the Foreign Ministers of the three Western Powers, signed his name against his country's black eagle seal on the 400-page document known as the Bonn Contractual Agreement. Much of this Allied-German treaty was incorporated in the Paris Agreement which, almost three years later, did eventually give the Bonn Republic the independence which Adenauer so much cherished.

At the time, however, all four statesmen who signed the treaty, Mr. Dean Acheson, M. Schuman, Sir Anthony Eden, and Dr. Adenauer, genuinely believed that within a few months the West Germans would be transformed from enemies into allies. Adenauer believed it was the greatest hour of his life. He was so moved that he could scarcely acknowledge the handshakes of the diplomatic corps and the German notables who attended the ceremony.

Adenauer believed that only seven years after 'Unconditional Surrender', he had won freedom for 50 million-odd West Germans in return for a pledge to contribute twelve German divisions to a European army.

In Paris, twenty-four hours later, he signed that pledge when he put his name to the European Defence Community treaty for the establishment of a European army to be controlled by a European Ministerial Council and a European Parliament. Like other treaties, the Bonn Agreement had to be ratified by the Parliament of all four contracting powers. There was, though, a further obstacle before it became operative. To allay chronic French fears that Germany would somehow shirk her responsibilities, the Bonn Agreement and the E.D.C. Treaty were made mutually interdependent. Before either became effective, *both* must be ratified by all concerned; the three Occupation Powers, Italy, and the Benelux countries, plus Germany. The whole interlocking diplomatic complex, required the ratification, of one section or another, by no less than eight national Parliaments. To many Allied and German officials who negotiated the Bonn Agreement, this criss-cross contrivance of oversubtle diplomacy seemed singularly ill-advised. So it was to prove when, two and a half years later, the French Chamber finally rejected the E.D.C. Treaty and the whole structure collapsed like a house of cards.

Adenauer seemed to have some such foreboding. For on the day of the signing of the Bonn Agreement, he declined to permit general rejoicing throughout the Federal Republic.

He categorically banned torchlight processions and other festivities planned to celebrate the signing of the Bonn Agreement, and his intense preoccupation when he left for Paris next day to sign the E.D.C. Treaty was widely noted.

The fundamental provision of this E.D.C. Treaty was that Western Germany should rearm only within the framework of a future European army to which the six powers concerned would contribute according to their strength.

To control this international force Adenauer, with his French and Italian 'European' friends, planned a supra-national commissariat, a council of ministers and a supra-national parliament drawn from the assemblies of the defence community countries.

This supra-national aspect of the European Defence Community, which was based on Adenauer's long-held ideas of European integration, was particularly cherished by the French supporters of the project as the only sure way of maintaining international control of German rearmament. It was precisely this supra-national aspect which would prove anathema to the members of the French Assembly who finally killed the European army.

Neither Britain nor America signed the E.D.C. Treaty, for neither had taken direct part in the negotiations. Both countries gave general guarantees to the E.D.C. powers. American non-participation was easy to understand, but the absence of Britain from the European Defence Community was much deplored in Paris.

Two years later, when this British non-participation had become the main criticism on which French opponents of E.D.C. relied, Sir Winston Churchill put the whole question into perspective.

'I am sometimes reproached,' he told the House of Commons, 'for having led France to expect that Britain would be a full member of E.D.C.' He explained that when in Strasbourg in 1950 he had proposed the creation of a European army, he had in mind the formation of a long-term grand alliance in which national armies would participate under unified Allied command.

'My conception involved no supranational institutions and I saw no difficulty in Britain playing her full part. But when the continental powers worked out the detailed scheme it took the form of a complete merger of national forces under a federal supra-national control.'

In the summer of 1952 the form which opposition to E.D.C. would take was still far from clear. Adenauer, however, was well aware that the two treaties he had signed were foredoomed to a stormy course, particularly in Bonn.

Adenauer at first talked about obtaining ratification of the two treaties before the summer recess. But the opposition shown by both the S.P.D. and his own F.D.P. allies during the first reading in the Bundestag disillusioned him, and he settled down to wait while various committees considered the two pacts.

The Federal President, Professor Heuss, and the S.P.D. were both much exercised by another aspect of ratification. They felt that the rearmament of the Bonn Republic might well be contrary to the provisions of the pacifist Bonn constitution. The President therefore asked the newly established Constitutional Court for advice, which he was not bound to accept. The court, which had been filled with political nominees of both main parties, neatly evaded the issue. But much more was to be heard of the constitutional problem and it finally led Adenauer into deep waters.

By that autumn, the treaties were still no nearer ratification and Adenauer concentrated all his armoury to achieve that end. By public speeches and inspired propaganda, and above all, by private persuasion and party pressure, he used all means to overcome the opposition which existed in both houses of the German Parliament. He realized, however, that the ultimate decision would lie with the French Parliament.

To influence that assembly from afar, Adenauer exploited every device of diplomatic persuasion and public encouragement. By soft words and assurances he tried to lull the widespread and understandable suspicions of the Paris parliamentarians. He tried to persuade them, unsuccessfully as was to be proved, that there really was a democratic Germany beyond the Rhine which had renounced aggression and was genuinely imbued with the European spirit.

With a public restraint and tolerance which astounded those accustomed to his often blunt and authoritarian ways, Adenauer declined to take offence at continued French prevarication, not to say provocation. With his own Parliament he was less tolerant. In the autumn he became nettled at the repeated S.P.D. insistence that he was more interested in Western unification than in German reunification.

Professor Ernst Reuter, the gallant Oberbürgermeister of Berlin was one of those who said so outspokenly, for members of all parties in the Reich capital were more than suspicious of Adenauer's attitude towards reunification.

When Adenauer visited Berlin for a C.D.U. conference, he hit back at Reuter. He alleged that these S.P.D. attacks were weakening his bargaining position in regard to the Western Powers. He continued with some heat, 'But for Signor de Gasperi in Italy, for M. Schuman in France and for the "thrice accursed Bundeskanzler in Bonn" Europe's problems today would have been left to the tender mercies of the Socialist International.' Adenauer's reference to his two distinguished European colleagues of the moment was not an accident.

The E.D.C. Treaty provided for a supra-national political authority and assembly. By the autumn of 1952 when it had become obvious that ratification, at the best, must be a long-drawn-out process, the three 'European' stalwarts decided that European unity must be approached from another direction.

With the other ministers of the Coal and Steel Community, the three members of the so-called 'Black Front' agreed that an immediate start should be made on drafting a treaty for European political unity, and a few days later a working party was set up in Strasbourg to investigate this project. This bold plan embraced one of Adenauer's most cherished ambitions, and he vigorously advocated such political integration.

Once again, he was bitterly attacked, and again accused of attempting to set up a 'little Europe'. The S.P.D., which had recently lost Dr. Schumacher by death, was particularly vehement in its denunciation of Adenauer's 'European' activities. For, however misguided the policies of the S.P.D. may have been on occasions, in those years the German Socialists never failed to emphasize one fundamental point. The basic weakness of all Adenauer's plans for the future of Western Europe was the absence of his old enemies, the British, from all the negotiations. Adenauer, of course, could scarcely be blamed directly for

British non-participation, but the S.P.D. analysis was basically correct. The British distrusted all the European projects because they stemmed from the 'Black Front'.

Soon Adenauer's European aims ran into more immediate problems – once again over the future of the Saar. Provincial elections were due in the Saar basin towards the end of 1952, and in an effort to end the Franco-German wrangling, he sent proposals to Paris for the 'Europeanization' of the Saar.

Adenauer's proposals, among other things, involved delaying the Saar elections. M. Schuman recognized Adenauer's proposals for what they were, a statesmanlike approach to an old problem. But European integration and M. Schuman's over-warm advocacy of it had begun to arouse misgivings in Paris, and the French Government declined to accept Adenauer's proposals. The elections went on in conditions which the Germans regarded as most unsatisfactory and tension continued between Bonn and Paris. This scarcely made Adenauer's position in securing ratification of the Bonn Agreement and the E.D.C. Treaty any easier in the German Parliament. But by using his powerful coalition majority, he scored a notable success on the second reading of the ratification bill.

This success was not unalloyed. On the eve of the second-reading debate, news reached Bonn that the Federal Constitutional Court was about to issue its long awaited judgement on the legality of German rearmament. Adenauer somehow heard a whisper that the judgement was likely to be adverse. After hurried consultation between Adenauer's office and the Federal Court the issue of the judgement was deferred until after the second reading. That only delayed the crisis. By the time the second reading was approved Adenauer knew that the judgement was adverse, that the judges took the view that German re-armament would be contrary to the strongly pacifist Bonn constitution.

At once an envoy of the Chancellor appeared before the court and asked for another adjournment. That same evening, in Bonn,

Adenauer was received by the Federal President, Professor Heuss, and later Adenauer saw the leader of the opposition, Herr Ollenhauer.

The key to the situation lay in the fact that the court's function was advisory. Its opinion was not constitutionally binding on the President. And the court had not yet issued any opinion. Next morning President Heuss informed the court that he wished to withdraw his request for an opinion on the legality of German rearmament. The court was not, therefore, called upon to issue any opinion. There was no crisis.

But by what methods had Adenauer averted the crisis and saved his policy? Were they constitutional? Still more, were they democratic? There was a storm in Bonn where all members of all parties took the view that his tactics were the reverse of democratic.

The Social Democrats accused him of aping the nefarious methods of the Nazis in interfering with the constitutional functions of both the Federal President and the Federal Constitutional Court. The Free Democrats in his coalition, including some of his uninformed and otherwise disregarded ministers who had known nothing of what he was doing, were equally outspoken. Even among some of his own supporters there was a strong suspicion that Adenauer had acted with an authoritarian disregard for the fundamentals of the constitution which he helped to frame. On one point all the Adenauer critics were united. It was inconceivable that Professor Heuss, who certainly did not share the Chancellor's autocratic tendencies, could have been any party to anything improper.

Adenauer's anxiety to avert a constitutional crisis on the rearmament issue, already complicated by the French attitude, was easy to understand. He honestly believed that the future of Germany, and possibly Europe, depended on the fulfilment of his policies. But he seemed to be perilously near the precept of some of his earliest Rhineland mentors that the end justified the means. His autocratic impatience with opposition and the devious tactics

by which he secured his ends showed a disregard for constitutional and democratic organs which was to obtain striking confirmation in his public statements at the time of the *Spiegel affair*
ten years later.

So tense was the domestic political situation caused by Adenauer's extra-constitutional activities, that President Heuss felt
bound to go on the radio and categorically deny that he had done
anything to give party advantage to the Chancellor. The whole
incident left an unfortunate impression of the thinness of the
veneer of German democracy, and did nothing in the Anglo-
Saxon countries to enhance Adenauer's reputation as a democrat.
Rather did it create an impression that Adenauer, like Hindenburg
before him, in a moment of national crisis might be ready to stray
from the path of strict constitutional propriety.

The S.P.D. moved a vote of 'no confidence' in the Federal
Chancellor. Adenauer was saved, as he was on other occasions,
by that fundamental provision of the Bonn constitution that the
motion of no confidence which removes a Chancellor must also
nominate his successor. At that moment there was almost certainly a majority of the Bundestag members against Adenauer.
But there was no other figure who could command the majority
necessary to secure election as his successor. So Adenauer remained for another decade, to gather even more power and to
become ever more autocratic.

By early 1953 the E.D.C. ratification was almost at a standstill.
In Bonn, Adenauer had made slow, but satisfactory progress.
Elsewhere, there seemed no enthusiasm for ratification. About
this time the French Government fell. M. Schuman disappeared
from the Quai d'Orsay, where his European policies had held
sway for so long.

The new French Government, in which M. Bidault became
Foreign Minister, at once demanded further guarantees about
future German action. Adenauer's advisers thought the French
went too far. The old man, however autocratic he might be
at home, was determined to be a liberal statesman abroad.

So painstakingly he prepared a series of letters covering the latest French requirements, which in due course the French accepted.

By March, 1953, Adenauer decided that in Bonn, at any rate, an end must be made to the apparently interminable process of ratification of the vital treaties. For the reluctant French were only too happy to use delays in Bonn as a reason for doing nothing in Paris. After a long debate, in which both sides repeated the speeches they had made earlier, the Bundestag at last completed the ratification of the Bonn Agreement and the E.D.C. Treaty.

It was an undoubted personal triumph for Adenauer. If, in the nine months' struggle for ratification, his methods had sometimes been open to question, there had never been any doubt of his fundamental aim. He genuinely believed that the future of Europe depended on restoring the Germans to the Western world where they belonged. And he let nothing stand in his way to achieve that aim.

Even in Bonn there were still complications. Some of the clauses required ratification by the Bundesrat, the Federal Council to which all the federal states sent their chief ministers. He had made many enemies in the upper house, some from Weimar days. After much negotiation and not a little backstairs intrigue, he obtained Bundesrat approval. The constitutional issue of the legality of German remilitarization remained. However, a German general election was in the offing and Adenauer decided to delay the issue pending an appeal to the voters. In the long run the constitutional issue fizzled out when it was overtaken by the French defeat of E.D.C.

In those long months of 1951 and 1952, while Adenauer first negotiated and then struggled to obtain the ratification of the Bonn Agreement and the E.D.C. Treaty, he achieved something which will be remembered in world history long after his passing political triumphs have been forgotten. Out of the fullness of his heart and without any pressure from the Western Powers Konrad Adenauer, on behalf of all Germans on whatever side of the Iron

Curtain, accepted responsibility for what Germany had done to the Jews. And he made what reparation was in his power.

Adenauer, unlike many Germans, was probably always pro-Semitic. Since his early years in the civic administration of Cologne when he was city treasurer, he had been a friend of the great Jewish international bankers who had made the city a centre of world finance. In the separatist days one of his close associates was Louis Hagen, alias Louis Levy, and the contacts continued as long as Adenauer was Oberbürgermeister.

In 1933 it was the Jewish banker, Danny Heinemann, who had lent him the money he needed so much, and without any security. When, in 1951, the Government of Israel sent a sharply worded Note to the three Occupation Powers demanding that Germany be forced to help with the construction of the new Israeli state, Adenauer quietly took note, although the Allies made no move.

He felt Germany had a deep moral responsibility to Jews for what had happened under the Nazis and, soon after the Note was sent, he sent a representative to London to contact the World Jewish Congress. A few weeks later, while in Paris, he invited the Israeli Ambassador and a government official to meet him. The Israeli representative took a very strong line with the Federal Chancellor, threatening international legal action. From any other source their words would have drawn a sharp retort. But during this exceedingly painful meeting he remained calm and dignified and assured the Israeli representatives that he would go further into the question.

The Jewish representatives in these various discussions had demanded that the German Government should accept responsibility for what the Nazis had done. He felt the demand was just. And in September, 1951, he made a formal statement to the Bundestag in which, on behalf of his Government, he expressed the immeasurable sorrow of the great majority of the German people for what had been done to the Jews in Germany and the Nazi-occupied countries. The German people, he said, had a duty to make what reparation, moral and material, was possible. His

Government proposed to pass a Reparations Law. But first he wished to sit down with representatives of world Jewry and the Government of Israel to find a solution to the problem of material reparations.

When he was in London, in December of that year, he had a friendly meeting with Dr. Nahum Goldmann of the World Jewish Federation, who had been selected as head of the Jewish commission dealing with claims against Germany. In a letter to Dr. Goldmann written after the meeting, he said that his Government felt it had a duty to restore the honour of the German people by doing everything possible to try to make good the evil done by the Nazis to the Jewish people. He therefore proposed that negotiations should begin as soon as possible.

The negotiations had just got off to a shaky start when in March, 1952, Jewish terrorists made an attempt to assassinate Adenauer. An untidy, badly-dressed man in a Munich street persuaded two Bavarian schoolboys to take a parcel to the post office. It was addressed to 'Dr. Konrad Adenauer, Bonn.' The sender gave a name and address in Frankfurt-on-Main.

The two boys thought the request strange and asked the advice of a tramway inspector. He summoned the police and the packet was taken to the central police station. The police suspected that something was wrong and sent for their explosives expert. He carefully unwrapped the parcel and found inside it a box containing a conversation lexicon. He had just started to open the box when a violent explosion occurred. The explosives expert lost both hands while his arms, legs and face were badly injured. He died four hours later. The German security services established that the packet had been sent by one of the Jewish terrorist organizations which had survived the establishment of the Israeli state, probably the rump of the Stern Gang. Adenauer categorically forbade that this should be revealed to the German public. He was determined that nothing should interfere with the reparations negotiations. He preferred to announce that the assassination attempt was the work of a madman.

The German-Israeli negotiations were resumed. Finally, in September, 1952, Adenauer met the Israeli Foreign Minister, Mr. Moshe Sharett in Luxembourg. They both signed a treaty by which the West German Government undertook to deliver goods worth nearly 3,500 millions Deutschmarks (nearly £ 300 million at the prevailing rate of exchange) as compensation for Nazi persecution of the Jews.

When Mr. Sharett returned to Jerusalem one of the more extreme anti-German fanatics in the Israeli Parliament asked in what language he had negotiated with Adenauer. The answer was truly classic – 'In the language of Goethe.'

The German-Israeli Treaty provided that delivery should be made over a period of twelve to fourteen years. The first cargo reached Haifa the following summer. Subsequently fifty ships totalling 500,000 tons, a floating dock, and great quantities of equipment for power stations, railways, steel mills and textile factories were delivered to Israel by Western Germany.

So honourably did Adenauer carry out his personal undertaking to Israel that the final cargo reached that country in the spring of 1963 – several months ahead of the scheduled date.

Whatever doubts there may be about some of Adenauer's policies, his treaty with Israel was the act of a great man.

CHAPTER TEN

The Great Might Have Been

Two EVENTS of world importance took place on the eve of Adenauer's ratification triumph in March 1953. 1. At the end of January the Republican administration of President Eisenhower took office, with Mr. John Foster Dulles as the new American Secretary of State. 2. At the beginning of March Josef Stalin died.

The two events in conjunction were to have profound consequences for Adenauer, and for Germany, in the months that followed.

The part played by Mr. John Foster Dulles as foreign affairs adviser of the Republican party in the days of the Truman bipartisan foreign policy has already been noted. Like Adenauer, he was a Conservative capitalist and reactionary. The only fundamental difference was that Adenauer was a devout, narrow Catholic and Dulles was a devout, narrow Presbyterian; oddly, both men had sons who were brilliant young Catholic priests.

Dulles had been an expert on German affairs since, as a nephew of Mr. Robert Lansing, the American Secretary of State at the Versailles Conference, he had been a member of the first Allied Economic Commission. He had been close to German bankers and big business ever since; as a Wall Street attorney, he had helped to float the Dawes and Young loans to Germany in the mid-twenties. To Dulles a man like Adenauer was the best type of German.

In the years before the Republicans took office in 1953, Mr. Dulles had learned much from his friends in the American army and U.S. High Commission about Adenauer's pro-American sympathies. His devotion to the Pentagon policy of German remilitarization had been noted with approval by the new Republican administration. President Eisenhower, too, had come to know and respect the Federal German Chancellor. In the months in 1951–2 during which the new President had served as N.A.T.O. Commander-in-Chief, he had formed a personal friendship with the veteran in Bonn.

Looming ahead was the German general election in the autumn of 1953. To both the President and the Secretary of State, Adenauer's continuance in office was a fundamental requirement of American political and military strategy in Europe. As soon as the Eisenhower administration took office, therefore, it was decided to make a public demonstration of the respect and trust in which Adenauer was held in Washington, and in so doing to give his election campaign a triumphal send off. Adenauer therefore was invited to make an official visit to the United States in April.

It was an invitation for which Adenauer had been angling almost since the first months after he took office in the autumn of 1949. But in previous years the Truman-Acheson administration had been curiously coy. They appreciated his support for the policy of German rearmament and had been willing to instruct their envoy, Mr. McCloy to make important concessions to him. But they preferred him in Bonn to Washington.

On an early April afternoon, therefore, Adenauer, accompanied by his daughter Lotte, at that time unmarried, left Bonn in an American aircraft. At Havre they joined the liner *United States*.

In New York they were greeted by Adenauer's very distant relative by marriage, the former High Commissioner, Mr. John J. McCloy. The presidential aircraft awaited the Chancellor. At Washington, on the steps of the White House, stood Adenauer's old acquaintance, the President himself, with a beaming grin and outstretched hand.

For three days the President and his advisers talked with Adenauer. The talks were more symbolic than intrinsically important; both sides were in complete agreement. During these talks Adenauer received confidential assurances, which were repeated after the French rejection of the E.D.C., *that Germany would be rearmed no matter what happened.* He was informed that equipment for some of his divisions was already in the pipeline between the United States and the Rhine. The equipment remained in the pipeline for a long time.

The talks did give formal acknowledgement, on the highest level, to the existing policy of the closest possible friendship between the two nations. Americans and Germans had often got on well together since a certain Baron von Steuben, whose grave was visited by Adenauer, helped the American colonists to throw out the British. Eisenhower and Adenauer were no exceptions. The Chancellor's sympathy with the policies and aims of President Eisenhower's Right-wing Republican administration was not difficult to understand. Adenauer's natural sympathy and admiration for the power of the United States had been strengthened by the enormous financial help which had contributed so much to Germany's recovery.

His American hosts felt equally that the German visitor was worthy of all the honour they could pay him. For Adenauer was the one statesman on the European continent, and maybe anywhere, who was in complete agreement with American policy. He was the only man in Europe, beyond the British whom many American administrations take for granted, on whom the Americans felt they could depend. Adenauer was the political boss of America's most important forward base in Europe. It may have been significant that, within a few weeks of his visit, the first American atomic cannon reached the Rhine.

It was in American interests, therefore, that President Eisenhower should bestow a signal honour on the German Chancellor, an honour seldom paid to a foreign visitor.

The ceremony took place, on a mild April morning, before the grave of the American Unknown Soldier in the Arlington National Cemetery at Washington. In the midst of a small group of American generals and German diplomats, stood the black figure of the German Federal Chancellor. His mask-like face stared straight ahead as a salute of twenty-one guns sounded across row after row of white crosses – memorials to American soldiers who had fallen in two wars fighting Germany. Behind the little group fluttered the Stars and Stripes and the black, red and gold emblem of Federal Germany. The old man stepped forward and placed his wreath on the American Unknown Warrior's grave. Then *Deutschland über Alles* echoed across the tombstones.

It was the same music which the victorious Allies under a very anti-German Eisenhower had publicly banned eight years before. It was the same national anthem which caused the fuss when played at Adenauer's request only three years previously, in Berlin. For once the stern old man wept openly. He murmured, 'This is the turning-point in history.'

By that symbolic act the most powerful nation in the world, 'only eight years after unconditional surrender', had taken Germany as an ally and demonstrated to the world that Adenauer was the leader of that great power. Adenauer could not conceal his emotion. For years he would continue to refer to the Arlington ceremony as 'the greatest moment' of his long life.

Adenauer was the first Chancellor to visit the United States during his term of office, and everywhere during his seventeen-day coast-to-coast tour he received a warm welcome. Speeches, Press Conferences, TV interviews and lectures followed each other in quick succession.

Throughout all these public utterances he had only two main themes: 1. His profound admiration for the emergence of the United States as the first world power, and the inevitable corollary, Germany's respect for American strength and wealth. 2. Germany's heartfelt appreciation of the part American generosity had played in what was soon to be known as 'the German miracle' only a few years after the notorious Morgenthau plan to 'pastoralize' the Reich.

After seven days of unprecedented triumph Adenauer flew home. By excellent stage management by his Christian Democrat party minions, he flew direct to a great C.D.U. rally at Hamburg to launch the 1953 election campaign.

The Germans worship success – and victory. Adenauer clearly had that in mind when, tired and pale, he opened his speech to his party a few hours after landing at Hamburg airport.

'I believe,' said the Chancellor, 'that my visit to the United States has had great results for Germany. I believe, too, that it has rarely happened that a victor has held out his hand to the vanquished who, and we cannot deny it, started the war.'

Then, like a prince of the Church denouncing a heresy, he castigated those of his countrymen who had fallen into the sin of anti-Americanism, then widespread in Europe.

'The average European,' he said, 'has I am afraid, an entirely wrong conception of the American people. People whose sole interest was business could not demonstrate such generosity as the United States has shown. Of course, the Americans are business-minded, but they also have a spiritual capacity and a concern for human freedom. I myself am convinced that the policy of the United States is based on the belief that liberty and justice are the only true basis for co-operation between peoples.'

Then the basic Teutonic truth was revealed:

'There is one power on top of the world today: that is the United States. Their aims and general views are close to ours. We Germans have made many mistakes in the past in the field of foreign relations. *We would make our biggest mistake now if we did not ally ourselves with the leading power on earth* which seeks to promote freedom and justice for all, including the Germans.' There was no doubt where Konrad Adenauer stood. If there was to be a third World War (Cuba was still nearly ten years ahead) the Germans were to be on the winning side for a change.

Adenauer was scarcely back in Germany before he set out on his travels again – this time to Paris. But there he had scarcely the success which he had experienced in Washington. Little progress was made at a meeting of 'The Six' Foreign Ministers on European unity, and over the Saar he was rebuffed.

M. Bidault, alas, was neither M. Schuman, nor General de Gaulle. The French Foreign Minister was not impressed by the German Chancellor. The day after Adenauer left Paris a new convention, in defiance of all his pleas, was signed between the French and Saar Governments. It was, as he commented with unwonted restraint, 'scarcely polite'.

It was at this moment, in the spring of 1953, that Sir Winston Churchill made his historic speech calling for a re-examination of the East-West conflict in the changed circumstances arising from Stalin's death a few weeks earlier. The Prime Minister proposed that there should be a European settlement along the lines of 'a new Locarno Pact'. This, he said, would guarantee the security of both the Soviet Union and Germany.

Adenauer was on the eve of his second visit to London and Sir Winston went out of his way to emphasize, with all his considerable power, that the Germans would not be sacrificed on the altar of a general European settlement but would remain masters of their fate. The German problem, he said, was the most important single problem in Europe. And because he realized that everything might hinge on the German Chancellor's attitude, Sir Winston deliberately described him as 'the wisest German statesman since Bismarck'.

What reports on the attitude of the new men in the Kremlin towards an easing of the Cold War formed the basis of Sir Winston's proposals for 'a new Locarno' will remain unknown until the British archives are opened decades hence. That he had some ground for believing that his historic proposals would not be unwelcome, is almost certain. In recent years it has become known that, within weeks of Stalin's death, hints reached Western capitals that the new leaders, notably Beria and probably Malenkov, favoured a liquidation of the German situation as part of a general European settlement.

Confirmation of this in general terms has been given to the

author in conversations beyond the Iron Curtain in the past two or three years. Well-informed East European sources have suggested that Beria, who in the spring of 1953 was striving desperately with the aid of his secret police to dominate Malenkov, Molotov and Khrushchev, favoured a radical solution of the German problem.

He is reported to have stated that the German East Zone Communists headed by Ulbricht would always be a millstone round the Russian neck. The East Germans would never become Communists, claimed Beria, and therefore he was in favour of liquidating the Soviet Zone of Germany on the best terms that could be obtained. This he proposed to use as a powerful card in negotiations with the Western Powers for a general European settlement. His views were strongly opposed by the marshals of the Soviet Supreme Command. Inter-continental ballistic weapons were still years ahead and forward short range rocket bases were still important. Beria throughout April, May and early June, 1953, is claimed to have pressed strongly for a settlement of European problems. Whether the details stated above are correct or not, it is certain that Beria and other Soviet leaders in the spring of 1953 were ready to do a deal, including a settlement of the German problem.

Indirect but official confirmation that the Soviet leaders were prepared to resolve the German question immediately after Stalin's death came ten years later from no less an authority than Khrushchev himself. The Soviet Prime Minister, addressing a conference of the Russian intellectual *élite* in the Kremlin in March, 1963, made this sensational revelation:

'In the early days after Stalin's death, Beria and Malenkov produced the provocative proposal that the German Democratic Republic [Russian Zone puppet government] be liquidated as a Socialist state; and they urged the S.E.D. [East Zone German Unity Party] to renounce the course of building up Socialism.'

Some hint of this may very well have reached Whitehall. Sir Winston Churchill, with his political flair and his enormous prestige not only in the West but among the Soviet leaders, realized that the psychological moment had been reached for a radical approach. The American administration, still in its first weeks of office, in spite of Mr. Dulles would clearly not have opposed such a settlement. The influence on the new President of the British Prime Minister, to whom he owed so much and who could have sent Eisenhower into obscurity after Tunisian reverses in 1942, was certainly considerable. The view of the divided French was scarcely decisive.

Adenauer, therefore, for all practical purposes held the key. There is not much doubt that the Prime Minister's flattering reference to 'the wisest German statesman since Bismarck' was not fortuitous. Future historians may well decide that Adenauer, in these spring weeks of 1953, held in his hands the golden opportunity which Fate seldom offers to any man a second time.

Immediate support by Adenauer of Sir Winston Churchill's initiative could well have proved decisive. A top-level four-power meeting could have been arranged within a matter of weeks. A settlement of the Cold War in Europe and the re-unification of Germany might very well have been achieved. In the three months after Stalin's death the Soviet leaders, still suspiciously watching each other, were almost certainly ready to do a deal.

Adenauer, in the event, was no Bismarck. Sir Winston Churchill's mention of a 'Locarno' had at once aroused his most profound distrust. A quarter of a century earlier he had attacked his great predecessor, Stresemann, for negotiating the Locarno Pact. Despite the most solemn assurances given him in No. 10 Downing Street fifteen months earlier, Adenauer still feared that the West would make a bargain behind his back. He cherished a strong suspicion that the Western and Eastern Powers who had united to overthrow Hitler were about to combine again. To Adenauer a Soviet *rapprochement* with the West could only be at the expense of what he regarded as Germany – the Federal Republic. He carefully refrained from expressing these views publicly before he left for London. He was given a much warmer welcome by the British people and Press than on his first visit. The British had become increasingly impressed by his support for the Western cause.

From German accounts of what took place it is evident that Sir Winston Churchill and Sir Anthony Eden did their utmost to allay the Chancellor's fears. He was again assured that no fundamental policy decision on Germany would be taken without his agreement. He was assured that he would be kept informed, in detail, of the course of any East-West exchanges.

Adenauer left London, apparently pacified. But his fear of a reconciliation between Russia and the West was basic and profound. Even the most solemn word of Winston Churchill was not enough. When, a few days later, the Prime Minister proposed a meeting between himself, President Eisenhower and the then French Prime Minister, M. Laniel, in Bermuda to prepare for a four-power conference, all Adenauer's narrow, provincial suspicions broke out again with renewed vigour. His response may well prove historically the most revealing statement of his long years as Chancellor.

The question of German security, he announced categorically, could not be solved by any treaty on the Locarno pattern. He doubted any real willingness on the part of the new masters of the Kremlin to negotiate. And he did not expect a four-power conference to be successful. He denounced any attempt to negotiate with the Russians on the basis of the Potsdam Agreement of 1945, the last four-power decision on a united Germany.

'Bismarck has spoken of his ever-present nightmare of a coalition against Germany. I too have a nightmare,' he confessed. 'My nightmare is called Potsdam. The danger (to Germany) of a collective policy by the Four Great Powers has existed since 1945 . . . *and has continued to exist since the founding of the Federal Republic.*'

His foreign policy throughout his period of office, he said, had been aimed at 'leading Germany out of the danger zone. If

Germany is left between the millstone of East and West she is lost.'

In simple terms, the Cold War must be continued at any price, and it would continue with the help of his greatest friend, Mr. Dulles, until a dynamic young Irish-American in the White House declined to permit the views of an octogenarian German to dominate American foreign policy any longer.

Adenauer added that he could never emphasize enough that the two treaties he had signed had brought Germany into the Western partnership and freed Germany from 'the nightmare of Potsdam'. By these treaties, he believed, the Western Powers were committed to strive for German unity. He did not add the obvious corollary, unity on his terms.

The Chancellor was still putting a spoke in the wheel of East-West negotiations when the situation was revolutionized by the gallant, but useless revolt of the German workers in East Berlin and the Soviet Zone on 17th June, 1953. Armed with sticks and stones, the German workers were ruthlessly shot down by Soviet tanks rushed into East Berlin when it became obvious that the Communist puppet government had lost control.

Within a few days Beria was dead, executed, it is rumoured, by some of his colleagues at a meeting of the Soviet Politburo in the Kremlin. What connection there may have been between the death of the Secret Police Chief responsible for much of the Stalin terror, and the East Berlin rising can only be a matter of surmise. If for no other reason, the revulsion of all free Germans headed by Adenauer at the massacre of their defenceless fellow-countrymen in East Berlin, eliminated any real chance of an immediate European, and with it a German, settlement.

The great opportunity had been lost. The chance of a new Locarno was gone, and with it any chance of German re-unification on reasonably acceptable terms for the rest of Adenauer's long period in office. The vital period was from mid-March to 17th June. If Adenauer during these three months had been as great, as wise, and as big a man as Winston Churchill, and grasped the chance offered by the Prime Minister's 'new Locarno' speech, the history of Europe, and of Germany, might have been different.

Any chance of German re-unification became even more remote when, in consequence of the 17th June deaths in East Berlin, all political leaders pledged themselves never to have any contact with those German Communists 'whose hands are red with the blood of German workers'.

In due course, representatives of the Western Powers met in Washington in July and sent a Note to Moscow calling for four-power talks. The abortive Foreign Ministers' meeting in Berlin early in the following year was the result.

As the Western delegates met in Washington, Adenauer had plunged into an electioneering tour in preparation for the forth-coming German general election. He was under strong attack. His tepid approach towards German re-unification became a major election issue. His opponents alleged that he was well content with his Bonn Republic as it was and that, despite all his protestations, he was still a separatist at heart.

The Social Democrats had long believed that in a united Germany, with the support of a Socialist Berlin and 'Red Saxony', they might well emerge as the majority party in a reunited Reich. They alleged that this was the main reason for Adenauer's opposition to re-unification. This taunt nettled the Chancellor. 'I would rather have a united Germany with an S.P.D. government than a rump Western Germany with a C.D.U. coalition,' he snapped.

His main attack, however, was on a neutralized, re-united Germany, a policy which some of his opponents and others in the West felt should be explored. Adenauer, in repeated speeches, showed that he was prepared for re-unification only on his own terms. Any future all-German government, he said, must be free from foreign control and at liberty to ally itself with any international grouping it chose – N.A.T.O., the Coal and Steel Community or 'the little Europe' of 'The Six' which was still only an Adenauer dream.

It was difficult to visualize Messrs Khrushchev, Malenkov, Molotov and Mikoyan, even in their most liberal frame of mind, ever accepting these conditions.

To those in the West, however, whose private nightmare was not a second Locarno but a second Rapallo (a German-Soviet pact), Adenauer's conditions were sweet music. He had opted for the West. And the closer his ties with the West became the more unlikely became the chance of German re-unification. With great clarity he explained this policy to 20,000 cheering supporters at Frankfurt-on-Main.

'Our country is a point of tension between two world *blocs*. Long ago I made a great decision. We Germans belong to the West and not to the East. Isolation is the concept of idiots; it could only mean the withdrawal of American troops from Europe.'

He urged that the German electors must demonstrate to the world their support of his policies and, above all, his efforts to create a united Europe. His words fell on fertile soil. By 1953 vast numbers of Germans were firm supporters of a united Europe, whether on the narrow, restricted lines conceived by Adenauer is open to some doubt.

Adenauer knew his Germans and as election day approached he had no doubt of the result. The Germans worship nothing so much as success, and make instinctive obeisance to authority (*Die Obrigkeit*). Adenauer was the embodiment of both. In his negotiations with the Western Powers he had gained great success. He had restored virtual independence to the Germans, or would do so when all the treaties were ratified. He had restored Germany to a position of respectability in the world. Under his leadership, if not his direction, the German economic miracle was taking shape. And his authoritarian rule in Bonn provided that Father Figure which the Germans instinctively respect and obey. He was sure that his combination of success and authority would prove irresistible.

His friend Mr. Dulles, in Washington, was determined to make sure. With that lack of tact which in the next few years would become historic he issued a statement warning the Germans that *they must vote for Adenauer*. And, curiously enough, the Federal Chancellor seemed to find nothing strange in the crass interference of a foreign politician in a German election. In any event Mr. Dulles's interferences proved unnecessary.

CHAPTER ELEVEN

Parliamentary Autocrat

IN THE AUTUMN of 1953 Adenauer won an overwhelming personal
triumph in West Germany's second general election. He was
returned to power with an absolute majority, in striking contrast
to the hairsbreadth win in 1949. In an electoral landslide the
great majority of the 50,000,000 free Germans voted, not for a
policy or a party but for a man. They were duly thankful for
what the superannuated Oberbürgermeister had achieved. In
the most elementary political terms they voted for Konrad
Adenauer, just as twenty years earlier they had voted for Adolf
Hitler.

For centuries, generation after generation of Germans had been
inculcated with the supreme Teutonic doctrine of *Die Obrikgeit*,
that authority was there to be respected and obeyed. That is the
fundamental political premise of German life, whatever the
intrinsic political system by which it may be administered. It
was not by chance that the Marxist doctrine of the overriding
paramountcy of the State stemmed from a German source. Over
the centuries the Germans respected and obeyed, if they did not
love, Frederick II, Napoleon, Bismarck, Wilhelm II and the Führer.
With all their basic instincts revived as the shock of unconditional
surrender wore off, they now felt they must again obey authority,
albeit a democratic authority. And in the rigid, narrow old man
with the firm hand and the wily political mind who for four years
had imposed his increasingly authoritarian régime on Bonn, they
recognized that authority for which they had been seeking since
1945.

Consciously or unconsciously Adenauer, beneath the thin

veneer formed by the outward essentials of parliamentary democracy, had sensed and exploited that German craving for authority. In four years he had succeeded in reviving that authoritarian
personality cult which had played such a decisive part in German
history over the centuries. The enormous electoral majority with
which the Germans swept Adenauer back to power in 1953 made
him the supreme autocrat of Bonn, and by a truly Teutonic
paradox the dictator of a democracy.

With the absolute majority accorded to his rigidly disciplined
C.D.U. party machine, coupled with the dangerous constitutional
powers which he had succeeded in evolving from the Bonn Constitution, Adenauer for the next decade was virtually a one-man
government. The outward trappings of democracy were, of
course, maintained. But neither his party, his coalition nor his
Cabinet ever decisively challenged his will. So little did the parliamentary Germans understand the fundamentals of true democracy that, no matter how outrageously Adenauer behaved, as he
did before the presidential election in 1959, and over the *Spiegel*
affair in 1962, only Dr. Heinemann in 1950 and the Free Democrat
Ministers who walked out of his government in the autumn of
1962, resigned on an issue of policy.

That did not imply that Adenauer's electoral victory was any-
anything but democratic and strictly constitutional. But that
sweep of Teutonic emotion which, within the framework of the
Bonn parliamentary system, carried Adenauer to autocratic
power in 1953, held a stern warning for the future when at last the
old man would go. That highly dangerous form of authoritarianism, evolved by Adenauer behind the screen of Bonn
parliamentary institutions, might provide a less fundamentally
benevolent and less pro-Western successor with a perfect
instrument to lead the Germans once again along those paths
of political extremism which they are so prone to follow.

The Adenauer metamorphosis was indeed remarkable. The
aged politician who had once been a loyal civil servant of

Wilhelm II, who twenty years earlier had been hounded from office by the Nazis, had become a major international figure supported by the vast majority of his fellow-Germans. Yet he never changed. He followed policies which, had his Imperial master survived 1945, would certainly have earned the approval of Wilhelm II. For the next decade this relic of a Hohenzollern past, with little contact and less respect for the views of millions of growing young Germans, was permitted to impose his will on the Federal German Republic.

So important had he become in the eyes of the world that a great American newspaper was sufficiently misguided to instruct its correspondent in Bonn that it wished to hear no more of German politics . . . 'for Adenauer is the only thing that matters in German politics'. In a curious way, the editor who sent that telegram was right.

Yet these same policies which had gained Adenauer his dominating position, at the very moment of his triumph were in danger of imminent collapse. The ratification of the Bonn Agreement and the E.D.C. Treaty signed sixteen months earlier seemed as far as ever. Germany was still technically an occupied country without those German soldiers for whom Adenauer had risked so much. In the autumn of 1953 Adenauer's policies seemed to lie in the hands of the French – as they did ten years later – and the French seemed to have no interest in ratifying the two treaties. It was with these problems in mind that Adenauer plunged into the difficult task of reconstructing his Cabinet, a process which was to have disturbing consequences.

Adenauer, it will be recalled, had still to settle the constitutional issue of the legality of German rearmament. To please Mr. Dulles and give the generals in the Pentagon the German troops they so ardently desired, it might be necessary to interfere with the four-year-old Bonn constitution. To Adenauer constitutions were something to be altered and amended to suit the needs of his own political policies. A change in the Bonn constitution, however, would require a two-thirds majority in the Bonn Parliament.

Despite his absolute majority he did not control two-thirds of the votes in Parliament. The Rhineland political boss at once took over from the international statesman.

Despite his differences with his former allies in the Free Democratic party, he once again renewed his association with that party. In the process he dropped his outspoken Minister of Justice, Dr. Thomas Dehler, who, whatever his faults as a politician, was a genuine independent German liberal and who, over the years, became more and more critical of Adenauer's authoritarian methods of government. Adenauer also renewed his association with the German Party (D.P.) which had also had ministers in the first Bonn Government. Finally, Adenauer made approaches to the Refugee Union (B.H.E.), the chauvinistic, revanchist refugee group which had appeared in the Bundestag for the first time.

Posts had to be found for leading personalities of all four parties which he proposed to bring into the new Government. After a month of hard bargaining Adenauer at last produced a Government with no less than nineteen ministries. The size of the Government was widely condemned, for the new administration was a repetition in exaggerated form of what had occurred four years earlier of 'finding jobs for the boys'.

There might even have been a twentieth ministry – of Propaganda. The former head of Adenauer's private office, Dr. Otto Lenz, had reached an understanding with Adenauer that he would be the new Dr. Goebbels. The German Press, unlike the Bonn ministers, never took Adenauer's dictatorship lying down. They fought back.

Astute as always, Adenauer quietly buried the proposal. He had no desire, yet, for a showdown with the German Press. There was also much public hilarity over his creation of a Ministry of Family Affairs, manifestly a sop to his Catholic friends. But these typical Adenauer political tricks were unimportant. Much more serious, not to say sinister, was a development which occurred during the horse trading which formed an inevitable preliminary to the formation of the second Adenauer administration. For at this point, eight years after the death of Hitler, Adenauer brought the Nazis back into the German Government. It was the signal for the Nazi revival in Bonn and throughout the Federal Republic.

Up to 1953 the former supporters of Adolf Hitler had been understandably coy about reappearing in public. During the 1953 election, however, a number of former Nazi and Hitler fellow-travellers of various complexions appeared as candidates. A few were in Adenauer's own Christian Democrat party. Most of them had been members of the Nazi party but not necessarily fanatical adherents of the Führer. More were to be found in the Free Democratic Party which, in northern Germany, had a distinctly Nazi fringe. The Refugee Group contained everything from Germans who just wanted to go home to the east, to notorious war criminals. It was led by a curious assortment of former S.S. officers and German ultra-nationalists who still dreamed of the *Lebensraum* in the east.

In the process of the Adenauer-sponsored Nazi come-back, four ministers of distinctly equivocal background appeared in the Bonn Government. Two of them were simply Nazis. A third, Professor Theodor Oberlaender, had been one of the 'eastern experts' of various Third Reich organizations.

The background of the new Minister of the Interior, Dr. Gerhard Schroeder, was less clearly defined. As one of these young German idealists who had been attracted by the more utopian side of the early Nazis, he had been a candidate member of the Storm Troopers. But in the course of his law studies he spent a year at the University of Edinburgh. Day-by-day contact with the Fathers and Brethren of the 'Kirk' and the citizens of 'Auld Reekie' may well have contributed to the change which began to develop. Young Schroeder became increasingly disillusioned. Subsequently he had enough character to wed a pretty girl with a partly Jewish background, no mean act of civic courage at the time. He was relegated to the East Front as an ordinary soldier. After the

German surrender he found employment as a lawyer in a Düsseldorf administrative office under the British military government.

When he became a minister for the first time in 1953 there were considerable doubts about Dr. Schroeder. It was widely believed that he was yet another of the Adenauer 'personal assistants'. After an uncertain period, however, Dr. Schroeder, in recent years, has emerged as one of the outstanding members of the Bonn Government. His appointment as German Foreign Minister in the fourth Adenauer administration in 1961 gave Germany her first strong Foreign Minister of the post-war period. He began to challenge Adenauer's dictatorial and increasingly disastrous control of German foreign affairs in the winter of 1962–3. By the end of the Adenauer era he was, with Professor Erhard, the Vice Chancellor and permanent Minister of Economics, the most prominent minister in the Bonn Cabinet.

More disturbing even than the Nazi come-back in the German Government was Adenauer's choice for the post of Secretary of State in his own Federal Chancellery. To succeed Dr. Lenz, the would-be Goebbels, Adenauer selected as his chief of staff a Catholic lawyer from the Rhineland like himself, Dr. Hans Josef Maria Globke.

When the Nazis took power in 1933 Dr. Globke, like Adenauer a member of the Catholic Zentrum party, was one of the bright young department chiefs of the German Ministry of the Interior. As Minister of the Interior, Hitler appointed the veteran Nazi, Frick, who was eventually to be hanged at Nuremberg. Globke was *never* a Nazi party member. As a member of the Zentrum he was apparently instructed by the Roman hierarchy to remain at his post, as a sort of Catholic spy on the Nazis. At that time the hierarchy did not believe the Nazis would last long, and the Zentrum voted *for the Enabling Act* which was the basis for Hitler's dictatorship.

Globke continued to serve in the Reich Ministry of the Interior and, within a few years, he became the co-author of a commentary on the Hitler Nuremberg laws against the Jews. He claimed later that he did so in an effort to ameliorate some of the worst provisions of the laws. Subsequently, in the years before the war, Globke helped to draft other anti-Semitic ordinances. He remained at his post until the eve of the Nazi collapse in 1945. During the war years his ministry became closely involved in the Heydrich-Eichmann operation which would gain world notoriety as 'The Final Solution' of the Jewish problem.

Globke's exact part is doubtful but he certainly helped to draft Nazi racial ordinances. According to documents produced at the Eichmann trial, Globke was present in January, 1941, at a conference which made the 'legal' preparations for the subsequent final solution.

Globke was photographed in uniform, in attendance on his Minister, Frick, at conferences in Occupied Europe where the extermination of the Jews was planned. He was on the Allied list of war criminals and was arrested in 1945. But after giving evidence at the trial of his former Nazi associates to the Nuremberg tribunal, Globke was released and found employment as a legal adviser at British Military Government Headquarters. In 1949, on the formation of the Bonn Government, he was summoned to the Federal Chancellery in Bonn.

Since then, an elaborate propaganda campaign to whitewash Globke has been carried on with all devices of modern propaganda. As demands for Globke's removal and trial from anti-Nazi sources in both Eastern and Western Europe increased, cardinals, American senators and ex-members of the so-called 'German Resistance' have been enlisted to prove that Globke was not what he seemed.

His apologists have suggested that, in fact, Globke was a Catholic secret agent in the very heart of the internal administration of the Reich throughout the Nazi period. He is claimed to have been a member of the anti-Hitler generals' plot responsible for the bomb explosion at Hitler's headquarters in July, 1944, and to have been selected for high office in the German Government which it was hoped would follow Hitler's murder.

At the end of July 1963 Globke was found guilty by the East Germar. (DDR) Supreme Court in East Berlin of being an accomplice in Nazi war crimes. He was sentenced – *in absentia* – to hard labour for life. The evidence was, however, of a type which would have been insufficient to prove Globke's personal responsibility before most West European courts.

On the day the East German verdict was announced the Federal German government pointed out that the West German legal authorities had already examined the charges made by East Germany against Globke but had found that in no case did they justify proceedings.

This, then, was the man who, in the autumn of 1953, Adenauer chose as his chief administrative assistant in the Federal Chancellery and to whom, in the face of violent international attacks, he clung as long as he was Federal Chancellor. Globke, a German civil servant of the highest qualifications and a brilliant administrator, seized his chance. Exploiting the peculiar opportunities offered by Adenauer's autocratic form of government, Globke became for the next decade, as his denunciators alleged, *the second man in the Bonn Republic*.

The enigma of Adenauer's sponsorship of the Nazi come-back and the installation of Globke and other equally equivocal figures from the Nazi ministries in Berlin in the seats of power has never been fully explained. Adenauer's own record as an anti-Nazi is so much a matter of history and his persecution by the Nazis so well-known, that any sympathy with the Nazis can safely be eliminated.

On the premise that the end justified the means the inclusion of some of the Nazi ministers, notably from the refugee group, in his second Government may be explained by the necessity of getting the German rearmament legislation through the Bonn Parliament. But the appointments of highly equivocal civil servants, and notably his fellow-Catholic Rhinelander, Globke, can be explained only by Adenauer's authoritarian methods of government, and his complete disregard for either his Ministers or his party.

By the autumn of 1953 the Chancellor, fortified by his electoral landslide, began to show open impatience with, not to say distaste for outspoken democratic advisers. Like all dictators, he wanted only 'Yes-Men', efficient subordinates who would carry out his orders without any quibbles. Who better than the Nazis and the men with a past like Globke?

They were only too willing to crawl back into high position on any terms that Adenauer might dictate. They had been the fellow-travellers and sycophants of their Nazi bosses. They were well accustomed to an authoritarian method of administration. It made little difference to these cynical men whether they obeyed Adolf Hitler backed by the Gestapo or the fundamentally benevolent Adenauer armed only with a superb political intelligence and the parliamentary subterfuges learned during a lifetime. In any case, it did not matter very much what the Nazi fellow-travellers and sycophants thought. By this time, Adenauer was so sure of himself that Nazis or non-Nazis were all the same to him. With the mellowness of advancing years, Adenauer may also have felt that the time had come when the division of the Germans into sheep and goats must end.

Whatever the explanation of Adenauer's actions, his sponsor-ship of the Nazi come-back in his Government marked the beginning of the Nazi revival throughout Western Germany. Thereafter, the men who had kept in the shadows returned openly to public life. Globke introduced his ex-colleagues from Berlin into key Government positions. Convicted war criminals became heads of some of Germany's largest cartels. Men who had run the Ruhr for Hitler's war effort were again to be seen in the board-rooms. Judges who had been responsible for judicial murder throughout Europe reappeared on the German bench. And hundreds of German police officers who, as members of Hey-drich's Einsatzgruppen, had murdered millions, reappeared in the German C.I.D. searching for petty criminals. It took the kidnapping of Eichmann and his subsequent trial in Jerusalem to jerk Adenauer out of his complacency sufficiently to stage a number of long delayed war crimes trials at which the most notorious of these men appeared. But little was done about the Nazi sycophants who once again thronged the ministries and other key departments in the Federal Republic.

As the leader of the Social Democratic opposition, Herr Erich Ollenhauer commented, 'There are many in high positions in Bonn who have little connection with democracy.'

Adenauer's part in the Nazi revival did not go unmarked. But although West Germany was technically still occupied, there was little inclination in the Western capitals to take any action.

Mr. Dulles in Washington had certainly no objection to Nazi big business men, for while Britain fought alone he had been in close contact with some of them. Even in London and Paris it would have been thought inexpedient, not to say churlish, to cavil at Adenauer's action. If the old gentleman had become so mellow that he had taken in a few Nazi fellow-travellers what of it?

For Adenauer, by the end of 1953, was the most devoted supporter of the Dulles policy of 'negotiation from strength'. His importance in the Western councils had been increased by the enormous majority which he had just obtained at the German general election. The Western Powers were especially anxious at this time not to upset Adenauer. Four-power negotiations with the Russians, after long diplomatic exchanges, were imminent and it was essential that the West should show a united front.

In preparation for this meeting, President Eisenhower, Sir Winston Churchill and the French Prime Minister, M. Laniel, met in Bermuda at the beginning of December, 1953. Germany was one of the main topics. Adenauer might well have taken part, but he was still technically head of an occupied country. But the absent Chancellor was much more a real participant than the ailing French premier, who took little part in what happened. From Bonn came telegram after telegram demanding immediate French ratification of the Bonn Agreement and the E.D.C. Treaty signed eighteen months earlier.

The French were not prepared to promise anything. Sir Winston Churchill, with much wisdom, therefore urged that the European army project be abandoned and a new solution sought. That is what eventually did happen a year later.

At Bermuda at the end of 1953 Mr. Dulles was so entranced by Adenauer's pro-American policies that the Americans would not budge. Eisenhower dismissed the Churchill proposal with a wave of the hand and added, according to good authority, 'We can't consider any alternative to E.D.C. *for that is what Adenauer wants!*' Adenauer had become the favourite ally.

Doubts about French ratification of the two treaties formed only a minor part of Adenauer's anxieties. With a four-power meeting on Germany imminent, he was once again obsessed by his 'Potsdam Nightmare', the fear of an Allied-Soviet agreement over Germany. And, probably with the encouragement of Mr. Dulles, he set out to sabotage any such possibility.

To the leaders at Bermuda he cabled his conditions:

1. German re-unification to be preceded by free all-German elections under international control.
2. The freely elected German Parliament would form a Government to negotiate a peace treaty with the four Occupation Powers – the peace treaty was still outstanding on the eve of Adenauer's retirement, ten years later.
3. The future German Government must be free to ally itself with any group it wished, and any question of a neutral Germany was out of the question.

These rigid conditions virtually ensured the failure of the conference before it met. But to make sure that there would be no backsliding, he systematically set out, by a series of calculated leaks, to force the Western Powers into a position from which they could not retreat.

Adenauer's tactics succeeded. Mr. Molotov reached Berlin fully briefed by Adenauer's indiscretions on the extent of the Allied negotiating position. The proposals put forward by Sir Anthony

Eden were based on Adenauer's demands. Adenauer need have had no fear of a deal behind his back. The Soviet Foreign Minister, despite the brief relaxation in the immediate post-Stalin months, was as rigid as he had ever been. The four-power meeting was a failure. Once again, the absent Adenauer had played a key role. The chances of German re-unification had begun to fade away.

The Berlin conference cleared the air. The Americans certainly did not want a settlement of the German question. Mr. Dulles shared the Adenauer view that the Russians were more likely to be accommodating when faced by twelve or more German divisions. The other Western Powers were certainly not upset at the indefinite partition of the Reich, and probably neither were the Russians. The Cold War seemed set for years to come. Adenauer and his 50,000,000 Germans had become firm allies. The Western nightmare of a new Rapallo, the always possible alliance between a resurgent Germany and the Soviet Union, had disappeared once again.

By the spring of 1954 the Allies were becoming alarmed by a serious slump in Adenauer's prestige in Western Germany. The failure of the Berlin conference to achieve any concrete results on which many Germans had pinned much hope had started the decline. With justice, the Germans blamed Adenauer for his lukewarm and rigid approach to the question of German re-unification.

Opponents began to revive the taunt of 'separatist' and to suggest that, with his American friends, he was very well content with Western Germany as it was. His growing arrogance became proverbial. There was widespread complaint at the manner in which he had concentrated much of the effective power in his own hands. All these things combined to make many Germans increasingly dissatisfied with the Adenauer régime. But for the constructive 'vote of confidence' clause in the Bonn constitution he might well have fallen.

In Washington and London it was realized that part of the

reason for the German disillusionment lay in the continued failure of France to ratify the Bonn Agreement and the E.D.C. treaty. The British, in an effort to encourage the Government in Paris, gave a promise that one British armoured division should be attached to the future European army for operational purposes.

France, torn by the Indo-China crisis, had little interest in Adenauer's two treaties. When in mid-summer M. Pierre Mendès-France, well known as no friend of E.D.C., became both French Prime Minister and Foreign Minister, Adenauer became alarmed. He realized that the policies to which he had devoted much of the first five years of his chancellorship were in serious jeopardy.

Within days of Mendès-France taking office Adenauer, certainly encouraged by Mr. Dulles, announced bluntly that 'Germany cannot wait for ever for independence'. To make sure that the message was understood in Paris he repeated the statement four times in as many days.

His fears received alarming confirmation when in provincial elections for the Parliament of North Rhine-Westphalia his C.D.U. party lost a million votes compared with the great total it had polled in the general election landslide in the previous autumn. Adenauer was now thoroughly alarmed. He was so excited that he sent for his old friend, M. François-Poncet – and according to Western diplomats – gave him this message for the new French Prime Minister:

'French delays have cost me a million votes,' he said. 'In a few months I may lose another million. *I am the only German Chancellor in history who has preferred the unity of Europe to the unity of the Reich.*'

The history of the next decade would but confirm that these were the truest words Konrad Adenauer ever uttered. Future German historians may well decide that it was the most damning public statement he ever made. As the débâcle early in 1963 over the British entry into the Common Market and his personal alliance with de Gaulle would prove, it was not for Europe that

Adenauer sacrificed the German Reich, but for the neo-Caroling-ian Reich in which no one believed but himself and his megalo-maniac fellow-authoritarian, de Gaulle.

In the summer of 1954 Adenauer was not alone in being alarmed. The Governments in Washington and London were not prepared to sacrifice the most pro-Western Chancellor they had ever known for the French. Therefore, when the American President and the British Prime Minister met in Washington at the end of June 1954, both realized that something must be done. The President and the Prime Minister decided that immediate steps must be taken to see that West Germany became inde-pendent, no matter what happened to the E.D.C. treaty. Once again, Sir Winston Churchill urged that E.D.C. be abandoned. This time Eisenhower was more receptive to Sir Winston's ideas.

They decided that France should be given one last chance to ratify the two treaties. However, Adenauer in private received assurances which went far beyond what was stated in the official communiqué. Mr. Dulles repeated what had been said during Adenauer's first visit to Washington fifteen months earlier, and added that *no matter what happened to E.D.C. Western Germany would be rearmed.* As though to give practical confirmation to this assurance, the Pentagon at once sent a military mission to Bonn to begin planning for German rearmament.

So much trust did Adenauer put in Dulles's words that he began to abandon his lifelong courtship of France—at least for a few years, until a more favourable atmosphere should once again dominate the Elysée. To one of his favourite German radio commentators he gave an interview which contained the final warning to France:

'Germany has earned her sovereignty,' he said. 'She has signed and ratified the treaties, and she cannot continue to suffer just because other states are behind with their ratification.

'Assuming, however, that France does finally reject the E.D.C. treaty the German Government will reject any attempt to offer Germany rearmament under unworthy or humiliating terms – a German army under tutelage.'

Then came what in Paris was described as 'Adenauer's ultimatum'. 'I am anxious to make it clear once and for all that the only alternative to E.D.C. is a German national army. There is nothing else for it.'

Adenauer knew he had Eisenhower, Dulles, Churchill and Eden behind him and, having delivered his broadside, he retired to a Black Forest sanatorium to await results. Mendès-France, having settled the future of Indo-China, by the middle of August intimated that he was prepared to meet France's E.D.C. partners in Brussels.

Through diplomatic channels the French Prime Minister indicated that he would propose major changes in the E.D.C. Treaty, with particular reference to its supra-national aspects in which the cultured liberal Frenchman did not believe. Fortified by a series of personal envoys from Dulles in Washington, Adenauer made up his mind to give no quarter. Like Hitler, his patience was exhausted. Either the French put an end to the farce or his friends in Washington and London would be forced to act.

Adenauer was in a gloomy mood when he set off in his gleaming black Mercedes for Brussels, as usual at breakneck speed. When he reached the Belgian capital he was at his dourest. The French Prime Minister, a few days later, stated that the conference degenerated into a 'humiliating experience'.

Mendès-France wished radically to alter the E.D.C. Treaty. He further asked for an undertaking that no German troops would be stationed in France. Adenauer's answer was simple, 'Take it or leave it.' For four days he stuck to his point. Then his dour stubbornness gained one concession. Mendès-France, a convinced opponent of the whole E.D.C. project, told Adenauer that without fail he would put the E.D.C. Treaty before the French Chamber within weeks. He would give no promise of the result. With all hope gone, Adenauer returned to his Black Forest sanatorium to await the inevitable.

M. Mendès-France was to prove as good as his word.

CHAPTER TWELVE

Saved by the British

ON A LATE summer evening in 1954 a telephone rang in the Black Forest sanatorium where Adenauer had resumed his cure. For hours the old man had waited in suspense. He knew that the French Chamber was at last to take a decision on the E.D.C. Treaty. Mendès-France had kept his word. But personally disapproving of the European army project and all its works, the French Prime Minister had, most properly, declined to make the vote a question of confidence in his Government.

Adenauer lifted the phone. At the other end was the German Ambassador in Paris. 'I have bad news, Herr Bundeskanzler,' said the agitated German diplomat. 'The French have rejected the E.D.C. Treaty by nearly 60 votes.' The Chamber, he added, had not taken the trouble to consider the treaty in detail but rejected it out of hand.

Torn between fury and despair, Adenauer put down the phone, unable to speak. He scarcely spoke for two days. Only twice in his life, when firstly the Nazis, and secondly the British had driven him from Cologne, had he suffered such a blow. The old man had never been so angry since he became Federal Chancellor. The white, parchment-like face, which so seldom revealed his true thoughts, could not conceal his profound emotion. All was gone. Not only the E.D.C. Treaty but the Bonn Agreement, and with them both independence for Western Germany and the possibility of German rearmament. Not only were his policies shattered and his prestige hurled into the dust, but he had suffered a deep personal blow from the country for whose reconciliation with Germany he had worked all his life. France had spurned the

hand which Adenauer had held out for so long. The dream of a
lifetime seemed to have disappeared for ever, and no one who
recognized his sterling services to the Western cause could have
anything but sympathy for him at that moment.

It took the embittered old man forty-eight hours of solitude
in his forest retreat to regain a semblance of his normal composure.
His anger, however, remained unabated. Peremptorily, he
ordered his whole Cabinet to drive the 200 miles from Bonn
to his sanatorium. For international propaganda purposes he was
anxious to show a broad front. They merely gave their assent to
what he had already decided, that he was now strong enough to
ignore France.

After the Cabinet meeting a statement was issued that was to
mark a turning-point in Adenauer's foreign policy for the next
half-dozen years. In the hours between the rejection of the E.D.C.
Treaty and the Cabinet meeting he had received new assurances
from his friend and ally, Mr. Dulles.

Adenauer announced, therefore, that his Government would
try and restore the seriously prejudiced international situation
*by immediate negotiations with the American and British Govern-
ments.* With authoritarianism now extended to the international
field, in his fury he had decided to ignore the French. Fortified
by Mr. Dulles's messages, he decided to ignore the veto
right, still technically held by the French as the third Occupation
Power.

That statement signified much more than it said. It marked
Adenauer's abandonment, for several years, of his lifelong ambition to achieve a Franco-German reconciliation. From that point
the Bonn-Washington alliance became the corner-stone of
Adenauer's policies. For the next half-dozen years, until the
advent of the Kennedy régime, he would be America's most
trusted ally in the Cold War.

Two days after issuing his statement of policy he amplified
his views. With great skill, he chose the London *Times* as his
medium. Under the mellowing influence of Sir Winston Churchill

his Anglophobia had become somewhat muted, and Adenauer was astute enough to appreciate that Britain might well hold the decisive role among the three Occupation Powers in the following few months.

'There is no question now of isolating France,' he told a correspondent of *The Times*. 'For France has isolated herself from Europe and the United States.'

'The goodwill which Germany has shown since the war, and the German desire to go forward in friendship and fellowship with France has been disappointed,' he continued. 'The Germans are now saying that Adenauer has negotiated with Schuman just as Stresemann negotiated with Briand,' he added, blaming the French for any renewed ultra-nationalism which might appear as a consequence. 'Must we Germans now assume, therefore, that the French do not wish for understanding between our two countries?'

In Western Germany, where Adenauer's entire prestige had been built up on his apparent success in extorting major concessions from the Western Powers, coupled with his European policies, his stock slumped badly. 'Those weeks,' he admitted in private, 'after the French rejection of the E.D.C. Treaty were among the most anxious of my life.'

However much his prestige did fall, Adenauer in the next few weeks, in private correspondence with Washington and London, persistently exaggerated the weakness of his position. The crafty old politician realized that the weaker the Americans and Britain believed his position, the greater would be the concessions he could wheedle out of them. In the weeks immediately after the French rejection of the European army he exploited this device with superb skill.

Adenauer suggested to the Governments in Washington and London that restrictions on German sovereignty contained in the Bonn Treaty signed more than two years previously were, by this time, anachronisms. Both Governments were inclined to agree in the prevailing international atmosphere. For the E.D.C. dèbâcle in Paris had produced serious concern in London, and something approaching near-hysteria in Washington.

The Americans had believed for so long that some time or other France would eventually ratify the E.D.C. Treaty, that the vote of the French Chamber left the American Government without a policy; just as de Gaulle's rebuff of Britain and America did again at the beginning of 1963.

After a week of numbed silence the State Department and Pentagon planners plunged into that 'agonizing reappraisal' with which Dulles had threatened France some time earlier. The Secretary of State and his Pentagon friends fluctuated from day to day between two diametrically opposed policies. One was to withdraw all American forces in Europe to a 'peripheral line'. The second was for a straight German-Anglo-American military alliance without France.

In London there was a more sober approach to the problem. The British had never concealed their dislike of E.D.C. with its complicated supra-national secretariat, council and Parliament based on the Adenauer-Schuman concept of a neo-Carolingian Reich in the form of 'Little Europe'. Successive British ministers had accepted the E.D.C. idea with misgivings, only because it seemed to be what both France and Germany wanted. For British statesmen, in private, had always been more than a little suspicious of the 'Black Front'. This was almost certainly the real background to the British reluctance to participate in various 'European' developments throughout the fifties. The British approach to the E.D.C. crisis, therefore, was less radical than solutions contemplated in Washington.

The British Government realized that urgent steps must be taken to retrieve the situation. Sir Anthony Eden set out on a surprise tour of the former E.D.C. capitals. He went first to Bonn, where he was effusively greeted by Adenauer who, for the time being, suppressed his lifelong Anglophobia.

The British Foreign Secretary put to Adenauer the essence of the British government plan:

1. That Western Germany be given full independence as soon as possible.

2. That Western Germany be rearmed within a revised and extended Western Union pact, originally signed in 1948 to prevent future German aggression.

3. That German troops in the Western Union alliance should come under the direct command of the American Commander-in-Chief of N.A.T.O. of which Federal Germany would become a member.

Adenauer could not have asked more if he had drawn up the plan himself. To the old man in the depths of despair the British solution seemed like a miracle. He at once told Sir Anthony Eden that he accepted the proposals, but within a few days he was less certain. Mr. Dulles had been at work.

Within a few hours of the departure of the British Foreign Secretary, Mr. Dulles sent to Bonn that doyen of American diplomacy, Mr. Robert Murphy, for long diplomatic adviser to Eisenhower and his successors as Military Governor. Four days later Mr. Dulles himself descended on Bonn. The Secretary of State was never able to see a colleague aloft without himself taking wing. As was so often the case elsewhere, Mr. Dulles in Bonn proved to be a disturbing influence. He confidentially repeated his previous assurances that Germany would be rearmed whatever happened. His solution to the immediate problem had that Dulles diplomatic simplicity which so often proved disconcerting. He merely proposed that the situation should be resolved by 'granting Western Germany complete independence, full point'. She could then re-arm in any way and to any degree that Adenauer wanted. Adenauer was delighted. He almost glowed as he stood at Bonn airport watching the Dulles aircraft disappear.

So elated was Adenauer by the Dulles proposals that he made one of his rare essays at a wisecrack, 'This is further proof, if that is necessary, that the best Europeans are in America.'

His enthusiasm was somewhat damped by reports from Paris of

continued French opposition to German rearmament. He reluctantly turned to the view that the British, after all, might be right and that the Eden plan held most prospect of a solution.

The visits of the British and American Foreign Secretaries had done little to counter the growing disillusionment in Bonn with Adenauer's failure. Not only the Social Democrat opposition, but his Free Democrat allies and some of his own C.D.U. members of the Bundestag, were loud in their criticism. From all sides there was a demand for a Bundestag debate. Parliamentary institutions never meant much to Adenauer; they were unfortunate necessities to be muffled as best could be. In the midst of delicate international negotiations Adenauer had no wish to be embarrassed by Bundestag outpourings. With an authoritarian gesture, he summoned his C.D.U. party managers and forbade the debate. Such was his domination over his sheeplike followers that they did as they were bidden.

Adenauer was determined to have no parliamentary criticism, for he had just received a British invitation to a nine-power conference in London at the end of September. It was, therefore, with a deeply divided German public behind him that he flew to London. It was his first meeting with Mendès-France since the E.D.C. dèbâcle and the stony Brussels meeting, and no diplomatic protocol could conceal Adenauer's deep distaste for the French Prime Minister. The feeling was reciprocated. The first two days of the meeting did little but emphasize Mendès-France's profound suspicion of all things German. Once again the conflicts which had dogged E.D.C. reappeared. The nine-power meeting seemed near stalemate, if not worse. Adenauer again was slumped in despair.

Suddenly, and without any warning, Adenauer was saved. To a completely unprepared and dumbfounded gathering of Western Foreign Ministers, Sir Anthony Eden announced that Britain was prepared 'to take a very formidable step' to save the situation.

Britain was willing, said the British Foreign Secretary, *to guarantee* to keep four B.A.O.R. divisions and the 2nd Tactical

Air Force in Europe *as long as the majority of the Western Union Powers* wished, subject to cases of emergency and the ability to pay for these forces.

Here was the guarantee which successive French Governments of 'good Europeans' had sought in vain. It was no accident that the guarantee was given to the most liberal, Anglophile French Prime Minister of the decade.

The British guarantee did much more, however, than merely resolve the immediate crisis. It was the key to the restoration of German independence, to German rearmament, and the ability of Western Germany to take part in all the European developments of the next few years. Without that guarantee West Germany would have remained an occupied country, and there could have been no European Common Market, something which both Adenauer and that other autocratic Anglophobe, de Gaulle were quick to forget in January, 1963.

The Foreign Ministers, including even the strangely subdued Mr. Dulles, were speechless. It was M. Paul Henri Spaak, the burly Belgian Foreign Minister, who was quickest to appreciate what had happened; which may have been why he toiled so hard to further Britain's entry into the Common Market in the face of French intransigence and Adenauer's scarcely concealed hostility in 1963. Turning to Mendès-France, Spaak almost shouted '*Vous avez gagné* ... You've won!'

None of the other Foreign Ministers realized that the historic British guarantee to participate indefinitely in *European* defence had been taken early that morning at a Cabinet meeting at No. 10 Downing Street after they had all left an official banquet given by Sir Winston Churchill.

There were still difficulties to overcome. But Adenauer, saved at the eleventh hour by the dramatic British intervention, showed his most statesmanlike approach. The French wanted some form of control of Germany's industrial rearmament. Adenauer, with great reasonableness, pointed out that such controls would be difficult to reconcile with German sovereignty. But he made some concessions and agreed that the question of a European Arms pool should be left to a later meeting of the Foreign Ministers in Paris, in October.

When he signed the Western European agreement he made an important concession. He promised that Western Germany, in return for all she had been given, would honour the *defensive* character of N.A.T.O.; he guaranteed that the Bonn Republic would never attempt to recover the German territory in the East or to change its boundaries *by force of arms*.

He also signed an undertaking that *Germany would not manufacture atomic, biological or chemical weapons*.

The details of the agreement and the difficult problem of the Saar were left to the next meeting of the Foreign Ministers in Paris, at the N.A.T.O. Council meeting a fortnight later.

Adenauer knew that he had been saved by his old enemies, the British. When, two days later, he reported to the Bundestag he was, for once, almost rhapsodic in his praise of Britain.

The British guarantee, he said, would go down to history as a revolutionary monument to British statesmanship. It was a far cry from the first election campaign of 1949 and 'The British are the enemies now'. It was even farther to the black January day in 1963 when some practical demonstration of that gratitude which he so effusively expressed in 1954 might well have countered the more extreme manifestations of Gaullist megalomania.

When Adenauer and the other N.A.T.O. Foreign Ministers met in Paris a fortnight later, the only outstanding problem between France and Germany was the future of the Saar. The French were determined to legalize, so far as possible, the *fait accompli* of the immediate post-war years when the Saar had been integrated into the French economy. The Germans stuck to their classic slogan *Deutsch ist die Saar*. (The Saar is German).

After years of fruitless negotiation, Adenauer believed that both sides must make concessions. But Mendès-France realized that Adenauer was literally desperate, after all the delays, to achieve both independence and German rearmament. So he outfoxed

'The Old Fox'. He produced his trump card – no French ratification of sovereignty, rearmament or anything else without complete agreement over the Saar.

The situation became even more tense. Once again the British
intervened. After a banquet at the British Embassy, Sir Anthony
Eden thrust the two contending leaders, like a pair of fighting
cocks, into the drawing-room of the Embassy and urged them to
make a deal. With the British Foreign Minister and the British
Ambassador standing outside the door, they remained arguing
until three o'clock in the morning. When they emerged they
announced that 'considerable progress has been made'. But at
what price? Cornered by the French, Adenauer, as had happened
before and would happen again in moments of crisis, decided to
follow an undemocratic if not unconstitutional line.

Because he had wished, for once, to have the whole of Western
Germany behind him, Adenauer had summoned to Paris the
leaders of all the main Parliamentary groups. They had reached
broad agreement on German policy in the Saar question. They
were not prepared to make major concessions.

Faced by Mendès-France in the British Embassy drawing-
room, however, Adenauer in a moment abandoned all his democratic good intentions, and made a decision in direct opposition to
the views of his Cabinet, his coalition, and his party, not to say
anything of the parliamentary opposition. He capitulated completely to Mendès-France – or so it seemed at the time. He
accepted the French proposals:

1. That the Saar basin be 'Europeanized' and that a neutral
Saar Commissioner be appointed.

2. That there should be a Saar plebiscite giving the 1,000,000
Saarlanders the right to opt for or against 'Europeanization',
but giving them no right to express any desire for re-unification
with Germany. In return, he obtained French agreement that
the hitherto banned German parties in the Saar should be free
to carry on political agitation.

That Adenauer was authoritarian in making that agreement with Mendès-France is beyond dispute; that he was as naïve as his opponents alleged at the time and gave in as supinely as even some of his supporters believed, is open to some doubt.

Adenauer knew his Germans; and the Saarlanders were German to a man. Almost certainly, the astute political veteran suspected that the plebiscite would be converted into a massive pro-German vote. And with the German political parties free to carry on the agitation for which they had proved their genius in the thirties, he must have guessed that the incorporation of the Saar into Western Germany could only be temporarily delayed. That analysis of the situation, if these were his thoughts, was to be justified. In due time the Saarlanders returned to Germany.

In retrospect, Adenauer may be given the credit for having had more political vision than his critics. And there is no doubt that his authoritarian actions were largely motivated by his desire to obtain French agreement to German independence and his country's rearmament.

At the time, however, Adenauer's single-handed settlement of the Saar problem was seen for what it was, the act of a self-willed, self-opinionated political authoritarian. He had not time to get back to Bonn before his outspoken, and not always tactful, ex-minister, Dr. Dehler, opened the Free Democratic attack.

'Adenauer's method of signing agreements without informing a single member of his Cabinet is not the way to take decisions of such far-reaching significance,' said Dehler. And another prominent Free Democrat Liberal from south Germany, Dr. Reinhold Maier, an Adenauer enemy from Weimar days, stated with great justice that Adenauer's concessions to France went far beyond the decisions of the German Parliament and the agreement on the subject made between the parties in the Adenauer coalition. Dr. Maier suggested that Adenauer had traded 1,000,000 Germans for a mess of potage, 'a most dubious political document'. That was the beginning of the campaign, in which the Social Democrats joined, against what in Bonn was known as 'Adenauer's Saar Sell-Out'. The criticism was well justified and to foreign observers it proved healthy evidence that the tender plant of German democracy still flourished in the midst of the Adenauer authoritarian flood.

Adenauer's decision to take upon himself, in the face of the diametrically opposed all-party advice which he had sought, the settlement of the Saar problem seemed to smack more than a little of the methods of Adolf Hitler. His attitude was, 'I know what's best for the Germans.' That remained his attitude for so long as he was Chancellor. Hitler thought the same, with consequences to Germany which may survive for generations. The only difference was that, while the method was the same, Hitler was diabolically-motivated and Adenauer paternally inclined.

But no one who watched the political development of Adenauer as Federal Chancellor could ever visualize the old man echoing to the Bundestag the historic words of Churchill at successive crises of the War, 'I am the servant of this House . . . you have the right to dismiss me when you please.'

The attack on the Adenauer autocracy was resumed when, towards the end of the year, the first reading of the new treaties came before the Bundestag. To the onslaught on his personal dictatorial methods of government was added the taunt that he had sacrificed the re-unification of Germany for an agreement with the West.

So bitter was the feeling against him that, for the first time in the history of the Bundestag, he was shouted down by the enraged opposition and some of his nominal supporters among the Free Democrats. It was nearly a quarter of an hour before order could be restored. Adenauer strode from the House, tight lipped and pale, to marshal his parties and to 'persuade' his turbulent allies with the personal files which Dr. Globke had already begun to collect. He was worried, nevertheless. Soon afterwards he announced that as soon as the London-Paris agreements were ratified, he would lay down the post of Foreign Minister. No one took him seriously. Everyone was well aware that a nominal change at the top of the Foreign Ministry would connote nothing, and so it proved when, in due season, he appointed Dr. Heinrich von Brentano as his 'personal assistant' in the Foreign Office, with the title of West German Foreign Minister. At the same time, he announced that as soon as the treaties were ratified, one of his main tasks would be 'to start negotiations with the East'.

His critics were unappeased. The onslaught on Adenauer was resumed when he literally man-handled the second and third readings of the Ratification Bill through the Bonn Parliament during an almost non-stop marathon week-end sitting. The members of the Bundestag wanted to go home. But the master cracked the whip and they duly remained to perform, to the delight of millions of TV viewers who watched the whole performances throughout Saturday and Sunday. And there was something to see.

The anti-Adenauer attack reached its climax in a slanging match across the floor of the house between Adenauer and Dr. Dehler. Dehler's bitter and wounding criticism was more than a manifestation of his personal venom against the Chancellor. There was a deep cleft in the coalition Government. Of the four Free Democratic ministers in the Government only the rather ineffectual Dr. Blucher, the Vice-Chancellor, who was completely under Adenauer's thumb, voted for the Government. Two other F.D.P. ministers abstained. One quite openly voted against the policy of the Government of which he was a member. That was not all. When the Saar clause was considered, one of Adenauer's own C.D.U. ministers abstained. He was the able and distinguished Jakob Kaiser, a survivor of the 1944 Bomb Plot against Hitler and Adenauer's one-time rival for the party leadership. He never made much effort to conceal his distaste for Adenauer. And, as Minister for Saar Affairs, he felt in honour bound to abstain.

In any normal democratic country the abstention of ministers on major issues of policy could only have led to the resignation of those concerned and the formation of a new Government under Adenauer or probably some less controversial figure. In fact, only one minister did offer to resign, the unfortunate Dr. Blucher, on the grounds, apparently, that he had voted for the policy of the Cabinet of which he was a member.

Adenauer did not care which of his ministers voted against him. As he had told the American High Commissioner years before, his ministers were negligible factors. He had achieved what he had set out to do and secured the ratification of the London-Paris agreements. His indifference to his ministers, which often verged on contempt, was so great that he did not even ask them to resign!

During these weeks Adenauer had one bad moment. Just before Christmas, 1954, the French Chamber rejected the ratification of the Paris agreement, just as it had done to the E.D.C. Treaty a few months earlier. The Federal Chancellor spent a most unhappy Christmas. But unlike other French politicians with whom Adenauer negotiated, M. Mendès-France once again proved that he was a man of his word. Having made a deal with Adenauer, he stuck to it. He gave the French Parliament a second chance, and in due course France ratified the agreements. The process was completed at the end of March, 1955, by the French Senate.

The last great obstacle to Adenauer's dream of German independence and a new army had gone. The United States quickly completed the ratification process. They were followed by the smaller European members of the Western Union which had awaited the French decision.

Finally, on 5th May, 1955 the three Western Occupation Powers formally lodged their instruments of ratification in Bonn. It was a great day for Adenauer. He seemed to weep as the Western Ambassadors formally handed over the ratification documents to him. At last he was head of a sovereign Government, recognized by the free world as the only legitimate Government of Germany.

The seal was set on his success a few days later when he took his seat for the first time at a meeting of the N.A.T.O. Council in Paris. And, as some sort of curious acknowledgement to the part which the British had played in his success, Adenauer wore the N.A.T.O. 'old school tie'.

CHAPTER THIRTEEN

Visit to Moscow

ADENAUER REACHED the climax of his long years as Federal German Chancellor at the beginning of May, 1955. At home and beyond he was applauded and acclaimed as a world statesman. He deserved the praise, but never again would he achieve such general approbation. He had restored freedom to 50,000,000 Germans. He had transformed the rump of the Reich into an equal partner and a trusted ally of the Western Powers for years to come. It was a considerable achievement, and the Adenauer legend was firmly established.

The Chancellor had shown great tenacity and not a little diplomatic skill in achieving his success. But amid the applause and the adulation, there was a tendency to ignore fundamental facts. Adenauer owed most to the policies of the Soviet Union in the decade which followed the Potsdam conference. The Russians were always his best friends. For Adenauer and the West Germans were always the main beneficiaries of the Cold War. Adenauer himself never doubted that, however much he may have averred to the contrary. In the years that followed the restoration of German freedom he was to prove the most rigid and uncompromising exponent of that Cold War.

By a paradox of international politics Adenauer, at that very moment when he had firmly integrated Western Germany into the Western alliance, was swamped by a flood of wishful thinking on German re-unification. As Western Germany's integration into the Western Alliance had become imminent in the spring of 1955, governments on both sides of the Iron Curtain recognized that a turning-point had been reached in post-war European history. Statesmen in Moscow and the Western capitals shared the view that radical changes of policy must follow. And, in the weeks just before West Germany attained sovereignty, discreet diplomatic soundings had begun between East and West.

The moment Adenauer secured independence for his people developments followed in rapid succession:

1. After years of diplomatic stonewalling, the Soviet Union suddenly agreed that Austria, divided between Western and Eastern Occupation Powers since 1945, should become neutral. Within a week or so of Adenauer obtaining his freedom the four Foreign Ministers met in Vienna to sign the long delayed peace treaty. The analogy between the so long divided Austria and the still divided Germany was obvious. Throughout Western Germany and elsewhere voices were raised demanding the settlement of the German problem by means of 'the Austrian solution'.

2. Adenauer was still attending the N.A.T.O. Council meeting in Paris in mid-May when the three Western Powers proposed to the Russians that a Heads of Government meeting should take place, probably in Switzerland, in the following few weeks. And almost at once Marshal Bulganin, who at the time held the post of Soviet Prime Minister, indicated that he favoured such a meeting.

3. The Soviet Government, despite the threats of what would happen if Western Germany was permitted to join N.A.T.O., opened secret negotiations with Bonn through its Paris Embassy, and within a short time a formal invitation was sent to Adenauer to visit Moscow.

Amid such a rush of revolutionary developments it was scarcely surprising that a wave of hope swept through Western Germany that at last some concrete progress might be made towards German re-unification. Whether Adenauer shared these hopes is uncertain. But, as always when the prospect of four-power top-level negotiations in Germany were imminent, he was

assailed with doubts and fears. He had retired again to his Black
Forest sanatorium for a rest, and there he became obsessed once
more with his 'nightmare of Potsdam'. His fears were almost
certainly groundless. Neither Adenauer, nor indeed any other
Western statesman, appreciated the fundamental change that was
taking place in Soviet policy.

Faced with the accomplished fact of a sovereign and free West
Germany inside N.A.T.O., an agonizing reappraisal had clearly
begun in Moscow. The ruling junta in which Mr. Khrushchev was
already the dominating figure, although not Prime Minister,
realized that all hope of re-uniting Germany on terms acceptable
to the Soviet Union had disappeared for years to come. Germany
could only be re-united by sacrificing the East Zone German
puppet government controlled by the faithful Soviet stooge
throughout the years, Walter Ulbricht. And the Russians were
not prepared then, or as long as Adenauer remained Chancellor,
to sacrifice the Ulbricht régime. The Soviet leaders had, therefore,
come to the policy of 'the two Germanies' which would remain
basic Russian policy for a long time to come and throughout the
repeated Berlin crises of future years.

Adenauer, of course, could know nothing of this. And to his
sanatorium at the Buhlerhoehe he summoned his Ambassadors in
London, Washington and Paris, along with Herr von Brentano,
who was about to become Bonn Foreign Minister, and the State
Secretary at the Foreign Office Professor Hallstein, much better
known in later years as President of the European Market
secretariat in Brussels.

Adenauer was alarmed that the Western Powers, in the wake of
the successful negotiation of the Austrian peace treaty, would be
prepared to settle the German problem in the same way. As his
advisers met, his obsessional fears were again lulled by a personal
message from Dulles and assurances from London and Paris.
Under no circumstances, said the U.S. Secretary of State, could a
policy of neutralization apply to Germany.

From his Black Forest retreat, Adenauer made known that he

would insist on two conditions for any future four-power negotiations on Germany.

There must be no question of the neutralization of Germany.

No restrictions must be imposed in advance on the freedom of action of any future German Government.

There must be no discussion of the Paris treaties.

Without knowing anything of the developments of Soviet policy, he had set the seal on the impossibility of attaining German re-unification by negotiation for years to come.

In Bonn, he was at once vigorously attacked by the Social Democratic opposition for the rigidity of his position. Herr Ollenhauer suggested with great truth that Adenauer, in fact, had now adopted 'a programme against re-unification'. He had, but it could not be finally confirmed until the reactions of Bulganin and Khrushchev had been tested.

With the four-power 'Summit' Meeting arranged for the middle of July in Geneva, the Governments in Washington and London tended to show a rather more flexible approach without in any way abandoning basic principles. And Marshal Bulganin, speaking in Warsaw, seemed to show a similar attitude, although he added the significant words that 'The Paris agreements have seriously changed the international situation and confronted peace-loving states with new problems'.

At once Adenauer's almost psychopathic suspicion of Western intentions again came into play. He suspected there might be waverers among his Western allies. By coincidence, he had a long-standing engagement to visit Harvard University. It was with real relief, therefore, that he flew to Washington to be assured that his fears were groundless by his good friends, the President and the Secretary of State. So anxious were the Americans to please, that Adenauer tended to dominate the talks. And the President and Secretary of State were unofficially reported to have been 'delighted at the vigour of his assurances' of his support for the Western Alliance.

Firm agreement was reached on the line to be taken by the

Americans at Geneva on matters affecting Germany. Equally firm agreement was reached on what Adenauer would do if and when he decided to visit Moscow some time after the Summit Meeting.

At a subsequent Press conference and in an address at Harvard, Adenauer gave the answers expected of him by an American public just beginning to recover from the wildest excesses of the McCarthy era. German militarism, he confidently asserted, had disappeared. They need have no fear of the new German army which he was about to organize. There was no thought of achieving German re-unification by force or violence. He rejected any suggestion of re-unification through neutralization. Such a course, he said, would make the Federal Republic eventually into a Soviet satellite which would benefit no one, least of all the Germans in the Eastern Zone. He sounded a warning about the forthcoming negotiations with the Russians. They might last a long time, he said, as much as two years.

In Bonn, the Social Democrats were quick to spot the real motive behind the reference to long years of negotiation. Herr Ollenhauer at once demanded that long drawn out negotiations should not be exploited in order to create a *fait accompli* of a re-armed Germany inside of N.A.T.O. while four-power talks were still going on.

Adenauer's opponents had plumbed the depths of his real approach to four-power negotiations. He was against any talks, at least until he had an army of his own to throw in as a bargaining counter. His tactical approach to the Summit Meeting, therefore, was simple. Let the Russians cool their heels and drag out the four-power negotiations until the first German divisions were in their barracks.

It was surprising how such an acute and analytical observer as Adenauer, like many of his critics in Western countries, had become bemused by the thought of a handful of German divisions. Even accepting the soundness of the Dulles-Adenauer doctrine of 'negotiation from strength', such a policy owed little to the mere irritant of a few German formations, and everything to the American nuclear deterrent delivered by the rapidly developing rocket ironmongery of the United States.

Adenauer's Washington visit had been a resounding success and he was in high spirits as he said good-bye. Asked privately why he thought the Russians had invited him to Moscow, he replied with one of his flashes of ironic humour, 'Ach! probably because they haven't seen a dictator since Stalin's death.'

Back in Bonn, he at last sent a reply to the Soviet invitation. He agreed on negotiations for the establishment of diplomatic, commercial and cultural relations between Moscow and Bonn. But his reply was studiously cool. He did not accept the invitation outright but suggested that the matters under discussion should be further explored by diplomatic exchanges in Paris.

He was much condemned in Germany for this lukewarm approach to the Soviet gesture. But, as always, Adenauer had a purpose behind his tactics. He had begun to appreciate the difficulties which faced him in carrying through the German Parliament the legislation necessary for the remilitarization of Germany. The Social Democrats were already demanding that no parliamentary steps be taken until after the Summit Meeting. The Federal Council, or Bundesrat, was showing equal doubts and hesitations.

Adenauer had no wish to go to Moscow empty-handed. Personally he would probably have preferred not to go at all, or at any rate, not until he had half a dozen divisions in existence. He felt that before he sat down round the table with Bulganin and Khrushchev he must have at least set in motion the machinery for the creation of the new army.

Now, the Summit Meeting at Geneva was imminent. To keep in close personal contact with the diplomatic delegation which he sent to Geneva, he moved his office to a villa in Muerren in the Bernese Oberland. On the eve of the conference came the first indication from Moscow of Soviet policy towards Germany. Moscow radio proposed a European security pact *based on the acceptance of the division of Germany* into two parts. The 'Potsdam nightmare' again dominated his thoughts. But the Western Allies had no intention of negotiating on such a basis. From Washington and London he received categorical guarantees that there would be no four-power agreement on European security *without making German unity a pre-condition*. The Western Governments also assured him that there would be no concessions to the Russians unless they were willing to abandon their control over the Soviet Zone.

In these circumstances, the four-power talks on Germany were a waste of time. From the outset of the Summit Meeting it was clear that there was ostensibly general agreement on the desirability of German unification, but an unbridgeable gap over the means and the timing.

Bulganin and Khrushchev, in private, gave increasing evidence of their distaste for re-unification by free elections. And in his final speech to the Summit Meeting Bulganin publicly confirmed the 'Two Germanies' policy of the Soviet Government by announcing, 'The time is not ripe for German unity.'

The Russians, however, were still not prepared to make an open break. And Bulganin, as technical head of Government, signed an official protocol which stated:

'The Heads of Government, recognizing their common responsibility for the settlement of the German question and re-unification of Germany, have agreed that the settlement of the German question and the re-unification of Germany by means of free elections shall be carried out in the interests of the German people and in the interest of European security.'

From Muerren, Adenauer watched with growing approval the collapse of all question of German re-unification. And he cabled his thanks to his allies. His thanks might better have been directed to the Kremlin. The Russians had again proved to be his best friends.

At the end of the Summit Meeting the four Foreign Ministers were instructed to continue negotiations on the German question.

But when they met again in October, the Western representatives ran into a stone wall. Russia by then had abandoned all pretence of favouring free elections, which inevitably must mean the liquidation of the Ulbricht régime. Molotov openly advocated the 'two Germanies' policy by insisting that re-unification could only be achieved by agreement between the two German Governments. His adamant refusal to budge from that position resulted in complete breakdown. From that point onward Russia demonstrated that the fundamental aim was to maintain her grip on East Germany at all costs. This policy of consolidation reached its culmination in the construction of the Berlin Wall in August, 1961.

Molotov's attitude, which wrecked the Foreign Ministers' Conference in October, was not fortuitous. By that time Khrushchev had written off any chance of a German settlement for years to come. For in the interval Adenauer had been in Moscow.

Early in September Adenauer, accompanied by an impressive delegation which included members of both the Bundestag and Bundesrat Foreign Affairs Committees, had travelled to Moscow. With his customary lack of tact he included in the party the Communist *bête noire*, Dr. Globke.

From the outset, Adenauer fell foul of Khrushchev. At the first plenary session in the Kremlin the Russians made reference to the atrocities committed by the German army in the Soviet Union and to the war criminals still in Soviet hands whose release Adenauer was desperately anxious to secure.

At once Adenauer took umbrage. It was true, he retorted, that many bad things had happened. But it was also true that the Red Army, in striking back had penetrated into Germany and many terrible things had occurred during the Soviet operations on German soil.

Khrushchev sat completely silent until Adenauer had finished only the movements of his fingers showing his anger. Then, with his face beetroot red, the torrent burst out.

'The German Federal Chancellor at the end of his statement has declared that Soviet troops during their advance into Germany were responsible for outrages. I deny that categorically. I consider that an insulting remark.'

Molotov intervened to add coldly, 'Yesterday, the Federal Chancellor told me that he had never seen Hitler but that he would willingly have strangled him with his own hands had they met. We understand the feelings of Herr Adenauer, but he must really appreciate the historical fact that it was our army which freed the German people from Hitlerism and Fascism.'

Stony-faced, Adenauer and the rest of the German delegation listened to the attack sparked off by the Chancellor's tactlessness. Clearly, the Russians would not tolerate the acid comments which the British and Americans had been accustomed to brush aside with a wisecrack. To many of the Germans it seemed that the conference had collapsed before it had begun.

That afternoon, however, when Adenauer again met the Russians in a *dacha* outside Moscow, once the home of Maxim Gorki, the tension eased. And during the week-end which followed, in the country and at the Bolshoi Theatre where Ulanova danced for the visitors, the Soviet leaders played the part of the genial hosts which they always are to distinguished foreign guests. Only Mikoyan was absent. Like Khrushchev, the formidable foreign-trading genius of the Soviet Union had lost a son in the war. He was widely reputed to have opposed the invitation to Adenauer during a meeting of the Soviet *praesidium*. He declined to take any part in the talks, although some years later he had modified that attitude enough to enable him to make an official visit to Bonn.

During these social exchanges Khrushchev formed a strong attachment to Professor Carlo Schmid, the deputy leader of the Social Democratic opposition and a member of the Bundestag Foreign Affairs Committee. Stout and extrovert, like Khrushchev himself, the half-Catalan, half-German scholar could joust and joke with Khrushchev in a way none of the other Germans could. The General Secretary of the Communist Party of the Soviet

Union at once christened the stout jovial professor 'Gospodin Great Germany.' It was a friendship to which Adenauer would owe much in the next few days.

As always on similar international social occasions, Adenauer told his hosts how the British had thrown him out of Cologne in 1945, exactly ten years earlier. And to the astonishment of the Russians he added, 'That was a lucky thing for me or otherwise I would be here.' Khrushchev was silent, but some of those who watched felt he might have had a certain sympathy for the British.

The Russians made an all-out effort to win over the Bonn delegation to the idea of future German-Soviet co-operation and the consequent weakening of ties with the West. They assured Adenauer that the most important thing was for the Germans and Russians to hang together, just as in the good old days of the Ribbentrop-Molotov pact, and farther back, of the Rapallo Treaty. If they did, peace would be assured for ever.

When Adenauer suggested that Germany was no longer as important as she had been and was now a second-class power, Bulganin retorted brusquely, 'Nonsense! You are still a great power.'

The Russians, even without Mikoyan, dangled the bait of future economic co-operation. Khrushchev pointed out that China with its 600,000,000 people had still to be industrialized. 'We cannot do that alone,' he said, 'but together we can. That would guarantee work and food for your people for the next fifty years.'

Adenauer was unimpressed. He had no intention of weakening those links with the West which had brought him such great gains. The Russian flattery and obvious attempt to sound out the possibility of a future German-Soviet alliance were summarily rebuffed. Khrushchev and Bulganin were very much aware of it.

When the conference resumed the following morning in the Kremlin, the two sides were as far apart as ever. Adenauer announced bluntly that there would be no question of establishing diplomatic relations without, at the same time, Soviet agreement to return the still imprisoned Germans and negotiate on the re-unification question.

Khrushchev, who had made it clear that he was the Soviet master, categorically rejected Adenauer's proposals. Briefly and bluntly he said Russia declined to make the establishment of diplomatic relations dependent on any factor whatsoever.

The temperature sank steadily. When the conference broke up for lunch most of the Germans thought it had collapsed. Aden-auer, in the private train which had been sent to Moscow to act as a German headquarters, decided to emulate Disraeli. At the Berlin Conference in 1878 the British Prime Minister won a diplomatic victory by letting it be known that he thought the position hope-less, and ordered his special train from the Prussian State Railways knowing that Bismarck would be immediately informed.

Against the advice of his most favoured confidants, Adenauer decided to try the same trick on Khrushchev. He gave orders that his two Lufthansa Constellations should be ready to leave the following day, twenty-four hours ahead of schedule. Khrushchev, too, had apparently studied the life of Disraeli. When the con-ference resumed, he was even tougher and more unforthcoming than at the forenoon session. He announced that if diplomatic relations were to be established this would mean the immediate exchange of ambassadors. As for the prisoners of war, they were all criminals who had murdered honest Russians. What would the Russian people think if he let such criminals go. That seemed the end.

Suddenly the southern accented voice of Professor Carlo Schmid the only Left-wing member of the delegation, intervened. Turning to Khrushchev he said that as a member of a nation who had committed unspeakable crimes against the Soviet people, it was not easy for him to speak. He was ashamed to plead. But he turned to Khrushchev across the table and said, 'At this moment you must not think only of these duly convicted war criminals, but of their mothers and of their children.'

They should be set free, urged Professor Schmid, not because of justice but because of magnanimity, that magnanimity which had always been one of the virtues of the Russian people. For ten seconds there was complete silence. Khrushchev stared intently at the big German whom he had come to like. Then his face brightened.

'Well spoken, Gospodin Great Germany, well spoken,' said Khrushchev, 'We will discuss the matter further.'

The tension eased, and when the Russians entertained the Germans at a banquet that evening in the St. George's Hall in the Kremlin, Khrushchev was still clearly impressed by Carlo Schmid's eloquent plea.

Adenauer sat between Bulganin and Khrushchev. After a toast in which the Soviet Prime Minister said he was sure everything would work out, Adenauer returned to the question of the 10,000 convicted war criminals whom the Russians agreed were in Soviet captivity.

Suddenly Bulganin turned to him. 'Good,' he told Adenauer, 'I give you my most solemn word of honour that eight days after the establishment of diplomatic relations these men will be on their way home.' And just to make sure of confirmation he leaned across Adenauer and asked 'Nikita, what do *you* think?'

'Yes I agree,' said Khrushchev. 'I also give my word of honour.'

Adenauer was as persistent as always. What about the other Germans who were still in Russia, he asked. At this time some German authorities alleged there were another 100,000. 'I have never heard of them,' said Bulganin. 'Have you, Nikita?' Khrushchev, too, knew nothing about any other Germans. But he was prepared to give his word of honour to send them home if their existence was proved.

When Adenauer reported the verbal undertaking which he had received to his advisers the following morning, there was bitter controversy among the German delegation. The professional diplomats saw that Adenauer was about to suffer a major diplomatic defeat. The Russians were determined to make him crawl, he would have to agree to the establishing of diplomatic relations between Bonn and Moscow without receiving, publicly at least, any *quid pro quo*. And with characteristic Teutonic mistrust they distrusted the Soviet leaders' 'word of honour'.

Adenauer was persuaded to ask Bulganin to put his promise in writing. When, an hour later, Adenauer put this request to the Soviet Prime Minister his reception was frosty in the extreme. The bearded, elegant Bulganin, who could always play the aristocrat with ease, was insulted. His word was his bond. Frigidly he assured Adenauer that his word, and that of Nikita Khrushchev, were as good as all the diplomatic agreements in Molotov's files. He presented an ultimatum. Letters would be exchanged agreeing to the establishment of diplomatic relations and the exchange of ambassadors. No mention of the war criminals would appear in any document. Adenauer could take it or leave it.

Adenauer asked for a further adjournment to consult the rest of the German delegation. At the outset, almost everyone opposed accepting the Soviet terms. Adenauer, however, was adamant. He was certain that he dare not go home empty-handed. There may have been another reason. During a private tête-à-tête Bulganin is alleged to have taunted Adenauer with not being able to accept the Soviet leaders' word of honour, because he must first receive permission from Eisenhower and Dulles. During the heated discussions in the German train, Adenauer turned on his critics and asked truculently, 'What have the Western Powers ever done for German re-unification?' The overriding reason, however, for his attitude was that he knew he *must* secure the release of the 10,000 German P.O.W.'s. At last he had come face to face with the facts of the Cold War. If he wanted something badly enough from the Russians he must pay the price. It was a far cry from the days on the Petersberg when the High Commissioners had leant over backwards to please him.

Adenauer, once again, took a major decision alone against the advice of his closest advisers. He returned to Bulganin and

Khrushchev and grovelled. Adenauer and Bulganin exchanged letters agreeing to the establishment of diplomatic relations between Bonn and Moscow. The letters said this would contribute to the solution of 'the main national problem of the German people, the establishment of a unified, democratic German State'. Adenauer had wished to insert the word 'immediate' before the reference to re-unification. Bulganin was blunt to the point of offence. But for the Paris treaties, 'aimed at integrating Germany into the hostile N.A.T.O. alliance,' the Russians would have agreed to the 'immediate' solution of the German reunification question. In view of what Adenauer had done, certainly not.

There was no reference in the letters to the Russian's verbal pledge to release the 10,000 German prisoners of war.

Adenauer dare not return to Bonn without disclosing that he had secured the release of the German prisoners. Before driving to Moscow airport, Adenauer hastily gave a Press conference at which he revealed the Khrushchev-Bulganin pledge. At the airport it was noticeable that Khrushchev did not appear. He and Adenauer had proved 'mutually incompatible'.

Adenauer flew back to Bonn to be greeted by weeping mothers who kissed his hand in gratitude for obtaining the release of the sons they had not seen for more than ten years. Adenauer was deeply affected. But the deep emotion produced by the release of the prisoners, and Khrushchev and Bulganin kept their bond faithfully, could not conceal the major diplomatic defeat which the German Chancellor had suffered at Khrushchev's hands. That marked the effective end of all chance of German re-unification for so long as Adenauer remained Chancellor. The great opportunity had been lost in the fleeting months of early 1953.

In the years which followed Khrushchev proved just as rigid as Adenauer. It was surprising, however, that so shrewd a tactician as Khrushchev made no real effort to exploit the discovery that, provided the bait was irresistible Adenauer could be forced into a deal against his own inclinations. If Khrushchev in those years before the creation of the Berlin wall had offered sufficiently attractive terms on German re-unification, Adenauer might well have had to face the painful choice of a reunited Germany or the Western Alliance. But the Russians were saddled with Ulbricht and his hopeless, bankrupt, so-called German Democratic Republic. The German situation would remain frozen until both Ulbricht and Adenauer disappeared from the German political stage.

Adenauer's deal in Moscow scarcely caused wild enthusiasm in the Western capitals. It was generally agreed that he had been forced into a corner and surrendered more than he had ever contemplated before leaving Bonn. And when he made his report to the Bundestag a few days later, Adenauer went out of his way to reaffirm his ties to the West after referring to critical reports from London, Washington and Paris.

Adenauer was not above exploiting for his own ends the disarray which he had caused in the Western camp. Soon after his return one of the more nationalist members of his Government said, 'What has happened has shaken confidence in us. It has been a terrible shock to the Americans.' 'Excellent,' said Adenauer, grinning, 'We have been tied to the apron strings of our American nurse too long. Now it is the nurse's turn to follow. At the Geneva conference we were trembling all the time lest the West did a deal at our expense. Now it is their turn to tremble.' Whatever he really did think Adenauer, as tortuous as ever, made certain that this conversation duly reached the Western embassies in Bonn.

Adenauer, by this time within a few weeks of his eightieth birthday, had been physically and morally exhausted by his first experience of Soviet *Realpolitik* in Moscow. The inevitable happened. After rioting, incited by the now uninhibited German parties in the Saar, had broken out Adenauer travelled to Luxembourg to meet the French Prime Minister, M. Fauré to discuss the forthcoming Saar referendum. Wearing only a thin raincoat, he sat shivering as his limousine twisted through the Eifel Hills. By the time he got back to Bonn he had bronchitis. Within a few days the old man was suffering from a serious attack of pneumonia. Like Churchill in similar circumstances, Adenauer was a bad patient. Irritable and impatient, he insisted he was the only one who could rule Germany. So ingrained by this time was his own individual development of Bismarckian personal rule that, even with his temperature at 102, he continued to govern from his sick bed.

He saw no one but his doctor and Dr. Globke, who commuted almost daily between the Chancellery in Bonn and the Adenauer private residence at Rhoendorf, on the other side of the Rhine.

For three weeks no one but the very doubtful ex-official of the Nazi Ministry of the Interior knew what decisions had been taken by the old man in bed. Smug, bespectacled, tubby Dr. Globke, although a civil servant, was for all practical purposes German Vice-Chancellor in contrast to the official incumbent, the Free Democrat Dr. Bluecher, whom Adenauer treated with good-natured contempt. For by the autumn of 1955 Globke had succeeded in seizing personal control of all the main functions of Adenauer's office.

The dominating position of the highly equivocal Secretary of State had begun to arouse concern in some Western capitals. At least one intelligence service was given the mission of investigating how much influence Globke exercised, and would continue to exercise as long as his autocratic master was the Federal Chancellor.

Discreet inquiries established that Globke had succeeded in concentrating into his own hands:

1. Control of all documents intended for Adenauer – on which he minuted his own opinion before passing them to the Chancellor for decision.
2. Co-ordination of all propaganda and information through the medium of the Federal Press and Information Office which formed part of the Federal Chancellery.
3. As secretary of the Cabinet, preparation of the agenda for all

Cabinet meetings and the co-ordination of all projects from the various Bonn ministries which required Cabinet, or more correctly, Adenauer's approval.

To these Globke, in the months just before Adenauer's illness, had added even more significant functions. He was the main channel of communication between Adenauer and the virtual head of the new German army, Hitler's ex-chief of operations, General Heusinger with whom Globke had been interned after the war.

More serious perhaps, Globke had recently become co-ordinator of all the West German Secret Services. As such, he was Adenauer's main link with the mysterious Gehlen organization, the fabulous secret service set up by the Americans after the war under the mysterious General Reinhard Gehlen, the wartime head of Foreign Armies East intelligence organization, who had handed over to the Americans the former German army spy networks in Soviet Russia and Eastern Europe largely intact. In the intervening years the Americans had spent truly fabulous amounts on the Gehlen organization. And in the months just prior to Adenauer's illness the Gehlen Secret Service, officially at least, had been handed over to the control of the Bonn Government.

It was from the Globke co-ordinated Secret Services that Adenauer drew much of that secret information on leading political and public figures in Western Germany filed in the Chancellery *Panzerschrank* – armour-plated safe. In the best traditions of Himmler and Heydrich, these secret files were the key to Adenauer's iron control over West German political affairs for nearly a decade and a half. For the contents of the *Panzerschrank* were ruthlessly used to 'persuade' any who might tend to oppose what Adenauer knew was best for Federal Germany.

Much of this was known to leading politicians in Bonn, and above all to the Free Democratic members of the Adenauer coalition which had four ministers in the Government. As

Adenauer's illness dragged on for week after week, alarm steadily rose. The Adenauer-Globke combination, which had concentrated almost all power into their own hands, came under increasing open attack. At the end of October, after Adenauer had been in bed three weeks and no one had any idea what was going on, the Social Democrats expressed what almost everyone felt, 'Globke bears no parliamentary responsibility and does not even possess the confidence of the Government coalition, far less the opposition.' They demanded what would have taken place weeks before in any truly democratic country, that Adenauer should delegate his powers either to the Vice Chancellor, Bluecher, or to a Cabinet Commission.

One very distinguished German Liberal shared these views. The day after the Socialist attack Adenauer had his first official sick visitor. The Federal President, whose powers regrettably were severely curtailed under the Bonn constitution, called at Adenauer's Rhoendorf home. He carried gifts to the sick Chancellor. But officials admitted that the two men discussed political affairs. Professor Heuss's devotion to true democracy and the German public good were so well known that there was no doubt that the President had spoken very frankly to the Chancellor.

The visit of the President at once unleashed a wave of speculation about the possibility of Adenauer's retiring. These hopes proved premature by nearly a decade. There were even discreet conversations between some of Adenauer's dissident followers and the Social Democratic opposition about forming a 'large coalition'. But for the constructive 'no confidence' clause in the Bonn agreement, Adenauer might very well have been swept from office in these last weeks of 1955. For on all sides, including among his own supporters, it was felt that the Adenauer personality cult was becoming intolerable.

Adenauer took the President's hint. In the following fortnight he saw a number of his ministers. And by the second half of November he was back in the Federal Chancellery ruthlessly disciplining by ways best known to himself the waverers among his own supporters. He even rebuked one minister who called on him with shoes showing rather less than a barrack room polish.

The growing anti-Adenauer rebellion was pushed underground for his eightieth birthday at the start of January 1956. For four days the occasion was somewhat hypocritically celebrated with all that Teutonic pomp and ceremony which by this time had become a Bonn tradition. For Adenauer the key feature was the first appearance of his new German army, in the form of the Bundeswehr military band, which serenaded him on the morrow of his eighty-first year. The celebration, however, merely papered over the cracks in his coalition.

In February the crisis broke. In the Ruhr province the Free Democrats were led by a group of 'young Turks' who had been manifesting an ever-growing distaste for the Adenauer authoritarianism for some time. They were particularly opposed to the acquiescent attitude of the Free Democrat ministers in the coalition in Bonn. For nine years the Free Democrats had been part of the right wing coalition in North Rhine-Westphalia headed by the much respected and often Adenauer-hostile Dr. Karl Arnold of the C.D.U.

In the first week of February the Free Democrats withdrew their support from Dr. Arnold who, all too clearly, was being martyred for Adenauer. Ten days later the Free Democrats, who were far from radical, joined the Social Democrats in forming a new government in North Rhine-Westphalia under a Social Democrat Minister-President.

The F.D.P. in Düsseldorf, taking the offensive, announced that the alliance with the S.P.D. had been formed 'to save the nation from Adenauer's authoritarianism and his efforts to establish a one-man party government'. But there were still four Free Democratic Ministers in the Adenauer Government in Bonn. Adenauer was livid. The vassals were in revolt. That same evening, in the Bonn Press Club, he asked truculently how the F.D.P. could remain in his coalition in Bonn and be

against his C.D.U. party in Düsseldorf, fifty miles down the
Rhine.

Adenauer's democratic dictatorship and his insufferable conduct towards his political subordinates had now become a matter
of international comment.

The *Manchester Guardian* correspondent, probably the best
informed Western observer in Bonn, explained the crisis by stating that there was a fear that Adenauer was developing increasing
authoritarianism and had surrounded himself with unsuitable
advisers.

'In intellectual and industrial circles there is a surprising degree
of resentment against Adenauer and his circle of "Catholic
janissaries!" . . . the Chancellor's principal confidant is Herr
Globke, a man with a dubious political past.'

The leader writer of the London *Times*, which at no time was
deluded by the American-propagated Adenauer legend, was even
more pointed; 'Dr. Adenauer is, by all accounts, becoming
personally more overbearing.'

Adenauer never took kindly to criticism, and more particularly
from what he called 'the island'. Determined to restore his
crumbling authority, he forced a showdown with the Free
Democrats. At the end of February the Free Democrat executive
withdrew, after seven years, from the coalition. An official statement justly said that 'Adenauer's methods of leadership' were
responsible for the break.

But despite the break up of the coalition, the four Free Democrat ministers and a handful of their supporters remained in the
Bonn Government – devotees of the Adenauer personality cult.
Office, with its dignities and its emoluments, frequently triumphs
over principle in the German political jungle. But that was not the
last showdown between Adenauer and the F.D.P. over his
authoritarian methods of government, as was to be proved in the
notorious *Spiegel* affair in the autumn of 1962.

Dr. Dehler, the Free Democratic party chairman, was not
finished with Adenauer. At the annual conference of the party in

mid-April, 1956, he launched the fiercest debunking attack on Adenauer hitherto made in the history of the Federal Republic.

No party had shown more willingness than the F.D.P. in co-operating in the coalition said Dehler. But Adenauer had refused to discuss with them even the most fundamental policy decision. The concealment of important facts and the release of half-truths, treatment from which the German opposition had suffered since 1949, had been increasingly extended to Adenauer's Free Democratic allies. That was what had broken up the coalition.

In a two hours' onslaught Dehler listed the major German policy decisions which Adenauer had taken without reference to either his Cabinet or his Parliament.

1. His decision to rearm Germany in 1950.
2. The Israeli compensation treaty.
3. The Saar Agreement.

Dehler also revealed that Adenauer in his Cabinet meetings would never give a straight answer as to whether or not he had promised to raise 500,000 German troops under the London-Paris agreements. He had still not raised that number in his last months of office in 1963.

Dehler then openly stated that Adenauer, in the months after Stalin's death, had permitted the chance of German re-unification to be lost. He reported that Adenauer, before leaving for Moscow the previous autumn, had assured his Cabinet that he would *not* agree to the establishment of diplomatic relations with the Soviet Union.

With a taunting reference to Khrushchev's famous de-Stalinization speech at the Russian Communist Party's twentieth party congress a few weeks earlier, Dehler summed up by commenting, 'Even in the Bolshevik world idol worship has been done away with.'

The anti-Adenauer campaign was not confined to the disgruntled Free Democrats. It extended right into his own party. At the C.D.U. party conference a few days later, at the end of

April, Adenauer suffered an open rebuff. There had been keen resentment among C.D.U. members in North Rhine-Westphalia over the 'martyrdom' of Dr. Arnold. For the first time in the history of the C.D.U. since 1949, Adenauer was defeated by his own party.

With an obvious hint to the Chancellor that the time was coming for him to retire and get out, the party elected no less than four vice-chairmen, including Dr. Arnold. All of them were aspirants to the Adenauer succession. One of the 'Catholic janissaries', on learning of the anti-Adenauer move, was so outraged that he spontaneously denounced the adverse vote as 'high treason'. He need have had no fear. The would-be Adenauer successors would have to wait a very long time.

Long before the party conference at which he took such a beating the 80-year-old Chancellor, still suffering from the after effects of his illness the previous autumn, had been forced to retire for further convalescence to Ascona on the Swiss shore of Lake Maggiore. It was there that he summoned an emergency meeting of his foreign policy advisers, following a statement made by the French Socialist Prime Minister, M. Guy Mollet, on his return from a visit to the Kremlin. M. Mollet indicated that after a long conversation with Khrushchev, he was certain that the whole question of German re-unification should be quietly buried until European and world disarmament had taken place. Khrushchev had told the French leader, without prevarication, that the Soviet Union preferred 17,000,000 East Germans within the Communist orbit to even a unified and neutral Germany.

Adenauer had no difference with Khrushchev on that score. But once again he suspected that the Western Powers, urged on by the French left wing, were contemplating a deal with Khrushchev behind his back. The 'Yalta and Potsdam' nightmares once again obsessed him. He was even more alarmed, at the beginning of May, when Khrushchev and Bulganin visited London.

From the garbled accounts of what Khrushchev was alleged to have said in London, it seemed that the Russians were threatening the West with a new Rapallo; or with a refurbished version of the Ribbentrop-Molotov pact, with Adenauer in the role of the Nazi Foreign Minister, against the West.

Adenauer was appalled at the thought. After the humiliations he had suffered at the hands of Khrushchev, a few months earlier, he had no desire to enter into further negotiations with the Kremlin. But whatever the contradictory versions of the new Soviet line, it seemed certain that Khrushchev was in a more conciliatory mood. Worse, the Russian desire for negotiation was being taken seriously, in London, Paris, and worst of all Washington. Adenauer's whole Cold War strategy was in danger.

Hastily, he sent his Foreign Minister, von Brentano, to tell the Foreign Press Association in Bonn that a separate deal with the Russians was out of the question.

'No German government,' said von Brentano, 'could contemplate a secret agreement with the Soviet Union at the expense of the West. We do not want bilateral agreements with the Soviet Union which would take us even one step beyond the obligations we have entered into with our Western allies.'

Still obsessed by grave fears and faced with a gathering crisis over his Conscription Bill for the new German army, Adenauer, early in June, departed for the more salubrious atmosphere of the United States.

President Eisenhower was in hospital, but all Adenauer's misgivings were removed by the unequivocal language of Mr. Dulles. American diplomats had the impression that Adenauer was by this time a more determined advocate of the Cold War than even the indefatigable Mr. Dulles with his periodic bouts of 'brinkmanship'. And if Adenauer was reassured by Dulles, the Secretary of State was certainly fortified in his basic beliefs by the Federal Chancellor.

The official announcement after the Adenauer-Dulles talks was the most uncompromising document to come from the State Department for some time.

No faith could be placed in the Kremlin's new line, said the announcement, until the Soviet leaders took action, in accordance with the four-power agreement, reached at the previous year's Summit, to end the 'brutal and unnatural division' imposed by the Russians on Germany.

Adenauer went out of his way to underline the American-German Cold War strategy when he spoke next day at Yale University.

The West, must not relax its vigilance for one moment, he warned, in face of the apparently more friendly attitude of the Soviet Union.

'Present Russian tactics are more dangerous than the former aggressive conduct of the Soviet leaders,' he added. 'The men in the Kremlin are not prepared to remove the main causes of world tension.' In ever more flattering references to the United States, Adenauer went on to say that a free Germany was essential for the integration of Europe, which in turn was essential to the freedom of the United States.

'America's fate,' he continued, 'is inseparably linked with the fate of Germany and Europe.'

In the eyes of Mr. Dulles the German alliance had replaced the traditional 'special relationship' with the British. Adenauer returned to Bonn well satisfied.

CHAPTER FOURTEEN

Election Ahead!

IN THE LATE summer and autumn of 1956, for the first time since he became Chancellor, Adenauer was reduced to the role of an international cypher. He did not take kindly to the change. These months were dominated by the Suez crisis, the Polish rising, and the tragic Hungarian revolt which followed. To these great events Adenauer's contribution was negligible but characteristically tactless.

At the height of the Polish crisis, when Poland seemed within an ace of becoming a Titoist state, Adenauer chose the moment for a singularly unfortunate intervention. With an eye to the millions of German refugees, whom he knew would be a key factor in the German general election twelve months ahead, Adenauer truculently announced that the day would come when these expellees would return to their homes, east of the Oder-Neisse line. That was the area of East Germany which the Poles, with Russian support, had occupied since 1945. Anything more likely to drive the Poles back into the arms of the Russians would have been difficult to conceive.

Ossified in his lifelong hatred of Socialism, Adenauer completely failed to appreciate what was taking place in Warsaw. He announced that he would not enter into negotiations with Gomulka, although he was willing to negotiate with a 'free Polish Government'. To the Rhineland ex-Oberbürgermeister no doubt it never occurred that, but for his own 'sabotage' of German re-unification in 1953, and the almost inevitable withdrawal of Soviet troops from East Germany and from their lines of communication from Poland which would have followed,

Poland might well have been able to throw off Soviet suzerainty in 1956.

His contribution to the Suez crisis was equally gauche. Germany, as a maritime power using the Suez Canal, took part in the London negotiations during the summer. The Bonn Foreign Minister, von Brentano, as on other occasions, faithfully echoed the zig-zag utterances of Mr. Dulles. Fortified by a combination of his traditional anglophobia and the Dulles alliance, Adenauer bitterly opposed the Anglo-French intervention. His mouthpiece, Herr Felix von Eckardt, attacked the British-French landings at Port Said. When eventually the cease fire took place, Adenauer returned to Bonn triumphantly claiming that he had played a crucial role in Paris in bringing the operations to an end.

At home his activities were equally muted. The only noteworthy event was the resignation from his Cabinet of the four Free Democrat 'deserters' who, after breaking with their own party, had clung to office as Adenauer ministerial sycophants. In the subsequent reshuffle Adenauer appointed as German Defence Minister a boorish, bellicose young Bavarian named Franz Josef Strauss who was at this time the Chancellor's blue-eyed boy. On more than one occasion in the half-dozen years before Strauss was at last forced from office for his part in the *Spiegel* affair in the autumn of 1962, Adenauer may well have regretted the appointment of the minister who progressed from one *contretemps* to another.

In January, 1957, the Saar basin at last was re-united with Germany, and Adenauer travelled to Saarbrücken to take part in the official ceremonies. His reception was cool. The Saarlanders had not forgotten his bargain with Mendès-France by which the Saar would have been 'Europeanized' instead of integrated into the Federal Republic. As his special train moved into the Saar, his welcome was modest and when he appeared outside Saarbrücken station, some of the noises from the crowd, if not openly hostile, were certainly less than respectful.

The return of the Saar to the Fatherland, which Adenauer in the previous year or two had done little to assist, was an event of historical importance, he admitted. He revealed his true interest, however, when he expressed satisfaction that the 'problem which had poisoned Franco-German relations for eleven years' had been solved. He ended by stating that he had not yet given up hope that some solution on a similar basis might be possible in the East.

That hint may well have been the reason for a letter which he received a few weeks later from Bulganin. After making the usual propaganda attack on the new Bundeswehr, the Russian Note, which seemed to owe a good deal to Mikoyan, suggested that Russia and Western Germany might well develop advantageous economic relations.

The Federal Republic, continued Bulganin, might look forward to large and favourable orders from the Soviet Union. Trade could provide a solid foundation for an improvement in political relations. That, in turn, might facilitate the re-unification of Germany. Events showed, continued the Soviet Note, that a solution of the German problem could be achieved only through a *rapprochement* between West and East Germany. In any such development the Soviet Union would be pleased to provide its good offices. The time had come for both Germany and the Soviet Union to take definite steps in this direction. Certain immediate questions, suggested Bulganin, should be discussed while European security might also be considered.

Soviet intentions in such an event are always difficult, if not impossible, to fathom. Adenauer rejected out of hand Bulganin's contention that there were two Germanies and that they must come together to discuss German re-unification. He had no wish for German re-unification except on the completely impossible terms demanded by himself and his *alter ego*, Dulles. For the Adenauer-Dulles 'Do nothing' policy, which in later years would have such tragic consequences for the 17,000,000 East Germans and the people of East Berlin, was by this time deep frozen. Adenauer would do nothing to ameliorate the Cold War, to which he owed so much.

Trade was another matter. The Federal Chancellor was passing more and more under the influence of various West German pressure groups. Political principles were not permitted to extend to economic fields. In an official reply to Bulganin, at the end of February, Adenauer proposed that trade talks between West Germany and the Soviet Union should begin at an early date. He assured the Russians that he was willing to make a sincere effort to improve relations. But, in the next sentence, he showed his real intentions by rejecting the Soviet contention that there were two German states, which was obvious to almost everyone except Adenauer.

Towards the end of March, Bulganin informed Adenauer that the Soviet Government was willing to open trade talks in either Moscow or Bonn within a few weeks. The Russians realized that any attempt at political negotiations with Adenauer was so much waste of diplomatic time and Bulganin resignedly expressed regret that Adenauer was unable to accept the existence of both German states. A trade pact was eventually negotiated and subsequently Mikoyan visited Bonn.

Even before the Soviet reply reached Bonn, Adenauer was moving towards a more congenial economic partnership. On 25th March, with the ministers of the other five 'Little European' states, he signed the Treaty of Rome setting up the European Common Market.

Some of the ministers present at the Rome ceremony, if not Adenauer, were anxious about the restricted membership of the new Common Market Community. The French Foreign Minister of the day, M. Pineau, expressed the views of most when he emphasized the desire of 'The Six' to associate with other West European nations still outside the Community.

'We desire particularly,' he said, 'to associate with Britain, without whom the Europe we wish to build cannot be complete.' That was a view which some of M. Pineau's successors in office and their ally in Bonn tended to forget.

When the new British Prime Minister, Mr. Harold Macmillan,

paid his first visit to Bonn as head of Government, at the beginning of May, the association of Britain and other members of what became known as 'The Outer Seven' with the Common Market Community was the main subject of discussion. Some months earlier, the British Government had proposed the creation of a European Free Trade area, and much of the Bonn discussions centred on how such a grouping could be co-ordinated with 'The Six'. Mr. Macmillan emphasized that British agriculture and British Imperial preference would be excluded from any negotiations, a preview of the basic difficulties which were encountered when negotiations for Britain's entry into the Common Market took place nearly five years later.

Adenauer was agreeable in general to Macmillan's proposal but he was adamant on one point. He stressed the delicate negotiations between 'The Six' themselves which had preceded the agreement on the Rome Treaty, and insisted that the treaty must be ratified by all six powers before any negotiations with Britain and other nations could begin.

The Anglo-German conversations took place in a cordial atmosphere, in marked contrast to the mutual incompatibility and profound distrust which would soon grow up between the two statesmen. Adenauer's courtesy, however, merely cloaked that deep distrust of Britain, and other countries like radical, Protestant Norway and Denmark, which underlay his insistence on ratification before any new negotiations with 'the Seven'. At heart, he had no real desire for Britain or any of Germany's north European neighbours to join the Common Market, a view which he held throughout the next few years, despite official protestations to the contrary. He had already appreciated, as de Gaulle would do later, the inherent danger to the Catholic-dominated, Right-wing 'Little Europe' which would arise from any expansion to include diametrically opposed countries such as Britain and the Scandinavian Socialist régimes.

By the time Macmillan reached Bonn, disarmament negotiations were taking place in London between Soviet Russia and the leading N.A.T.O. powers headed by the United States and Great Britain. As always when Britain and America sat down round a table with Soviet Russia, Adenauer was obsessed with a pathological fear that a deal was being fixed behind his back. He was also worried by the British policy decision to concentrate on a nuclear deterrent and the consequent decision to cut the strength of the British Army of the Rhine to the bone. Mr. Macmillan was able to reassure him, as Mr. Duncan Sandys subsequently reassured Herr Strauss in London, that Britain was not about to 'tiptoe out of Europe'.

Adenauer was even more alarmed by the policy trend of his American allies. The United States delegate to the London talks, Mr. Harold Stassen, in negotiation with the Russian delegate, Mr. Zorin, was showing a highly regrettable tendency towards flexibility, even to the extent of discussing military inspection zones in Europe, which smacked of the Eden proposals or the Rapacki plan.

In a speech to the C.D.U. in Hamburg in mid-May, Adenauer went so far as to say that he was agreeable to some form of military inspection-zone in Central Europe 'provided it is not restricted to Germany'. Subsequent public utterances showed that this was nothing more than a pre-election gambit made to please the C.D.U. party managers, who were anxious about the sterility of the Adenauer policies. Later exchanges with Mr. Stassen, which developed into something near a feud, demonstrated that he had never seriously departed from this opposition to anything which would ameliorate the Cold War.

It was an alarmed Adenauer who, in the last week of May, took wing for Washington, where even his fellow Cold War Ironside, Mr. Dulles was showing regrettable signs of heresy towards Adenauer's doctrine of 'negotiation from strength'. Serious divergences of approach between Adenauer and the other leading Cold War protagonist became evident from the difference of emphasis which emerged in the public statements of the two men at the close of the Adenauer visit. That the German Chancellor prevailed in Washington there can be no doubt, for as Dulles's enlightened Democrat opponents openly declared, 'American foreign policy is now decided in Bonn.' Mr. Dulles went so far as to state publicly that it was not for him 'to qualify Adenauer's view', adding significantly, 'Dr. Adenauer's positive views can hardly fail to influence American thinking.'

Dulles showed little enthusiasm for the Four Power Summit meeting which Adenauer, with an eye to the forthcoming German elections, had publicly proposed. But Adenauer did get a public assurance that there would be no European disarmament at the expense of German re-unification, or, as it was more succinctly expressed in London, 'Adenauer has secured the right of veto in the London disarmament talks.'

In Germany, his political opponents of both Right and Left rightly judged his 'Washington success' for what it was, a new blow against both German re-unification and European disarmament, coupled with open American intervention in the German election campaign. He was attacked from all sides for the aridity of his international policies and the growing authoritarianism of his 'democratic dictatorship'.

The Free Democrats, in an open letter, denounced American intervention in the election, and denied that Adenauer's defeat would mean the end of N.A.T.O. as State Department officials were trying to suggest. They accused Adenauer of a 'Führer complex', and gave the German people a stern warning of the inherent dangers of the Adenauer régime to German parliamentary democracy. With much justification, the F.D.P. said that Adenauer's contempt for the often inefficient, but nevertheless fundamental procedures of parliamentary government was creating the very rock on which the Weimar Republic was wrecked.

'If the United States is truly interested in stability in Western Germany,' said the F.D.P. open letter, 'it should think again before supporting a one-man government. Germany has never had a real chance to develop parliamentary skills. Procedure is now being permitted to decay because Adenauer never takes the trouble to tell the Opposition of his legislative programme. He treats ministries as private clubs, parliament as his private secretary, and debate as a farce.'

Adenauer was indifferent to home-based attacks on his quasi-fascist form of administration but criticism of his international policies from the Western capitals nettled the old man. To a rally of cheering C.D.U. supporters, he made the amazing assertion that only he and the C.D.U. stood 'between Western civilization and a new Goetterdaemmerung'.

Developing his role of a Western St. George single-handedly facing the Communist dragon, Adenauer, in a speech to a gathering of chauvinistic irredentist refugees from the 'lost territories' of the east, reached a new height of political fantasy:

'If a European security system is created,' he claimed, 'the German people will be robbed of American protection and Germany will become a Soviet satellite. We wish to stay in the Atlantic Community under the leadership of the United States.'

At this point, Mr. Khrushchev in East Berlin had characterized Adenauer, with some justice, as 'the man who was preventing the re-unification of Germany'. Worse still, Khrushchev, taking a leaf out of the Dulles book, seemed to be backing the Social Democrats, and spoke approvingly of some of the points in the S.P.D. election manifesto. '*If Germany chooses an S.P.D. Government,*' shouted Adenauer to the cheering meeting of the Refugee party, '*she will become a Russian satellite.*'

Campaigning politicians during a general election are forgiven much in all democratic countries. But the reaction in the Western capitals to the spectacle of the Rhineland political boss – who more than any other man had sabotaged all attempts at European disarmament – posing as the saviour of Western democratic civilization was icy.

International disapproval was reflected in the scathing descriptions of his lordly election progress in a luxuriously equipped private train which appeared in the more balanced sections of the Western Press. All the foreign correspondents who travelled with him in his highly guarded train spoke of the astonishing figure of the 81-year-old man who had been on the road for a month and who had made five major policy speeches, in four days, in cities as far apart as Lubeck and Stuttgart. The correspondent in Bonn of the London *Times*, in an epic of political reporting, commented that 'the tour has all the characteristics of an inspection by a colonial governor of a restive province.'

'This is a pity, because Dr. Adenauer has a tremendous zest for the hurly-burly of the hustings, a kindness which appeals to the voter, and a wit (*Teutonic*) devastating to the heckler. Had his forebears emigrated to America, he could have held his own at any party congress or on any whistlestop tour without the help of coonskin caps or other gimmicks.'

Describing a meeting at the North Sea port of Bremerhaven, *The Times* correspondent noted that the audience (by ticket only) was obviously a section 'of the German middle class which demands from authority only the right to be left alone to enjoy the rewards of its shopkeeping and small manufactures. A social historian would probably have blamed them for all the misfortunes which had befallen Germany since the Frankfurt assembly of 1848. But they remain the backbone of German social life. There was no political idealism, and', said the British correspondent, 'Dr. Adenauer showed them that they were living under a strong benevolent government – as no doubt they had always believed!'

Adenauer told them there were now only two problems, economics and foreign affairs. This was at the height of the 'German miracle', and Adenauer, ignoring Professor Erhard, announced that *he* had solved the economic problem. Germany was prosperous as never before.

'Indeed,' commented *The Times* correspondent, 'The audience had all the ugliness of sudden prosperity. The market-place outside was filled with new cars. Were they going to throw all this away, asked Adenauer. The applause indicated that they would not be ungrateful.'

Adenauer told the Bremerhaven burghers that the remaining problem of foreign affairs amounted essentially to a struggle between the two giants, the United States and Russia.

'When he had met President Eisenhower in Washington . . . the audience sat in silent respect before the man who had the confidence of Mr. Dulles,' continued *The Times* dispatch. 'Then the band struck up *Deutschland über Alles* and Dr. Adenauer was borne away to continue his lonely struggle for their well-being.'

The Adenauer train and the foreign correspondents continued along the Weser estuary to the great port of Bremen.

'At Bremen,' continued *The Times* dispatch, 'stood groups of young men in the aisles ready to defend democracy against Socialism. They quickly went into action against a solitary heckler – almost inaudible because of the blare of loudspeakers. Fists rose and fell – *only the rubber truncheons were missing*. Dr. Adenauer intervened . . . distressed by such misplaced enthusiasm.'

The electioneering Chancellor then painted a rosy picture of the amount of meat which the Germans were eating under his chancellorship. 'The audience sat back,' reported *The Times*, 'apparently dreaming of ever-increasing piles of Schnitzel and German sausage.' Finally, it was necessary for the Press to leave to catch Adenauer's train. The muscular young men had their own ideas of democracy. Nobody could leave while the Chancellor was speaking. It was apparently undemocratic.

'The situation was patiently explained, but the leader was non-plussed by the contradictions of democratic practice. Hysteria threatened . . . and finally the correspondents were jostled.'

Another Western commentator, disgusted by Adenauer's Führer-like progress through his domain, wrote disparagingly of the 'cold arrogance' with which Adenauer treated his political opponents and his *'primitive political philosophy'*. The commentators in the liberal German Press – and they were many – were equally disrespectful. One, noted for his long-standing denunciation of Adenauer's undemocratic tendencies, wrote that Adenauer had reduced the democracy to which he had reconciled the Germans 'to no more than a caricature'. The same commentator accused the Federal Chancellor of treating the Bundestag as little more than 'an applauding infant school'.

As the campaign reached a climax, Adenauer became ever more reckless of the facts. In justification of his own tepid attitude towards German re-unification, he had the impertinence to tell an adulatory C.D.U. audience in Catholic Mainz that the British Labour Party was equally opposed to German re-unification. He did so despite the 'Gaitskell Plan' issued a week or two earlier. The Labour Party leader, Hugh Gaitskell, in statesmanlike proposals had suggested that all foreign troops, including the British and American, be withdrawn from Germany as a prelude to all-German free elections. The united Germany should, thereafter, be linked with Poland, Czechoslovakia and Hungary, cleared of all Soviet troops, in a central European neutral zone guaranteed by the four great powers.

By that time, however, on the eve of the poll in mid-September, Adenauer, with an overbearing arrogance which only a German politician could ever attain, was impervious to criticism at home or abroad. He was quite sure he would win his third general election. The German economic miracle was approaching its peak, although it owed singularly little to his efforts. The Germans were well fed as they had never been before. They were prosperous as never in history – and, once again, increasingly self-satisfied and arrogant. They had no desire for change. Adenauer's undemocratic practice suited them well enough. He was the 'Father-Figure' who had restored them to wealth and power. That was not all the story. Adenauer had taken every possible step to see that his Germans recognized these things.

German big business, through Dr. Pferdmenges, had levied tribute to pay for Adenauer's fabulously expensive electoral campaign, a campaign whose cost was wildly beyond the statutory figure permitted in the United Kingdom. The Catholic Church, through the agency of 'Herr Frings', the Cardinal

Archbishop of Cologne and German Primate, with whom he had enjoyed a curiously barbed relationship since the days of his Cologne Oberbürgermeistership, had openly intervened in Adenauer's favour. Even the German trade unions, with their members earning ever more and more, had refused to endorse the S.P.D. party platform, and thereby given Adenauer oblique support.

The result was not in doubt. Once again, on election night Adenauer retired to bed in his Rhineland home, certain that dawn would see him Federal Chancellor for the third time. The election results confirmed his confidence. He was returned to power with an even greater absolute majority than in the 1953 landslide. His Christian Democrats and their Christian Socialist allies in Bavaria gained 244 seats in the new Bundestag, an increase of 20. The S.P.D., however, significantly made an equal advance. The Socialists improved their representation in the Bonn Parliament from 151 to 169 seats. All the attacks on Adenauer had not fallen on deaf ears; something approaching half the electorate was far from being mesmerized by Adenauer and his 'German miracle'.

The Free Democrats, for all their outspoken criticism, or perhaps because of it, and the German Party (D.P.) were the main sufferers. The political splinter groups, the Refugee party and the post-war rump of the old Catholic Zentrum, disappeared from the Bonn Parliament.

On the morrow of victory, the convoy of cars with flashing blue lights in which Adenauer was accustomed each morning to roar through Bonn in defiance of all speed limits, and at sight of which all honest Bonn burghers hastily took cover, for once crawled at funeral pace to let the Chancellor wave graciously to the admiring populace.

When he reached his office in the Palais Schaumburg, he announced that his success guaranteed another four years of stability in Germany's domestic and foreign policy. He was curiously coy about *the real victor*, his economics minister Professor Erhard, the one man who, more than any other, deserved credit for German prosperity. The more critical sections of the German Press left the Germans no doubt about what had really happened.

The Social Democrats put a different emphasis on Adenauer's victory. They attributed his success to 'the desire of the Germans for a Führer-Figure who will relieve them of the need to think and act politically, and who removes the deep-seated unconscious fear that German re-unification must entail great sacrifice'.

How much of the 1957 electoral victory can be attributed to Professor Erhard and how much to the Germans' subconscious desire for a 'Führer-Figure' is arguable. The S.P.D. statement, however, was a profoundly accurate analysis of the true state of German 'democracy' then and for a considerable period thereafter.

Adenauer's third election success seemed to give him a feeling of internal self-confidence which he had often lacked. In the weeks immediately following the election he noticeably mellowed. He began to emerge once again as the benign statesman, more concerned with the future of German democracy than with the hurly-burly of daily political life.

The attacks on the 'Führer-Figure', particularly in the more responsible Anglo-Saxon journals, had gone home. He sought advice. He had known the British Ambassador in Bonn, Sir Christopher Steel, since the very early days of the occupation. He regarded Steel as a friend. During the later months of 1957, Adenauer had a number of quiet conversations with the British Ambassador on British democratic practice. He was particularly interested in the working of the British Cabinet. He asked many questions on British joint Cabinet responsibility. By the Bonn Basic Law, as in earlier German constitutions, the Chancellor alone is responsible for the formulation of policy. Joint ministerial responsibility, as practised in Whitehall, is unknown to the Germans. The principle of a minister taking full responsibility for, and if need be resigning because of, the actions of his ministry is equally unknown in Bonn. Adenauer pondered all these matters.

His new mellowness took another form. For five years he had pointedly ignored the estimable leader of the Social Democrats, Herr Ollenhauer, and in the recent election campaign, Adenauer had made undeserved and unworthy attacks on the Socialist leader. He seemed to regret these. Having learned of the official position of the Leader of H.M. Opposition in the U.K., he let it be known that he wished to consider Herr Ollenhauer on the same footing. It was a strange transformation and, as the London *Times* commented, 'Perhaps he is feeling his 82 years a little.'

That may well have been true. He always showed a tendency to become depressed and take to his bed towards the end of the year. At the beginning of December, he had to cancel a visit to London because of his annual pre-Christmas attack of influenza. But the 'New Adenauer' did not last long. With the advent of the spring of 1958, the old man became his old self again, arrogant, offensive and as authoritarian as ever.

CHAPTER FIFTEEN

The Old Feud Revived

ON HIS eighty-second birthday, at the beginning of 1958, Adenauer seemed to be approaching the apotheosis of his career as a great German and a world personality. To many Germans, deeply impressed by his overwhelming electoral success a month or two earlier, he was not only the 'Father-Figure' but the very embodiment of Germany itself. The fate of the Fatherland seemed bound to his inexorable advance into octogenarianism. Little more than a dozen years after 'unconditional surrender', he stood at the head of a German state which he had raised to a major force in world affairs. In N.A.T.O. Germany was no longer on probation but a full member of the club who spoke with a strong voice.

The new role which he seemed intent on taking in international affairs had been indicated by his surprising initiative at the N.A.T.O. Council meeting in Paris a week or two earlier. To the consternation of Dulles and the other Cold Warriors he had proposed that a new approach be made to the Soviet Union. He had been instrumental in persuading the N.A.T.O. Council, including Eisenhower, to pass a resolution calling for a four-power Foreign Ministers' meeting.

As patriarch of the Western World it seemed as though the German Chancellor, divorced by advanced age from his narrow provincial past, wished to mark the termination of his political career by broad statesmanlike measures aimed at the peaceful resolution of the major problems of the time. Physically strong despite his years, overwhelmingly supported by his fellow-countrymen, honoured through the Western world, and secure in the wisdom, or cynicism of great age, it seemed he would make his exit from the international stage full of honour and achievement.

So alarmed were the transatlantic Cold Warriors by the new Adenauer and his new spirit of reconciliation towards the Soviet Union that the *New York Herald Tribune* felt constrained to warn that 'the greatest danger is the spirit of neutralism'. Mr. Dulles, worried but submissive, wrote in *Life* that 'there is little to be done for the present offer of a Foreign Ministers' meeting voices the desire of many in the Western camp.'

Even the Russians seemed to be impressed. Bulganin, still officially Soviet Prime Minister, sent Adenauer a series of letters. They contained nothing particularly new, but they did seem to indicate a Soviet willingness to meet Adenauer part of the way and to re-examine, once again, the outstanding problems of East and West.

Only the British were cynical. A somewhat irreverent British observer who watched the Adenauer birthday celebrations, which by this time had become a Bonn institution, observed, 'He is not only approaching the zenith of his career – but of his own belated political development.'

The illusion of the patriarch of the West did not last long. By mid-January when he broadcast to the German people the mantle was slipping somewhat. He observed that, while he would study Bulganin's letters, he was under no illusion about their real purpose.

On the following day the leader writer in the London *Times*, never among his greater admirers, emphasized British doubts about the change of heart.

After pointing out that it was three years since the last Summit meeting in Geneva and that there was a general feeling that the four leaders should meet again, *The Times* continued, 'Dr. Adenauer is right that there is little point in such a meeting without careful diplomatic preparation. The Atlantic Council has recommended a meeting of Foreign Ministers. The size of the meeting is crucial.' The leader writer went on to comment that

Bulganin's proposal for a gathering of thirty heads of state provided no hope of achieving any result and clearly had been 'thrown out as a cockshy'.

'Dr. Adenauer is right in restating the opposition of his Government to Bulganin's proposals for the future of Germany. But *he went too far* when he appeared to reject out of hand the Rapacki Plan for an atom-free zone in Germany, Poland and Czechoslovakia. This he claimed would be the end of N.A.T.O. and the liberty of Western Europe. It is certainly not the intention of the West to adopt proposals to destroy N.A.T.O. as Adenauer suggests. But the idea of a nuclear-free zone might well be the key to reopen the door to confidence.'

His German critics were equally unimpressed in the foreign affairs debate which took place in the Bundestag a week or so later. He was openly accused of political failure, duplicity and worse. His one time Minister of the Interior, Dr. Heinemann, alleged that the Chancellor had falsified a Cabinet minute, while Dr. Dehler said that not only had Adenauer never made any serious effort to secure re-unification but on one specific occasion he had done his best to prevent it.

Weary and obviously feeling his years, Adenauer retired to the south of France for a long holiday. No sooner did the cat disappear than the C.D.U. mice in Bonn started to bicker. The carefully concealed doubts about his foreign policy were revealed all too clearly. He was furious. In mid-March, reinvigorated by the Mediterranean sun and looking like a man twenty years his junior, Adenauer returned to Bonn – like a case-hardened sergeant-major come to discipline restive recruits.

Having restored order, in mid-April he flew to London, accompanied by von Brentano and Erhard, for a four-day visit. Part of the talks were devoted to the hardy annual of Anglo-German ministerial meetings, the squabble over support costs for the British Army of the Rhine. Adenauer's main conversations with Mr. Macmillan and other British ministers concentrated, however, on the Summit meeting which Khrushchev was loudly demanding, and which it was generally assumed would be held during the summer of 1958.

The British soon realized that Adenauer was unchanged. His basic policy was 'Do nothing'. He emphasized that a Summit meeting should take place only after long diplomatic preparation. Surprisingly, he laid no emphasis, in the privacy of the top level meetings, on German re-unification. In fact, he did not even press for re-unification to be on the agenda of a Summit meeting. His attitude was that if security in Europe was discussed, the issue of German re-unification must inevitably arise. With justice he pointed out that there could be no permanent improvement in European security if Germany remained divided. But he seemed singularly unwilling to agree to any concrete step towards that security.

The Times bluntly asked, 'Is it really possible to hope that simply by remaining strong and united behind their bastions the Western allies will eventually reap the reward of Russian concessions?'

A communique issued at the end of the visit said that Adenauer and Macmillan were agreed on the desirability of holding a Summit meeting, and recalled the Soviet undertaking, given at Geneva in 1955, that the re-unification of Germany must be based on free elections. The communique also referred to the talks then proceeding between 'The Six' of the European Common Market and the seven members of the European Free Trade Area, and emphasized the importance of these negotiations, under the chairmanship of Mr. Reginald Maudling, which it was hoped would prevent the division of Europe into two *blocs*.

Despite the hackneyed reference to agreement in the communique, there was considerable disillusionment in important British circles – where it was hoped that a Summit meeting would lead to a general easing of tension – about Adenauer's all too obvious desire to hot up the Cold War.

While his great service to the Western cause was generally agreed, it was felt that Adenauer and his West Germany state were becoming more and more a creation of the Cold War with all that implied. The more the West viewed with horror the prospect of total nuclear war, and the greater the desire to reach a global understanding with the Soviet Union, the less harmony there was in London with Adenauer and what he stood for. Important British personalities, aware of the tenor of his statements, hesitated to accuse him of war-mongering. But it was widely felt that tension between East and West formed the foundation of his political life work, and that the talks in London showed that he would fight hard to prevent that life work being endangered. From that basic premise, the British realized, stemmed all Adenauer's passionate opposition to any talk of a neutral zone in central Europe, such as was envisaged in the Eden, the Rapacki and the Gaitskell proposals. As he flew back to Bonn there was a widespread feeling that his main aim, far from a reduction of international tension, was to hot up the Cold War in order to secure atomic weapons for West Germany.

Adenauer was quick to sense the British hostility to his Cold War advocacy. It was openly expressed by commentators of diverse political views. But he was pathologically incapable of understanding that pragmatic British approach to international affairs which was the complete antithesis of his own primitive ideological conception. His suspicion and growing resentment fitted easily into lifelong Anglophobia. It was some months before he openly expressed his anger. But among his confidants in Bonn, he openly expressed his growing distrust of Mr. Macmillan and the British policy of seeking a lessening of tension through direct talks with Mr. Khrushchev. For some years the Adenauer-British feud had been dormant if not quite dead. From the spring of 1958 the old distaste and distrust, if nothing stronger, reappeared, intensified by the calcification processes of extreme age.

At that moment, as British-German relations began to deteriorate, General de Gaulle became Prime Minister of France. De Gaulle had long been regarded as a strong opponent of the

European integration movement which was contrary to his conception of 'La France' and its *'gloire'*. Adenauer was in something approaching despair. Among his closer friends of the diplomatic community he did not try to conceal his feelings about the disappearance from French public life of the 'good Europeans' with whom he had worked so long. With the revolt of the French officers in Algiers, the dream of the 'Little Europe', conceived by de Gasperri, Robert Schuman and himself nearly a decade earlier, seemed to have disappeared into thin air. At the same time the talks between 'The Six' and the seven countries of the Free Trade area, which had already encountered serious difficulties because of the French attitude, were suspended. Adenauer's European policy seemed in ruins.

Adenauer felt that he must meet the new master of France and ascertain the intentions and the policies of the enigmatic general as soon as possible. Soon after de Gaulle took office, the Chancellor, through diplomatic channels, suggested a meeting. He was rebuffed. Cool and haughty as always, 'the general' had more important matters than that of Franco-German relations to settle in the early summer of 1958. That could wait, along with the future of Europe, while he decided the destiny of France. Adenauer, accustomed to the easy acquiescence of Eisenhower and Dulles, was insulted.

In Bonn official spokesmen were markedly hostile. Difficulties of protocol, it was suggested, prevented any possibility of a meeting in the near future. One Bonn official reached the heights of formal hypocrisy when he announced that the Chancellor 'in his frail state of health' could scarcely be expected to travel all the way to Paris to meet a new arrival fifteen years his junior. No one else had noticed the Chancellor's enfeebled physical state, and he had made a day trip to Paris at least a dozen times in the previous few years.

The impasse dragged on into the summer while the great powers were embroiled in a new crisis in the Lebanon. Both men were proud and stubborn. It was obvious that each was highly suspicious of the other. Gradually, however, Adenauer began to be swayed by the advice of those whom he trusted. As the senior statesman in Western Europe, it was suggested, he could afford to be gracious. He relied much on the British Ambassador, Sir Christopher Steel, from whom no doubt he got much good advice, based on British experience of dealing with the intractable, pig-headed man who now ruled France.

In August, Adenauer once more retreated to the south, as he was to do more and more in the future. This time he chose a villa at Cadenabbia on Lake Como which, for the remainder of his period of office, was to be the second capital of the Federal Republic for months each year. It was there, mellowed once again by the warm Italian sun, that the old man felt he could lose nothing by being gracious and generous to his junior colleague in France. He agreed to make a friendly gesture. A meeting was arranged for mid-September, not in the French capital but at de Gaulle's private residence at Colombey-les-deux-Eglises, approximately half-way from the Rhine to Paris.

As Adenauer left Baden-Baden and drove into France by the great Rhine bridge at Strasbourg, he still felt much disturbed by recent events in France and highly suspicious of de Gaulle's policies, above all, of his well-known opposition to the European movement. He knew that the talks would be difficult, both personally and diplomatically, and was shrewd enough to appreciate how alike de Gaulle and he were in many respects.

They were both proud and stubborn and far from young. They had both great achievements in the past to their credit. Each could hide his thoughts behind an impassive countenance and had developed during the years in the wilderness a habit of establishing clear objectives and picturing the road in fundamental principles, usually simply expressed. At the same time both could be wilfully obscure and mystifying on points of detail. And though they were gifted with great breadth of vision they were restricted in action by an equally high sense of national mission.

Both men inevitably were very reserved and showed a formal

politeness at this first encounter which smacked somewhat of an earlier and more elegant age. They were quick to realize that they had much in common. From devout Catholic families, they were both products of a jesuit system of education, and were still true sons of the Church. In their correct, formal and authoritarian approach to affairs they were curiously alike.

After luncheon in the family dining-room, Adenauer and de Gaulle spent three hours together with only interpreters present. The conversations were intentionally exploratory. Neither man took up any strong position. They discussed the integration of Europe and the problem of whether the first major cut in tariffs in the Common Market would come into operation at the beginning of the following year. They talked about Algeria and the French atomic weapon. No decisions were taken. As the French Ambassador in Bonn, M. François Seydoux, observed: 'What they talked about is unimportant. The main thing is that they enjoyed themselves and didn't sulk.'

The two men were joined by von Brentano and the French Foreign Minister, M. Couve de Murville, whom Adenauer had come to know and trust as French Ambassador in Bonn, and after dinner the German party drove to spend the night at nearby Chaumont where Adenauer was warmly welcomed by the local people.

When the Chancellor returned to Bonn, he was an immensely relieved man. To a Press conference the 82-year-old veteran reported that his 67-year-old host had seemed 'quite hale and hearty' (*sehr frisch*). After announcing the usual official cliché on such occasions, that 'full agreement had been reached on all points', Adenauer warmed to the subject of de Gaulle. He said that contrary to earlier fears (notably his own), General de Gaulle's antipathy to a united Europe had been exaggerated. The general, he said, was most anxious to develop friendly relations between the former enemies. The meeting had confirmed the wisdom of German (he meant his own) policy of strengthening co-operation between the two countries.

Adenauer assured the Press conference that General de Gaulle was *not* a nationalist. On the contrary, he had found the general very well informed on foreign affairs, and especially on the importance of harmonious Franco-German relations, not only to the two countries themselves, but for Europe and the rest of the world. General de Gaulle had pointed out the complete change in the relationship between France and Germany. Fears of a new attack by Germany – which had been strong in de Gaulle's mind in 1945 – were now over and done with.

Adenauer said that they had discussed the European Common Market and he was convinced that it would become operative at the beginning of 1959. He said he also hoped that the European Free Trade Area would become effective in the same year. He revealed that both de Gaulle and himself were in favour of the Free Trade Area, and added significantly that both of them hoped *to see Britain linked to the Common Market by the Free Trade Area.*

In spite of the decisive role played by the French a few weeks later in the collapse of the negotiations between 'the Six' and the European Free Trade Area led by Britain, there is strong evidence to suggest that Adenauer, on that occasion in the autumn of 1958, expressed the fundamental view of both himself and de Gaulle to Britain's association with the Common Market. Both of them were in favour of Britain being *linked to the Common Market – but not of it.*

There is strong evidence from the German side to suggest that the statement made by Adenauer after his first meeting with de Gaulle was an accurate reflection of both men's fundamental thinking. The publicly expressed doubts of Adenauer during the 1961–2 negotiations would confirm this. De Gaulle's statement at the Press conference in January, 1963, which precipitated the breakdown of the talks, was consistent with the view he appears to have expressed to Adenauer at Colombey-les-deux-Eglises in September, 1958.

Adenauer, in the autumn of 1958, was certainly genuinely

concerned about the danger of Europe splitting into two contending economic *blocs* and when the negotiations between 'The Six'
and the Free Trade Area collapsed in November of that year, he
at once asked de Gaulle to meet him. He had already been warned
by his friends in German industry that, unless 'The Six' had
access to the British market, German exports eventually were
bound to suffer. When he met de Gaulle for the second time, at
Bad Kreuznach at the end of November, both men agreed that
every effort should be made to avoid the economic division of
Europe. France remained opposed to the Free Trade Area but de
Gaulle suggested that some solution might be found through
O.E.E.C. Adenauer was adamant that new negotiations must
take place, and exploratory talks were started with the O.E.E.C.
countries, but without much result.

Even as the two statesmen met, Adenauer's inflexible 'Do
nothing' Cold War policies were coming home to roost. For the
previous fortnight the Western Alliance had faced an infinitely
more serious international crisis – a new Soviet threat to the
future of Berlin.

First hint of trouble had come in the second week of November
when the Polish Prime Minister, Mr. Gomulka, visited Moscow
to realign Polish-Soviet policy on Germany. In a joint communique, Khrushchev and Gomulka attacked Adenauer for his support
of 'revenge-seeking elements which openly proclaim their
territorial demands on other countries', a reference to Adenauer's
far from discreet support of some of the more chauvinistic German
refugee groups from territories now incorporated in Poland.

Khrushchev, in a speech at the same time, announced that the
'correct thing would be to hand over control of the whole of
Berlin to the East German Government'. All that remained of the
Potsdam agreement of 1945 was the four-power control of
Berlin which, he said, permitted the three Western Occupation
Powers 'to meddle in the affairs of the East German capital and
permitted them to have road, rail and air lanes through East
German territory'. Despite that, continued Khrushchev, the

Western Powers refused to recognize the existence of the German Democratic Republic (D.D.R.).

Khrushchev's statement was strictly correct. At the time of the formation of the Bonn Republic in 1949, the British, American and French Governments had carefully excluded Berlin, in particular the three Western sectors, from the Bonn administration. Legally, Berlin remained – as long as Adenauer was Chancellor – an occupied city under four-power control, although for more than a decade the Russian (east) sector of the city had been in effect under independent administration. The four-power Kommandadtura, nominally responsible for the administration of the former German capital, like the Allied Control Council which remained the legal government of the Reich, had not met since prior to the start of the Berlin blockade in 1948. Adenauer, therefore, was not strictly involved in the administration of Berlin. The Western sectors of the city, under their doughty ruling Mayor, Herr Willy Brandt, were in fact closely linked, both politically and economically, with the Federal Republic.

Khrushchev's comment on the non-recognition of the D.D.R. struck directly at Adenauer who had adopted the pretence, and would continue to do so as long as he was Chancellor, that the D.D.R. did not exist, a standpoint which he had persuaded the three Western Powers to accept.

Within twenty-four hours of Khrushchev making his speech, Adenauer summoned the Bonn Cabinet to consider counter measures should a new Berlin blockade seem imminent. He had a powerful weapon in his hands. It was well known that the always shaky economy of the D.D.R. could be seriously jeopardized by a major stoppage of lucrative inter-zone trade which, despite the official non-existence of the D.D.R., had gone on for years between the two halves of Germany. He was careful not to adopt a bellicose attitude. When, a day or two later, he sent an official reply to a Soviet Note received in September, he was conciliatory and urged the Russians to adopt a 'realistic approach' to the solution of the German problem. He added that he had 'noted with pleasure' that the Soviet Government had adopted the idea of forming a four-power working group to prepare the draft of a German peace treaty.

His conciliatory approach availed nothing. Next day the Soviet Ambassador in Bonn, Mr. Smirnov, informed Adenauer of the steps which his Government proposed to take 'to liquidate the occupation status of Berlin'. Adenauer, in reply, emphasized to the Ambassador that four power rule in Berlin – in which the West German Government had no part – was based on international agreement to which Soviet Russia was a party. Finally, twenty-four hours after the Adenauer-de Gaulle meeting at Bad Kreuznach, Khrushchev took a decisive step. It was less drastic, however, than had been feared in the Western capitals and gave a breathing space of six months. In Notes handed to the three Western ambassadors in Moscow and to their West German colleague, the Soviet Government proposed that within six months West Berlin should become a 'free city', without political links to either part of Germany, but with guaranteed freedom of access and freedom of trade.

At the same time Khrushchev took the almost unprecedented step of holding a Press conference in Moscow. He said that West Berlin had become a 'cancerous tumour' in the heart of East Germany and must be liquidated whatever the reaction of the Western Powers. He denied that he was issuing an ultimatum; there would be no change in the status of the inhabitants of West Berlin unless they themselves wished a change. The best solution for Berlin, he said, would follow the re-unification of Germany in accordance with the Potsdam treaty, with West Germany withdrawing from N.A.T.O. and East Germany from the Warsaw Pact in terms of the four-power agreement to keep Germany demilitarized. Failing that, the Western Powers had no right to remain in Berlin.

The next best solution would be for the whole of Berlin to be incorporated within the East German state, but the Western Powers would not agree to that. The only remaining solution, therefore, was for West Berlin to become a demilitarized 'free city', politically independent. It was clear that the Russian initiative marked the opening of a long and arduous struggle, but Khrushchev, by giving the Western Powers six months' grace, showed that he proposed to move cautiously.

Adenauer took the initiative in proposing a meeting of the Western Foreign Ministers which was at once accepted. But then, as had happened so often in the past, he took steps to limit the West's field of negotiations. To the consternation of the Western Governments, he started to lay down conditions. At a meeting of the C.D.U. parliamentary group Adenauer announced categorically that *there could be no negotiations with the Soviet Union on a peace treaty until the question of Germany's eastern frontiers had been settled.* He added that a peace treaty, in any case, could only be negotiated with a freely elected German Government.

In diplomatic correspondence with the Soviet Government in the previous few weeks he had appeared to show a willingness to discuss a peace treaty. His speech to the Bonn parliamentarians, however, confirmed the view of Western cynics that such protestations had been for home consumption. Why, at this moment, he should have chosen to introduce the highly controversial question of the Oder-Neisse line was anyone's guess. In the Western capitals it was felt that Adenauer seemed determined to make more difficult a situation which was already complicated and dangerous. He had ignored the Oder-Neisse line for a long time. Now, he seemed determined to have nothing to do with reunification until the 'lost territories' included in Poland and the Soviet Union had been returned to Germany. As one well-informed British commentator stated: 'That opened up prospects which all the Western Governments would have rather avoided.'

The speech, which some Western diplomats described as 'culpably reckless' in the circumstances, was a measure of his fear, based chiefly on foreign Press comment, that the Western Powers might try to settle the Berlin problem within a framework of a general European settlement.

He was once again obsessed by his 'Potsdam Nightmare'. He was certain that the weak and wobbling British, on the slightest encouragement, would come to an accommodation with Khrushchev which would involve some sort of recognition of the hated East Zone puppet régime of Ulbricht.

The Chancellor was equally alarmed by the attitude of his principal American allies. President Eisenhower had declined to be panicked by the Russian moves into abandoning his favourite Georgian golf course; Mr. Dulles, now far from well, had returned reluctantly from a fishing holiday in Canada. Worst of all, when Mr. Dulles did get back to Washington, he seemed to be affected by 'British appeasement'.

The Secretary of State said that in the question of access to Berlin 'the United States *might well deal with the East German authorities as agents of the Russians'*. He was careful to qualify that statement by adding that a clear distinction must be drawn between such *Modus operandi* and the *de facto*, still less *de jure* recognition of the East German régime. It was all a question of how the East Germans acted or functioned – or, as an American commentator put it more succinctly – 'Nobody's going to start a war about who stamps the paper on the Berlin *autobahn*.'

To Adenauer in Bonn all this was heresy. Even Mr. Dulles had been seduced from the straight and narrow path. Deeply worried by the apparent treachery of his closest allies, Adenauer flew to Berlin for what was claimed to be a morale-boosting visit. Like other Rhinelanders, he was never really at home in the Reich capital and, as on former occasions, he was not at his best. The value of his visit was somewhat nullified by the Berliners awareness that, long before the crisis had blown up, he had planned an electioneering trip to Berlin to help his C.D.U., the junior partner in the Socialist-dominated city coalition. His visit was not a success. Worried and depressed, he returned to Bonn to take to his bed – as he usually did in mid-December.

At the start of 1959, Mr. Mikoyan, on a reconnaissance to attempt to arrange a Khrushchev visit to the United States, reached Washington. The shrewd and able veteran of the Soviet praesidium gave private assurances that there was no question of a new Berlin blockade. There would be no interference with Allied access to the city as in 1948–9. But he stuck to Khrushchev's point that a solution must be reached by the end of May.

Mr. Dulles, seriously ill but cheered by the accommodating attitude of Mikoyan, observed casually that there might be ways of reuniting Germany other than by free elections. Adenauer's obsessional '*angst*' at once swamped his more reasoned processes. The American Ambassador in Bonn was summoned to the Chancellery. By this time, Adenauer did not even trust Dulles to stick to 'the hard line'. He told the Ambassador that he did not wish to interfere in American politics, and then proceeded to do so. He asked the Ambassador to pass on to Mr. Dulles his conviction that Mikoyan's assurances and promises were no more than bait to lure the more gullible elements in the West – he clearly had the British in mind – down the slippery slope of compromise. A soothing answer came from Washington. Once again, the old man seemed reassured.

Nevertheless, Mr. Dulles was filled with a spirit of compromise, which may have owed much to the private realization of how limited were his days in office, and remarked that 'we should all be delighted to achieve re-unification of Germany by any means'. He fought shy of the word 'confederation' which the Russians had been suggesting as one solution of the German problem. But, Dulles added, 'The real heart of the matter is to reunite Germany in freedom.'

His remarks seemed not only unexceptionable, but praiseworthy. But Adenauer was suffering from an acute compulsive obsessional mistrust neurosis, directed at the British *in toto* and the Americans in part, the symptoms of which were to reappear frequently following the advent of a new American President. In Bonn Allied diplomats realized that he feared any compromise at all on the German question. Confederation was regarded as a

serious trap which could only result in the East Germans, with
Soviet support, gaining control over the whole Reich. So far did
Adenauer believe in his own Bonn democracy! Those who came
in contact with him observed a most noticeable backing away
from German re-unification *in any form*. Adenauer was just not
prepared to negotiate about anything. A combination of political
instinct, provincial background and great age had made him
incapable of appreciating, still less initiating any move at all.
The combination was to lead to dire consequences for the
17,000,000 Germans in the D.D.R. and the people of East Berlin
when the showdown came more than two years later. For the
Rhineland ex-oberbürgermeister was pathologically incapable of
understanding that, despite a willingness to co-operate in any
plan which would lessen European and, still more, global tension,
the Governments in Washington and London were quite as well
aware of their basic interests as he was.

The Adenauer near-panic continued. Finally, Mr. Dulles, ill as
he was, gallantly offered to fly the Atlantic to soothe the German
Chancellor. At the beginning of February, the Secretary of State
flew to Bonn for the week-end, and spent five hours in private
conversation with Adenauer. The visit was notable for the display
of mutual admiration. Dulles said he always felt great satisfaction
when he visited the Chancellor in Bonn. Adenauer replied that he
deeply appreciated the visit at a time when the Secretary of State
was so much needed in Washington.

Dulles accepted Adenauer's suggestion that there should be a
meeting of the Western Foreign Ministers as soon as possible;
and that an East-West conference should take place, if possible,
before the end of May when Khrushchev's 'period of grace' for a
settlement of the Berlin problem was due to expire. The Secretary
of State conceded Adenauer's demand that any negotiations with
the East must be governed by the basic principle of 'no concessions without counter concessions'. At the airport, however,
before he left Germany for the last time, Dulles was careful to
water down Adenauer's condition by stating that it would not

prevent the West from being conciliatory in any East-West negotiations.

Mr. Dulles had bowed to Adenauer's demands without any reference to the other Western Allies. Under the influence of drugs and gravely ill, the Secretary of State was anxious only to soothe the anxieties of his old friend and fellow Cold Warrior, but on his return to Washington it was widely reported that there was an impasse among the Allies on how to deal with the Berlin crisis. It was widely known that the British were ready to talk.

Adenauer's near-panic in the preceding weeks, although apparently started by his distrust of his American friends, had an even deeper basis. During the last weeks of 1958 and early in 1959, he had become aware of a confidential British approach in Moscow. A combination of his lifelong, primitive anti-Bolshevism coupled with his chronic Anglophobia at once revived the symptoms of his anxiety neurosis.

In February, his worst fears were realized when it was announced officially that Mr. Macmillan − complete with astrakhan fur hat − was about to pay an official visit to Khrushchev. Bitterly he resented the British Prime Minister's initiative, and although it was some weeks before his venom became public, even as Mr. Macmillan flew to Moscow, British observers in Bonn were aware that the Chancellor viewed Macmillan's approach to the German and European problems with much distrust.

Adenauer's agitation, in the event, proved pointless. Mr. Macmillan, although conciliatory and proposing a four-power ministers' meeting, proved more unyielding on *basic principle* than Mr. Dulles. Khrushchev, unlike Adenauer, was quick to appreciate it. Mr. Macmillan was still visiting Soviet industrial plants outside Moscow when Khrushchev, with an obviously deliberate breach of normal diplomatic courtesy, bluntly rejected the Western proposal for a Foreign Ministers' meeting.

A four-power Foreign Ministers' meeting was just a waste of time, announced Khrushchev in a major policy speech in Moscow. Instead, he proposed a Summit meeting at which the well-known

Soviet draft peace treaty for Germany should form a basis of discussion. He repeated the basic Soviet promise that, once the 'Big Four' powers had brought the leaders of the two German states together, they should have to hammer out a re-unification settlement for themselves.

'Let the Germans sit round a conference table and decide this question for themselves,' he said. 'We shall not intrude. The West only wants to inveigle us into diplomatic talk – that labyrinth of which we have had so much experience. It is a bog without a way out.' Khrushchev, said the Soviet Foreign Minister, was much too busy to waste time on such a meeting. It would be much better for the heads of the four great powers to discuss the question soberly and make decisions.

Relations between Macmillan and Khrushchev became noticeably cool. The Soviet leader cancelled a visit with Macmillan to Kiev because he had to visit the dentist! The Anglo-Soviet talks ended, leaving the gulf over the Berlin question as wide as ever.

Macmillan had announced that he proposed to visit both Paris and Bonn, immediately he returned from Russia, to report to de Gaulle and Adenauer on his conversations with Khrushchev. Adenauer, fearing that de Gaulle might be persuaded to back the British line, hastily arranged to beat Macmillan to the post. He organized a visit to Paris on the eve of Macmillan's arrival. On 4th March Adenauer met de Gaulle at a hunting lodge at Marly-le-Roi outside Paris. He confirmed what he had suspected, that de Gaulle also favoured a strong line over Berlin. The French leader shared Khrushchev's view that a Foreign Ministers' meeting was so much waste of time. He wanted a Summit meeting. When the two men parted, French diplomats said that a 'firm Franco-German front had been established over Berlin'.

On the same day Khrushchev arrived in East Germany and announced that he proposed to sign a peace treaty with East Germany alone, if Adenauer refused to participate. But he seemed to regret the abruptness with which he had treated Macmillan in Moscow. Khrushchev now emphasized that there was no question of an ultimatum over Berlin. There must be a peace treaty, but if the West would agree to reasonable negotiations, the date for the transfer of control of communications to the East German authorities could be postponed until July. The Russians would retain their control of communications until a peace treaty had been signed, he said. This was the first of several Soviet postponements by which Khrushchev staved off a Berlin crisis until the showdown came in August, 1961.

A few days later, in East Berlin, Khrushchev gave further indications of Soviet policy. He said he was not opposed to the three Western powers *plus Soviet Russia* maintaining a minimum number of troops *in West Berlin* to guarantee its status as a free city. He favoured West Berlin becoming a free city because it had developed differently from the D.D.R. and there must be bitter changes were it to be integrated in East Germany. If the West refused to sign a peace treaty with both German states he reiterated that he would sign a peace treaty with the D.D.R. alone, whether Adenauer liked it or not. If Adenauer refused, it would prove that his basic policy was one of preparing for war, against the D.D.R. presumably.

On 12th March, Macmillan arrived in Bonn for a two-day visit. Officially there was nothing but sweetness between the Chancellor and the British Prime Minister. The two official spokesmen insisted that there were no differences between British and German attitudes towards the procedure and principles to be followed in the forthcoming weeks; the public relations officers claimed that there was complete agreement in principle on Berlin, the German problem, and European security.

This was a strange statement. Macmillan's presumption in taking the initiative in anything affecting the future Germany and, still more, his gentlemanly and somewhat dilettante manner infuriated Adenauer whose Red Indian-like visage nevertheless remained as impassive as ever. The Prime Minister had scarcely left Bonn when Adenauer launched into a tirade against Macmillan to a group of his political sycophants. It was high time, he told some of the C.D.U., that the British learned that they were no longer the leaders on the continent of Europe. 'Germany and France are the leaders in Europe now,' he is reported to have concluded.

Denigrating comment on British policy in Europe continued to flow from officially inspired spokesmen in Bonn. On the other hand, de Gaulle's revolutionary acceptance of the Oder-Neisse line as Germany's eastern frontier, which might well have been expected to cause loud protest, was permitted to pass almost without comment. British newspapers, not surprisingly, replied to the Adenauer-inspired anti-British campaign. He was furious. And in a broadcast early in April all the venom, conditioned by a lifetime of Anglophobia, was poured out.

'A lot has been mentioned – and in the German Press as well as elsewhere – about our relations with Great Britain and, in particular, that my personal relations with the British Prime Minister are troubled. First of all, so far as my personal relations with Macmillan are concerned, everything that has been written is pure fantasy,' said Adenauer.

'I have sometimes asked myself if there are wire-pullers somewhere who deliberately try, for reasons of policy, to impair the relations between the British and the German people. Unfortunately, for some considerable time, a long time before Macmillan's journey to Moscow and before the start of the recent Washington (Foreign Ministers') conference, the atmosphere towards Germany in Britain has been, one might almost say, systematically impaired.

'When Prime Minister Macmillan visited Bonn on 12th March, I drew his attention openly and frankly to the systematically contrived impairment of the British attitude towards Germany. I told him how much I regretted this development, and how inexplicable I found it, even from the British point of view. For the fate of Britain and Germany, like the fate of the other states linked in the Atlantic Pact, are inseparably and insolubly bound together.

'In such a situation I lay great importance on the memory of the war years being finally buried and an end being made to that aversion to Germany which is fed from various quarters. On the German side, everything will be done to avoid anything which might contribute to adding fuel to the anti-German feeling in Britain.'

Adenauer claimed that after the talks with Macmillan the German delegation had been reproached for refusing to discuss the British proposals for the creation of a frozen zone in Europe. 'I have now once again made a very careful check of whether Great Britain ever made such a precise proposal. I have established that this matter was mentioned only in a vague way so that no discussion of it was possible,' Adenauer pronounced.

So much for the official claim that there had been 'complete agreement'.

Adenauer said that attacks on General de Gaulle in Britain, which arose from certain differences of opinion, had been kept within moderate limits. 'Only against the Germans, and against me in particular, are these attacks being made ever more strongly. My view is that we have become companions in fate and such superfluous and disturbing factors should be eliminated from political discussion.'

Adenauer had hated the British Press – as he hated all free organs of opinion – with all his heart and soul ever since that day in the spring of 1949 when he had been sent about his business by the British correspondents in Germany. It was beyond the scope of his aged, authoritarian intelligence to understand that the British Government and Mr. Macmillan had virtually no control at all over what British newspapers and political periodicals wrote about Germany and himself. In simple terms, he did not understand one of the basic institutions of free speech and democracy.

But the Chancellor's anti-British broadcast showed that he was thinking of more than just the British Press. By implication the speech was a direct personal attack on Mr. Macmillan. In semi-private conversation in Bonn, Adenauer had never concealed his view that the Prime Minister's visit to Moscow was nothing more than 'a shameless and dangerous electioneering trick' in preparation for the British general election in the autumn of 1959.

Adenauer's venomous outburst inevitably drew a sharp reaction in Britain. In the House of Commons, Mr. Dennis Healy, M.P. for the Labour party pointed out, amid wide approval, that nothing would do more to increase criticism of Germany and of Adenauer himself than 'the arrogant and dictatorial tone of his broadcast'. But the British Government believed that the unity of the West was more important than the irresponsible outburst of an aged Rhineland politician suffering from an attack of wounded vanity. For H.M. Government Mr. R. A. Butler gave the classic British answer in such circumstances; the reports of differences had been 'grossly exaggerated'.

CHAPTER SIXTEEN

Presidential Candidate

On 7TH APRIL 1959, Western Germany was struck by a bomb-shell. 'Adenauer to Go', screamed headlines on special editions of the evening papers and radio announcers breathlessly broke into regular programmes.

To the amazement of his fellow-countrymen and the gratifica-tion of a considerable section of his own party, he announced that he had decided to resign as Federal Chancellor in order to become the C.D.U. candidate in the forthcoming West German Presiden-tial Election. The Western World was equally thunderstruck. No one had believed that the old man who had been the absolute ruler of West Germany for a decade would go of his own accord.

Since the previous autumn, when it had been appreciated that by the Bonn constitution President Theodor Heuss would be debarred from standing for a third term, there had been inter-mittent discussion about the C.D.U. candidate. Adenauer had been mentioned several times, chiefly by his party foes. He had always brushed off the suggestion. Professor Erhard, his Econo-mics Minister and the most popular man in West Germany, had been the next choice. Adenauer, whose distaste for Erhard as a politician was common knowledge, had summarily quashed that proposal. By the beginning of April, the C.D.U. were aware that the choice of a C.D.U. candidate was becoming urgent.

The party managers pointed out to Adenauer that the S.P.D. had already selected the genial and popular Professor Carlo Schmid, and that a strong C.D.U. candidate was necessary. Adenauer agreed but dismissed hints that he was the obvious choice. Something approaching a 'palace revolt' now developed in the higher ranks of the C.D.U. Many of the more independent party leaders, notably the Protestants, had become weary of the intolerable and interminable Adenauer dictatorship. The urgent need to nominate a C.D.U. Presidential candidate gave them the opportunity to 'work him out'. The anti-Adenauer tacticians deployed their forces.

On 6th April, Adenauer received a small party delegation of whom the most important members were his fellow-Catholic and old crony Heinrich Krone, a pre-Nazi Zentrum party hack, and the formidable Premier of Schleswig-Holstein, later German Defence Minister, Herr Kai Uwe von Hassel, much of whose youth had been spent in the British mandated territory of Tanganyika.

They formally put to Adenauer a proposal that he should become C.D.U. Presidential candidate. He declined the nomination. But when the delegations departed, he had a sudden idea. His faithful shadow in the Federal Chancellery, the Third Reich civil servant, Dr. Globke, was told to make a rapid survey of the constitutional powers of the Federal President.

When Adenauer went home that evening to his villa at Rhoendorf, he seriously discussed his future with his son, Monsignor Paul Adenauer, who had become perhaps his 83-year-old father's closest counsellor. Monsignor Adenauer, concerned for his father's health and anxious that he should spend the evening of his life under less exacting conditions than the previous ten years, strongly urged his father to retire as Chancellor. To the devoted son it seemed an admirable solution for his father to end his great political career as Head of State.

All that night Adenauer, on his own admission, could not sleep. He pondered his future. He realized the wisdom of his son's counsel. He was certainly conscious of the fact that, with Mr. Dulles's resignation imminent, he was the last of the Cold Warriors. The Western Powers seemed determined to follow a more flexible line towards the East than the tension-charged policy which he favoured. He was now regarded in London and

Washington as an obstructionist. His bitter differences with Mr.
Macmillan and his growing estrangement from the Eisenhower
administration indicated that he was increasingly isolated at the
council table of the West.

The following morning, when he met the Council of the
C.D.U., he was still undecided. To the surprise of most of his
party colleagues, he made an hour and a quarter speech (facts
provided by Globke) on the dignities and duties of the Federal
President, an office which hitherto he had regarded with ill-con-
cealed contempt.

The Bundestag President, the Protestant Church official and
anti-Nazi resistance leader, Dr. Eugen Gerstenmeier, never one of
his greater admirers, commented, 'In view of the importance you
have attached to the office, Herr Bundeskanzler, there can only be
one choice for Federal President – yourself.' To this attempt to
rush him into acceptance, Adenauer retorted with a categorical
'Nein'. He then left the meeting to receive a French general in
the Federal Chancellery.

Over a cold buffet the sixty-three-man Council of the C.D.U.
canvassed the question of Adenauer as candidate. Dr. Gerstenmeier, Premier von Hassel and others did their utmost to further
Adenauer's candidature – it seemed the one sure way of kicking
him upstairs. They were successful. When Adenauer returned to
the meeting after lunch, he was faced with the news from Gerstenmeier that he was the unanimous choice of his party. He was
obviously nonplussed. He seemed to weaken. He spoke of
'doing his duty'. Then suddenly on an impulse he announced,
'I'll do it.'

The following day, he went on the German television and radio
to assure the Germans that there would be 'continuity' in Bonn
foreign policy when he became Federal President as seemed
inevitable; thereafter he launched into his philippic against the
British in general and Mr. Macmillan in particular to which
reference has already been made.

To the many critical commentators in the German Press the

reference to 'continuity' had a slightly sinister ring. They were far from convinced that the sudden decision to retire from the hurly-burly of political life signified any desire to vacate the role of supreme autocrat in Bonn. When, a few days later, Adenauer stepped into his special sleeping-car for his Easter holiday at Cadenabbia, with a copy of the Bonn constitution under his arm, his motives were suspect.

He realized that he had been outmanœuvred temporarily at the C.D.U. council meeting. As he later told intimates, he was 'rushed into a decision'. Now that the decision had been taken, it was obvious that he was bent on transforming Western Germany into 'a Presidential state'.

The commentator in *Der Spiegel*, Jens Daniel, – often reputed to be the proprieter Herr Augstein – always one of his most outspoken critics, commented that Adenauer was hoping to ape de Gaulle by becoming Head of State with supreme power.

'No real disservice will be done to the departing Chancellor,' he wrote, 'if one recognizes that by "continuity" he means nothing else than his own personal power.'

That prognosis was correct. Before he left Bonn, Adenauer told the always pliable Globke to make a full report on the powers of the presidential office. For Adenauer had begun to consider whether, by exploiting the powers of the Presidential office as he had exploited the powers of the Federal Chancellorship, he could still exercise authority over the Government, and especially over its foreign policy.

Globke, the obedient civil servant under all circumstances, was soon able to produce what appeared to be a satisfactory legal justification for what his master wanted to do. It reached Adenauer at Cadenabbia before Easter. The Chancellor was delighted and Globke is reported to have said, 'The Federal Chancellor was most impressed when he realized just what difficulties the Federal President can create for the Government, and all that he actually has the power to do – if he wants.'

His State-Secretary also carefully selected all the evidence and criticism made in recent years of the over-concentration of power in the Federal Chancellery and of the burden of work on the present incumbent. The aim, no doubt, was to provide justification, should it be required, for one of those modifications of the Bonn constitution which Adenauer always proposed at the moment it suited his own purpose.

Day after day, in his garden by Lake Como, Adenauer pondered on the possibilities of the Federal Presidency. Globke, in fact, was a poor constitutional lawyer and, as Dr. Gerstenmeier stated subsequently, 'It is clear that Adenauer read all the negatives in Globke's report as positives.'

Despite all the legal casuistry of the Globke report, Adenauer was politically acute enough to see that his plan rested on one fundamental fact; if he were to succeed in wielding supreme power as President, the next Federal Chancellor must be a stooge. After surveying the possibilities among the ranks of the C.D.U., he decided that his colourless and trustworthy Finance Minister, Franz Etzel, would be most easily brought to heel.

By private teleprinter from Lake Como to the Federal Chancellery in Bonn, Adenauer began long-distance soundings on Etzel's chances. The response was unfavourable. Daily reports reaching Italy from Bonn emphasized that the undoubted choice of the C.D.U. as next Chancellor would be Professor Erhard, the Vice-Chancellor. This hit Adenauer at his most vulnerable point. The idea that he would be kicked upstairs while a man whom he openly regarded as 'politically negligible' stepped into his shoes as Chancellor was too much.

From that moment of realization at Cadenabbia, Adenauer began to play a game of political trickery, paralleled in recent European history perhaps only by the activities of Lloyd George. For while publicly maintaining the lie that he would stand as C.D.U. candidate in the Presidential election, *Adenauer had ninety-nine per cent decided that he would remain Chancellor.*

According to well-informed political sources in Bonn, at Cadenabbia he revealed his innermost thoughts to his Minister of the Interior, Dr. Gerhard Schroeder, who at that time was still very much under the old man's domination. To his old Zentrum party friend Dr. Krone he expressed what he described as doubts about going on with the candidacy for President. Krone, blunt and honest, answered, 'That just won't work. It would be the end of your political career.'

Adenauer's secret intention was fortified by further news from Bonn, that Erhard had made it clear to the party 'kingmakers' that, in the event of Etzel becoming Chancellor, he would not remain as Minister of Economics. Adenauer returned to Bonn in mid-May and to some, but not all of his Cabinet colleagues he confided that it was 'ninety per cent certain that, due to the foreign affairs position', he would not be a Presidential candidate. Those in his inner circle knew that he meant what he said. The others believed that this was just another of the 'Old Fox's' tricks to force Etzel on the party as Chancellor.

To maintain the pretence that he was still a Presidential candidate, however, Adenauer devised a stratagem which would have been of little credit to him, even as the most junior Beigeordnete in Cologne half a century earlier. As a connoisseur of German wines, he began to express anxiety about what would happen to the splendid selection of Rhine and Mosel vintages which he had gathered in the cellar of the Chancellery, in the Palais Schaumburg. He indicated that he was concerned that when he moved next door to the Villa Hammerschmidt, the Presidential residence, he would be unable to take his collection of vintages with him. With discreet propaganda on the higher levels of the Government, he instructed experts of the Finance Ministry – Etzel's ministry – to work out a plan for transferring the wine.

A week after his statement to his Cabinet colleagues, Adenauer summoned Erhard and then Gerstenmeier to the Chancellery. On Erhard he urged that he should drop his opposition to Etzel as Chancellor. Otherwise he would reconsider his decision.

According to members of the C.D.U., he suggested to Gerstenmeier that he should bring pressure on Erhard to accept Etzel.

Bluntly the Protestant Church official answered, 'No one can force you, Herr Bundeskanzler, to propose what you don't want. But you cannot force the Bundestag to vote for your candidate. Don't let it come to a test of strength. Then you've had it!' Adenauer retorted, 'No one has spoken to me so bluntly. I must now consider all the consequences.'

From that moment, Adenauer's battle for his protégé, Etzel, was no more than shadow boxing – if it had ever been any more since he returned from Cadenabbia. His mind was firmly made up to remain Chancellor. At a meeting of the committee of the C.D.U. parliamentary party on 25th May, after some hesitation, he indicated that he would continue to be the party candidate for the Presidency. Gerstenmeier demanded to know whether that was to be so in all circumstances, even in the event of the C.D.U. choosing Erhard rather than Etzel as his successor. Adenauer answered arrogantly, 'Not at all.'

Twenty-four hours later, at a full meeting of the parliamentary party, he again attempted to blur the issue. When Krone told the meeting, 'I am certain that the Chancellor will stand as candidate,' Adenauer remained silent. From this meeting Adenauer drove straight to Bonn airfield and climbed into a special aircraft chartered to take him to the funeral of his great friend, John Foster Dulles, who had finally succumbed to cancer, a few weeks after his resignation. As he disappeared, one of his more irreverent ministers commented, 'When he comes back he will say that Eisenhower pleaded with him to remain as Chancellor.'

On Saturday, 30th May, Adenauer returned from Washington where he had had some conversation with Mr. Gromyko and the three Western Foreign Ministers, who had flown from the four-power meeting at Geneva to the funeral. Adenauer spent the weekend resting at home, but on Monday morning, he received Erhard, who was about to leave on a week's trip to the United States.

They discussed economic affairs for several hours. When Adenauer wished his Economics Minister a pleasant trip, he gave no hint of the decision he had already taken. Erhard was still on German soil when Adenauer told Krone and Gerstenmeier, during a meeting in the Bundeshaus, that he had reached an irrevocable decision; he would remain Chancellor and abandon his candidature for the Presidency. Both said they would report his decision to the party office-bearers.

Gerstenmeier, according to C.D.U. sources, was so incensed by Adenauer's jesuitical double-dealing and play acting of the previous few weeks, that seizing the Chancellor by the arm, he dragged the old man into a vacant room and banged the door. There, a showdown is reported to have taken place between the German Federal Chancellor and the Speaker of the German Parliament. But the high official of the Lutheran Church was preaching to deaf ears. To his prophecy of what would happen to Adenauer and the party, Adenauer retorted, 'My authority will be unimpaired.'

He knew his Germans, and the C.D.U. politicians. On the following day, Adenauer gave his decision in black and white to the C.D.U. 'kingmakers'. The Foreign Ministers' meeting in Geneva on the Berlin question was still dragging on, and Adenauer declared that, 'because of the deterioration in the foreign political situation', he could not leave his chair at such a critical phase in events.

In a panic, the party leadership resolutely kept silent about his right-about-turn. The most formidable of the party vice-presidents, Premier von Hassel, was summoned from Kiel to try and persuade Adenauer to stick to his pledged word and stand for President. Herr von Hassel received a stony reception when he reached the Chancellery. By the evening of 4th June the news could be concealed no longer. The second Adenauer bombshell in two months hit the German capital.

Bonn was in turmoil. The C.D.U. seethed with a combination of furious anger and frustrated hopes. The bolder spirits were out for blood. Next afternoon Adenauer, dour, formidable and more intransigent than at any time in the previous ten years, faced the hostile phalanx formed by the office-bearers of his parliamentary party. They wanted to get rid of him. He knew it. In any normal democratic country the spectacle could have had only one conclusion, the resignation of the detested Federal Chancellor.

With that contemptuous authoritarianism, which by this time was innate, Adenauer scarcely deigned to consider their hostility. Like Hitler, he believed that he was indispensable for the future of Germany. In the famous words of Lord Acton; power had corrupted. There was no one fit to succeed him. He had delusions of infallibility. He might well have repeated the remark made to Paul Henri Spaak in 1954, at the height of the European Army crisis, '*Mein Gott*, what will happen to Germany when I am not there.'

According to C.D.U. officials, he told his hostile audience that he had decided to change his mind because the world situation had deteriorated since he had first made the decision to stand for the Presidency on 7th April. A change in German foreign policy at this moment was out of the question, he told the C.D.U. office-bearers. Clearly, no one else was capable of directing German foreign policy.

The speaker, Dr. Gerstenmeier, said with calculated offence; 'None of your arguments has impressed us in the least, Herr Bundeskanzler.'

Frigidly the old man retorted, 'There is no question of my *wishing* to be Federal Chancellor. *I am Chancellor.* If that doesn't suit you, you know what to do – move a vote of "constructive no confidence" against me in Parliament.'

That was a key moment in German post-war history. German democracy cried aloud for a Leopold Amery; for a German like the veteran British minister who, in the House of Commons on 7th May, 1940, told his lifelong colleague, friend and Prime Minister, Neville Chamberlain, in the terrible words Oliver Cromwell used to the Long Parliament: 'You have sat too long here for any good you have done. Depart, I say, and let us have done with you. In the name of God . . . Go!'

Alas, there was no Leopold Amery in the C.D.U., or in the German Bundestag! Had there been but one, German democracy today might be placed on firmer foundations, and German foreign policy in the last months of Adenauer's Chancellorship would not have been in the dead end into which he led it.

If there was no German Amery there was, however, a certain Dr. Gerd Bucerius, the Hamburg publisher of both the influential political periodical, *Die Zeit* and also of the biggest of the mass circulation German picture weeklies, *Der Stern*.

Unlike so many of the C.D.U., Dr. Bucerius was a man of political courage. The confidant and friend of Professor Erhard, he rallied a hard core of twenty C.D.U. democrats who were determined, if they could, to oust Adenauer and save the honour of their party. Before the meeting of C.D.U. office-bearers, Bucerius and his fellow-conspirators, greatly daring, agreed to make an all-out onslaught on the Chancellor and his double-dealing. They believed that given a clear lead, the weak-kneed sheep who formed the majority of Adenauer's party might, for once, nerve themselves to defy the will and fury of the octogenarian autocrat. Adenauer quickly brought his C.D.U. flock to heel.

Comparatively few Germans and still fewer German politicians, as the history of the past half-century has proved, are noted for either political or, still more, civic courage. Office is dear in a country dominated by 'Herr Doktor snobbery'. The great mass of the C.D.U. deputies were, and continued to be, very average Germans. Adenauer, in diametrical contrast, was one of the historical 'Führer-figures' whom the Germans through the centuries have instinctively obeyed.

By the exercise of an iron will and open manifestation of contempt for the vacillating opposition, he soon squashed all resistance. It was a grim portent of what one determined Teutonic autocrat, without either Adenauer's devout Catholic principles or personal benevolence, might achieve with a democratically elected majority of the German Bundestag in years to come.

But Adenauer's authoritarian disregard of democratic and parliamentary practice was not allowed to go unchallenged. The great body of the German Press, always the true defenders of German democracy in contrast to the craven politicians, unloosed an onslaught on the impossible old man in the Federal Chancellery.

Die Welt, the organ of multi-millionaire Axel Springer, whose publications as a whole were normally far from anti-Adenauer, asked, 'How can the highest offices of the State be respected after they have been juggled with in this manner?'

Adenauer, said *Die Welt*, had sacrificed to his lust for power 'some of the bonds between him and his party, some of the dignity of the two highest offices of State, and some of the confidence of his parliamentary colleagues'.

Der Spiegel, despite its faults probably the freest and most outspoken German publication, called him a 'power-obsessed old man'. The news magazine of Herr Augstein, with whom in due course Adenauer was to come to open battle, then demanded what most of Germany felt; members of all parties in the Bundestag should show enough political guts to sweep Adenauer from office, and by a massive vote of 'constructive no confidence', nominate Professor Erhard as the new Federal Chancellor.

Everything now seemed to depend on the stand taken by Professor Erhard, the Economics Minister, who was breathing fire from the other side of the Atlantic. Abandoning the remainder of his trip, Professor Erhard flew by way of London to Düsseldorf where he was greeted by an army of newspaper, TV and radio reporters. The normally friendly, tubby economics expert made no effort to disguise his fury. He said that he would certainly take no initiative to meet Adenauer and that he would not necessarily remain Vice-Chancellor in the Adenauer Government.

Adenauer had hinted that Erhard's appointment as Chancellor would lead to a less firm German foreign policy, and that the

Economics Minister was less than whole-hearted in his support of European integration. In reply, Erhard demanded that 'this historical lie' should be put right.

Behind the scenes in Bonn, Adenauer's faithful retainer, 'Papa' Krone, was desperately striving to avoid a major split. To and fro he went between the completely relaxed Adenauer in the Federal Chancellery and the agitated Erhard and his friends and supporters in the Economics Ministry. Finally, five days after Erhard's return to Germany, the Chancellor and Vice-Chancellor met. According to what later leaked out, it was a frigid meeting. The two men only discussed Erhard's visit to America; not a word was exchanged about the blazing row between them.

By the basic traditions of democratic practice in all free countries, any Deputy Prime Minister who had been so abominably treated by the head of Government as Erhard had been, would have immediately resigned – and precipitated a major Government crisis. His self-respect, if nothing else, demanded it. But German politicians know little of democratic practice and less of self-respect. Erhard continued to puff and blow in his ministry.

Once again, the party political jobber Krone attempted to mediate. He was joined by the Speaker Gerstenmeier, whom Adenauer had accused to his face of being 'full of hate'. All that afternoon there was much to-ing and fro-ing between the private rooms of the C.D.U. in the Bundestag. Finally, Adenauer, Krone, Gerstenmeier and Erhard appeared in a row. Gerstenmeier had in his hand the result of the afternoon's horse-trading. He described it, somewhat euphemistically, as a 'declaration of honour'.

It stated that the C.D.U. parliamentary party had welcomed a declaration by the Federal Chancellor that any question of denigrating the Economics Minister had been far from his mind. The party assured Professor Erhard of its particular esteem, and deprecated statements aimed at damaging his reputation. For the benefit of the photographers, Erhard actually shook hands with Adenauer!

As the party broke up, Erhard muttered, 'I am finished with that man,' but no one seriously believed him. The political wits of Bonn pungently summed up the situation by christening Erhard 'The Rubber Lion'. That sarcastic but unfair appellation would stick. Four years later, after unparalleled denigration and insult from the Head of Government, Erhard was still in office as Minister of Economics.

While he acknowledged Erhard's skill as an economist, Adenauer's respect for the Vice-Chancellor as a politician was nil. He made little effort to hide that view. He expressed neither regret nor apology for his intolerable conduct, and at the first meeting of the Bundestag, he arrogantly told the members that his decision to change his mind had been 'an exercise of democratic freedom'. Non-Germans would have preferred to describe it as a cynical and unscrupulous demonstration of a lust for personal power.

He added that the deciding factor had been the unfavourable course of the four-power ministers' conference in Geneva, and the death of Mr. Dulles. The last statement held the core of the matter. Without Dulles he believed that the West was heading for disaster if he gave up control of German foreign policy and the veto which, for so long, he had succeeded in imposing on Western policy towards the East. For he had been in a state of near-panic when a rumour reached him from the German delegation in Geneva that Mr. Macmillan was on the point of making a lightning visit to Khrushchev in Moscow, to try to end the East-West deadlock over Berlin.

The Bundestag was unimpressed by Adenauer's arguments. After Erhard had given his account of the events of the previous few weeks, some members showed enough disregard for parliamentary practices to mount the rostrum, ten yards from where Adenauer sat at the end of the government 'jury box', and to call him 'liar' to his face. But not a single member of any party rose to move a vote of no confidence against him!

Adenauer had reason to be confident. To emphasize his complete disregard for Erhard, the party and the so-called 'Declaration of Honour', a week later he opened a new attack on his Vice-Chancellor. To a correspondent of the *New York Times* he said that it was possible to be an excellent economics minister without having any experience of foreign affairs.

He personally would refuse to become Minister of Economics, because he did not understand economics – which the previous ten years had shown to be the truth. He did not doubt for a moment that Professor Erhard was an especially gifted man, and he had no doubt that the Vice-Chancellor in time would acquire the requisite political experience. In any case, concluded Adenauer, the 1961 general election had still to be won, *and he would not retire before 1962 at the earliest.*

Once again, Adenauer brought the C.D.U. to the verge of revolt; it never went farther than the verge! Erhard was apoplectic. Again, he puffed and blew and threatened resignation. The cartoonists had made their own estimate of the value of the Vice-Chancellor's threats. He was shown, lion-like, roaring threats and then like a deflated rubber toy, with a pin stuck in its side, flat on the ground ... 'The Rubber Lion'. In due course, he was appeased by an equivocal letter of semi-apology from Adenauer. He would continue to puff and blow hot air for the next four years until, after an identical performance at the time of Britain's exclusion from the Common Market, the C.D.U. a few weeks later finally rebelled and nominated Erhard as next Chancellor (in defence of Adenauer.)

The question of the future Presidential candidate had been forgotten amid the party in-fighting. At the end of June, Adenauer summarily solved the problem by nominating as C.D.U. candidate the feeblest and most insignificant of his Cabinet Ministers, Dr. Heinrich Lubke, the Federal Minister of Agriculture, who could be safely relied on not to exercise these presidential obstructionist powers which had so fascinated Adenauer a month or two earlier.

Dr. Lubke was duly elected Federal President. If he had none of the distinction of his predecessor, Professor Heuss, he and his talented wife, carried out their official duties with great dignity. Having disposed of Erhard and the C.D.U. rebels, Adenauer once more returned to his favourite target, the British. Mr. Gromyko, the Soviet Foreign Secretary, had demonstrated all too clearly at Geneva the disarray in the Western camp. Adenauer, with the deepest distrust of what Mr. Macmillan, on the eve of a British general election, might do, blamed the British as usual. He felt that not only had they shown a deplorably pusillanimous approach, but that the British Prime Minister tended to lead his wartime colleague, President Eisenhower, now without Mr. Dulles, far from the true faith.

Mr. Macmillan, as so often in the later years of Adenauer's chancellorship, was the main whipping boy when Adenauer poured out his fears to an American correspondent who was visiting Bonn on the way from Geneva conference. To the American, Adenauer confided that Macmillan should understand that, if he belonged to an alliance, he must be prepared to sacrifice some of his own views.

To that offensive reference were added others. To visitors who could be relied on to relay his remarks to the British Embassy Adenauer continually referred to Britain as 'the weak link in the Western Alliance' and added that it ill-behoved Macmillan 'to try and outdo the German opposition'.

The British were well aware of all this; they had come to know Adenauer very well. It was just the old man's Anglophobia again. There was nothing to be done. But his Foreign Minister von Brentano and the German diplomats who had worked in the closest co-operation with their British colleagues in Geneva were worried. They felt that the non-stop anti-British campaign, sooner or later, might produce some re-action in London. They had no desire to force the British into an openly anti-German policy in the presence of Khrushchev at some future Summit meeting. Under strong pressure from the German Foreign Office, Adenauer was persuaded to write to Mr. Macmillan. Whether he made amends for what he had said in the previous few months is open to question. But there was an exchange of personal letters in the second half of July. Adenauer's Anglophobia was suppressed, but not for long.

President Eisenhower, too, was aware of the disarray in the Western camp. He decided to attempt to close the ranks by a personal tour of the principal European capitals at the end of August. For Adenauer and the Germans the mere fact of a visit of an American president to Bonn magnified the occasion far beyond its intrinsic importance. To the Chancellor and most of his people it seemed to symbolize the return of the Germans to full membership of the Western family, and the visit did much to allay, for the time being, that deep-seated German feeling of insecurity and inferiority.

Adenauer, emphasizing that the previous American President, Mr. Truman, had also visited Germany – to sign the hated Potsdam agreement – did everything to make the brief visit a gala occasion. The effect was somewhat spoiled by chauvinistic and irredentist banners demanding the return of the 'lost territories' of the east, along the President's route from the airfield to the Federal Chancellery. So outrageous was one banner, which demanded the incorporation of the Sudentenland which had never been German, that even Adenauer was constrained to have it removed before Eisenhower's arrival. The banners must have reminded the President, with memories of earlier days in Germany, that the Germans were not the cosiest of allies.

Much of the President's brief time in Bonn was occupied in discussing the increasingly awkward attitude of Adenauer's close friend de Gaulle to American leadership of N.A.T.O. It was a problem which, in the end, was to reduce Adenauer's foreign policies to chaos.

The President, as Mr. Dulles had done so often in the past, was able to dispel the Chancellor's doubts and fears, but only temporarily. Adenauer had scarcely returned to Cadenabbia to resume his interrupted summer holiday when he was obsessed by the realization that, within a week or two, Khrushchev would discuss the whole German problem with Eisenhower across a table in Washington. 'The Potsdam Nightmare' was seldom far below the surface.

CHAPTER SEVENTEEN

The Turning Point

THE SUMMER of 1959 marked the turning point of Adenauer's Chancellorship. Neither his prestige nor his policies ever recovered from the events of these months.

At first, Adenauer was like a small boy who had stolen the jam and got away with it. With the impertinence of what may well have been the onset of second childhood, he gloried in the success of his Machiavellianism. Soon after the *Machtergreifung* – as sarcastic Germans referred to the comparison between his Byzantine political antics and Hitler's seizure of power in 1933 – Adenauer received one of those postcards so dear to the instincts of Teutonic thrift. It was anonymous. But unlike most German cut-price postcards of the same sort, it contained, apart from his name and address only three words, scrawled in the Cologne dialect which he had known since childhood, '*Du Alter Jauner*' ... You old Rogue! That was just how he felt.

It was not until the quiet weeks by Lake Como after the Eisenhower visit to Bonn that it dawned on 'the old rogue' what had really happened. He realized at last that he had done himself irreparable harm. Both at home and abroad his prestige had slumped to the lowest point since he had become Federal Chancellor ten years earlier. The open manifestation of his all-consuming lust for power marked the end of the unchallenged supremacy of Adenauer and his policies, both in Western Germany and in the Western Alliance.

Never again would he be accorded that honour and respect in which, despite the intermittent criticism of his authoritarian ways, he had been held for so long. Adenauer, at last, had shown his true colours. Even his greatest admirers in Germany and beyond were shocked.

At home in the Federal Republic, opinion polls showed a disastrous drop in his personal prestige. One poll showed that over ninety-four per cent of West Germans were against him. The Hamburg publishers were again the mouthpiece of the people. In Dr. Bucerius's *Die Zeit* a commentator stated that hitherto it had been believed that German policy was decided by the Chancellor's judgement; now it had been discovered that it was only his prejudice. Herr Augstein's *Spiegel* stated bluntly that he was 'an obstinate old man'.

The wave of anti-Adenauer feeling marked the start of that slump in his once enormous prestige which would lead to the major setback in the general election two years later; and which would reach its nadir in the winter of 1962 and the spring of 1963, when he became something approaching anathema to great numbers of his fellow-countrymen.

Adenauer had never set much store on German opposition to his will. When he returned to Bonn in the second half of September he proceeded to re-assert his authority as usual, but to an almost unprecedented extent. In his absence the C.D.U. had been behaving like a normal democratic party. Individual ministers had started to carry out their duties as if they had some individual responsibility. At once he restored discipline and brought them to heel. First casualty was Professor Erhard's plan for attempting to avoid the economic division of Europe. Whatever its intrinsic merits, it stemmed from the Vice-Chancellor. Adenauer was not prepared to tolerate Professor Erhard's growing popularity. The plan was jettisoned. Next came the C.D.U. Some of the brighter spirits, in his absence, had drawn up plans for reforming the party organization, and limiting his power. These he rejected out of hand without reference to the other party leaders. To limit any future tendency towards restiveness, he indicated that he proposed to curb the power of the party machine in the federal provinces,

where there had been widespread signs of incipient revolt against
his leadership.

Beyond Germany, his most devoted admirers, with the sole
exception of the occupant of the Elysée, had been even more disillusioned by the events of the summer. His intimate, personal
ties with Washington had ended with the death of Mr. Dulles.
The President, as he showed during his visit to Bonn, was friendly
and understanding; he had never been an Adenauer intimate.
Even the Chancellor's firmest supporters in the White House, the
State Department and the Pentagon were shocked by his flagrant
disregard for even the common decencies of political convention.
The Washington correspondent of the London *Sunday Times*,
Henry Brandon, in a masterpiece of British understatement, commented: 'Recently Dr. Adenauer has lost a good deal of authority
in Washington and, particularly since he reversed his decision to
resign from the Chancellorship, faith in his judgement has
declined.' More brutal commentators suggested that the Eisenhower administration, with an eye on the presidential elections
little more than twelve months ahead, found his badly tarnished
reputation, and his reputation as the last of the Cold Warriors,
a distinct embarrassment.

Outside of Washington the Adenauer slump had gone even
farther. In the months ahead, a high-powered firm of New York
public relations consultants were retained to try and restore the
'Adenauer image' in the eyes of the great American public.

Not only had Adenauer's prestige slumped disastrously. His
foreign policy, to which he would devote of his remaining years
as Chancellor, was in disarray. From the moment the aura and the
assurances of the Eisenhower visit had faded, the old man
seemed troubled and, for the first time since he had become
Chancellor, muddled and confused – as the record of his zigzag
course in the following few months would confirm. As he sat by
the side of Lake Como, the fundamental policies on which he had
based everything for a decade seemed in jeopardy. This is what
faced him:

1. Khrushchev was on a triumphal tour of the United States after discussing global, European *and German* affairs with Eisenhower in an atmosphere of cosy cordiality. A Summit meeting of the Big Four, at which he could not be present and on which his influence at best would be limited, would certainly take place within the next few months. As always, when Mr. Dulles was no longer at hand, Adenauer was again beset by deep suspicion of Eisenhower's painstaking efforts to increase the odds in favour of peace.

2. The impressive marksmanship of the Soviet moon rocketeers, in which at first he had refused to believe, and Khrushchev's obvious refusal to be impressed by American power, had led Adenauer to have serious doubts, for the first time, about that American military supremacy on which he had based virtually everything since the start of the Korean war nearly a decade earlier.

3. Already partly mesmerized by the *'gloire'* of de Gaulle, the Chancellor was still far enough away from his subsequent state of hypnosis by all things French to be troubled by the enigmatic and awkward ways of his fellow-authoritarian.

While the French President stood side by side with the German Chancellor in presenting a hard front to the Soviet Union in Central Europe, de Gaulle, with characteristic disregard for his partner, had struck two blows at fundamental Bonn policies; he had recognized the Oder-Neisse line as the eastern frontier of a future United Germany, and he was doing his best to wreck N.A.T.O., which to Adenauer had long seemed the ultimate bastion of Western defence.

Then, as usual, there was Macmillan. On the eve of a British general election, the Prime Minister seemed in his approach to European and German affairs more unreliable and more untrustworthy than ever. To crown everything, Adenauer's own Foreign Office in Bonn, worried over the inherent contradictions of American and French policy, had lined up with the British. To his intimates at the daily game of *boccia* in the garden of his lakeside villa, Adenauer confided that his two main opponents in the Western camp were the Bonn Foreign Office and the British, in that order.

The sophisticated and experienced diplomats of the Koblenzer-strasse had already begun to mark the dangers of Adenauer's double headed policy of maintaining the alliance with the United States and, at the same time, coming to an ever-closer understanding with the increasingly anti-American French President. They were to be proved correct.

It was that same, inherent, basic contradiction which would reach its inevitable and ultimate conclusion in January, 1963, when Adenauer, in defiance of the advice of almost everyone in Bonn, signed his personal treaty with de Gaulle within a few days of the French President's anti-Anglo-Saxon blast at the Press conference which ended Britain's approach to the European Common Market.

Adenauer's uncertain state of mind had first become obvious within a few hours of Eisenhower's departure from Bonn. As soon as he arrived in Italy, he published the text of a letter which he had sent to Khrushchev very obviously as a result of the President's persuasion. It seemed to mark a new and positive development in German foreign policy, for it proposed a resumption of negotiations on disarmament from the point where they had been left by the United Nations sub-committee which had met in London in 1957.

In this 'new look' approach to the Russians he brushed aside all other problems, most significantly the question of German re-unification and Germany's eastern frontier, and asserted that the only decisive problem was controlled disarmament.

About the same time, on the anniversary of Hitler's attack on Poland in September, 1939, Adenauer expressed his sorrow for Poland's tragic history. The Poles were not impressed, and accused Adenauer of 'crocodile tears'. The Soviet Prime Minister, however, reacted more propitiously. He stated that Adenauer's letter, on a first reading, created a favourable impression. The correspondence between Adenauer and Khrushchev dragged on for some time until, towards the end of 1959, Adenauer suddenly dropped it. By then Adenauer knew definitely that a Summit meeting was to take place within a few months. He also realized that both the United States and Britain were prepared, if opportunity offered, to negotiate a new agreement on Berlin, which he considered both unwise and undesirable. He was incapable of contemplating any new approach to an old problem. His only contribution to Western counsels was a dogmatic reassertion of the necessity of maintaining the *status quo*; and realizing that his views were in disfavour, he withdrew into that defensive shell which his detractors described as intransigence and inflexibility.

Weeks before he reached that point, the zig-zags of his foreign policy had taken him in the most unexpected direction of all, to London. The British Government had long deprecated the series of insults and rebuffs which it had suffered at Adenauer's hands over a long period. In the interests of Western unity it was essential that the breach should be healed, if that were possible. Mr. Macmillan was world statesman enough to sink any personal rancour he might naturally have felt, in the interests of a reconciliation with the German Chancellor.

The British are bad haters, and after Adenauer's return to Bonn in late September, the British Ambassador, Sir Christopher Steel, whose personal friendship with Adenauer had remained unaffected by Anglo-German squabbles, sounded out the possibility of an Adenauer visit to London. The proposal was strongly supported by the Foreign Minister, Herr von Brentano, and by Professor Erhard and the leaders of German industry, who were increasingly concerned at what appeared the imminent division of Western Europe into two mutually hostile trading *blocs*.

Adenauer had profound doubts. He had deep-seated reservations about Mr. Macmillan and about British foreign policy in general. He feared what the British might propose at the forthcoming Summit and suspected that they wished to settle the

Berlin question without reference to the German problem as a whole. He was equally doubtful about the equivocal position which existed between London and Paris over the failure of the negotiations between 'The Six' and the seven nations of the European Free Trade Area.

But the Chancellor was under pressure from all sides. Not only did his Foreign Office and his Economics Minister urge a *rapprochement* with London; German public opinion had begun to be openly critical of his well-known Anglophobia, which was held responsible for the state of Anglo-German relations.

The important, and often pro-Adenauer, *Frankfurter Allgemeine* pointed out that it was high time that Anglo-German relations were put on a solid basis of common interest. 'Bonn should count itself lucky,' commented the German leader writer somewhat tartly, 'that it has to deal with a British Government which approaches questions between the two countries soberly and positively. The Chancellor should seize with firm hands the opportunity in London which now presents itself.'

With the British general election out of the way and Mr. Macmillan returned to office with increased authority, Adenauer finally decided to accept the British invitation. The main reason was perhaps his confused state of his mind. But he was close enough to German big business pressure-groups to realize what a division of Europe could mean to German exports – something which the hypnotized old man completely forgot when de Gaulle embraced him in Paris at the beginning of 1963.

When Adenauer reached London in mid-November, both sides were genuinely anxious to end the carping and the hostility of the previous few months. Whether Adenauer and Macmillan would ever be mutually compatible was more doubtful, but the spirit of the meetings at No. 10 Downing Street and at Chequers was much improved, and when the German Chancellor left Victoria Station, a British crowd quite spontaneously sang, 'For He's a Jolly Good Fellow,' as he shook hands with the Prime Minister. It was a surprising contrast to the muted self-conscious clapping and the odd individual cheer that had been heard on his arrival three days before.

The talks did much to clear the air but as was admitted later they were still dominated by the Adenauer-Macmillan discord. According to what became known in London and what Adenauer permitted to leak out through German sources subsequently, there was frank talking on two main subjects, how Britain could become associated with the European Common Market, and Allied policy on Germany and Berlin at the forthcoming Summit meeting.

Adenauer confirmed what was being widely discussed at the time, that 'The Six' proposed to push forward plans for a political union. Both men agreed that a political union between 'The Six' must not be permitted to develop into a political *bloc* which would injure the Western Alliance as a whole.

On the question of Britain's future association with the European Common Market Adenaucr, if German sources can be trusted, appears to have shown more sympathy to this idea than he had done in the past, or than he was to show in the final months of 1962 when keen bargaining was in progress in Brussels between British ministers and the Common Market representatives. Macmillan seems to have given Adenauer some hint that he was already pondering that policy which culminated in the decision in 1961, when Britain applied to join the Common Market.

Adenauer assured the Prime Minister that he favoured 'The Six' trying to meet British wishes, so far as the political aims of the Community would admit. He went on to add that 'The Six' were determined to reach agreement with Britain and that, sooner or later, *negotiations between Britain and 'The Six' must be started.*

On the forthcoming Summit both men agreed that a *detente* should be sought by way of disarmament, but not at any price. On the question of Berlin the Prime Minister accepted Adenauer's main premise that Berlin must be treated as part of the German problem as a whole.

Against his better judgement and basic instinct Adenauer appeared to accept one important British qualification, that an *interim* agreement on Berlin should be accepted if the Western leaders at the Summit were able to reach some sort of *modus operandi* with Khrushchev.

Whatever ostensible agreement Adenauer may have given to this pragmatic British suggestion amid the easy atmosphere of Chequers, he realized, as soon as he returned to Bonn, that it was the thin edge of the wedge. Such a proposal would permit Eisenhower and Macmillan, in the event of failure to achieve any progress on the German question as a whole, to make an agreement on Berlin alone for which big sections of the public opinion in both Anglo-Saxon countries were clamouring. It was in search of an ally for his 'Stand Firm' policy that he travelled to Paris, ten days later, for a two-day meeting with de Gaulle. Most of the meeting was devoted to the all-too-public differences between Adenauer and de Gaulle, with his well-known opposition to integrated defence, over the future of N.A.T.O. When the somewhat discomfited Chancellor got back to Bonn, he had to admit that he 'had not ascertained General de Gaulle's view of a *detente* on the Soviet side'. He added that he saw no sign of any thaw on the Russian side which, no doubt, was why he ended his correspondence with Khrushchev a few days later, and retired into his shell.

But no one could ever accuse the German Chancellor of a lack of persistency. He was a convinced follower of King Robert the Bruce of Scotland, who watched the spider try seven times before it achieved success. Before Christmas, Adenauer was back in Paris to attempt to impose his 'Do nothing' pre-conditions for the Summit on Eisenhower, Macmillan and de Gaulle, all of whom had gathered in the French capital for the annual council meeting of N.A.T.O.

He failed, chiefly because Macmillan, and to some extent Eisenhower in his determination to try and ease tension before he demitted office, refused to be pinned down by what were now generally recognized to be simply the old man's intractable political prejudices. As Mr. Richard Crossman, M.P. aptly commented, Adenauer was a political primitive.

Most of the four-power discussions centred round the forthcoming Summit. Before the talks ended, letters were sent to Khrushchev suggesting that the Summit meeting be held in Paris, probably about the end of April, 1960. At the same time, the three Allied Ambassadors in Moscow were told to put it to the Soviet Foreign Minister, Mr. Gromyko, that the agenda should include disarmament, Germany (including Berlin) and East-West relations.

At the end of the meeting Adenauer, Eisenhower, de Gaulle and Macmillan issued a statement reaffirming the general Western policy on Germany and Berlin agreed twelve months earlier in Paris. Adenauer at once repeated one of his time-honoured tactics. He attempted to put the Western leaders at the Summit into a diplomatic straitjacket by ordering his spokesman to claim that Western policy had hardened. The spokesman alleged that by virtue of this innocent communique, the Western Powers were, in effect, withdrawing a number of concessions made conditionally to Gromyko at the Foreign Ministers' meeting at Geneva during the previous summer.

He was rebuffed. The Americans privately, and the British openly, had become weary of Adenauer's constant attempts to dictate what Eisenhower and Macmillan should say to Khrushchev. British Foreign Office spokesmen gave Adenauer the lie by announcing categorically that there had been no change in British policy at least. The Americans tacitly agreed.

Adenauer was with his family celebrating the traditional German Holy Eve on 24th December, when suddenly the grim shadow of Germany's immediate past loomed over the Federal Republic. On Christmas Eve, as millions of Germans lit the candles on their Christmas trees, swastikas and that slogan of terrible memory, '*Juden Raus*', were daubed across the walls of the Cologne synagogue. The city's memorial plaque to the Cologne victims of the Nazi holocaust was desecrated in the same way.

It was a personal blow at Adenauer himself. The outrage had taken place in his own native city, where he himself had been persecuted, and where only the previous October at the opening of the synagogue, he had spoken of the general German rejection of the small anti-Semitic element which still existed in the Federal Republic. The Chancellor was deeply disturbed. He interrupted his Christmas to apologize: 'It is with deep abhorrence that I have heard of the outrageous act which I, and all decent Germans condemn.'

The Cologne outrage acted like a toxin to latent anti-Semitism throughout Western Germany. Within hours, a wave of anti-Semitic and neo-Nazi incidents were reported from all parts of the Federal Republic. All evoked terrible memories of what had been commonplace in the terrible years of the Third Reich. Adenauer ordered that the strongest measures be taken to protect and defend the small number of Jews in Western Germany and their property. Police guards were placed on synagogues, Jewish cemeteries and memorials to the victims of the Nazis.

The example set by the two young fanatics of the Deutsche Reichspartei, an extreme right wing group on the lunatic fringe of German politics, who had been arrested within twenty-four hours of carrying out the original outrage in Cologne, spread like wildfire. Anti-Semitic outrages and demonstrations were reported from all over Europe. There was some evidence that they might be linked with the new Nazi underground international. Soon anti-Jewish slogans had been scrawled on walls from Melbourne to London.

Liberal opinion right round the world was outraged. More and more incidents were reported from the Federal Republic, where estimates put the number of new Nazis at around 100,000. In Western countries, where largely because of Adenauer's services, there had been a tendency to forget, if not to forgive, the Nazi past, there was a sudden shock at the revelation that many prominent members of the 'Brown scourge' were firmly esconced in high office in Bonn. Liberal opinion in Germany held that Adenauer and his Government must accept at least some part of the responsibility.

One of the leaders of the small Jewish community in Germany, Herr Galinski of Berlin, expressed the views of many liberals and democrats when he accused Adenauer's Government of having done little to eradicate the spirit of Nazism in Germany.

'Adenauer is too much concerned with foreign affairs,' said Herr Galinski, 'and has neglected what is going on at home.' Nazism was dead, said the Jewish leader, but there were many former Nazis in high places. With reason he complained that many State school teachers and parents had done nothing to eradicate the Hitler spirit. Many West Germans, notably the Social Democrats, whose anti-Nazi record fills one of the finer pages of recent German history, shared the view of the Jewish community.

Adenauer was accused of being too patient with the former Nazis. He was attacked for having two Nazis in his Government, Dr. Schroeder, the Minister of the Interior, and Professor Theodor Oberlaender, the Minister for Refugee affairs. Much emphasis was placed on the fact that he had permitted many former Nazis to throng the Bonn ministries and the West German judiciary. The Chancellor was inclined to ignore the attacks by the Social Democrats and other political opponents. But the accusation, widely expressed in many Western countries, that he had become pro-Nazi, wounded him deeply.

Finally, in mid-January, he could remain silent no longer. He went to the German television and radio studios and poured out his feelings in one of the most remarkable speeches of his political career. With a lack of restraint unparalleled in his years as Chancellor, he told the Germans to be just as authoritarian as himself *and take the law into their own hands*. Most of the anti-Semitic incidents, he claimed, had been the work of young hooligans. To the millions of Germans who were watching and listening to him, he said, 'Whenever you get your hands on one of these louts deal with him, there and then, on the spot. Give him the good hiding he deserves.'

'Four times I was on the extermination lists of the Nazis,' he added. 'It is only by a miracle that I survived and am here now.' Then he acknowledged a great truth – that he was pro-Semitic. When his family was in financial difficulties, he said, the Jews had been the first to offer help. When he became Chancellor, he had worked with all his strength to reach a reparations agreement with Israel.

'I want to tell the whole world that the Germany of to-day totally rejects anti-Semitism,' he concluded. He really meant that.

To prove his sincerity he travelled, a fortnight later, with his old friend Dr. Nahum Goldman, the German educated president of the World Jewish Federation, to what had once been the Belsen concentration camp. There, on the memorial to those who had perished in the last weeks of the war, he laid a wreath. At a Press conference in a nearby British Army barracks, he explained that he had come to Belsen publicly to honour those who had died and those who had suffered misery in the death camp.

Denouncing the anti-Semitic outbreaks, he said he would personally promise that all those responsible for the outrages would be severely punished. To all the Jews who had returned to Germany, he gave a guarantee that they could live there in 'safety and respect'. Adenauer's sincerity was obvious. A month later, he impressed no less a Jew than Ben Gurion, Prime Minister of Israel, with that same sincerity when, for the first time, they met in a New York hotel where both happened to be staying.

Both of them dictatorial and awkward, and accustomed to having their way, the two old men, speaking in German, formed an immediate bond. The two hour tête-à-tête behind closed doors was perhaps the most satisfying political interview of Adenauer's whole career. He was much moved by meeting the man whom he described as 'the chief architect of modern Israel and its remarkable development.' The Israel Prime Minister was equally impressed.

He said, that after meeting Adenauer, he was sure that the 'Germany of today was not the Germany of the past.'

Adenauer later told members of his staff that he had seldom enjoyed a talk more; for indeed, so enthusiastic were the two veterans that they refused to stop talking even when reporters and cameramen broke in to take pictures and record the historic occasion.

Adenauer's manifest honesty and sincerity in his unrestrained broadcast to the German people, at Belsen, and with Ben Gurion in New York, merely served to intensify the great Adenauer enigma. How could a man who, with members of his family, had been a Nazi victim not only tolerate, but encourage the great Nazi comeback in Western Germany which, by early 1960, was an international scandal?

The key may well be found in a statement which Adenauer made to the Bundestag in Bonn as far back as October, 1952:

'The time has come to abandon the smelling out of Nazis,' he said. 'If we once start on that, nobody knows where it will end.'

He continued to hold that view in the years which followed, and at the time of the anti-Semitic outrages at the beginning of 1960, he told his intimates that he considered it impossible to deny former Nazi officials employment. He considered it equally impossible to continue to consider millions who had once been members of the Nazi party as political outcasts. He hoped, he is reported to have said, that the spirit of Nazism would die out with the older generation, and that Germany, within the Atlantic alliance, would develop into a decent, democratic country. Time, he said, rather than surgery was the solution.

That showed admirable sagacity and a praiseworthy under-standing in an octogenarian German who had four times been within an ace of death at the hands of Hitler's thugs. Most of his Western admirers shared the view that something like half the population of Western Germany could not go on indefinitely being regarded as political outcasts. Clearly they had to live and, provided they remained decently in the background and kept quiet, no one would cavil at his charitable understanding.

But why these guilty men should have been restored to public office and elevated to the great offices of State under an unquestionably anti-Nazi Chancellor, will long remain the mystery of the Adenauer era. Not only were there two ex-Nazis in his Cabinet, one of them, Dr. Schroeder, admittedly not a very good one, but in the early months of 1960, at the time of the anti-Semitic outrages throughout Western Germany, the main ministries in Bonn were largely dominated by high civil servants who had held important office in the Third Reich – and in many cases had been card-carrying members of the Nazi party.

As years passed and Adenauer more and more confined himself to the direction of German foreign policy, the situation became steadily more disturbing. Headed by the equivocal Dr. Globke, a group of top civil servants from the Third Reich concentrated into their hands more and more of the day-to-day administration of the Bonn Republic. The Ministry of the Interior, at that time headed by Dr. Schroeder, provided refuge for a formidable phalanx of ex-Storm Troopers and their like. In other ministries the total of State secretaries, ministerial directors and similar mandarins with a Nazi past varied according to the liberal principles or otherwise of the ministers concerned. Even the Economics Ministry of Professor Erhard had two top officials who had been card-carrying Nazi party members and had occupied important posts under Hitler.

The Nazi comeback in Bonn, however, was but a small part of the whole picture. Scattered throughout the federal provinces were thousands of ex-Nazis resurrected into positions of authority. The Nazi resurgence in the State police forces was notorious. In the province of North-Rhine-Westphalia alone, hundreds of police officers, including the chiefs of various Criminal Investigation Departments, were relics of the Nazi Reichssicherheitshauptamt. In one Ruhr district was a group of senior officers who, as members of the infamous Battalion 316 of the Einsatzgruppen, had been responsible for the murder of many thousands of Jews, Communist and others in Nazi-occupied eastern Europe.

The situation in the various German secret services, all 'co-ordinated' by Globke, was even more sinister. Some of the leading officials of the so-called Security Group in Bonn were ex-minions of the late Reinhard Heydrich, either from the Gestapo or the Nazi S.D. (Security Service). One of them at least, Saevecke, who led the *Spiegel* action, had long been wanted in Italy for alleged war crimes. Other ex-Nazis were Russian double agents.

The administration of so-called justice in the Federal Republic was even more sensational. The state of the West German judiciary was an international scandal. After allegations from Eastern Europe about '1,200 Nazi judges', followed by the automatic denial from the Adenauer administration of this 'Communist-inspired propaganda', high authorities in London decided to find out the facts. One organ of the British Intelligence was ordered to make a detailed secret investigation of the state of the German judiciary. It was established that there were *not less than fifty* West German judges against whom, *prima facie*, a charge could be brought *under British law* of being accomplices after the fact in judicial murder. All of them had presided over what euphemistically were described as 'Hitler's special courts'.

In the provincial administrations the situation varied. In the most northerly territory of the Federal Republic, Schleswig-Holstein, Herr von Hassel, the Prime Minister and one of the deputy chairmen of the C.D.U., had carried Adenauer's policy of tolerance and forgiveness to its ultimate. As one Nazi scandal followed another in quick succession, Schleswig-Holstein was openly referred to by many liberal Germans as 'the half-Nazi State'.

In Bavaria, where Adenauer's Christian Socialist allies and his friends of the Roman hierarchy wielded overwhelming influence, the position was quite as bad as in Protestant Prussian Schleswig-Holstein. Subsequent revelations showed that at least one high Government official was a former senior officer of the Nazi S.D. *who had already served a sentence of several years penal servitude for war crimes.* Others had been more discreet. The Bavarian police, where Himmler and Heydrich as heads of the Munich force had tried their prentice hands in 1933, was notorious for the number of ex-Nazis permitted to slip through their fingers. The pay-off came, a year later, when a Jugoslav business-man was arrested in Munich for murder – because as a Tito partisan *he had shot and killed the German invaders during the war on his own native soil.*

In the private sector of German life the Nazi comeback was just as extensive. Intrinsically the situation was bad enough. But the damage done to German morality by the cynical way in which men with a sinister past had been permitted to return to high office would last long after Konrad Adenauer had disappeared.

By 1960, the Adenauer-tolerated Nazi revival in Western Germany had induced throughout German life a standard of double morality which was the despair of serious-minded and honest Germans. In private affairs the old German virtues persisted. In public life amorality prevailed. Honest, decent, middle-class Germans, who had not, and never would commit any crime beyond reckless driving, could see nothing strange in convicted war criminals and other guilty men of the Third Reich holding high office in the Federal Republic.

Mesmerized by the fantastic prosperity and the sordid materialism of the 'German miracle' – which was just reaching its peak – solid German burghers could see nothing wrong in men with a criminal past continuing to hold high office.

Highly respectable, church-going, middle-class families protested violently when fathers and brothers, who as members of a Nazi occupation authority had signed the death warrants of hundreds of innocent people, or as judges in a 'special court' had sentenced eastern slave-labourers to death for a minor racial peccadillo, were driven from office.

This cynicism developed into a wave of corruption, unequalled since the Weimar Republic in the twenties or in France at the time of the Stavisky scandals in 1934. About the time of the anti-Semitic outrages, Dr. Schroeder, the Minister of the Interior, admitted that in a period of six years more than fifty senior officials, from departments ranging from Adenauer's own Chancellery to the Bonn Foreign Office, had either been convicted of, or were awaiting trial for corruption.

Pastors of the Lutheran Church and Catholic priests were shocked and disturbed by the double standards of morality which they had found among even the most devoted members of their flocks. To their credit, many courted much unpopularity and, sometimes, open contumely by resolutely refusing to accept the standards of morality current in the new democratic Germany of Konrad Adenauer.

The wave of protests in Germany and beyond, triggered off by the Cologne anti-Semitic outrage and the revelations which followed, inevitably demanded a scapegoat. The most obvious victim was the Federal Minister for Refugee Affairs, Professor Theodor Oberlaender.

Oberlaender was probably neither better nor worse than dozens of other ex-Nazis in high office in Bonn at the time, but he was unlucky. Unlike others, he readily admitted that he had been a member of the Nazi party. As an officer of the far from pro-Nazi military secret service, the Abwehr of Admiral Canaris who died for his part in the anti-Hitler conspiracy of 1944, Oberlaender was one of the Third Reich's leading 'eastern experts'. It was no doubt in that capacity that Adenaeur employed him in a refugee ministry which was not unconcerned with espionage in Communist-occupied Eastern Europe.

In 1946, Oberlaender had been released from a P.O.W. camp at Amersham in Buckinghamshire after the Allied authorities had decided there were no grounds for holding him. At his subsequent denazification trial in Germany, he had no difficulty in producing witnesses who were ready to testify that he had been under observation by the Gestapo, as many Abwehr officers were, and that he had been sacked from the German army in 1943, after criticizing Nazi policy in Eastern Europe.

It was unfortunate for Oberlaender that he was alleged to have been in the Polish Ukrainian town of Lvov at the end of June, 1941, when a massacre of Polish and Jewish intellectuals, including many professors of the famous Lvov University, occurred. At the time, he was associated with the so-called 'Nightingale' Battalion of Ukrainian partisans linked with the Abwehr's Brandenburg division, a sabotage formation. Also in the city at the time was one of Heydrich's Extermination groups – or Einsatzgruppen – whose part in the massacre needs no amplification. Oberlaender denied that he had any part in the massacre. In support of this, he cited the categorical order of Canaris, whose humanity was almost a byword, that the Ukrainian militia must behave in exemplary fashion as it would form the core of a Ukrainian national army to fight the Bolshevists.

Even before the wave of anti-Semitic outrages in Western Germany at the beginning of 1960, Oberlaender had been accused in a German court, by the Association of the Victims of Nazism (V.V.N.) of being implicated in the Lvov massacre. And as the international scandal about the ex-Nazis in Bonn reached a climax in early 1960, the East German Communist régime published a propaganda brochure entitled *The Truth About Oberlaender*. The interest of the Communist authorities in removing Oberlaender from office was obvious. He was an outstanding expert on Eastern Europe, with ties far behind the Iron Curtain. He was, no doubt, a formidable opponent on the level of clandestine operations. His subsequent trial, *in absentia*, before an East German Court and his conviction and sentence to life imprisonment was probably a legitimate part of the Cold War.

By the time Adenauer made his 'I was a Nazi Victim' broadcast, he was under strong pressure from many quarters to sack Oberlaender. The old man resisted strongly, no doubt partly from loyalty and partly because Oberlaender was a most efficient specialist at the head of a key Cold War ministry. In addition they were both primitive anti-Bolshevists.

The Social Democrats were determined to use the Oberlaender

affair to discredit Adenauer and his Government. Adenauer fought back for he shared an interest in certain proselytising groups with which Oberlaender was associated. Finally, the Social Democrats proposed the establishment of a Bundestag Parliamentary Commission to fully investigate Oberlaender's Nazi past. Under the Bonn constitution such a committee had power to hold public hearings.

To Adenauer, a public parade of the events of Oberlaender's Nazi career, at a time when his Government was under bitter attack from Moscow, could be nothing but a disaster. At the beginning of April, he finally bowed to the storm. Oberlaender, who to his credit had announced that he was perfectly willing to leave the Government, went on leave prior to his resignation a month later. He was entitled to a substantial minister's pension. Subsequently, he was cleared in Western Germany of all charges of having participated in the Lvov manoeuvre.

Oberlaender remained a highly equivocal figure. Following his dismissal by the Nazis – and, according to one version of his career, being sentenced to death – he became a professor in the *German* university in occupied Prague which was an instrument for the so-called 'Germanization' of the Czechs. Correspondence, now in the Czech State Archives in Prague, shows he was a subordinate of the 'One-Eyed Monster of Prague,' the Reich Protector Karl Hermann Frank, hanged as a war criminal in 1946.

Why Adenauer should have chosen and sustained a man with such a record is but one facet of the great mystery.

It was not until a few weeks later, when the Israeli secret service kidnapped Adolf Eichmann, that Adenauer was at last jerked out of his complacency. Belated measures were started against former Nazi police, judges and others – but not against the top Nazi civil servants in Bonn who run his Government.

CHAPTER EIGHTEEN

The Interregnum

ADENAUER expected little if any good to come out of the Summit conference scheduled to meet in Paris in mid-May; and as winter passed into the early spring of 1960, he became ever more anxious about the trend of Western policy. Once again the Chancellor was obsessed by his 'Potsdam nightmare'. He was convinced that some of his allies were plotting to do a deal with Khrushchev behind his back. He was certain that, if it were possible, the Allies would try and reach a compromise on Berlin despite all his attempted vetoes.

He felt helpless. In London and Washington his policies – or, rather, the lack of them – were considered to be a major impediment to any East-West settlement. Only in Paris did he have a trustworthy ally. President de Gaulle was as adamant as himself in pursuing the Cold War line in Central Europe although from a somewhat different standpoint.

It was the Americans who caused Adenauer most anxiety. It was not so much that he doubted their good intentions. He doubted rather the ability of President Eisenhower and the Secretary of State, Mr. Herter, to handle the negotiations in the right way. He felt that, with a presidential election in the offing later in the year, the President was showing signs of listening more carefully to the American citizens than to the Federal German Chancellor. As was often the case in his later years, he was deeply concerned about the American public, which he believed was going soft.

In mid-March, therefore, the 84-year-old Chancellor once more set off across the Atlantic to try, according to his subordinates, 'to put a little backbone into the Americans, just in case American resolution might be weakening'. Before he left Bonn, he repeated the demand that he had voiced in London a few months earlier; there must be no separate negotiations, and particularly 'no surrender' on Berlin.

Alas, the Federal Chancellor no longer enjoyed that power of veto which had hamstrung western policy in the great days of the late John Foster Dulles. The President, perhaps as a result of his great wartime career as Allied commander-in-chief, was pragmatic in an almost British way. He was polite and helpful to his old friend from Bonn, but he declined to let Adenauer dictate American policy. The State Department, under the patrician hand of Mr. Herter, showed an equal resistance to Teutonic pressure. The statement issued at the end of the Adenauer-Eisenhower talks was a measure of how the Chancellor's influence had declined since the death of Mr. Dulles almost a year earlier. The statement reiterated the mutual resolve of the two countries that 'preservation of the freedom of the people of West Berlin and their right of self-determination must underlie any future agreement affecting the city'. But there was no suggestion that a settlement of the Berlin problem must be decided within the German question as a whole, as Adenauer had demanded.

Adenauer had been rebuffed. He was well aware of it, despite his claim that he was well satisfied, as he set out across the Pacific for an official visit to Japan, which seemed to have little purpose except that it indulged an old man's vanity.

He was still worried about the forthcoming Summit meeting when he got back to Germany in April. In the main he was concerned with the 'weakness' of Macmillan, afraid that he would lead astray his wartime comrade when they got together in Paris.

To the Mayor of West Berlin, Willy Brandt, he confided the thought that he had already bandied about among his confidants in Bonn; 'Let me assure you, Herr Brandt, you can never rely on the British'.

Herr Brandt, one of these gallant German democrats who had carried on the fight against the Nazis from outside of Germany, was as broad in his outlook as Adenauer was narrow. As the right hand of that great German, the late Professor Ernst Reuter, he and everyone else in Berlin had been fed by the R.A.F. and the American Air Force in 1948–9.

Brandt was not prepared to accept this new denigration of the British by Adenauer. He flew back to Berlin, and twenty-four hours later publicly gave Adenauer the lie. The people of Berlin, said Brandt, would never forget how steadfast and ready for sacrifice their British friends had been in the blockade of 1948–9. Suspicions and suggestions that the British were not just as ready to make sacrifices for the safety of Berlin in the spring of 1960 were grossly untrue.

But Adenauer remained an intransigent Cold Warrior. When at the end of April he addressed the ninth C.D.U. party congress at Karlsruhe, he repeated parrot-like the demand for the only policy which he seemed to understand, 'Negotiation from strength'. Harking back to Mr. Dulles, he claimed that the only possible policy at the forthcoming Summit was the one he had followed for the previous ten years.

'Anyone who wants a relaxation of tension, and that is something that we too want, my friends, and those who, in consequence, seek peace must be in favour of strength; for one can deal with Soviet Russia, Communist China and the others only if one is at least as strong as they are.' He was gracious enough to admit, however, that the 'strength' on which he based everything was not German, but the strength of those American people whom privately he thought required backbone.

The inherent contradictions of his foreign policies once more became apparent when swiftly he went on to praise President de Gaulle for the way *he had supported the German view in Washington.*

'The friendship between France and Germany,' said Adenauer, 'and not only between two men but between the two peoples, is the most significant instrument for the future that we have created in all these ten years.'

It was through his ally de Gaulle, therefore, that he attempted to keep his finger in the Summit pie. To the consternation of more than one Western *chef de protocol*, he succeeded in manœuvring a meeting in Paris with the French President at the very moment when the Summit delegations were due to arrive in the French capital. So tactless was Adenauer that it was discovered, almost at the last minute, that the Federal Chancellor's plane would land at Orly airport at precisely the moment Khrushchev would fly in from Moscow. There were panic telephone calls. Adenauer delayed his arrival for an hour or two and, in the light of what happened a few days later, a highly embarrassing encounter was averted.

Adenauer had a talk with de Gaulle and departed. He need have had no fear of the outcome of the Summit meeting. Even before the delegates reached Paris, a spanner had been thrown into the works.

A week before the Summit was due to begin, an American U-2 'spy plane' on a flight from Pakistan to northern Norway, was shot down over the Soviet Union and the pilot, Captain Gary Powers, taken prisoner.

With a scarcely credible gaucheness, the American administration played straight into the Russians' hands. When Khrushchev reached Paris, he announced that there would be no Summit unless Eisenhower apologized for the U-2 flight. He was adamant. Eisenhower, whose transparent honesty had led him into a diplomatic dead-end, did not know how to retreat. Unavailingly the British Prime Minister tried to mediate. The Summit conference collapsed before it started. The end was marked by one of the most sensational Press conferences in recent history. For two hours the Soviet Prime Minister poured out his venom to three thousand half booing, half cheering journalists in the Palais Chaillot.

The boos from a substantial section of the audience as Khrushchev mounted the rostrum provoked an immediate tirade. His outburst left little doubt that, despite his theatrical anger at the

U-2 incident, he regarded Adenauer as his real enemy. It was on the 'imperialist lackeys of Adenauer' that he unloosed his wrath as he started his long, declamatory and angry statement. 'Adenauer has sent his riff-raff here,' he said, referring to rows of booing reporters in front of him. 'They do not appear to appreciate that they were defeated at Stalingrad,' he continued, giving vent to his basic anti-Germanism, which the British had appreciated ever since his visit to London in 1955.

'This group here represents people of whom the Germans themselves will be ashamed.'

In Khrushchev's long, rambling philippic, German affairs occupied a considerable part. Asked if he intended to sign a separate peace treaty with East Germany, he replied, 'Yes'. Then, speaking with extreme emphasis and firmness, as though to make his answer seem more positive than it really was, he added, 'The Western Powers will be deprived of their occupation rights (in East Berlin).'

'Just as the United States signed a peace treaty with Japan without us, although we fought in the war against Japan (in fact for only the last day or two), we are almost at the end of our patience in our attempts to sign a German peace treaty along with the United States. Now we shall do it alone.'

He added that the Soviet proposal to make West Berlin a free city was the only reasonable solution. All foreign troops would be withdrawn. West Berlin would be left to choose whatever social system it wished and to maintain the freedom of its links with the outside world.

The Soviet threat to sign a peace treaty with East Germany and, more important still, to end the Western occupation rights in Berlin, seemed to threaten the Western Powers with a major crisis.

When Khrushchev reached East Berlin twenty-four hours later, he had regained control of his temper. At once he resumed that caution which had been manifest since soon after his first ultimatum over Berlin in the autumn of 1958. To the visible annoyance of the East German Communist dictator, Ulbricht, whom Khrushchev personally, according to East European Communists, cannot tolerate, he announced that the time was not yet ripe for a separate peace treaty with East Germany.

He made it clear, to the point of repetition, that there would be no separate peace treaty before another attempt had been made to reach agreement with the West at a new Summit conference after the American presidential election in November. For Khrushchev had decided to write off the Eisenhower administration for the months it would remain in office.

Adenauer in Bonn for once was silent. His spokesman, Herr von Eckardt, declined to make any comment on the implications of either the collapse of the Summit or Khrushchev's speech in Berlin. In fact, Adenauer was profoundly relieved by what had happened and retreated to Cadenabbia in a mood of great satisfaction.

It was there that he admitted his true feelings to a peripatetic visitor from the *New York Times* – that the collapse of the Summit Conference *had been a gain for the West as it had removed a number of possible sources of embarrassment.*

This brutal exultation in the failure of an attempt to reduce the European, and world tension on which his whole policy and his international prestige had been founded, was widely deplored. At once, he issued one of his usual semi-denials. From Cadenabbia it was announced that he had merely had a talk, and not an interview with his American visitor, and that afterwards the correspondent had been free to put his own interpretation on the Chancellor's remarks.

Khrushchev's view that there was little to be done on the international stage until a new American President took office in the following January, was generally accepted. For the remainder of 1960 there was a hiatus in East-West affairs, except in the Congo.

With his basic Cold War policies out of danger for the next few months, Adenauer started to tie up loose ends. The most obvious problem was the cleavage which existed in the C.D.U. as a consequence of his antics the previous summer, and which would continue to exist as long as he was Chancellor. Professor Erhard was invited to visit him at his Italian holiday home to which the Government of Western Germany had been transferred. What was claimed by the Adenauer sycophants as a reconciliation took place. In fact, nothing was changed. He continued to regard Erhard as a political lightweight, and made little effort to conceal his opinion.

The lull in East-West tension did not suit the last of the Cold Warriors. Back in Germany at the beginning of July, and with an eye no doubt to the German general election a year ahead, he decided to stoke up the fires of German irredentism.

He chose for his characteristic act of crass political irresponsibility a mass rally of 70,000 East Prussian refugees, summoned to Düsseldorf to recall the fortieth anniversary of the East Prussia plebiscite after the First World War.

The band – somehow the Bundeswehr had become involved in irredentist propaganda – played *Deutschland über alles* and the East Prussian hymn. Hundreds of fair-haired young Prussians, none of whom had any personal memories of the Baltic province, paraded stiffly in East Prussian costume, waving black and white flags in a manner which brought a shudder to foreign observers who recalled 1933.

Then Adenauer launched into one of the most cynical and cheap vote-catching speeches in his whole political career. Ignoring that nothing but nuclear war could ever free the Baltic province, which since 1945 had been divided between Poland and the Soviet Union, he declared that none had the right to determine the future of East Prussia until an all-German Government could negotiate Germany's future at a peace conference.

Though he was careful to remind the vast crowd that a solution of the German problem must await until tension had been relaxed, he whipped them up to a Nazi-like hysteria by shouting that the 'lost province' of East Prussia, too, must have the right of self-determination. For a man who had hated Prussia all his life, his devotion to the cause seemed dangerously near 'crocodile tears'.

His ranting, chauvinistic outburst to the East Prussian refugees had a frigid reception in Western capitals. Then, as so often was the case with the schizophrenic political personality of the Federal Chancellor, a phase characterized by cheapjack vote-catching and an almost parochial political irresponsibility was succeeded at once by a period of high statesmanship.

By the summer of 1960, Adenauer was thoroughly alarmed by the increasing megalomania of de Gaulle. The French President seemed determined to arrogate to himself the leadership of the neo-Carolingian Reich for which Adenauer and the other 'little Europeans' had striven so long. The more de Gaulle saw himself as emperor of the new Europe with Paris as its capital, the more anti-Anglo-Saxon he became. Adenauer was quick to appreciate the danger; de Gaulle's obsession could divide Britain from the rest of Europe and jeopardize the American position in the Atlantic community.

The built-in dilemma of his foreign policy, a dilemma which was to reach its climax at the beginning of 1963, was already obvious. But in 1960 he was determined to avoid a situation where he would be forced to make a choice.

Adenauer and de Gaulle were at one in trying to maintain and improve the economic basis of 'The Six'. The French President, however, while hostile to supra-national institutions, was anxious for a closer political association of independent sovereign states with France at its head. Adenauer was firmly opposed to anything which would endanger the Atlantic alliance and which, in consequence, would widen the division of Europe and inevitably antagonize the British. He suggested to de Gaulle that they should meet in August. The President was haughty. He was going on holiday in August. If the German Chancellor wished to see him, he had better come at the end of July. In the end a meeting was arranged at the Presidential hunting lodge at Rambouillet.

The exchanges between Paris and Bonn had aroused in Adenauer's mind an apprehension which was rapidly changing to consternation. And at the same time that the appointment at Rambouillet was fixed, Adenauer informed the British Prime Minister of what was happening and invited Mr. Macmillan to visit Bonn soon after his own return from Paris.

To those in his immediate circle Adenauer made it clear that he was highly alarmed about de Gaulle's intentions and concerned for West German relations with both Britain and the United States. He was determined to try and make new arrangements which would guarantee the unity of the Western Alliance and which would mean an important step towards European unity.

There was no question of changing the 'special relationship' which he had built up between de Gaulle and himself, but Adenauer was not prepared to endanger the Western Alliance. At this point, as opposed to the early months of 1963, he was anxious not only to associate Britain in Western Europe but to modify French ideas – which he realized would not be easy.

Adenauer knew from his private exchanges that de Gaulle was still distinctly cool to Britain, claiming that there could be no political co-operation *until Britain joined the Common Market.* He had told Adenauer that Britain must choose between Europe and the United States. Adenauer appreciated that Britain would never make the choice in favour of Europe alone, a view with which, at this time, he tended to sympathize. For in 1960, prior to the advent of the Kennedy régime, he was not prepared to prejudice his relations with Washington for a rapprochement with France.

The old man dutifully flew to Paris at the end of July, and little good it did him. There were various accounts of what happened behind the closely guarded and barricaded doors of the Château de Rambouillet. Some of them were highly sensational. According to one well-informed German source, the Federal Chancellor found his host had 'become somewhat strange'. Western diplomats with access to secret information described the meeting as 'catastrophic'. Whatever did transpire, Adenauer had no desire for a repeat performance of the de Gaulle monologue for some considerable time to come.

It was with an unwonted warmth that he drove to Bonn airfield ten days later to greet the British Prime Minister, ostentatiously addressing him, for the first time, as 'My Friend'.

The meeting was almost certainly the most successful ever held by the two men. Adenauer, in his most statesmanlike mood, assured the Prime Minister that he had abandoned all thought of a 'little Europe' at the expense of Britain. The conversion seemed genuine though British cynics wondered how long it would take him to fall from grace. So sympathetic was he to Britain's problems of association with the Common Market, that he made a truly magnanimous gesture. He told Mr. Macmillan that he was ready to try to find a way round one of the major obstacles to Britain joining the Common Market, how the preferential entry of Commonwealth products into the U.K. should be assured if Britain should associate herself more closely with Europe. Herr von Brentano and the new British Foreign Secretary, Lord Home, were instructed to investigate the problem.

Adenauer's generous statesmanship at his meeting with the British Prime Minister in Bonn in the summer of 1960 marked a decisive step in the approach of the British Government to the European Common Market. In Whitehall it was recognized that so long as President de Gaulle remained in office, Adenauer's role in the Common Market negotiations would probably prove decisive. The estimate was, and remained fundamentally correct. When the final showdown did come in January, 1963, Adenauer alone, with the enormous political and economic power of Germany behind him, could have stopped de Gaulle in his tracks.

In the summer of 1960, however, the German Chancellor, as a result of his acute anxiety over French policy, was more than willing to back Britain's entry. As Mr. Macmillan flew back from Bonn, authoritative British sources suggested that two days of conversations had made it possible to contemplate an association between Britain and 'The Six' that, only a few weeks earlier, would have seemed impossible.

The Prime Minister, when he reached London, suggested the same conclusion. He said that in a few hours' conversation it was impossible to reach a final answer. 'But we have decided to continue our discussions together, to exchange ideas in full loyalty, each of us to our own partners; in the case of the Germans to the partners in "The Six", and in our case to our partners in the Commonwealth and the organization "The Seven".'

'I say we have not found the answer – *but I do think we have made the first step.*'

Officials in both London and Bonn were curiously coy about future visits by either leader to Paris. It was indicated that the French Government would be informed through the much neglected 'normal diplomatic channels'.

President de Gaulle proved even more difficult than was his wont. By the time the French Prime Minister, M. Debré, reached Bonn, in early October, relations between Adenauer and the French were more strained than at any time for years. The two men completely failed to reach agreement on any of the main issues, the future of the European Community or of N.A.T.O. A truculent speech by de Gaulle demanding Franco-British-American control of N.A.T.O. had thoroughly antagonized the German Chancellor. For the first time since the war, he was not prepared to make a single concession to France. It was not until the beginning of the following year that tension eased and Adenauer again met de Gaulle face to face.

In October, 1960, the German Chancellor had a more serious preoccupation. He was much concerned about who would be elected in the American presidential election in November. His own choice was undoubted. He hoped that the Republican Vice-President, Mr. Richard Nixon, who had been part of that Republican administration whose European policy Adenauer had largely dictated for the previous eight years, would be returned and that the Adenauer-Republican axis would go uninterrupted.

He was alarmed by the prospect that his fellow-Catholic, John Fitzgerald Kennedy, might become President. For Kennedy, according to German diplomatic reports, could scarcely be described as pro-German. It was reported that Senator Kennedy had been much attached to his eldest brother who had been killed by the Germans. Adenauer also could not forget that the young Senator, in 1957, had called on Bonn to accord diplomatic recognition to the Communist Government in Poland, 'For America must remove from Poland its fear of Germany.'

The Kennedy 'brains trust' of Harvard radical intellectuals increased the Chancellor's anxiety. The prospect that the former Democratic presidential candidate and one of the world's outstanding radicals, Mr. Adlai Stevenson, might become U.S. Secretary of State filled Adenauer with something approaching horror.

In the election campaign during the previous weeks Mr. Stevenson, with considerable justification, had observed that 'for the past ten years Adenauer has been American Foreign Minister'.

Adenauer and his closer collaborators in the Bonn Cabinet at this juncture were less than discreet. The stormy petrel of the German Government, the Bavarian Catholic Defence Minister, Franz Josef Strauss, whether with Adenauer's approval is uncertain, ordered the German generals to make a staff study of the consequences of a Kennedy victory. A month before the presidential election, the Bonn Government had in its possession a three-page secret document entitled 'A Survey of the Consequences to American Policy of a Kennedy Victory'.

The contents were explosive. It was openly and avowedly pro-Nixon and emphasized the serious consequences, to Adenauer's policies, of a Kennedy victory. The authors viewed, with something akin to panic, the prospect of 'Egg Head' Stevenson talking over the office of Secretary of State where Mr. Dulles had once reigned. The secret document added that 'Stevenson is generally understood to be in favour of disengagement' and other liberal policies which the Germans described as 'irregularities'.

Somehow, a copy of this remarkable document reached the *Baltimore Sun*. Towards the end of October, that distinguished American journal came out with banner headings: 'Nixon More Acceptable to Germans!' Senator Kennedy and his friends in Washington could scarcely be expected to be unaware of what was published in nearby Baltimore.

The German Ambassador, displaying normal German diplomatic tactlessness in such a *contretemps*, hurriedly announced in Washington that 'the memorandum is in no way an official document'. It was difficult to see what else it was. He would have been better employed suggesting that it was just 'another Strauss indiscretion'.

The Bonn correspondent of the *Baltimore Sun* was not to be denied. He retorted by quoting still further denigration of Mr. Stevenson in particular, and the Kennedy 'brains trust' in general. Relations between the Kennedy camp and the Germans virtually ceased to exist. Adenauer was much troubled. He was aware that, following the publication of the 'Strauss indiscretion', should Kennedy be elected it would be many months before even normal relations between Bonn and Washington could be restored. On the night of the presidential election he slept badly. To quote *Der Spiegel*:

'In the West German province of the American *Imperium* uncertainty over the plans of young Kennedy caused the oldest and trusted ally of the United States to pass a troubled night.'

The German Embassy in Washington had been ordered to send him the result by the fastest and shortest route, no expense to be spared. At eight o'clock in the morning in Bonn, when Kennedy seemed to have just got the edge over Nixon, and the world Press was already announcing a Kennedy victory, Adenauer refused to accept it. There was still hope for Nixon. 'The result is not yet certain,' he announced. Hour after hour, as messages from the United States suggested that a recount in key states might yet give Nixon victory, Adenauer tried to convince himself that there was still hope for the Adenauer-Nixon axis. It was not until late afternoon, by which time the whole world had accepted Kennedy as the new President, that Adenauer sadly conceded defeat. Belatedly, after almost everyone else, he sent a formal telegram of congratulation to the new President. But faced by what he regarded as a major catastrophe to the Western cause, the old man suddenly decided that he had not a moment to lose. He must get his oar in at once. Within hours, he announced that he proposed to visit the United States in mid-February to attend a meeting of the German-American Council. He stated that he would also visit the new incumbent in the White House – just three weeks after his installation. The reaction of Mr. Kennedy to this classic Adenauer effort to gatecrash was noticeably cool. At his first Press conference after election, Mr. Kennedy made it obvious that things had changed in Washington, and that Adenauer could wait until he was invited to the White House.

That marked the end of the Adenauer-U.S. axis. It was the end of Adenauer's domination of American policy in Europe. From that moment, his role as a world statesman declined. He still remained a much respected leader of one of the principal Western Allies, but no more. He had lost his decisive voice.

In the meantime, President Kennedy left the old man to cool his heels. The attitude of the new American administration was scarcely helped by Adenauer's reluctance to meet American proposals to try to restore the U.S. States balance of payments. It was not until mid-April that he reached Washington, his eighth visit, in response to an invitation from the White House. His arrival was overshadowed by Gagarin's historic flight, and the start of the Eichmann trial, which did little to foster pro-German sentiments in the United States. Four days after he reached the American capital, the unfortunate 'Bay of Pigs' invasion of Cuba took place. The President had little time for the Federal German Chancellor. Adenauer spent the last two days of his visit with the Vice-President, Mr. Lyndon Johnson, *on a ranch in Texas.*

Before leaving to inspect the cowboys, however, he had realized the new role of Western Germany. It became apparent to him that, as America and Britain alone owned the strategic deterrent, decisions in Western strategy inevitably would tend to be in their hands. He would have little or no say. President Kennedy lectured him on the importance of Germany building up her conventional forces, and he was forced to agree with an American proposal that there should be no further deliveries of tactical atomic weapons to the Bundeswehr pending further discussions.

Adenauer had achieved virtually nothing in Washington. And when he emerged from his aircraft at Bonn, carrying a Texas ten-gallon hat, he was weary and discomfited. He knew that never again would he wield authority over the American Government as in the halcyon days of Mr. Dulles. Next day, *Die Welt* described his policies as 'full of confusions and contradictions'.

In the interval of waiting to be summoned to the White House, he had reverted to his role of the 'great European'. In the first few months of the new year he strove hard to find some solution to the two apparently intractable problems of European unity, de Gaulle's ever increasing hostility to N.A.T.O. and American leadership, and his conditions for a British association with the European Common Market.

At the end of January, the Chancellor, after much encouragement by the British Ambassador in Bonn, steeled himself for another face to face encounter with the French President. After an interval of six months, he again travelled to Rambouillet. The General, despite his reputed immovability, had come to recognize that in Adenauer he had encountered stubbornness and persistence as determined as his own. He was considerably more accommodating than in the previous summer. Adenauer was able, for the time being, to avert the formation of a French-led 'Little Europe' *bloc* inside N.A.T.O. But he was unable to shake the General from his deep suspicion of any British association with the Common Market. And when Adenauer visited London three weeks later, he was only able to tell Mr. Macmillan that 'everything depended on de Gaulle ' – as was indeed to prove the case.

CHAPTER NINETEEN

Disaster and Defeat

IN FEBRUARY, 1961, the Soviet Ambassador in Bonn, Mr. Smirnov, returned from Moscow bearing a memorandum from Khrushchev to Adenauer. It was remarkably different in tone, although depressingly similar in content, to previous communications from the same source. The memorandum was extremely courteous in its references to Adenauer personally, and Khrushchev urged him to display his 'statesmanlike wisdom' and to tell his people 'the true facts'.

Western diplomats, noting Khrushchev's unwonted courtesy to Adenauer, speculated on whether the Soviet Prime Minister really did want a settlement of the German question. Subsequent evidence suggests that he did. By the early months of 1961, the internal situation in the D.D.R., which had originally precipitated the first Berlin ultimatum in the autumn of 1958, was near crisis point. Khrushchev had to do something.

Adenauer, calcified in his obsession that the Russians would never do anything so long as the Western Powers stood to their guns and insisted on the *status quo*, was cynically unimpressed. The courteous Khrushchev memorandum, like so many others in the previous dozen years, was written off as just another Soviet trial balloon.

Adenauer had thrown away his last chance. By rejecting Khrushchev's courteous *demarche* the Federal German Chancellor had deserted the people of East Berlin and left his 17,000,000 fellow-countrymen under Communist rule to their fate. It was the climax to his Cold War policies which future Germans would almost certainly long hold against his memory.

He was still wallowing in the self-righteousness of his own policies when, in June, President Kennedy and Mr. Khrushchev met in Vienna. It was not a particularly successful encounter. At the talks Khrushchev handed over a memorandum, obviously prepared during the year since the abortive Summit since which time the Soviet leader had been prepared to let the German question simmer. Khrushchev's main points were:

1. The summoning of a conference and the conclusion of a German peace treaty by the four Occupation Powers 'without delay'.
2. Negotiations between the Adenauer and Ulbricht administrations within the following six months.
3. Final settlement of the German frontiers.
4. Normalization of the position of West Berlin on the basis of 'sensible consideration for the interest of all concerned'.
5. The Soviet Union did not propose to change anything in Germany or in West Berlin in favour of one state or any group of states.

The nub of the matter was reached when the memorandum stated that if the two Germanies failed to reach agreement 'then measures will be taken to conclude a peace treaty with both German states, *or with one of them*'.

This would mean the end of the occupation régime in West Berlin with all the consequences resulting therefrom. What Khrushchev meant was that future access to West Berlin by land, water and air, would have to be negotiated with the East German Communist Administration, whose existence the West did not recognize.

Khrushchev, however, emphasized that West Berlin should remain strictly neutral. In a curiously ambiguous passage which seemed to provide a starting-point for further negotiations, he suggested that signature of a peace treaty with Germany by all four Occupation Powers would not necessarily involve recognition of East Germany by all concerned. This seemed to suggest that he would be prepared to accept *a Berlin settlement without involving real recognition of the East German Communist régime.*

Khrushchev's memorandum offered a basis for a new round of negotiations on Berlin and the German problem, and in London and Washington the experts began serious study of his points.

Adenauer would have none of it. To a rally of refugees from the 'lost province' of Silesia at Hanover, he announced categorically that the Federal Government would never agree to Khrushchev's demand for a conference between West and East Germany. The prospect of sitting down at a table with a man he regarded as the modern anti-Christ, the Soviet puppet, Ulbricht, induced something near apoplexy in the normally restrained old man. Russia's real aim, he said, was to cement the position created at the end of the Second World War.

'We want freedom and self-determination for the whole German people,' he shouted, which was no doubt excellent if he could get it. For Adenauer, the pragmatic British axiom that 'Politics are the art of the possible', would always be beyond his comprehension.

In Washington, the White House and the State Department were impressed by Khrushchev's statement that he was 'honestly striving to eliminate the causes which have resulted in tension . . . and to move forward to constructive friendly co-operation'.

Apprehensive over reports of American willingness to negotiate, Adenauer sent a special envoy to Washington to persuade President Kennedy to follow what was known as the 'Adenauer hard line'.

Like a schoolmaster admonishing a wayward sixth former, he told the President that the West must react strongly to any Soviet attempt to close the Allied military, or the German civilian access routes to Berlin. He also proposed economic sanctions against the Eastern *bloc*. The American administration, as had been made clear to him in the previous six months, did not intend to have its foreign policy dictated from Bonn. Officials in Washington tartly suggested that there was nothing to prevent the Federal Chancel-

lor beginning with unilateral sanctions, such as stopping the
lucrative trade between West and East Germany. The Governments in both London and Washington indicated that they would
take some weeks to prepare a detailed answer to Khrushchev's
memorandum, which was accepted as forming the basis for a
renewal of negotiations.

In the meantime, the East Germans started to panic. From
rumours which spread across East Berlin and the D.D.R., they
were certain that Khrushchev was about to permit decisive action
which would cut them off from contact with the West. Vast
streams of refugees started to pour westwards, principally
through the gaping gaps in the Iron Curtain along the sector
boundaries in Berlin. East Germany, whose economy was already
in a parlous state, faced a catastrophic loss of manpower. It was
obvious that a major crisis over Berlin was imminent.

In Moscow the Warsaw Pact leaders met and planned action of
which rumours seeped through to the West. At the end of July,
President Kennedy's special adviser on disarmament, Mr. John
J. McCloy, former High Commissioner in Bonn and Adenauer's
distant relative by marriage, visited Khrushchev at Sochi on the
Black Sea coast. The Soviet leader lent him a pair of bathing-
trunks and the two elderly men discussed East-West tension in
the comfort of Khrushchev's bathing-pool. The Soviet Prime
Minister developed the theme of his growing anxiety about the
stream of refugees from East Germany. Unless something was
done, he said, it would lead to incidents which could trigger off a
war. That would do no one any good.

By the beginning of August, while Adenauer holidayed at
Cadenabbia, the stream of refugees into West Berlin had become a
flood. At the same time intelligence reports reaching Western
capitals warned of impending action.

The Allied Military Missions to the Soviet Commander-in-
Chief at Potsdam learned of the movement of Soviet armoured
formations across the Russian zone towards Berlin. To confirm
the significance of these deployments the veteran Red Army

Marshal Koniev, who, as generalissimo of the wartime First Ukrainian Front, had been one of the two Soviet commanders who took Berlin in 1945, was recalled from retirement and appointed Commander-in-Chief in the Soviet Zone. When, on August 10th, he entertained the representatives of his wartime comrades in arms, the three Western military commandants in Berlin, he assured them that *whatever might happen in Berlin* the rights of the three Western Allies would be fully respected. Marshal Koniev and the Soviet Government, duly honoured that undertaking.

In Paris the Western Foreign Ministers were considering the Allied reply to Khrushchev's memorandum. Some of them, according to what later leaked out in Washington, were more concerned about how a way could be found to keep the East Germans in East Germany. The mass flight was becoming a major threat to peace.

Although well informed of what was happening, the American administration, as subsequent public statements indicated, followed a cautious line. Like the British Government, the Kennedy administration steadfastly refused to be panicked into precipitate action. Adenauer, back in Bonn, was profoundly dissatisfied. Differences between Bonn and Washington were now a matter of common knowledge, and Adenauer, on the point of embarking on an electoral grand tour of the Federal Republic in preparation for the general election little more than a month later, was alarmed by the possible effect on the electorate of any discovery that his voice no longer carried decisive influence in the White House. At Kiel in Schleswig-Holstein, where he started his election campaign on 11th August, he dismissed all reports of differences between the German and American Governments as 'utterly false'. He continued his electioneering the following day and then set out for his Rhineland home which, tired and exhausted, he reached around midnight.

At four-thirty in the morning of Sunday, 13th August, two hours before he had arranged to be called to go to Mass, Adenauer was awakened by his housekeeper. Dr. Globke, she said, was on the phone. He insisted on speaking to the Herr Bundeskanzler.

Wearily, the old man lifted the receiver by his bedside – to learn of the greatest defeat he ever suffered. From the highly agitated State Secretary he gathered that, an hour earlier, the Soviet sector of Berlin had been sealed off from the Allied Western sectors by a barbed-wire barrier. 'The Wall' would follow in days.

Adenauer's opponent for Chancellor in the general election, Willy Brandt, Mayor of West Berlin, was also electioneering. When the Communist People's Police sealed off the entrance to the Brandenburger Tor and the Unter den Linden, he was in a sleeping-car on his way from Nuremberg to Kiel. At five o'clock in the morning S.P.D. colleagues dragged him from his berth at Hanover. An hour later, he flew on the first plane of the British-American 'shuttle service' back to his crisis city.

In the Bonn Foreign Office and other interested ministries there was that hysteria with which many Germans face a major crisis. Only in the villa at Rhoendorf, where the Federal Chancellor remained almost incommunicado, was there still and quiet.

The Cold War vultures had come home to roost. Adenauer's 'hard line' had reached its logical, and almost inevitable, conclusion. As *Der Spiegel* observed, 'At the Brandenburger Tor Adenauer was given the answer to his mistaken policies of the previous twelve years.'

The Chancellor did not seem to know what to do. In simple fact, there was very little he could do. Berlin was a military-occupied city. Despite the attempts of his Parliamentary Council in 1948–9, the three Western occupied sectors were not part of the Federal Republic. He had no legal status in Berlin, and no constitutional authority to intervene. And, as an American spokesman in Washington pointed out, no action had been taken against the Western sectors and no attempt made to cut West Berlin's links with the West. In all justice to the old man, much of the criticism which poured down on him for his failure to do anything at that moment was unfair. He was in the hands of the Western Allies.

Politically, Adenauer was hamstrung. Personally, he was a free man and a German. One thing he could have done; he could have flown, that same Sunday morning to Berlin and, side by side with his opponent in the election campaign, Willy Brandt, appeared before the wire barring the Brandenburger Gate, so that the East Berliners on the other side could have seen that all Germany stood shoulder to shoulder with them. Adenauer's closest political adviser, Dr. Krone, who with Globke and an American radio reporter from Berlin were the only visitors he saw on that historic Sunday, urged him to fly to Berlin at once. Great, generous and all-German gestures, however, never came easily to the old Rhinelander and at 85 he was probably too shocked to do anything. He made no move for more than twenty-four hours.

It was not until the following afternoon that Adenauer, in company with a wildly flapping Brentano, appeared before the German television cameras. It was a sorry spectacle. Neither of them seemed to know what to say. Adenauer muttered that there was no need for panic. N.A.T.O., he assured the Germans, would deal with the Berlin crisis, and the situation would be mastered. Brentano, always 'his master's voice', duly repeated the Adenauer platitudes. The barrenness of their thoughts was manifest. As the opposition *Frankfurter Rundschau* commented next day, 'Neither of them were quite the glowing figures on the election posters', which stared down from every wall in the Federal Republic. 'Their faces were grey and they looked broken men. What they said merely confirmed that their policies had proved a fiasco.'

At the same moment, the Bonn Foreign Office spokesman deprecated any suggestion of 'taking rash counter measures'. Twenty-four hours before East Berlin had been sealed off, Adenauer had ranted at Kiel about 'immediate economic sanctions'. After dispatches from Washington and London, and a meeting between Brentano and the Western Ambassadors in

Bonn, he began to change his tune. It had already been made very plain to him that the British and Americans were opposed to any action which would provide the Russians with an excuse to start a second Berlin blockade. American and British policy, as was to be amply demonstrated, was dominated by one single fact, a realization; that neither people was prepared to fight a nuclear was *for the Germans in East Berlin.*

It was, perhaps, his growing frustration over Allied caution, for which he was being condemned by the Germans, that decided Adenauer, less than forty-eight hours after the erection of the barbed wire, to resume his electioneering, and to abandon the East Berliners to their fate. Late on that same Monday afternoon, he flew to a long-arranged C.D.U. election rally at Regensburg in Bavaria. After a brief and cautious reference to the Berlin crisis he turned his big guns on his S.P.D. opponents in the election. Then, in order that the Berlin tragedy should not be without comic relief, the German patriarch decided to take a crack at the Berlin bürgermeister, 'Herr Brandt, who is so distinguished'.

The inhibitions placed on him in the election campaign by the fact that his principal opponent was Ruling Mayor of West Berlin had long irked Adenauer. Now, gripped by frustration, and jealous of the praise being heaped on Brandt as a result of 'The Wall' and of his courageous stand at the head of the Berliners, Adenauer's venomous tongue outstripped his discretion.

'If ever anyone has been treated with the greatest consideration by his political opponents,' he sneered, 'it is *Herr Brandt alias Frahm.*' With his own peculiar sense of delicacy the Federal Chancellor was revealing that the gallant chief magistrate of Berlin was the illegitimate child of a shopgirl named Frahm. Brandt, working closely with his C.D.U. allies in the city government of Berlin, was deeply wounded. But, with natural dignity, he ignored the gutter attack. The more responsible C.D.U. leaders were quick to disassociate themselves from the Chancellor. Professor Erhard publicly denounced 'personal defamation' in the election campaign; Dr. Gerstenmeier, in a TV discussion group, said it would be deplorable if the election campaign were 'to be burdened by intolerable personal abuse'.

The *Stuttgarter Zeitung* expressed what most decent Germans felt when it commented, 'In these days since the start of the Berlin crisis, the Berlin bürgermeister has cut a much better figure than *the election orator alias the Federal Chancellor.*'

Behind the scenes Adenauer had been bombarding the White House and the U.S. State Department with demands for counter-action. How much these demands were motivated by concern for the East Berliners and how much by fear that he might lose the general election if no steps were taken, only Adenauer can answer. In any event, when he got back to Bonn from Bavaria, he found that he faced another, and more important crisis, a major row with the Anglo-Saxons.

In both Washington and London there was much sympathy for German emotion over what had occurred in Berlin. But Adenauer's intense pressure was sharply resented. His non-stop demands, along with those made in a more understandable letter from Brandt, were regarded in Washington as downright dangerous.

President Kennedy, much better informed than Adenauer about the probable effect of a nuclear war over Berlin, made his policy plain in diplomatic exchanges. In complete agreement with the British Prime Minister, the President indicated that the United States was prepared to go to war *only over the safety of West Berlin.* He was not prepared to start a nuclear war over the closing of the sector boundaries. The security of West Berlin was regarded as a vital and non-negotiable American interest. The President was determined to try and negotiate an agreement guaranteeing the security of West Berlin. But counter-measures, which Adenauer kept hysterically demanding, were regarded in Washington and London as something which should be reserved for such time as the access to West Berlin was blocked, and not to provide an excuse for the Russians to block it.

There was, however, an easily understood 'crisis of confidence' in the Western sectors of Berlin and this the chief of the U.S. Information Service, Mr. Ed. Murrow, the noted TV commentator, reported to the White House after a rapid sortie to the city. The American Government sympathized with the anxieties of the West Berliners and President Kennedy took immediate steps to bolster up morale. Troop reinforcements from Western Germany moved along the *autobahn* across Eastern Germany to the city. They were followed by the Vice-President of the United States, Mr. Lyndon Johnson, and the one man above all others whom the Berliners trusted, General Lucius D. Clay, the 'Father of the Airlift' in 1948–9. Hundreds of thousands of Berliners turned out to welcome the Vice-President and to cheer General Clay, who stood with tears in his eyes, as they drove through the streets. The Vice-Presidential party had made a brief stop at Bonn airport. Adenauer suggested that he should accompany them to Berlin. The Americans had no wish for the highly unpopular Federal Chancellor to gatecrash an American demonstration of solidarity with the Berliners. He was rebuffed. It was not until nine days after the East sector had been sealed off by 'The Wall' that the Federal German Chancellor flew into the city. He was frigidly received by Herr Brandt. Waiting reporters jokingly suggested, 'Just wait and see the Old Man forget himself, and say, 'Tag, Herr Frahm!' Outside Tempelhof airport there was a less restrained welcome. Rows of placards on poles carried by lines of marchers announced, 'Hurrah, the Saviour is come at last.' Other cockney-like Berliners carried banners announcing laconically, 'Too Late.' In contrast to the vast crowds who had welcomed Vice-President Johnson and General Clay a day or two earlier, there were only groups, chiefly women, to wave to the Chancellor as he drove to 'The Wall'.

His visit to Berlin, like others before it, was not a success. He was deeply depressed. His influence on international events was steadily declining. By the last week of August the Anglo-Saxon powers by virtue of sole possession of the deterrent had made plain that they proposed to negotiate with Khrushchev over

Berlin. The U.S. Secretary of State, Mr. Dean Rusk, and the Defence Secretary, Mr. Macnamara, told the four-power working group in Washington – of which the German Ambassador Professor Grewe was a member – that as they were 'carrying the atomic risk', they proposed to 'accelerate negotiations'.

Adenauer and his faithful echo, Brentano, were once again obsessed by the nightmare of an East-West bargain behind their backs. The German Foreign Minister in Bonn did not hide his Government's fears. To a wide circle he admitted that the Western Powers were determined on East-West negotiations. The Federal Government, he admitted, was highly alarmed because 'the Anglo-Saxons are ready to make concessions provided their rights in Berlin remain undisturbed'.

In a desperate bid to influence Western policy, Adenauer wrote a confidential letter to President Kennedy. The Western Alliance was far from united for, so far as oracular utterances from Paris could be interpreted, de Gaulle was even more insistent on 'No surrender' than Adenauer. The Chancellor's gambit was to offer the White House his good offices in the Elysee in trying to secure a united Western front. The response from Washington was not encouraging. To Adenauer it seemed that Herr Brandt in Berlin had much more influence in the White House than the German Chancellor in Bonn. Once again, the old man was consumed with jealousy and rage, and a fear for what might happen at the general election only a fortnight hence.

At Hagen in Westphalia, during an electoral tour of the Ruhr, he seemed to lose control both of his tongue and his senses. 'I will tell you something about Berlin,' he announced to a C.D.U. rally. 'Listen carefully – everything that has happened in Berlin since 13th August *was planned by Khrushchev to help the S.P.D.*'

Officials at the American and British embassies in Bonn were astounded when they read his sensational allegation on the ticker tapes. They were sure it was a mistake. They could not believe that the head of the Federal German Government could say such a thing. They phoned the international news agencies to get confirmation before passing on this provocative titbit to their Governments in Washington and London. It was no mistake. A few hours later he returned to the charge. At Gelsenkirchen he said, 'To me it is perfectly clear. The Soviet Union wishes to help the S.P.D. in the election.'

In the next week the entire German Press – from Right to Left – fell on him. The editor of the Bucerius-owned *Der Stern* suggested that it was 'a political Sauerbruch case'. (The great German surgeon, Professor Sauerbruch, at the end of his life could not be persuaded to stop operating, with the result that several of his patients lost their lives.)

Once again, Adenauer was disowned by his party. Professor Erhard said it was an execrable thing that the fate of Berlin and the Russian Zone could have been degraded into a party political row. Dr. Gerstenmeier, as Speaker of the Bundestag, on behalf of the great majority of C.D.U. disowned the leader of his party. In Berlin, Herr Brandt had the last word: 'I don't wish to attack the Chancellor – on the contrary I wish him nothing more than a peaceful evening to his life. I don't think the old gentleman grasps the situation any more.'

As election day approached, it was clear from public opinion polls that Adenauer's stock, and with it that of the C.D.U. had slumped badly. His TV appearances following 13th August did nothing to improve the position. In contrast, his S.P.D. opponent, appearing almost nightly on the TV screens in the midst of his doughty Berliners, became something of a national, and international hero.

The party managers realized the worst. The C.D.U. saw that, contrary to 1953 and 1957, Adenauer was no longer Election Winner No. 1. On the contrary, he had become an electoral liability, as the record of the next eighteen months would confirm. A week before the poll, the *Deutsche Zeitung* of Cologne, a newspaper fanatically devoted to the Chancellor, admitted that the S.P.D. was well ahead in the election campaign. 'For the first time – and dangerously close to polling day – the C.D.U. is on the defensive,' wrote the paper's leader-writer.

The rapidly rising anti-Adenauer wave, which first began to sweep through Germany in the autumn of 1961, was not due solely to the catastrophic collapse of his East German policies and the consequent tragedy of 13th August. The long campaign carried on by the genuinely democratic and radical forces in Western Germany had penetrated to the German man in the street. There was deep disillusionment and something approaching alarm at the *Kanzler-Demokratie,* as his authoritarian method of government was abusively described. The Free Democrats, quick to recognize and exploit this deep-seated political reaction to twelve years of Adenauer authoritarianism, were on the crest of the wave. Middle-class Germans, more and more disillusioned with Adenauer and 'his Catholic janissaries', turned with relief to the successors of what had once been the German Liberal party. Political pundits were convinced that Adenauer would almost certainly lose his absolute majority in the Bundestag.

The Party leader, Dr. Erich Mende, voiced the feeling of the thousands of new supporters of the F.D.P. when he categorically announced, 'No coalition with Adenauer.'

The complete disillusionment of millions of Germans with the man who had ruled them since 1949 was mirrored by *Der Spiegel* in a verbal onslaught seldom equalled against a democratic head of government. The commentator, Moritz Pfeil, widely assumed to be the proprietor, Herr Augstein himself, wrote:

'But the Federal Republic is not a well-established democracy. At its head since it was founded has been a man who has treated and addressed the Opposition as though they had been a gang of malignants; who in discussion with friend and foe has substituted for point and counterpoint preposterous childish jokes and irrelevant platitudes, because he has no ideas to articulate; who in his twelve years of office has never shown a single fine generous impulse and who has testified to his own "foxiness" (*Gerissenheit*); who has played off his own ministers against pressure groups and who has made provincial premiers bow down like lackeys; who has degraded the office of Federal President to that of a next-best appointment, who has jostled the Federal provinces, and who has censured the Federal Constitutional Court in front of the whole people "for a false verdict". Just because of these attributes he has gained a position among the Germans that has enabled him to become the absolute master of the C.D.U.-C.S.U. (and at the same time to become a master of narrowmindedness).

'His party knows that the 85-year-old man is incapable of being at the head of a modern industrial state. They know, too, that in a crisis that has brought us to the edge of war, his policies have got us into a mess about which he does not know what to do.'

Brandt, said the commentator, could not be expected to be able to repair the damage done by Adenauer.

'But democracy under an S.P.D. government and under Brandt,' concluded the *Spiegel* commentator 'has still a chance – perhaps only one chance and maybe the last chance'.

Adenauer would reply to Herr Augstein in due season, in kind and in the old man's characteristically tortuous manner.

The Federal Chancellor was too old and experienced a political realist not to realize that the tide was running against him. He asserted that he still believed that he would gain an absolute majority, the only person in the C.D.U. who did. But after the polling stations had closed on 17th September, Adenauer, for the first time in four general elections, decided to wait up for the results. By early next morning he knew he had suffered a resounding personal defeat. The Germans were weary of their 85-year-old Chancellor and his 'Stick in the mud' policies. The defeat was all the more personal because the C.D.U. and their allies in Bavaria had managed to avoid a landslide.

The C.D.U. and its Bavarian sister party, the C.S.U., lost its absolute majority in the Bundestag although remaining the largest single party. Both the Social Democrats and the Free Democrats made substantial gains, although not all at the expense of the C.D.U. The full extent of the C.D.U. reverse, however, was concealed by the complicated German electoral system. Half the candidates are elected by direct mandate and half by proportional representation from the party list.

The real sensation of the election was the success of the Free Democrats. The F.D.P., by succeeding beyond its leaders' fondest hopes, had raised its representation in the Bundestag from forty-one to sixty seats and thereby gained the balance of power in the new German Parliament. Many *bourgeois* German voters, especially the younger ones, had become weary of twelve years of C.D.U. rule and the never-changing octogenarian dictatorial Chancellor. They had been determined to express the deep-seated national dissatisfaction and had salved their *bourgeois* consciences by voting for the F.D.P.; for in Germany a dramatic switch to the Socialists would have been unthinkable.

The fundamental decision of the German electorate was clear. 'Adenauer must go.' The equally fundamental question of German politics, and it would remain so for nearly two years was – 'But how?'

Although Adenauer was still at the head of the largest single party in the Bundestag, a clear majority of the West Germans had rejected him and his policies. At best, only the toleration of his political opponents would allow him to continue as Federal Chancellor. His party felt he must go, for the Germans are ruthless towards leaders who have suffered defeat whether they be called Wilhelm II, Adolf Hitler or Konrad Adenauer. Had the old man's sagacity matched his age, he would have retired in 1961, surrounded by honour and respect, to become the Patriarch of all Germans as long as he lived. He would have averted what in all charity must be described as the Adenauer tragedy of the last two years. For in the autumn of 1961, in his eighty-sixth year, he was obsessed still by the thought which he had once expressed to Paul Henri Spaak years before, and which would dominate him so long as he remained German Chancellor: '*Mein Gott*, what will happen to the Germans after I have gone?'

Those who asserted in September, 1961, that the Adenauer

era was at an end were somewhat premature. On the other hand, the election result clearly marked the beginning of the Adenauer *Daemmerung* (Twilight). But few if any of those at the heart of Bonn political life, still less the leaders of the C.D.U., would have believed that the *Daemmerung* would last something exceeding two years. For what the old man lacked in sagacity he made up by sheer dogged perseverance and obstinacy. On the morrow of the election his days seemed numbered. Even his former 'wonderboy' the unpredictable extrovert, Franz Josef Strauss, turned on him. As head of the C.S.U., the Bavarian wing of the C.D.U., Strauss announced with characteristic crudeness that, while it was ready to acknowledge Germany's great debt to Dr. Adenauer, the C.S.U. would support Professor Erhard, the Economic Minister, as the next Chancellor. Dr. Mende, whose F.D.P. held the balance of power, repeated what he had so often declared during the election campaign that *he* would not take part in any coalition headed by Adenauer. The F.D.P. was in a position to dictate terms, and there seemed no reason why Dr. Mende should relent.

Cynical foreigners who knew their Germany recalled the Bismarckian dictum that 'there is never so much lying as before an election and after a hunt'. They were tolerably sure that some sort of compromise would be cobbled together, permitting Adenauer to become Chancellor for a 'brief period' and then disappear.

There followed a period of two months of political chaos which clearly confirmed Herr Augstein's assertion that democracy in the Federal Republic was 'a tender plant'. In no other Western democracy, apart, perhaps, from the France of the Third and Fourth Republics, would such a deplorable display of political fatuity have been tolerated.

Adenauer was determined to remain Chancellor – no matter what it cost his party, his policies, or his pride. So long as he could manœuvre a majority in the new Bundestag, he would come to any accommodation for, in the maxim of his youthful mentors in Cologne, the end justified the means.

Within ten days of the poll he had completely reasserted his hold over the weak-kneed C.D.U. and C.S.U. which had kept him in office for a dozen years. All the elaborate internal manœuvres designed to put forward Professor Erhard as his successor collapsed in a heap. Erhard, after the manner of his submission to Adenauer's will in the presidential election campaign of 1959, gave in meekly and resigned himself to another undefined period in the uncertain role of crown prince. Even the bellicose Herr Strauss, after breathing fire for a week, duly toed the line.

Before the C.D.U. drill sergeant restored order in the party ranks, however, he had begun exploratory talks with his enemies of a lifetime, the S.P.D. Whether he would ever have taken the German Socialists into a coalition is an open question. If it had been the only way to keep himself in office, Adenauer might well have done so. But his much publicized meeting with Herren Ollenhauer, Wehner and the others was almost certainly propaganda. He aimed at intimidating Dr. Mende and the F.D.P., who were manifesting an obstinacy almost equal to his own. It worked. By the beginning of October, the second round in Adenauer's horse-trading started. The F.D.P., if not Dr. Mende, began to weaken.

Although the F.D.P. subsequently strongly denied the charge, there was some reason to suspect that they, too, had been called to order by the 'Ruhr barons' and other big business supporters who had provided the bulk of the party's election fund. While the German industrialists were ready to support the F.D.P. as a useful and salutary corrective to the C.D.U.'s social and economic policies, they were not prepared to countenance an Adenauer-S.P.D. Government if it could be prevented.

With that over-subtlety which is so often a weakness of German politicians, the F.D.P. agreed to discuss policies, but not personalities with Adenauer. By mutual agreement the key question, whether or not they should serve under him as Chancellor, was ignored. The F.D.P. was on the slippery slope. Principles so clamorously asserted during the election campaign were discreetly forgotten.

In the midst of the tortuous negotiations, in mid-October Adenauer suddenly sprang a sensation. He told a private meeting of the C.D.U. parliamentary party that he would not remain in office for the next Parliament's full term of four years, which would have taken him well into his ninetieth year! *He announced that he would retire*, early enough to give his successor ample time to prepare for the general election of 1965. That was little enough, but it proved decisive. A week later, the F.D.P., but not Dr. Mende personally, to his credit, agreed to serve in another Adenauer coalition. *Der Alte* had got his way again; he had managed to cling to office. But he had to pay a price. The F.D.P., distrusting the 'Old Fox', extorted from him a complicated secret agreement on policy plus a written undertaking to retire as he had promised. They also demanded a scapegoat for the catastrophic collapse of his foreign policy demonstrated by the Berlin Wall. They demanded the head of Brentano. Whatever his other defects, Adenauer was always loyal to his subordinates as his often unwise defence of Globke proved. He fought hard for Brentano.

When he realized that he must have a new Foreign Minister, he offered Brentano another seat in the Cabinet. Herr von Brentano, as Foreign Minister, had been seldom more than an agreeable cypher. But as a member of a great Frankfurt family renowned in German history, he had a dignity rare in German political life. He declined the offer of further office and, in due course, was elected head of the C.D.U. parliamentary party. His exclusion from the Bonn Cabinet meant more than his mere removal from office. It may very well have ended Adenauer's cherished hopes of securing the appointment as his successor of another Roman Catholic like himself.

Finally, in mid-November, no less than two months after the election results had become known, the coalition pantomime came to an end. Adenauer presented a new Government, which included five F.D.P. ministers, to the Federal President. The most important appointment was the new Foreign Minister, the able and ambitious Dr. Gerhard Schroeder. As Minister of the

Interior he had seemed a trusty Adenauer acolyte. But his appointment to the Bonn Foreign Office brought major changes. For the first time since 1949, Adenauer lost complete control of West German foreign policy.

The first reaction to the formation of Adenauer's fourth Government was a feeling of intense relief both in Bonn and beyond. As *The Times* pungently observed, 'Neither West Germany nor the Western Alliance could have afforded much more delay. It is now urgent that the West should agree on a firm position from which to negotiate on Berlin – and then negotiate.'

It was indeed time! In the months when Adenauer had devoted himself predominantly to political barter, the Governments in Washington and London had become more and more irritated by his disturbing, not to say contradictory, foreign activities.

On the very eve of the German general election in September, as the Western Foreign Ministers discussed the Berlin crisis in Washington, they had received news of a conciliatory move from Moscow. The Soviet Foreign Minister, Mr. Gromyko, had indicated that he was prepared to have an exchange of opinions with the U.S. Secretary of State, Mr. Rusk, when he was in New York for the U.N. General Assembly meetings.

De Gaulle was strongly opposed to any negotiations and his Foreign Minister, M. Couve de Murville, demonstrated that wintry countenance which was to become something of a permanent feature of international gatherings in the next year or two. Adenauer showed equal distrust. But the U.S. Secretary of State, backed by the British Government, in defiance of the unyielding Cold War policies of the Bonn-Paris axis, met Mr. Gromyko for a series of talks. The same Soviet-American series of talks, after many ups and downs, were still in progress eighteen months later when Adenauer announced his firm intention to retire.

During the America-Soviet exchanges, President Kennedy had a talk with Mr. Gromyko in the White House. Reports, some incorrect, of what was alleged to have been said at this meeting, sent by the German Embassy in Washington, at once aroused

Adenauer's deepest suspicions that a deal was about to be done behind his back. The German attitude was so unco-operative that, at the four-power working group meetings in Washington during October, the American and British representatives did some very blunt talking to the German representatives.

According to what later became known in Washington, the German Ambassador, who was becoming *persona non grata* to the Kennedy administration, became alarmed by a statement alleged to have been made by the British delegate, Lord Hood. The British representative had indicated that, should any settlement be reached on Berlin, it was fairly obvious that 'the authority of the East Zone Government must, at least, be respected'. When the report of this British view reached Bonn, it fell on Adenauer like a douche of cold water. In the next few weeks there developed an incident which has never been fully or satisfactorily explained. The evidence suggests that Adenauer, infuriated by the 'appeasement' of the Anglo-Saxon powers, and increasingly jealous of the initiative shown by the young man in the White House and his own consequent relegation to a back seat, began to toy with a hazardous game.

Almost at the same time as Gromyko had proposed Soviet-American talks, Mr. Khrushchev, on the day after the general election, had cabled his congratulations to Adenauer on his re-election. This hint of a *rapprochement* certainly owed something to the excellent personal relationship which the Russian-speaking German Ambassador in Moscow, Dr. Hans Kroll, had succeeded in establishing with Khrushchev. The tough, highly ambitious, professional diplomat, Dr. Kroll, was much distrusted in the Bonn Foreign Office, but he had the personal ear of the Federal Chancellor with whom he was known to be in private contact.

During October at least one meeting took place between Mr. Khrushchev and Kroll. On whose initiative the talk took place is uncertain. By the beginning of November, however, rumours were permitted to leak out of Bonn Government offices hinting at a Khrushchev-Adenauer meeting.

From Press dispatches from Moscow it then became known that at their meeting, Khrushchev and Kroll had discussed a somewhat nebulous four-point plan to end the Berlin crisis. Again, it was never clear from which side the initiative came. There were sharp reactions in the Western capitals. Adenauer, after blocking Western attempts at a settlement for years, was now widely suspected, as a consequence of the battering he had received at home for the failure of his foreign policy, of trying 'To go it alone'. Doubts as to whether he was in earnest, or whether this was characteristic Adenauer blackmail aimed at trying to force the Kennedy administration to accept his views, merely served to increase the annoyance of Western leaders.

In the Bonn Foreign Office, which seemed to know little or nothing of what its ambassador in Moscow had been doing, there was confusion. The firm hand of Dr. Schroeder was not yet at the helm. Kroll was recalled to report to Adenauer. There was uncertainty as to whether he should be permitted to return to Moscow. He did go back to his embassy, but not for long. Dr. Kroll was much too ambitious a diplomat to be left alone in such a highly sensitive diplomatic post as the West German Embassy in Moscow.

As the 'Kroll scandal' broke, Adenauer had announced that he would visit Washington as soon as his Government was sworn in. But the suspicion and irritation engendered by Dr. Kroll's activities were scarcely conducive to even friendly relations. When, once again, Adenauer crossed the Atlantic, in the third week of November, the distrust was mutual as was evidenced by a speech made by the new Foreign Minister, Dr. Schroeder to the National Press Club in Washington:

'It has been said that the three Western Powers cannot remain inactive in this dangerous situation (in Berlin) and that he (Adenauer) should evolve fresh ideas. But I do think that it would be dangerous to renounce the rights vested in the Allies as a result of the military occupation of Germany and to replace them by an arrangement under which the Western Powers' rights would be based on an agreement with the Soviet Union. Such a substitution of original rights by negotiated rights,' suggested Dr. Schroeder, 'would amount to a deterioration in the Western position'. In plain English, Adenauer had nothing new to offer. He was still clinging to the 'Do nothing' policy of the Dulles era.

During the talks in the White House, Adenauer did one right-about-turn. For years he had insisted that Berlin was a problem which could only be settled within the framework of a general German settlement. Now he agreed that in talks with the Russians, Berlin alone should be discussed.

Some sort of compromise was patched up; how long it would endure the cynical Americans were uncertain. The Kennedy administration was far from happy about Adenauer and his apparent determination to maintain his blocking tactics to the very end. They felt, however, that they had nudged him a bit towards a more flexible attitude, at least over the question of negotiating on Berlin. With a man all too clearly incapacitated by age from any initiative, even that was some sort of progress.

If the Kennedy administration was cynical, Adenauer's basic suspicions had, if anything, been increased by his experience in Washington. He returned to Bonn weary and looking his age. In Washington he had contracted a head cold and, as had become customary at this period of the year, he retired to his bed. It was not until Mr. Macmillan paid yet another visit to Bonn, a few days after the Chancellor's eighty-sixth birthday at the beginning of 1962, that he exhibited any activity. The meeting took place in a mellifluous atmosphere which could not cloak the mutual incompatibility between the two men in their approach to East-West problems. British officials made no effort to hide this when they stated, 'There is no use pretending that differences don't exist.'

The differences between Adenauer and London and Washington, sharp as they were, were comparatively minor beside those which separated the Anglo-Saxon powers from de Gaulle, who had become ever more isolated in the Atlantic alliance. No settlement on Berlin, however, was possible without the third

Occupying Power. For France, despite her defeat by the Germans in 1940, had been regrettably introduced into the German scene in 1945 by Winston Churchill because he feared that the Americans would pull out of Europe.

Adenauer was the obvious envoy to Paris. The old man's vanity was warmed by the thought that he alone might be able to persuade his fellow authoritarian to rejoin the Western concert. In mid-February, 1962, he had an unexpected meeting with the French President in Baden-Baden. He went with the firm determination to persuade the Frenchman to co-operate over Berlin. But that strange mesmerism which de Gaulle increasingly exercised over Adenauer again came into play. The Chancellor returned to Bonn more set in his opposition to the Anglo-Saxon powers' East-West ideas than ever.

The Soviet-American talks, meanwhile, had been transferred to Moscow, with the American Ambassador Mr. Llewellyn Thomson representing Mr. Dean Rusk.

To a C.D.U. meeting Adenauer confided that the Gromyko-Thomson talks were 'getting nowhere'. He said he was very dissatisfied with the progress of the talks and the instructions given by the White House to the American Ambassador. Proposals for internationalizing the access routes to Berlin he regarded as the thin edge of the wedge. They might well lead to a loosening of the ties between West Berlin and West Germany, 'which is the main aim of the Soviet policy'. He ended by telling his C.D.U. friends that he was sure he could put the brake on such Anglo-Saxon projects.

Inevitably, his C.D.U. friends in the classic manner of Bonn 'open diplomacy', leaked his whole speech to the German Press. The German Ambassador, Professor Grewe, was summoned to the White House. 'An unusually frank exchange of views occurred between the President and the Ambassador', according to American official statements. Less official versions gave a much more highly coloured account of what occurred in the President's study. Following this encounter, President Kennedy took the almost unprecedented step of ordering the State Department to sever official relations with Grewe and to pass all official communications to the Bonn Government through the American Ambassador in Bonn.

Adenauer, showing signs of the intermittent onset of political dotage, was genuinely astounded by the American reaction. He failed to realize for some days that German-American relations had reached their post-war nadir. Mr. Robert Kennedy, the President's brother and U.S. Attorney General, flew the following week-end to Bonn to ask the Federal Chancellor bluntly what policy he proposed to follow.

Adenauer was incorrigible. He was in the midst of his annual late winter bout of pessimism, and of distrust of American policy in particular. He told the younger Mr. Kennedy that he was deeply wounded about the course of American policy towards Russia. He insisted that the Moscow talks should not be permitted to go on indefinitely. And, for good measure, he suggested to Mr. Robert Kennedy that 'the President seems more interested in self-determination in Africa than in Europe'.

CHAPTER TWENTY

Political Throwback

By early 1962, age had caught up at last with Konrad Adenauer. In appearance, he seemed virtually unchanged; the leathery visage was thinner, more lined, but he remained upright as a guardsman. His physical energy remained astounding. At Baden Baden in February, it was de Gaulle who seemed the elder; Adenauer still undertook the work of a man twenty years his junior. Up at five in the morning to read the newspapers, he returned home in the late evening with his brief-case crammed with papers, after a day filled with meetings and receiving visitors.

But, now, his mental energy began to lag. The moral defeat of the previous autumn's general election, coupled with the after-effects of two prolonged bouts of influenza during the winter left him weary and depressed and he seemed unable to recover his wonted vitality. Visitors to the Chancellery echoed what had been said of the aged Marshal Pétain during the last war; in the morning he was the dynamic figure he had always been, after lunch he became a weary old grandfather, only half aware of what he did.

Decisions, which once he would have taken in a few minutes, were now, for the first time, passed to ministers, or pushed aside indefinitely. He was interested only in his own private foreign policy, which encountered ever more opposition from Dr. Schroeder in the Foreign Office. Internal policies demanding decisions for a Germany well past the peak of the 'German miracle' (Wirtschaftswunder) were, despite the efforts of Professor Erhard, left indeterminate. More and more was pushed on to Globke who, by this time, had unsuccessfully attempted to resign five times. Because of Adenauer's habits of one-man rule

cabinet government was virtually an impossibility. Western
Germany had an administration rather than a government, as the
failure to tackle serious problems such as the growing balance of
payments problem indicated. Day to day administration fell more
and more into the hands of a 'cabal of guilty men', a round dozen
of high functionaries in key ministries who, whatever their intrinsic merit or efficiency, had all been either card-carrying members of the Nazi party or had held office in the Third Reich of
Adolf Hitler.

Throughout Western Germany there was rising opposition,
not only to Adenauer's Government, or, more correctly, the lack
of it, but also to his foreign policies, which seemed aimed at
creating a major showdown with the Kennedy administration in
Washington. When, in mid-March, Adenauer set out for Cadenabbia, exhausted and deeply pessimistic, it was not surprising that
Bonn was beset by doubts and confusion.

The decline in Adenauer's prestige inside the Federal Republic
since the tragedy of the Berlin Wall in the previous August was
phenomenal. Young Germans, to whom Adolf Hitler was little
more than a name, demanded to know why their country was
dominated by this antediluvian relic. Pastors and officials of the
Lutheran church, outraged by the systematic appointment of
Catholics to high posts in a basically non-Catholic country,
openly denounced the Chancellor. Those in close contact with
fellow-Protestants beyond the Iron Curtain transmitted their
plea: 'Can't you do anything to get rid of Adenauer and do something to help us here in the D.D.R.?' Millions of Germans, from
the Alps to the North Sea, shared a deep-seated sense of national
frustration: 'The old man must go!' was the cry everywhere.

The pusillanimous Bonn parliamentarians could have removed
him in twenty-four hours – *if they had got together*. The S.P.D.,
with its foreign policies reformed and purged of Marxist ideology,
was ready. The C.D.U. as usual lacked guts. The F.D.P., after
its bellicose noises in the election campaign of the previous
summer, sought only the fruits of office.

Dr. Dehler, always one of the rebels of the F.D.P. and now a vice-president of the Bundestag, said what millions felt when, in March, on German television he accused the Chancellor of 'primitive anti-bolshevism', a description which could scarcely have been bettered.

The Germans, said Dr. Dehler, should learn from the British and develop a policy of pragmatism towards the Soviet Union. For the past thirty years, he said, coupling Adenauer and Hitler, Germany had devoted its energies to an ideological crusade against the Soviet Union, instead of seeking a constructive policy of co-existence.

Dr. Dehler had put his finger on the rawest spot in the C.D.U. discontent. For many of Adenauer's own party privately agreed with much of what the stormy petrel of the F.D.P. had said. There was a characteristic outburst from the pro-Adenauer faction leaders headed by Brentano. They described Dehler as a 'national catastrophe', and publicly questioned the propriety of his being permitted to preside over future sessions of the Bonn Parliament. Their fury merely demonstrated to the outside world just how much the so-called Christian *Democratic* party understood about true democracy.

It was in the midst of this period of political confusion and doubt that Adenauer, at the beginning of April, broke his holiday to return briefly to Bonn in a Luftwaffe transport, for a budget debate. He had better remained by Lake Como. His rambling interventions confirmed the widely-held view that he was losing his grip. The C.D.U. was much relieved when, once again, he disappeared to the other side of the Alps. In the following weeks it became noticeable that ministers began to function with normal responsibility. There was no 'pilgrimage' to Cadenabbia as in former years.

By the time Adenauer returned to Bonn, early in May, his party was in a ferment. Control was fast slipping out of his hands. The growing rebelliousness against his old-fashioned authoritarian ways stemmed from the appreciation that his days were numbered. It would still be a long time before the timid and craven C.D.U. finally braced itself for a decision. How long, was to be the problem of the next twelve months.

From his Italian retreat, the Chancellor had been watching the continuance of the Soviet-American conversations in Moscow with growing apprehension and he was determined to sabotage any chance of a *rapprochement*, however unlikely. In the past he had shown a certain finesse and guile in such tortuous operations but this time his tactics were childish, and all too obvious to Washington. A clearly concerted campaign against the talks began to appear in some German newspapers. When that had no effect, the contents of an American draft of points for negotiations with the Russians, a copy of which had been passed to the Germans, was 'leaked' to German newspapers. No one in Washington believed official German denials that Bonn was not responsible for the leak. Relations between Washington and Bonn steadily deteriorated, although in public the Americans showed admirable restraint.

On his return to Bonn, Adenauer at once came out in the open. He repeated what he had said two months earlier, prior to the visit of Mr. Robert Kennedy to Bonn, that he did not believe any result would come from the Moscow negotiations. Despite mounting anger, the Washington authorities continued to show caution. But Adenauer, less discreet than ever he had been, seemed determined to pick a row with Washington and travelled to Berlin, a day or two later, to embark on a series of either calculated indiscretions or open blunders seldom equalled in his period in office.

There he repeated that he did not believe that any results could come from the Moscow talks, adding sarcastically, 'I am surprised I am reported as saying anything new. All I can say is that I evaluate events differently from others. The Soviet-American talks have shown no results as yet. I can see no reason for their continuance.'

Under his impassive surface he was seething at the thought of the Kennedy administration defying him. With what was seen as a calculated insult, he then casually announced that he 'was in favour of a change in the German diplomatic representation in Washington', and that it would 'take place soon'. That was the first that anyone, including his own Foreign Ministry knew that the unfortunate Professor Grewe, the German Ambassador in Washington, was to be recalled. The Kennedy administration certainly had no desire for the German Ambassador, officially described as 'incompatible', to linger in Washington, but Adenauer's tactics seemed a regrettable throwback to the worst habits of Ribbentrop's diplomacy.

Within twenty-four hours, the administration in Washington reacted. Adenauer's remarks about the very genuine American efforts to reach an interim solution on Berlin were much deprecated, especially as they had been made half a mile from the Wall. The State Department coldly announced that the Moscow talks would continue and would not be delayed, whatever Dr. Adenauer's objections.

There was now a deep crisis between Adenauer and the U.S. administration, the worst since President Kennedy had taken office fifteen months earlier. Well-informed foreign correspondents in Washington were encouraged to say so in print. Adenauer was furious. In his temper he turned on an old enemy, the British Press. The correspondent of *The Times* in Washington had reported the facts with admirable objectivity. Back in Bonn, the Chancellor turned on the British newspaper: 'There is no crisis between the U.S. and Bonn, nor is there one on the horizon ... and I am sorry to have to disappoint *The Times*', he announced with unconcealed rancour.

Next day, President Kennedy, at his Press conference, tried to pour oil on the troubled waters of Washington-Bonn relations. He said that he had never expressed optimism about the talks, and denied allegations that he had ever proposed either the *de facto* or *de jure* recognition of the East German régime. He made no direct reference to Adenauer. When asked about some of the Chancellor's statements, the President discreetly suggested that he was sure Dr. Adenauer had been misquoted. In Washington, too, it was suspected that the German Chancellor was becoming senile.

Despite the marked restraint of his statement, Mr. Kennedy ended by stating firmly that the Soviet-American discussions would continue to seek an interim solution of the Berlin problem.

The President had no desire to widen the breach in the Western Alliance. Nevertheless, official spokesmen in Washington indicated that there was virtually no diplomatic contact between Washington and Bonn and repeated that there was an inspired campaign in Western Germany against American diplomacy.

German-American relations were still tense when, from foreign Press reports, it became evident that Adenauer had not confined his Berlin indiscretions to East-West relations. Privately he had expressed strong views on the negotiations to enable Britain to join the European Common Market which had been going on in Brussels for the previous nine months. He feared that his original concept of 'Little Europe' would be endangered by the admittance to the European Community not only of Great Britain but of other countries such as Ireland and the Scandinavian countries. He said that the Common Market *must not be permitted to grow so big* that it would be unable to function effectively. Some reports claimed he advocated that the British should *be permitted to enter the Common Market only as associate members.*

Although he denied subsequently that he opposed British entry, Adenauer's comments in Berlin foreshadowed the explanation which he gave to his Ministers, after the final breakdown of the Common Market negotiations in the following January, to justify his support of de Gaulle's ban on British entry. Whatever his precise words, however, Anglo-American officials in Germany had little doubt that he had voiced growing misgivings of which the first indication had been given two months earlier, in an interview published in *Le Monde.*

The dismay of the British Government was easy to appreciate. The Kennedy administration was equally alarmed, for the United States Government was anxious that Britain should become a full member of the Common Market as part of President Kennedy's 'Grand Design'.

To officials in Washington it seemed that the old man's statements revealed an almost frightening degree of mental confusion. But his indiscretions in Berlin seemed to have a more serious background. He appeared to be attempting, unsuccessfully, to reconcile in his own mind the inherent contradiction of his foreign policies. There seemed to be some link between his growing apprehensions about Britain in the Common Market and de Gaulle's conception of the future of Europe. As one Western official, with great prescience, pointed out, it was clear that at the decisive stage of the Common Market negotiations – despite the warm support of both Professor Erhard and Dr. Schroeder – Britain *could not expect the German Government to take any initiative to put pressure on de Gaulle.*

The American Ambassador in Bonn, Mr. Walter Dowling, was instructed to call on Adenauer and try to ascertain just what his policy was on two fundamental points: 1. The East-West conversations on Berlin in Moscow; 2. Britain's entry into the Common Market. The Ambassador got little change out of the old man. A week later, the U.S. Under-Secretary of State, Mr. George Bull, flew to Bonn as the President's special envoy. American diplomats openly said that he had been sent because Adenauer's indiscretions in Berlin had aroused serious doubts in Washington, and also in London, about his attitude to fundamental Western policy. Mr. Ball talked very frankly to Adenauer who, ten days later, at a C.D.U. national congress in Dortmund, retraced his steps – part of the way!

As a conciliatory opening gambit he attacked his old scapegoat, the foreign Press, for making difficulties between himself and President Kennedy. Then he stated categorically that he was *now in favour* of the British joining the Common Market. He probably was, at that moment, but no one could predict with certainty what he would favour in a fortnight. As though to emphasize the vacillations of his weary mind, he at once added that he was, however, opposed to the entry of the Commonwealth into the Common Market. He seemed to fail to appreciate that none of the self-governing states of the British Commonwealth had applied to join the Common Market. He added that Britain's role as leader of the Commonwealth 'presents exceedingly difficult problems to the British and to The Six'.

He turned gratefully to a more congenial subject which had become the dominant obsession of his octogenarian mind – his growing friendship with President de Gaulle. In contrast to the difficulties caused by the British, he stated, the friendship which he had now established with France was 'the most valuable single factor of these troubled times'.

That brief phrase, which contained the very kernel of everything for which he would strive during the remainder of his period in office, did not go unmarked. In Washington and in London there was growing concern at the success of de Gaulle in weaning the ageing German Chancellor from the Atlantic Alliance into an anti-Anglo-Saxon European *bloc* with France at its head. Towards the end of June, the American Secretary of State, Mr. Dean Rusk, arrived in Bonn in a bid to combat the French President's growing influence over Adenauer.

The Kennedy administration was extremely irritated by Adenauer's activities during the previous few months, but nothing was to be gained by beating a dead horse. His indiscretions were therefore studiously ignored. Mr. Rusk with charm and tact set out to smooth his ruffled feathers and restore Adenauer's confidence in the Kennedy régime which had been seriously shaken. The Secretary of State went out of his way to soothe the octogenarian's political vanity and to rebuild the bridges to Washington which Adenauer had half-destroyed in the previous six months. A banquet was held for members of all German political parties and leading industrialists at which the Chancellor was guest of honour. And after numerous references to 'the great man' in their midst, Mr. Rusk ended by hailing Adenauer as 'one of the world's greatest statesmen'.

The old man's vanity was indeed touched by American flattery – for a week. At the beginning of July, however, Adenauer travelled to France for what, but for the niceties of protocol, would have been described as a State visit. He was welcomed by the French President with the highest courtesy and much deference. Side by side with 'The General' in uniform he inspected joint French-German manœuvres across the old battlefields of Champagne. Together they knelt at mass in the great cathedral of Rheims. Most Germans instinctively make obeisance before a great patriarchal military leader whether his name be Hindenburg or de Gaulle. Whether Adenauer, perhaps the most pacifist of all German heads of government, shared that basic Teutonic instinct is uncertain. As the two old men travelled together they talked and talked. The problem of Algeria was at last out of the way and 'The General' with all the charm of which he was capable explained how he planned to reorganize Europe, determined to win over the old German who must be his key ally. Adenauer was impressed or, perhaps, mesmerized by de Gaulle's oracular projects.

But Adenauer was far from enamoured by all de Gaulle's policies. He deprecated the repeated efforts of de Gaulle to set up a three-power Franco-British-American directory to control N.A.T.O. He deplored de Gaulle's increasing efforts to split the Atlantic Alliance. In the previous few months de Gaulle had shot to shreds Adenauer's plan for an integrated Western Europe. Only a month or two earlier the last of the disgruntled French 'European Old Guard' had walked out of de Gaulle's Government in disgust. They had been infuriated at his determination to substitute his own nebulous association of European sovereign states for the closely integrated supra-national European institutions favoured by themselves – and by Adenauer.

However much Adenauer disagreed with de Gaulle on the emphasis and details of European integration, he did share the

French President's fundamental aim of establishing a neo-Carolingian Reich, a new Holy Roman Empire of basically Catholic and conservative European states. What Adenauer in the enthusiasm of great age did not appear to comprehend was that, in de Gaulle's scheme of things, Germany would be relegated to the role of the No. 1 satellite of France. Under the pervasive influence of the remarkable man who ruled France Adenauer was obsessed by only one thought; to realize at last through the creation of an Adenauer-de Gaulle axis the fondest hope of his political life.

At that point in his eighty-seventh year, the German Chancellor seemed to develop a throwback to his political past. Under the near hypnotic influence of 'The General', the octogenarian Rhinelander lapsed into what was not so much second childhood as a second middle-age, from the depths of his aged subconscious were resurrected policies which had dominated him in his middle forties. The policies of 1918–23, the long forgotten dreams of the separatist days, took on a new form and substance. At last, after waiting forty years, the old Rhinelander saw the chance of creating a Franco-German alliance, based on the closest possible association between France and his old Rhine-Ruhr state of 1923 (somewhat enlarged to extend as far as the Elbe).

In the months which followed his visit to France in the summer of 1962, the inherent dangers of leaving near-dictatorial powers in the hands of a man in his eighty-seventh year were again demonstrated to the Germans – as they had been by Hindenburg in the years between 1932 and 1934. In open defiance of most of his ministers, the bulk of his party, and a majority of the German Parliament, the headstrong old man proceeded to alter radically the course of German foreign policy.

The German-American alliance, despite his repeated assertions to the contrary, was no longer the corner-stone of Adenauer's foreign policy. In a divided Germany, in which the power of the United States must always remain vital to the security of the Bonn Republic, Adenauer wilfully and recklessly fractured those ties which had held Bonn and Washington together since the West German Government was founded in 1949. For that fundamental alliance he substituted, so far as he was able, a treaty of friendship nominally with France, but actually with a fellow-authoritarian in his seventies who was the object of repeated assassination attempts. Again in defiance of his ministers, party, and Parliament, Adenauer obliged his friend in Paris by reversing his own, and his Government's, decision to do everything possible to aid the historic step of bringing Britain into the European community.

Some hint of the future was contained in the communiqué issued at the end of Adenauer's visit to France. His talks with de Gaulle had reinforced Adenauer's already strong misgivings about the wisdom of permitting Britain into Europe but at that stage de Gaulle had not yet made up his mind to use his veto power in 'The Six' to prevent it. But the underlying doubts of both men were implicit in the statement which expressed only 'hope' that the Brussels negotiations would succeed in resolving the problems raised by Britain's request to join the Common Market.

Throughout the summer Adenauer revealed in private conversation his deep reservations about the consequences of Britain entering the European Community. At a meeting of the C.D.U. parliamentary executive committee towards the end of August, he advocated a rough line in negotiation with the British. His views proved unpopular. Dr. Schroeder, who had begun to emerge as the 'strong man' of the Bonn Government, insisted that, on the contrary, Britain must be brought into the Common Market as soon as possible. When the executive issued a public statement expressing Schroeder's standpoint Adenauer found himself in a minority in his own party executive. The rebuff nettled the old man. He was determined to show who was the leader of the C.D.U., and who decided policy. Once again, in a state of fury he turned on the British.

About a month earlier, Mr. Macmillan, in reply to a question by Mr. Gaitskell, had assured the Leader of the Opposition that there was no question in the Brussels negotiations of giving any political undertakings which went beyond the preamble of the Rome Treaty. Four days later, the Prime Minister had written a friendly, eight-page letter to Adenauer on the question of the Brussels negotiations. In this Mr. Macmillan had expressed benevolent interest in the progress of The Six towards closer political union. He had gone on to assure the German Chancellor that it was the desire of the British Government, as soon as the Brussels negotiations had been brought to a successful conclusion, to join in this project.

Three days after his rebuff at the hands of the C.D.U. executive, Adenauer recorded an interview for the German television network on film. After saying he wished to say a few words on the problem of Britain's entry he launched into a five minute monologue, in the course of which he accused the British Prime Minister of double dealing.

He alleged that Mr. Macmillan in his private letter had said almost the complete opposite of his statement in the House of Commons four days earlier. Adenauer said that he *did* favour Britain entering the Common Market but that her association with a future European political union must be treated as a separate problem. But in view of Macmillan's 'double dealing', he continued, 'we do not know at present whether Britain really wants' to take part in the political union.

In the interval between the recording of the interview and its transmission over the German TV, the British Embassy in Bonn heard a whisper of the Chancellor's personal abuse of the Prime Minister. A counter campaign was launched in the German Press. As soon as the Federal Chancellery realized that the British knew what was in the interview, desperate efforts were made to persuade the German TV editors to remove the offending passage from the film. To their professional credit the administrations of the German TV networks stuck to their principles. The interview in full, complete with the allegation that the British Prime Minister was two-faced, was shown all over Germany.

Mr. Macmillan replied by taking an unprecedented step. Through the Foreign Office he issued the exact text of the relevant section of his private letter to which Adenauer had referred.

As *Der Spiegel* observed, 'What the Chancellor blabbed out would have been untactful enough if it had been true – *but it was false.*'

More charitable British and German diplomats who strove to play down the indiscretion agreed in private that clearly 'the old man is losing his grip'. The problem was to persuade the pusillanimous C.D.U. and F.D.P. to do something about that obvious fact.

In all the Western capitals, including Bonn but excepting Paris, there was much sympathy for the British Prime Minister, clearly the victim of the German Chancellor's chronic anglophobia. His hatred of all things British had now become a byword even in Germany: 'No other people, with the exception of the Soviets, have so been insulted and abused by Konrad Adenauer in recent years as the British,' stated *Der Spiegel*.

The Times observed that 'Adenauer's clumsy remarks about Britain and European political union have caused one of these needless disputes'. In remarkably few words he had dealt a double blow, suggesting that he was not eager to have Britain in a political union and slamming Mr. Macmillan for chopping and changing on the question. *The Times* suggested that Adenauer's outburst had been caused by a realization of how fast the sands of time were running out for him. If he had to leave office in 1963 he was more determined than ever to crown his life's work by a Franco-German reconciliation cemented in a political union.

Final steps towards the consummation of that reconciliation were taken a week later when President de Gaulle arrived in the Federal Republic for a State visit, which was rapidly transformed into an imperial progress through the easternmost province of the Carolingian Reich. It was a remarkable spectacle, and when de Gaulle spoke in robust and extremely creditable German, the crowds went mad. From the Rhine to the Elbe, from the North Sea to the Alps, hundreds of thousands of Germans cheered, and shouted, and clamoured for 'The General' with an enthusiasm unseen in Germany since the disappearance of Adolf Hitler. To foreigners with recollections of the Nuremberg rallies and other Nazi festivals devoted to Führer worship and mass hysteria, it was a disturbing reception. Given a German general possessed of a Teutonic rather than a Gallic mystique, German democracy already badly bruised by the authoritarian activities of Konrad Adenauer, might fare ill in the future.

Adenauer was unmoved by these manifestations of popular mass hysteria but de Gaulle's state visit realized his fondest hopes. Though there still remained serious differences between the two men, de Gaulle formally presented his views on future Franco-German unity and the final steps were taken towards the goal towards which Adenauer had striven so long, a Franco-German *rapprochement*.

The seal was set on those years of striving at a banquet in Schloss Bruehl, near Bonn. Deeply moved, and with his face aglow, the French President announced, 'The two countries are united. The time has come for negotiations on political union.' The hereditary hate which had separated Teuton and Gaulle for centuries had come to an end. The German Chancellor almost wept. Despite the emotion on both sides, however, the practical details had still to be worked out. The other members of 'The Six' had still to be reconciled to the grandiose project, and over all hung the shadow of the British! It was not until de Gaulle had wiped away that shadow that the two old men were able to meet in Paris and formally sign their personal Franco-German treaty. But that was still several months ahead.

In the autumn of 1962 there was an understandable and widespread satisfaction that reconciliation with France had at last been reached, but no one was quite sure what had passed between Adenauer and de Gaulle in private. Adenauer's Cabinet remained in the dark. There was an ineluctable suspicion that the price of reconciliation had been German surrender to de Gaulle's now morbidly hostile attitude to both the Anglo-Saxon powers.

When Adenauer returned to Bonn in the autumn from an extended visit to Cadenabbia, there were virtually two German foreign policies: 1. Adenauer's increasingly pro-French course. 2. The policy of the majority of his ministers, headed by Erhard and Dr. Schroeder, which followed a pro-American, pro-British line in general, and in particular supported British entry into the European Community as rapidly as possible.

Negotiations between Britain and 'The Six' in Brussels had reached an advanced stage. Adenauer began to show something near panic about what would happen should Britain be permitted to join the Common Market. He became ever more isolated within his Cabinet. The Foreign Minister, Dr. Schroeder, was finally constrained to announce what the Chancellor could not bring himself to say, that not only did the German Government favour Britain's entry into the Common Market, but it also hoped that the British would co-operate in some future political integration.

Discontent with Adenauer, however, was not confined to his ministers. Inside his own party, in that of his Free Democrat coalition allies, among a broad section of the German Parliament, and throughout the country there was rising resentment at the old man's pig-headed refusal to get out and give place to a younger man.

This national frustration and discontent suddenly burst into open conflagration at the end of October when Herr Rudolf Augstein, the proprietor of *Der Spiegel*, and a handful of his top editorial and management executives were arrested in a classic Gestapo operation for alleged 'treason'.

For years *Der Spiegel* had carried on a campaign of denigration against the turbulent Minister of Defence, Franz Josef Strauss, believed by many to be the most dangerous demagogue in Western Germany. Recently the news magazine had accused Strauss of irregularities arising from contracts in his native Bavaria in what became known as the 'Fibag' and the 'Onkel

Aloys' affairs. Furthermore, Herr Augstein had long been a leading opponent of Adenauer and his policies and, as previous chapters have indicated, *Der Spiegel* had consistently denounced the Chancellor both for his authoritarian ways and his barren Cold War policies.

Some weeks earlier *Der Spiegel*, in a further attempt to disparage Strauss as Defence Minister, had 'leaked' what were claimed to be serious reflections on the efficiency of the German Bundeswehr made in a secret report on a N.A.T.O. exercise called Fallex 62. It was the same report from which, six months later, the so-called British 'Spies for Peace' quoted sections. Early in October, the anti-Strauss campaign was continued in an article on the Inspector-General of the Bundeswehr, General Foertsch. This officer had the somewhat equivocal background of having been sentenced by a Soviet military court to twenty-five years' imprisonment for alleged war crimes in German-occupied Russia before being rescued with other 'War criminals' by Adenauer in 1955. This article was alleged to reveal German military secrets. The attention of the Federal judicial authorities was drawn to it. Action was instituted and Strauss, who was thirsting for revenge against *Der Spiegel*, blurted out that he would soon get even with the recalcitrant news magazine.

During the last week-end of October, as the world teetered on the verge of nuclear war over Cuba, Herr Augstein and his executives were arrested in an operation which would have brought joy to the heart of that great authority on nefarious police activity, the late Obergruppenführer Reinhard Heydrich. And well it might. The *Spiegel* operation was headed by one of Heydrich's former pupils, Police Commissioner Saevecke of the so-called Security Group in Bonn. Saevecke, only one of many former Gestapoists to find refuge in Adenauer's secret services, was discovered a few weeks later to be wanted by the Italian authorities for alleged war crimes in Italy prior to 1945.

Contrary to the specific safeguards of the Bonn constitution, the secret police swooped on the homes of *Der Spiegel* executives in the middle of the night. Children were pulled from their beds, families put in a state of alarm, and all the terror of arbitrary arrest which all Germans had come to know and fear in the years from 1933 to 1945 reappeared.

Simultaneously other secret police swooped on the Hamburg head office of *Der Spiegel* and sealed off the building while so-called experts searched the fascinating archives built up over the years for 'incriminating material'. An effort was made to seize the next issue of the magazine and prevent publication. But due to a massive demonstration of solidarity by Hamburg publishers headed by Dr. Bucerius, *Der Spiegel*, snarling and scratching at Adenauer, Strauss and all its enemies, came out on schedule – and doubled its circulation!

As a result of a truly Gestapo-like bungle the secret police at first failed to find Herr Augstein. The next morning the *Spiegel* proprietor, with dignified disdain, presented himself formally at the Hamburg police headquarters and was promptly arrested for treason.

One of the homes raided where children were put in a state of terror was the Hamburg residence of Herr Conrad Ahlers, an assistant editor of the magazine and its recognized expert on defence affairs. On learning to their consternation that he was in Spain – in fact, holidaying with his wife near Malaga – the secret police decided that 'the fugitive had fled'. This discovery was passed within minutes to the Ministry of Defence in Bonn and, in the middle of the night, several urgent calls were made to the German Embassy in Madrid. Finally, the German Military Attaché in the Spanish capital was contacted. About the same time a telegram which grossly abused the statutes of Interpol was sent by the Federal Criminal Office in Wiesbaden to its opposite number in Madrid ordering the arrest of Ahlers. The unfortunate Ahlers was dragged away from his wife in Torremolinos, taken to Madrid by the Spanish security authorities and 'hijacked' to Frankfurt in a Lufthansa Super-Constellation in a manner which would have done credit to the kidnappers of Eichmann.

All this was carried out in the classic Nazi way by '*Nacht und Nebel*' (night and fog) without the knowledge of the Federal Minister of Justice, Herr Stammberger, or the Minister of the Interior in North Rhine-Westphalia who was responsible for police activities in Bonn. The operation took place behind their backs because they were Free Democrats and therefore, in the view of some unidentified high personality in Bonn, were unreliable and could not be trusted.

The executive officials responsible for the affair were the Justice Minister's own State Secretary, and the State Secretary in the Ministry of Defence, both C.D.U. supporters who became the scapegoats and were temporarily suspended from duty. What precise part Defence Minister Strauss took in the arrests is still unclear, despite the efforts of a parliamentary committee of inquiry to find out. It is beyond dispute, however, that during the early morning he contacted the German Military Attaché in Madrid in connection with the arrest of Ahlers, and passed on a remarkable rumour that some of the *Spiegel* executives were about to flee to Cuba, at that moment threatening the United States with Soviet medium range rockets. The inference was clear. Strauss concealed the entire operation in Spain from his colleague, the Foreign Minister, Herr Schroeder, who might reasonably have expected to be informed of what was happening in his own embassy in Madrid.

Even more uncertain is what part Adenauer took in the *Spiegel* affair. He certainly knew of it and, as his subsequent parliamentary utterances showed, highly approved of it. Three months after the *Spiegel* arrests, while Herr Augstein, without a charge against him, still lay in prison, it was claimed in a parliamentary written answer that Strauss was acting on the Chancellor's orders when he telephoned the Military Attaché in Madrid. As though to emphasize the prevailing confusion in the Bonn Government, Adenauer's private office said that the Chancellor was informed three times of the progress of inquiries prior to the arrest. It was claimed that he gave no specific orders but insisted that as treason was involved, the inquiries must be pursued rigorously.

Within hours a wave of protest spread over Western Germany. Thousands of young Germans who had heard only terrible rumours of the Gestapo marched through the streets of the chief German cities. They demanded the release of Herr Augstein and his friends and the restoration of the freedom of the Press. The Social Democrats, with their historic anti-Nazi record, joined in the fray. In many ways it was a heartening demonstration.

All over the world the Adenauer Government's throwback to Gestapo tactics caused genuine alarm. Telegrams of solidarity with Herr Augstein poured into his Hamburg office now partly freed from the secret police. The true significance of Adenauer's enigmatic support of the Nazi comeback was realized in many countries, and notably the United States, for the first time. Herr Augstein and *Der Spiegel* became heroes all over the democratic world. There was doubt as to how much Adenauer had known about the '*Spiegel* scandal'. Many of his admirers suspected that the brash, ruthless Strauss might have secured his nominal consent in some moment of mental fatigue but any sympathy which there might have been for the old man vanished in seconds when, ten days later, he intervened in a parliamentary row over the arrests.

When the Social Democrats suggested that his judicial authorities had acted, probably within the letter, but certainly not in the spirit of the law, he became livid. He marched to the speaker's rostrum four times to intervene. Thumping on the desk with his fist, he shouted, 'We are faced in this country by an abyss of treason wilfully practised by publication for financial gain. This man, Augstein, prospers on treason and thrives on discord in the coalition. I find it utterly appalling.'

He went on to attack those who subscribed to *Der Spiegel* and those who inserted advertisements in the magazine. Herr Augstein and his colleagues, when condemned by Adenauer, had not even been charged—far less tried—for their alleged treason.

In the midst of the *Spiegel* crisis, which was now threatening the very existence of his Government, Adenauer departed for the United States, where he received the most frigid reception of his career.

Adenauer was never a Nazi, yet future historians may well debate whether, despite his democratic guise throughout his career, he was not a natural fascist. His telegram of congratulation to Mussolini on the signing of the Concordat between the Vatican and Fascist Italy, now discreetly forgotten in Bonn, may well have been significant. Given the opportunity, Konrad Adenauer, with policies based on reformist papal encyclicals, might well have developed a political system parallel to that of his fellow-veteran authoritarian, Dr. Salazar.

At the National Press Club in Washington he was forced to defend himself against accusations that he had used Gestapo tactics in a bid to destroy the freedom of the Press; and that he had attempted to put *Der Spiegel* out of business because Herr Augstein had become a thorn in his flesh.

Behind him, in Bonn, Adenauer left a major government crisis. His existence as Chancellor was threatened. The unfortunate Minister of Justice Stammberger had suffered a minor stroke and with the other four F.D.P. ministers had walked out of the Government. The F.D.P. caucus was laying down stiff conditions for further participation in an Adenauer coalition. The principal demand was 'Strauss must go,' for the Defence Minister's mis-leading statements and gross prevarications in Parliament, had become a national scandal. The F.D.P. – as it had proved during the disgraceful eight weeks of horsetrading a year earlier – was devoted to the spoils of office. Better for the party's reputation and principles had it joined forces with the S.P.D. and swept the aged authoritarian out of office.

Adenauer, after inclusive talks with President Kennedy, re-turned determined to end the crisis *and stay in power at whatever cost*. He knew the F.D.P. and was not especially worried about their imprecations and threats. But in the last eighteen months he had become increasingly disillusioned with his one-time Bavarian wonder boy, Herr Strauss. He had not forgotten Strauss's support for 'Erhard as Chancellor' in the party crisis after the previous year's election. Since then, the old man had enlivened German Cabinet meetings by turning his acid wit on the unpopular Minister of Defence, to the joy of the other ministers. After one of the Minister's more than usually turgid expositions of Straussian strategy, the Chancellor, with a malicious glint in his eye, observed; 'That is very interesting indeed, Herr Strauss, but I didn't understand a word of what you were talking about!' Adenauer's doubts about his Defence Minister had been reinforced by the discovery in Washington that the tactless and aggressive Strauss was almost as much out of favour among the Americans as he was in Bonn. The Kennedy administration and the new brooms in the Pentagon, headed by Mr. Macnamara and General Maxwell Taylor, were weary of Strauss's never-ending clamour for atomic weapons for his German army. President Kennedy and his advisers – for long regarded in Bonn as anti-German – had no intention of repeating the mistakes of the Russians in Cuba by giving the Germans such dangerous playthings. The lessons of Cuba were only three weeks away. Instead the President lectured Adenauer on the importance of the new German armed forces fulfilling a conventional role in European defence.

Adenauer took the hint. He returned to Bonn determined to sack Strauss. At one stroke he could relieve himself of a minister who was uncongenial, give satisfaction in Washington, meet the demands of the F.D.P., and *keep himself in power*. As always, he was the very personification of foxiness. Provincial elections were due in Bavaria. Strauss was prominent in the C.S.U., the Bavarian wing of Adenauer's party. The dismissal was delayed but in due course Strauss was summarily sacked. As a sop he was elected as head of the Bavarian C.S.U. parliamentary group – and as such was to play a prominent role in forcing Adenauer's acceptance of Professor Erhard as his successor five months later. He was succeeded by a minister whose political sophistication was beyond doubt. The new Defence Minister was a one-time resident of British mandated Tanganyika, Herr Kai Uwe von Hassel, a formidable Prussian who, with conspicuous success, had headed for several years the government of the half-Nazi province of Schleswig-Holstein.

Adenauer once again had managed to cling to office, but at what cost! Throughout Germany and in Berlin, loathing and disgust at the political clowning of the octogenarian Chancellor mounted. Provincial elections in the following few months would prove that abundantly.

Sheer self-interest at last shocked the C.D.U. into realization that, unless they got rid of Adenauer quickly, the party would be dragged to political disaster by the ancient at its head. His party and their allies were still pusillanimously pondering this discovery when, at the beginning of 1963, Adenauer entered his eighty-eighth year. Within a few days the German Government – if not the Federal Chancellor – got a much bigger shock.

The negotiations preparatory to Britain entering the European Common Market had entered a decisive stage.

Then President de Gaulle announced that he would give one of his rare, and usually oracular Press conferences. With Machiavellian intent he summoned the Press conference a few days prior to Adenauer's arrival in Paris for the signing of the new Franco-German treaty of friendship. The treaty was based on a memorandum handed to the Chancellor in Bonn during the previous autumn's imperial progress.

American diplomats in Europe had something more than a foreboding of what was afoot. How much Adenauer was told beforehand by de Gaulle is uncertain, but bitter American officials alleged that the German Chancellor had been exceedingly well informed of what de Gaulle would say.

The French President with unwonted clarity announced that he proposed to use his veto within 'The Six' to bar British entry to the European Common Market. His grounds were political

rather than economic. He indicated that his main reason was that
Britain was an island, and that the British were as yet still unfit to
join Europe. He further hinted that he saw in the British an
American 'fifth column' which, once inside the European com-
munity, would menace his Grand Plan for the future of the
European continent. The President made it clear that all Anglo-
Saxons were politically obnoxious to him..The firm manner in
which his megalomania had been squashed by Churchill and
Roosevelt still rankled. Like Adenauer, he was an historical
Anglophobe in the broadest possible meaning of the word.

He was furious about the agreement, made at Nassau just before
Christmas by President Kennedy and Prime Minister Macmillan,
for co-operation in the use of their nuclear deterrents. He was
determined that he, France – and his Europe – should go it
alone. He took a vicious swipe at President Kennedy's 'Grand
Design' and American domination of the Atlantic Alliance.
With a few ill-chosen words he split the Atlantic Alliance wide
open.

De Gaulle, as always, had carefully chosen his own moment to
stage the crisis which no doubt he had turned over in his mind for
some time. The key to everything was Adenauer. The French
President shrewdly calculated that the half-hypnotized old man
would do nothing at the last moment to prejudice his cherished
dream – the treaty of reconciliation with France. De Gaulle
realized that, after the *Spiegel* affair, Adenauer's days were numbered, and a government headed by the pro-Anglo-Saxon Erhard
and Schroeder would be much less pliable clay in his hands. His
double blow at the Anglo-Saxons had to take place while the
veteran Chancellor was still in more or less effective command.

De Gaulle was not alone in appreciating the decisive role of
Germany and its Chancellor. The other four members of 'The
Six', summoned to Brussels for the showdown, knew that only
the massive industrial might of Germany could offset the power of
France in the councils of the European community.

Adenauer was now under intense pressure from all sides. His

own Government, headed by Erhard and Schroeder, bluntly warned him that German public opinion was now totally opposed to his signing a treaty with de Gaulle, unless the French President modified his policies; and from all over Western Europe, the German Chancellor was under equally intense pressure from his 'good European friends' who had been outraged by de Gaulle's brutal rejection of Britain.

He was also under fire from heavier artillery. According to American reports, which his official apologists subsequently attempted to deny, during his visit to Washington in the previous November, Adenauer had made some sort of promise to President Kennedy that the Franco-German treaty would do nothing to injure the Atlantic Alliance. Some days before the de Gaulle Press conference, the Americans had warned Adenauer, apart from what he may have known from de Gaulle in secret, of the substance of what the French President would say. He was asked how, in view of his private assurances to the President, the French ban on the British entry into the Common Market would affect the treaty; and Washington is alleged to have exerted pressure to persuade Adenauer *not to go to Paris*.

But the befuddled Adenauer was incapable of perceiving anything at that moment beyond the realization of his lifelong dream. Other policies, above all, friendship with the United States to which he owed everything as Chancellor, were pushed into the background. On January 22nd, in defiance of his Cabinet, his coalition, his party, the Bonn Parliament, and the German people, Adenauer travelled to Paris to plight his political troth with de Gaulle.

Most Germans welcomed reconciliation with France but not at the price of de Gaulle's dictation of the future of Europe. *Die Welt*, which had often shown more sympathy for Adenauer than other Hamburg publications, expressed the national feeling: 'For the second time within a few months the question must be asked – are we a democracy? How can a man in this way defy the declared will of the people and the Bundestag? De Gaulle is

France . . . but Adenauer is not Germany, especially if at the end of his era he is determined to smash his life's work.'

Although his spokesman in Bonn paid lip service to the idea that Britain should still join the Common Market, Adenauer, impelled by his own Anglophobia, sympathized deeply with de Gaulle's suspicions that the British might prove to be a 'Trojan Horse', and would accept advice from no one. It was some weeks later that Adenauer's real view was blurted out by his Defence Minister, Herr von Hassel, to a private C.D.U. meeting in Kiel – with what political intent was a matter of some diplomatic speculation! Von Hassel declared that the German Chancellor shared de Gaulle's suspicions, not from any fear that the British would be an American 'fifth column', but because he believed that Mr. Macmillan would lose the next general election! The Social Democrat Scandinavian countries had also applied to join the European Common Market and *Adenauer was haunted by the spectre of a Socialist—and Protestant – dominated Western Europe headed by a Socialist Britain.* The two elderly Catholic reactionaries could not contemplate such a possibility. Three times they met tetê-à-tête. Then they signed their personal treaty of friendship. Adenauer made little or no effort to halt de Gaulle's anti-British course.

A week later, the inevitable sequel took place. President de Gaulle's faithful envoy, M. Couve de Murville, travelled to Brussels and at a frigid meeting of the Council of the Six, finally barred British entry into the European Community for an indefinite period. The two German delegates, Professor Erhard and Dr. Schroeder, fought hard but unavailingly. Adenauer, as always, knew best.

Die Obrigkeit, in the guise of a pigheaded, provincial politician obsessed by primitive personal prejudices and with the vanity of great age had prevailed. Adenauer had struck a blow at the European Community which he had done so much to create, the full consequences of which only time would reveal. The German-American alliance, to which he owed his power and his prestige, would never be the same so long as he remained Chancellor. Still he clung to power, but the writing was on the wall. His days were numbered.

The Christian Democrats suffered, in rapid succession, major reverses in provincial elections in Berlin, in Hessen, and finally in the Catholic and C.D.U. stronghold of Rhineland-Palatinate. When, in March, Adenauer once again retired to Cadenabbia, the party was at last determined that he must go. But still the tragic old man fought back. He still believed he knew what was best for Germany. But further provincial elections were due in the traditionally anti-C.D.U. province of Lower Saxony. The C.D.U. leaders in Hanover were prepared to stage a showdown. At last, a few days before Easter, Adenauer on television made the announcement that all Germany was waiting for. A fortnight later, against his wishes, Professor Erhard was nominated as his successor. From that moment, Western Germany had two Chancellors.

In a parting gesture the Bundestag a few weeks later finally ratified Adenauer's treaty with de Gaulle. Its true worth was demonstrated the following July during de Gaulle's 'catastrophic' visit to Bonn when two elderly authoritarians failed to agree about anything. Adenauer by this time was a shadow of his former self. The Bundestag had gone far from the days when a majority of its members accepted his word as law. The Bonn Parliament only approved the treaty after a somewhat contradictory preamble, pledging loyalty to the Atlantic, and by implication the American, alliance had been written into the ratification bill. For however much Adenauer by his international antics in the previous two years had strained the German-American friendship, the Bonn parliamentarians were determined to demonstrate their acceptance of fundamental fact that the existence of the Federal Republic depended in the ultimate on the United States, and the continued presence of American armed forces in Europe. The clamorous welcome given to President Kennedy at the end of June during his hero's progress through Germany, when in Berlin the hysterical jubilation paralleled the frenzy shown on the night Hitler took power in 1933, showed that millions of Germans shared the pro-American sentiments of the Bonn Parliament.

The Kennedy visit was a tremendous triumph, but not for Adenauer. Despite the usual trite tributes to 'one of the world's greatest statesmen' and the usual protocol courtesies, the jubilations seemed to take place almost in spite of the Chancellor. As Adenauer stood white faced and obviously near the end of his physical reserves he seemed almost jealous of the virile young man by his side, untired after the triumphal drive from Cologne to Bonn. In Berlin where the old man had to give precedence to his electoral rival Willy Brandt the Chancellor's discomfiture was even more marked. Even before Kennedy arrived there had been a squabble about where Adenauer should sit in the presidential car. And while the beaming Brandt sat next to the President, Adenauer was relegated to third place. His manifest annoyance increased when in the midst of his speech he was forced to end abruptly and give place to the American hero whom the vast crowd were hysterically demanding. Thereafter his main effort seemed directed to jostling with Brandt to get in front of the television cameras.

That and the unhappy visit of de Gaulle soon afterwards was virtually the end. He disappeared more and more into the background to emerge briefly to throw doubts on Khrushchev's good faith in signing a test ban treaty with the Anglo-Saxons.

Once the Germans felt certain that they were about to get rid of the old man at last they became sentimental as they always do. There was a natural tendency to recall only his great and devoted service to the German people.

But the great enigma remained. Was Konrad Adenauer a great man with almost unbelievable lapses into parochial pettiness; or was he just a little man inspired by the crisis of his people to periods of real greatness? History would decide.

Index

DATE DUE

MAR 1 8 '65			
AUG 3 '67			
AUG 3 '67			
AUG 7 '67			
GAYLORD			PRINTED IN U.S.A.